Can God Save My Village?

A Theological Study of Identity among the Tribal People of North-East India with a Special Reference to the Kukis of Manipur

Jangkholam Haokip

© 2014 by Jangkholam Haokip

Published 2014 by Langham Monographs
an imprint of Langham Creative Projects

Langham Partnership
PO Box 296, Carlisle, Cumbria CA3 9WZ, UK
www.langham.org

ISBNs:
978-1-78368-981-1 Print
978-1-78368-979-8 Mobi
978-1-78368-980-4 ePub

Jangkholam Haokip has asserted his right under the Copyright, Designs and Patents Act, 1988 to be identified as the Author of this work.

All rights reserved. No part of this publication may be reproduced, stored in a retrieval system or transmitted, in any form or by any means, electronic, mechanical, photocopying, recording or otherwise, without the prior written permission of the publisher or the Copyright Licensing Agency.

Unless otherwise stated, Scripture quotations are from the New Revised Standard Version Bible, copyright © 1989 National Council of the Churches of Christ in the United States of America. Used by permission. All rights reserved.

British Library Cataloguing in Publication Data
Haokip, Jangkholam, author.
  Can God save my village? : a theological study of identity among the tribal people of North-East India with a special reference to the Kukis of Manipur.
  1. Kuki (Indic people)--India--Manipur--Ethnic identity.
  2. Kuki (Indic people)--India--Manipur--Religion.
  3. Ethnicity--Religious aspects--Christianity.
  4. Colonization--Religious aspects. 5. Christianity and culture--India, Northeastern. 6. India, Northeastern--Church history. 7. India, Northeastern--Colonization.
  I. Title

275.4'17-dc23

Cover & Book Design: projectluz.com

Langham Partnership actively supports theological dialogue and a scholar's right to publish but does not necessarily endorse the views and opinions set forth, and works referenced within this publication or guarantee its technical and grammatical correctness. Langham Partnership does not accept any responsibility or liability to persons or property as a consequence of the reading, use or interpretation of its published content.

Rethinking traditional theology puts the identity of the people in crisis, but at the same time it reaffirms the necessity of local theologies in sustaining the cause of marginalized people. These days many such local theologies are being written that shall eventually enrich the theological spectrum of the 21st century. Dr Jangkholam Haokip has done an excellent job by documenting the theological voice of 'Kukis' of Manipur in India. In him I see a rising star of the theological world of North-East India provided he continues his work of theologizing from Kuki perspective with the same verve and spirit.

Professor Dr (Habil) James Massey
Director of Centre for Dalit/Minorities Studies (T), New Delhi; Chairperson, Navjyoti Post-Graduate & Research Centre, Delhi; Member, Assessment & Monitoring Authority (Planning Commission of India), and Former Member of National Committee for Minorities (NCM), Government of India

The people of North-East India demonstrate enthusiastic and dynamic Christianity, which is deeply embedded in their culture and religiosity. Research on the identity of the people in this region is a welcome addition to studies of world Christianity and mission in general, and of Indian Christianity in particular. Dr Jangkholam Haokip, in this significant monograph, discusses historical, socio-political and theological perspectives on the Christian identity of the Kuki people and presents a theology of identity drawn from his interaction with Dalit theology and tribal theology. This book contains rich material which is thoroughly researched, clearly presented and convincingly argued. It should therefore be on any must-read list for theology and mission studies in India.

Professor Sebastian Kim
Chair in Theology and Public Life, York St John University

Contents

Foreword xi

Abstract xiii

Acknowledgements xv

Abbreviations xvii

Introduction 1

Part One: Setting the Scene 9

Chapter 1 11
Survey of the Geography and History of North-East India in Ancient Times; The State of Manipur – Its Peoples and the Socio-Political and Cultural Context
- 1. 1. The Pre-Colonial Context 11
  - 1. 1. 1. The Name 'North-East' 12
  - 1. 1. 2. The Geographical Description 12
  - 1. 1. 3. Population 14
  - 1. 1. 4. The Socio-Political Life 16
- 1. 2. The British Annexation 17
  - 1. 2. 1. The Yandabu Treaty 18
  - 1. 2. 2. The British policy on Tribal people 18
  - 1. 2. 3. The Administration 19
  - 1. 2. 4. Immediate Impact of the Annexation 20
- 1. 3. The Post-Independence Experience 21
  - 1. 3. 1. Scheduled Tribe: A Wounded Identity 21
  - 1. 3. 2. Economic Situation of North-East India ... 28
  - 1. 3. 3. Demographic Change 32
  - 1. 3. 4. Politics of Containment 33
  - 1. 3. 5. Hindutva: A Self-negating Identity 35
  - 1. 3. 6. Insurgency: Search for Alternative 41
- 1. 4. Tribal Situation in Manipur 47
  - 1. 4. 1. The Land, the People and Their Settlements 47
  - 1. 4. 2. Political and religious context of Manipur 49
  - 1. 4. 3. Contesting Identities 58
- Conclusion 62

Chapter 2 65
    Concept of Identity: A Sociological Study
    2. 1. Defining Identity 66
        2. 1. 1. Primordialist View 68
        2. 1. 2. Instrumentalist View... 73
        2. 1. 3. Ethnic Group as Social Construct 75
    2. 2. Context and Identity Construction.. 83
    2. 3. Indigeneity, Indigenouse or Indigenous People.................... 87
    2. 4. Challenges and Opportunities in North-East India 92

Part Two: Kuki People and Their Struggle for Identity 97

Chapter 3 99
    The Kuki People of Manipur and Their Struggle for Identity
    3. 1. An Overview of the Kuki People: The Background 99
        3. 1. 1. The Homogeneity of the People............................... 100
        3. 1. 2. The Traditional Territory.. 101
        3. 1. 3. The Problem of Disintegration................................ 104
        3. 1. 4. The Use of the term 'Kuki' in this Publication 110
    3. 2. The Kukis of Manipur: Origin and Settlement..................... 112
        3. 2. 1. The Story of Origin 112
        3. 2. 2. The Khul Story 113
        3. 2. 3. Origin in Current Research..................................... 114
        3. 2. 4. Settlement and Traditional Rule in the
              Hills of Manipur 117
    3. 3. The Kuki Traditional Society... 122
        3. 3. 1. The Patriarchy, the Family Lineage and
              Formation of Clans 123
        3. 3. 2. Chieftainship: The Administration.......................... 124
        3. 3. 3. Social Relationship System....................................... 131
        3. 3. 4. Religion 135
        3. 3. 5. Worldview 142
        3. 3. 6. Khankho.. 144
    3. 4. The New Administrations and Kuki Identity........................ 147
        3. 4. 1. The British Rule.. 147
        3. 4. 2. Independent India: Contradiction in Terms? 154
        3. 4. 3. The Kuki Identity, Kuki Identity Movement and
              a Task for Theology 160

Chapter 4 167
History of Evangelization: A Study of Christianity among the Kukis of Manipur in Relation to Their Identity Crisis
    4. 1. The Background..168
        4. 1. 1. The Catholic Missionaries in North-East India 169
        4. 1. 2. The Serampore Mission 170
        4. 1. 3. The American Baptist and Welsh Presbyterian Missions...171
        4. 1. 4. The Arthington Aborigines Mission........................174
    4. 2. The Coming of Christianity to Manipur.............................177
        4. 2. 1. Northern Manipur: The American Baptist Union........177
        4. 2. 2. Southern Manipur: The Thado-Kuki Pioneer Mission ... 180
        4. 2. 3. Conflict between Missions and the Implications
            for Kukis...184
    4. 3. The Work of Evangelization 192
        4. 3. 1. Mission Approach..193
        4. 3. 2. Methods of Evangelism.......................................194
    4. 4. The Role of Colonial Rule in Mission 202
        4. 4. 1. The Rationales for Relationship 202
        4. 4. 2. Cooperation for the War in France 206
    4. 5. The Work of Evangelization Among the Kukis......................210
        4. 5. 1. Inception and Growth 210
        4. 5. 2. Mission and the Chieftainship...............................216
        4. 5. 3. What does a Christian Kuki look like? 219
    4. 6. Christianity from Kuki Identity Viewpoint 222
        4. 6. 1. The Way in which Christianity Came 222
        4. 6. 2. Lack of Integral Approach to Theology 227
        4. 6. 3. Opportunities and Scopes...................................231

Part Three: A Theological Response **233**

Chapter 5 235
Dalit Theology in Response to Dalit Struggle for Identity
    5. 1. The Context of Dalit Theology 236
        5. 1. 1. The Caste System and Dalit Oppression 236
        5. 1. 2. The Neglect of Dalit Experience in Indian Christian
            Theology 242
    5. 2. Methodological Concerns of Dalit Theology......................249
        5. 2. 1. Definition of Theology 249
        5. 2. 2. The Understanding of God 251
        5. 2. 3. Hermeneutics: A Dalit Reading of the Bible 253

    5. 2. 4. The Goal of Dalit Theology 255
    5. 2. 5. Sources of Dalit Theology 257
    5. 2. 6. The Subject of Dalit Theology 261
  5. 3. An Evaluation from a Tribal Perspective 262

Chapter 6 265
Toward a Theology of Identity in Kuki Context
  6. 1. Theology and Cultural Identity in North-East India: Current Scenario 266
  6. 2. Biblical Basis for a Theology of Identity 272
  6. 3. Proposals for doing Theology in Kuki Context of Identity Struggle 277
    6. 3. 1. The Theological Vision 277
    6. 3. 2. Preference for the Term 'Local Theology'. 277
    6. 3. 3. Re-visiting Kuki History and Culture 282
    6. 3. 4. Khankho: An Avenue for Local Theology 287
    6. 3. 5. The Bible and the Gospel in Local Theology 296
  6. 4. Theology of Identity and Identity Construction 305

Conclusion 311

Bibliography 313

Appendix 1 337
The Tribal Population of Manipur in 2001

Appendix 2 339
Operations Against Kuki Tribes

Appendix 3 341
The Five Hill Districts of Manipur and their Population

Appendix 4 343
Lists of Schedule Tribe in Different States of North-East India
  Manipur 343
  Meghalaya 345
  Mizoram 347
  Nagaland 348

Appendix 5 349
Letter of Directors to Revs. D. E. Jones and Dr Fraser on 16 February 1912

Appendix 6 351
Letter of Roberts to Fraser

Appendix 7 353
    Letter of Fraser to Rev T. W. Reese

Appendix 8 355
    Sunrise in Manipur

Foreword

At the very end of this book the author writes: 'What was once silenced as primitive needs to be given a chance to speak for the good of all'. In fact, that is precisely what Jangkholam Haokip achieves in this major study of his own Kuki people and their historical, religious and socio-economic context in North-East India. Through this volume, which is based on years of careful and painstaking research, the Kuki (and the many other groups classified as 'tribals' in modern India) are given a voice as the story of their experience of the modern world, including their incorporation into British India, their evangelization by Protestant missionaries, and their present situation in a post-colonial world in which they find themselves divided by international borders between India, Bangladesh and Burma, is told with both scholarly accuracy and moral passion.

The story is full of surprises. At the most basic level it brings to light the history of large numbers of people who belong to traditions, which anthropologists and historians of religion have described as 'primal'. There are vast numbers of such people around the world, yet their stories have often gone unnoticed and their frequently tragic plight remains unknown, in part because the ideologies of both Western modernism and some major religious traditions, continue to treat them as 'backward', uncivilized, or worse. What this book does is to shine a light on the reality of the traditional beliefs and way of life of one such primal group and, in so doing, it demonstrates not only the positive elements in the primal worldview, but suggests that, in its sense of community and its relationship with the non-human creation, the pre-Christian world of the Kukis had much in common with the biblical narrative and can today offer a corrective to the scientific and rationalist way of life which increasingly poses a terrible threat to our planet.

A second surprise concerns the presence of very significant numbers of Christians throughout the tribal areas of North-East India. It is doubtful whether many Christians in the Western world are aware of the fact that they have so many brothers and sisters within the borders of the nation of India and not the least significant aspect of this book is its revelation of the astonishing reality of World Christianity in areas in which its existence remains largely hidden and unknown in the West. However, the story of the evangelization of the Kuki told here also contains information which is disturbing and deeply challenging for Christians committed to mission. It reveals the negative outcomes of the work of evangelists who, while driven by a sincere desire to preach Christ, nonetheless, failed to recognize the extent of the cultural conditioning of their own understanding of the gospel. In particular, British missionaries operated hand-in-glove with colonial power in ways in which, as Haokip describes in detail, were tragic then and seem sobering and disturbing now.

Finally, this study is an example of the emergence of a truly local theology. Building on the significant example of Dalit Christian theology in India (which is brilliantly summarized here), Haokip provides what is a pioneering effort at addressing a whole nest of extremely difficult problems from the perspective of the gospel of Jesus Christ. This is not an abstract, 'armchair' theology, but is rather the beginning of an articulation of the good news of Christ in a context characterized by a crisis of identity, by severe socio-economic distress, and by the temptations of violence so common to our globalized world. While this book reflects its author's gifts as theologian, teacher and Christian leader, the reader should know that his theology is applied in practice in ways that provide a striking model of Christian discipleship in a context of human suffering and need. I count it a privilege to know the author not simply as a student, but as a friend and I gladly commend this book to the reader without reservation.

Dr David Smith
Senior Research Fellow
International Christian College, Glasgow, UK

Abstract

This publication investigates the struggle for identity among the tribal people of North-East India with a special reference to the Kuki people of Manipur. It explores the cultural and religious traditions of the people and the changes brought to them in the process of western colonial administration and Christianization in early part of the twentieth century. It also investigates the socio-political and cultural situation of the people under the Independent India. The work explores debates within sociology between primordialist and constructivist theoretical perspectives and concludes that, while identity is a social construct, it reflects the real socio-economic, cultural and political context within which it emerges and real struggles for justice and dignity on the part of marginalized peoples. It is in this light that the current ethnic movements in North-East India are understood and their limitations are described and shown to result from the lack of a critical theological reflection. This study demonstrates that Christianity, although playing an important role in the formation of the peoples' identity in the new setting, neglected their traditional cultural values and hence became a factor contributing to the people's identity crisis. Dalit theology is taken as a dialogue partner in search of a relevant theological response to the issue, but it is pointed out that while they have much in common, the additional task for tribal theology is to take into consideration the primal religious past as well as the difficult and complex socio-political realities shaping their present experience in a post-colonial, globalized world. The work outlines aspects of Kuki tradition which may contribute to a local theology and, in that process, can shape a new sense of identity, restoring dignity to the Kuki, while respecting the freedom and humanity of other peoples.

Acknowledgements

First of all, I should like to record my heartfelt gratitude and appreciation to the International Christian College, Glasgow for the generous grant which made this research possible. I would like to thank especially Rev Dr Tony Sargent, then Principal of ICC and the concerned committee of the college for making it possible. Likewise, I am grateful to Ms. Edith Barbour for her financial support toward my living expenses and the Church Mission Society for their generous support toward my fieldwork. I also would like to thank the Union Biblical Seminary, Pune, for granting me leave for my study.

In the same way, I would like to record my deepest gratitude and appreciation to my two supervisors: Dr David W. Smith, a Senior Research Fellow at the International Christian College, Glasgow who not only read each section of my work supplying his valuable comments, but also offered his pastoral support during my difficult time, and to Dr Sebastian Ch. Kim, Professor at York St. John University, who offered valuable comments especially during the early part of my research. Besides my two advisors, Dr Andrew Smith at Glasgow University has been very much part of my journey particularly by giving his comments in the section on sociological study of identity. I am grateful to him indeed. I am also grateful to John Jeacocke and Elizabeth Clarke for their help in proofreading and the library staff at ICC for their untiring support in acquiring the materials that I needed.

There are friends who are part of this journey, bearing my burden with me in times of both frustrations and happy moments. I would like to record my sincere thanks to Christopher Anderson, Dave McCaulay and his family, Chris and Rachel Lawton, Paul and Hannah Worth, Donald and Katrine Inverarity, and Derek McPhail for their untiring encouragement and prayers. I am also grateful to my church at Glasgow, St. George's Tron, Rev Dr William Philip, my minister in particular, for their encouragement and valuable prayer support. In the same way, I would like to thank my siblings for their priceless support: Heu Hejang and his family, Heu Kam and his family, Vavah and her children, Haopu, Henei and her family, Lelet and Ruth and Boisi and her family. I am also grateful to my parents, the late Mrs Lamkhochin Haokip and the late Mr Jangkhongam Haokip, for the undying inspiration for *Khankho* they imparted to me through their lifestyles. I am much indebted to my wife, Boinu, for her unfailing support, particularly during those days when I had to work extra hard into late nights. It is to them that this publication is dedicated in gratitude and to the glory of God.

Abbreviations

ABFMS	American Baptist Foreign Mission Society
BMS	Baptist Mission Society
CBCNEI	Council of Baptist Churches of North-East India
CDS	Centre for Dalit Studies
CMA	Calvinistic Missionary Archive
KNA	Kuki National Army
KNO	Kuki National Organization
LMS	London Missionary Society
NEIGM	North East India General Mission
NNF	Kuki National Front
TKPM	Thado-Kuki Pioneer Mission
WCMFMS	Welsh Calvinistic Methodist Foreign Mission Society

Introduction

"Pathen in kagalmiho a kon'a keima leh kakho eihuh doh jou louleh, milim kaki sema kahou ding ahi."

(Translation: If God cannot save me and my village from my enemy's attack, I will make idols and worship them.)
– An anonymous villager.

The felt-need for this research arose from the conversation I overheard quoted above in my hometown in Manipur between two ordinary villagers during the recent ethnic conflict. What became clear to me from this conversation were, first, the radical belief in and total dependency on God for everything the two people had in their lives, including for the safety of their villages. It is a good thing that within the last one hundred years, Christianity has become the dominant religion of the Kuki people in Manipur and that God is taken very seriously in all aspects of their lives. The second and disturbing reality reflected in the quotation is the risk of denouncing that faith if the villages are not protected from being burned down. Christianity, as understood and practiced among the tribal people inherited from the missionaries, comes to its crisis, facing the highest test of relevance in the current context of identity struggle. The question for me as a theologian and a pastor is, "how do I respond to these two men's situation?" The nature of the conflict was such that there was no time to reflect on the issue and respond to the two villagers. Regrettably, before I could at least go and talk to them, the two disappeared from my sight, leaving a deep and lasting question in my heart, which eventually led me to undertake this study.

Identity assertion and conflicts are not confined only to the tribal people of North-East India. With all its inhumane acts of holocaust and ethnic cleansings, the twentieth century has been termed the ethnic century. The power of ethnicity continues to dictate human behaviour despite the high intellectual developments and tremendous achievements in the present day. The cases of Northern Ireland and former Yugoslavia in Europe, conflicts in Sudan, Rwanda and Kenya in Africa, and those in Sri Lanka and Burma in Asia are only the tip of the iceberg.

In the context of the world's largest democracy, India, the so-called tribal country, and for that matter, the Dalit people's struggle, is for basic human rights and dignity. Besides the hierarchical social structure, with the rise of the assimilative *Hindutva* movement and the imposition of 'development projects' by the government, such groups feel threatened with the loss of their cultural traditions, and as a result, the tribal people often react to this situation in ways that are ethnocentric and even violent.

In fact, the North-East region of India has not seen a single decade of calm political atmosphere since the country's independence in 1947. The Mizo National Front (MNF) in Mizoram, the Naga Socialist Council of Nagaland (NSCN), the United National Liberation Front (UNLF) and the Kuki National Army (KNA) in Manipur can be mentioned here as examples of people's movements in the North-East created in order to safeguard their cultural identities. New movements of political unrest emerge every new decade showing various degrees of strain in accepting and adjusting to the idea of national integration proposed by the majority Hindu India. The undercurrent behind all these movements is a shared vision for life free from the threat of cultural assimilation and the recognition of their distinct identity.

The role of Christianity, as understood and practiced in this situation, is a complex one. In the process of Christianization in India, the people have experienced a radical decline of their traditional practices and values. The early converts of Indian Christians in central India constructed a local theology, later known as 'Indian Christian Theology', however, it was done in the light of the Brahminic tradition hence the experiences of the marginalized groups including tribals and dalits were not taken into consideration. The conviction behind this research is that a fresh articulation of the Christian message in the context of the people's search for identity is of fundamental significance. Hence the aim of this research is to propose a theological response to identity struggle in a way that will enhance the people's identity, while at the same time promoting peaceful co-existence in a multi-ethnic context such as North-East India.

For this task, the Kukis of Manipur were selected for the following reasons. The Kuki people were once the monarch in the hills of Manipur. The changes brought about by the colonial administration side by side with the Christian missionaries disadvantaged the people. While the former suppressed the Kuki spirit or national pride, the latter sought to replace their religious identity with that of a Christianity which was formulated in the West. The so-called '1917–1919 Kuki rebellion' was part of their struggle for the recognition of their distinctive culture, and at the same time, the beginning of their identity struggle. Secondly, with the coming of Christianity, the Kuki traditional way of life was suddenly disrupted through an evangelization which replaced the traditional worldview with that of the missionaries. What was there before Christianity was considered to be unholy, devilish, and sinful, and needed to be destroyed. The life of the people was oriented to a new way of life that concerns spiritual new birth, denunciation of the things concerning life here and now, the nearness of the Second Coming of Christ and the salvation of the lost souls. It was a faith movement that sought for a complete change of one's life from a human-world-God related worldview to other-worldly worldview. Moreover, unlike the cases of some other groups, Christianity among the Kuki people contributed to the gradual disintegration of the people through Bible translations into dialects, which are intelligible to each other. In this way, their new faith, as understood and practiced, failed to prepare the people to address concerns of their identity. Under the subsequent independent administration, the people found themselves further alienated from their traditional culture and identity.

In response to such a situation, there have been socio-political movements among the Kukis in the recent past, demanding political recognition within the Indian Constitution. However, such a movement without critical theological reflection risks both the Christian message of peace and non-violence as well as the altruistic cultural values which they sought to protect. This precisely is the danger leading to a situation which we called 'the crisis of Christianity' above.

The need therefore is a critical theological reflection on the issue of identity, including the historico-cultural, socio-economic and political context within which it emerges, to show the way forward. This is important because, first, for good or for ill, the society has now become a 'Christian society' and hence what is said in Christianity has a wider impact on the society. Second, a study of identity in its given context will enable a better understanding of the phenomena, enabling discernment of how they might be addressed. Finally, a sound biblical and theological grounding is crucial for the understanding of ethnic identity for peaceful co-existence in a multi-ethnic context such as in North-East India. The benefit of this will be seen in the following four ways. One, a more balanced view of identity will emerge from viewing the phenomena in the light of the biblical and theological perspective; two, the people will be reconnected to their cultural past, hence putting us in a better position to see a fuller picture of God's involvement in the people's history creating a basis for a critique of culture as well as enrichment of its transformative elements; three, when the transformative cultural values are reaffirmed in the light of the Christian message, the dignity and rightful place of the people will be restored which will further pave the way for their participation in and contribution to a wider community; four, a local theology that is relevant in a given context without disconnecting from others will reaffirm the translatability of the Christian message in all cultures.

It is difficult to carry out a study of this nature within a single discipline because of the wide-ranging concerns the subject touches, and the way it requires the project to be carried out. Therefore, this study adopts an interdisciplinary approach to the issue, involving historical, sociological and theological approaches. The nature of this study is descriptive and analytical. The limitation of this approach lies in the difficulty in satisfying the demands of any particular discipline adopted due to space.

The following methods are used in this study. Library research was undertaken using resources available in the libraries of International Christian College, the University of Glasgow, the University of Edinburgh, including the New College, University of Aberdeen, and the Bodleian Library, in Oxford. In addition, published resources relevant to the study of Indian Christianity, Dalit theology, and the religious, historical and cultural context of North-East India, most of which are available within the Indian sub-continent, were extensively researched. Besides the library research, Archival studies and field works were carried out. The archives of the British Library, London, especially the colonial records, including maps, related to the people's history, traditional administration and the Kuki-Uprising were studied, as well as the National Library of Wales in Aberystwyth, containing the records of Welsh missions in Mizoram, particularly that of Dr Peter Fraser which includes information regarding Watkin Roberts, the first missionary among the Kuki people in southern Manipur. Visits were also made to Regent's Park College, Oxford, in order to explore materials related to the work of the Arthington Aborigines Mission, the agency which sent the first three missionaries to Assam, including William Pettigrew, who became first and sole recognized missionary to Manipur, concentrating particularly on the northern part of the state. During my field trip I spent time at the library of the Council of Baptist Churches in North-East India in Gauhati, Assam, India, investigating the official documents of the American Baptist Mission, the only recognized mission agency in the state and which adopted Pettigrew and supported his work in Manipur. Fieldwork included attending conferences, both in Manipur (Youth Conference of the Evangelical Churches Association in February 2007 & The Centenary Celebration of the Coming of Christianity in Southern Manipur in February 2010), and in Delhi ("Writing Northeast: New Perspective", January 2009, an International Conference organized by Jawaharlal Nehru University). My fieldwork also included conversation with select church leaders and theologians in Manipur, including retired pastors and converts about the work of the missionaries and their subsequent impacts on the people. The decision to engage in conversation with these elderly Kuki Christian leaders was taken because their memories reach back to the missionary period and so represent a valuable oral tradition. I also made a visit to the Centre for Dalit/Subaltern Studies and Community Contextual Communication Centre, New Delhi, and had an insightful conversation with Dr James Massey, a well-known Dalit theologian and Director of the Centre.

The work is divided into three main parts. Part one is the background study and includes chapters 1 and 2. Chapter 1 surveys North-East India and the state of Manipur, highlighting the socio-economic, political and cultural context of the people. It shows how the people of North-East India as a whole struggle to preserve their identities under the new administrations, namely, the colonial administration and the present Indian state. Having surveyed the identity situation of North-East India as a whole, this chapter describes the situation of Manipur, with which this study is primarily concerned, demonstrating how all the communities, including the majority Hindu Meiteis in the valley, the Kukis and the Nagas in the hills, struggle to preserve their identities. In order to understand the complexity of identity and identity movements in North-East India, chapter 2 explores a sociological concept of 'identity', or ethnic identity, and attempts to assess the socio-political movements of North-East India in the light of the concept. It discusses the traditional debate between two approaches: Primordialism and Instrumentalism and observes that while the two arguments have their own valid points, the complexity of the phenomena cannot be fixed into rigid categories. Having noted complexity of the concept and the lack of precise definition of the term, this chapter identifies with the Weberian school of thought and suggests that it is more appropriate to understand identity assertion as a social construct influenced by a given socio-political and economic context within which it emerges. That is illustrated through the experiences of identity constructions in North-East India, including the 'Kuki' and the 'Naga'.

Part two, which incorporates chapters 3 and 4, describes in particular the Kuki people and their struggle for identity in the process of change in their socio-political and religious life. Chapter 3 describes how the traditional Kuki people, once the monarchs in their own territory in Manipur, with their own system of administration and rule, suffered decline in the process of modernization brought about by the colonial administration. The chapter seeks to demonstrate that the colonial administration not only suppressed the Kuki spirit, or national pride, in the response to what was called the Kuki Uprising in 1917–1919, but also created a lasting impact on the people's continuing identity struggle. This chapter also shows how, in the subsequent Independent India, the Kuki people continue to experience alienation from their culture as the result of new policies and systems. Chapter 4 examines the history of evangelization with a view to showing how far Christianity, as understood and practiced by the missionaries and their converts, affected the people's identity concerns. It demonstrates that although Christianity came to fill the vacuum created by the colonial administration and hence was considered a success story, the way it came has contributed to the people's identity struggle. It argues that while Christianity came to the Kukis of Northern Manipur as crumbs fallen from a rich man's table, it came to the southern part of Manipur through a back door with far reaching impact on the people at such a crucial time of transition from traditional to modern. It also argues that while the positive contributions of the missionaries cannot be ignored, their activities had the impact of breaking, or at least loosening, the connection of people with their cultural past. At the same time, this chapter also argues that Christianity provided a means for reconstruction of the people's identity and it is with the help of this that we must respond to the people's present identity struggle.

Part three, which is chapters 5 and 6, attempts to provide a theological ground for identity construction in a multi-ethnic context. Chapter 5 engages in dialogue with Dalit theology, a pioneer theology from a marginalized perspective in India, with a view to drawing insights for the articulation of the Christian message in the context of Kuki identity struggle. It suggests that both Dalits and tribals can share much in common particularly in the field of theological methodology, the emphasis and approach in theologizing. However, this chapter also argues that tribal theology has an additional task of taking into consideration both the cultural and geographical realities of the people in theologizing. Chapter 6, which is the final chapter of this publication, is a proposal for theological response to identity struggle. This chapter argues that the issue of identity needs to be reflected critically in the light of the biblical and theological insights and attempts to show how it might be done. It proposes a way of contextualizing the gospel in the cultural context of the people in a manner which affirms the identity of the people while at the same, relating their identity to that of their neighbours and placing it within the broader context of all the nations and peoples who together make up the one human family which, according to the Bible, God loves and seeks to create a unity in love and justice.

Part One

Setting the Scene

CHAPTER 1

Survey of the Geography and History of North-East India in Ancient Times; The State of Manipur – Its Peoples and the Socio-Political and Cultural Context

1. 1. The Pre-Colonial Context

The tribal people of North-East India share similar experiences of alienation and identity crises because of their distinct cultural background, history and geographical isolation. The aim of this study is to situate the identity problem of the people of North-East India, particularly the Kukis of Manipur, in this context and make proposals for developing a theology that will enhance the identity of the people and at the same time, enrich a Christian theology.

This requires a brief survey of the history of North-East India with a view to highlighting the socio-political and religio-cultural context of this region. Further to understand the context of the Kuki identity struggle in particular, it also requires a description of the socio-political and cultural context of the state of Manipur in more detail where the concerns of our study lie. This chapter first surveys the geography and history of North-East India both in ancient and modern times and situates the Kuki identity struggle in a broader context. And having shown the wider context, secondly, it also describes the state of Manipur – its people and their socio-political and cultural context – from a minority viewpoint.

1. 1. 1. The Name 'North-East'

The name 'North-East' refers to the geographical area to the North and East of the modern state of India, extending to the east of Bangladesh and bordering Myanmar. During the colonial period, in which the region was brought into one administration with India, the use of the term 'North-East' or 'North-East Frontier Tracts' was limited to the region which is now called Arunachal Pradesh. In the post-colonial period, the term refers to a wider geographical area as a categorization for a 'better' administration. B. P. Singh, an experienced Indian Civil Servant in the region writes, "With the passage of the North-Eastern Areas (Reorganization) Act, 1971, the region emerged as a significant administrative concept with a North-Eastern Council (NEC) as its regional planning and security organization, replacing the hitherto more familiar unit of public imagination: Assam."

Being a post-independence invention, the term is more than a mere geographical reference. For its geographical location, cultural entity of the people, and their struggle for identity in the new setting, the term North-East also refers to the distinctiveness of the people's cultural background from that of the dominant groups and the need for a special way of dealing with them.

1. 1. 2. The Geographical Description

The region designated as 'North-East India' lies between Bangladesh and Myanmar in the south and China and Tibet in the north. The entire area covers 254,994 square kilometres which is 8.06 per cent of India's total landmass and it is joined with the rest of India through a thin corridor of land between the north of Bangladesh and Tibet. Within this region, the state of Manipur lies on the extreme east on the Myanmar border and shares boundaries with the Indian states of Nagaland on the north, Assam on the west, and Mizoram to the south. The total geographical area of the state is 22,327 square kilometres. The greater part of the region is hilly or mountainous while the smaller plain area includes the Brahmaputra and the Barak valleys in Assam, the Tripura plain and the Manipur plateau. The majority of the people live in the valley.

The region 'North-East India' consists of states including Assam, Nagaland, Meghalaya, Manipur, Tripura, Arunachal Pradesh, Mizoram

Survey of the Geography and History of North-East India in Ancient Times

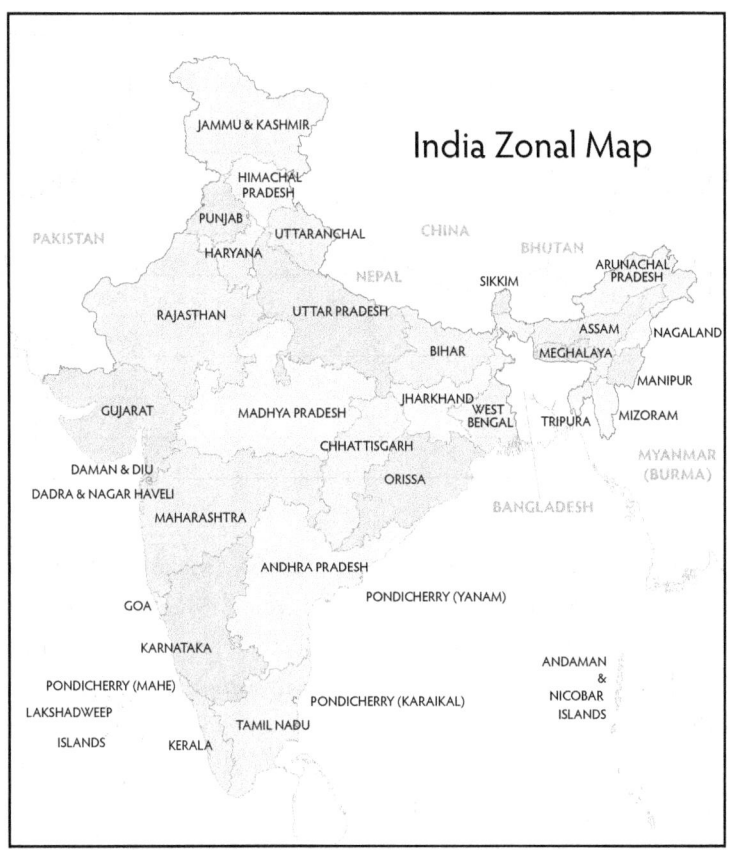

Map 1: States of India

and Sikkim in the Eastern Himalayan mountain range.[1] It used to be known as 'Seven Sisters', referring to the seven states, until Sikkim was added in 2003. Sikkim was once an independent Himalayan kingdom and it only became part of India in 1973. For this reason, Sikkim has a different historical experience from that of the other seven states and on that account the state of Sikkim is not included in this survey.

---

1. See map 1, States of India.

1. 1. 3. Population

The 2001 Census of India, which is the latest record of the population, shows a state-wise population as follows:[2]

Sl. No.	Name of State	Population
1	Assam	26,638,407
2	Tripura	3,191,168
3	Manipur	2,388,634
4	Meghalaya	2,306,069
5	Nagaland	1,988,636
6	Arunachal Pradesh	1,091,117
7	Mizoram	891,058

The population of North-East India as a whole makes 3.73 per cent of the total population of India.[3] Within the region, Manipur stands as the third most populated state wherein the tribal people formed one-third of the population. We shall come back to this in section 4.

Although the whole North-East region is categorized into a single entity for governance, the composition of the population is complex. It can be loosely divided into three distinct groups of people: the hill tribes, the plains tribes, and the remaining population, although it should be kept in mind that the term tribal is imprecise.

B. P. Singh observed the multi-ethnic situation and its ambiguity:

> To an outsider a person living in Assam is an Assamese, in Nagaland a Naga, in Mizoram a Mizo, in Manipur a Manipuri, and so on. But the real situation is baffling, and purely from the angle of ethnic variety the people of North-East India have

---

2. Population Figures of the North-East States (Census of India 2001). http://mha.nic.in/nemain.htm [Accessed 20 June 2007].

3. Sanjib Baruah, "Postfrontier Blues: Towards a New Policy Framework for Northeast India", *East-West Center,* Policy Studies, no.33, 6. http://www.eastwestcenter.org/fileadmin/stored/pdfs/PS033.pdf (Accessed 30 May 2010).

a greater variety to offer than perhaps any other part of the globe.⁴

Map 2: Districts of Manipur ⁵

Downs likewise notes the same as he observes each village as a kind of village-state and an autonomous unit.⁶ Linguistically, various languages are spoken including Assamese in Assam valley, Tibeto-Burman and Austro-Asiatic languages among the hill people. In this complexity, Downs finds an alternative categorization of the people as those who were or were not sanskritized before the British annexation in the 1820s.⁷ Sanskritized

---

4. Singh, *Problem of change*, 28.
5. Population: 2001 Census http://india.gov.in/knowindia/districts/andhra1. php?stateid=MN (Accessed on 8 November, 2010).
6. Downs, *History of Christianity*, 5.
7. Ibid., 2. Sanskritization refers to the process of the influence of the Aryan culture through Hinduism to the weaker 'tribal' people. Downs adopts the term 'sanskritized'

groups are found mostly in the plains areas while non-sanskritized, or Christians, mainly settled in the hill states due to the fierce nature of the tribal people and the remoteness of their settlements.[8] Down's classification is based on the popular understanding that the Aryans of northern India penetrated the weaker cultures, including those of the Mongoloids on the plain of Assam, but were prohibited from going further into those who settled in the hills including the Kuki people who later were Christianized under then British administration. This may be one possible way of classifying the people but again, there cannot be a rigid categorization based on this theory.

1. 1. 4. The Socio-Political Life

The region now known as North-East India was a home to numerous indigenous tribal people in pre-colonial times. Although there is no agreement among the scholars about the origin of many of these groups, it is believed that they migrated to this region during the last three or four thousand years.[9] The people have possessed their own cultures and customs which underwent drastic changes with the coming of modernization.

It is a popular understanding that Aryan culture from North India expanded among the tribal people of Assam. One example is S. Barkataki who writes:

> The Brahmins from northern India succeeded in absorbing into Hinduism all the tribal people of the plains including the powerful Ahoms . . . who in course of time not only adopted the Hindu religion, discarding their own, but also forgot their own Shan language and adopted Assamese [an Aryan Sanskritic language].[10]

---

from M. N. Srinivas who introduces the term in 1952 in his work, "Religion and Society among the Coorgs of Southern India". Srinivas prefers sanskritization to other terms such as 'hinduized' or 'aryanized.'

8. Ibid., 3.
9. Ibid., 1.
10. Quoted in Downs, *History of Christianity*, 3.

In this regard, O. L. Snaitang, a well-known historian in North-East India, contends the "imposition of an Aryan culture was a primary factor that led to the exclusion and oppression of the tribal people."[11] The spread of Hinduism among the tribal people continued until the British annexed the region and introduced 'Inner-line Permit'[12] which prohibited the free entry of the non-resident Hindus of 'mainland' India.

Politically, prior to the British annexation in the 1820s, Assam was ruled by the Ahoms for over six hundred years while Manipur and Tripura were ruled by their own kings and chiefs. The Ahoms were an "offshoot of the Shan or Tai races in the northern and eastern hill tracts of upper Burma and western Yunnan"[13] and they were said to have migrated to Assam in the thirteenth century under the leadership of Sukhapa (AD 1228–1268) and established themselves as a dominant power in the Brahmaputra Valley by the seventeenth century.[14] Under them Assam had developed as one nationality with Assamese as a *lingua franca*.[15] Later, Assam went through change as the Ahoms became weakened and other people, namely the Burmese, became interested in the region. It was at that juncture that the British seized the opportunity and annexed the area in the 1820s and gradually brought the whole region to become part of India.

1. 2. The British Annexation

The British annexation had a wide and lasting impact on the society. In this section we shall highlight the British policy on the tribal people in the hills, their administration and the implications of it.

---

11. O. L. Snaitang, "In Search of a Tribal History", *Asia Journal of Theology* Vol. 18, No. 2 (October 2004): 398–411.

12. Downs, *History of Christianity,* 4.

13. Sajal Nag, *Roots of Ethnic Conflict: Nationality Question in North-East India* (New Delhi: Manohar Publications, 1990), 15.

14. Ibid., 15.

15. Ibid., 29.

1. 2. 1. The Yandabu Treaty

The weakness of Ahoms in Assam during the early nineteenth century suited the purpose of the East India Company. From 1817 the gradual increase of Burmese dominance in Assam concerned the British East India Company since it threatened their business interests.[16] The British accordingly entered Assam and expelled the Burmese. As the result a treaty was signed at Yandabu, near Mandalay in Burma, on 24 February 1826 and the Burmese ceded to the British three provinces, namely Assam, Arakan and Tenasserim.[17] The region was thus brought under the same administration with India for the first time. Similarly, other parts of the region were gradually annexed: Cachar, which is presently Assam, in 1930; Khasi Hills, now called Meghalaya, in 1933; Naga Hills, now known as Nagaland, in 1835; Garo Hills, now part of Meghalaya, in 1872–3; and Lushai Hills, which is now called Mizoram, in 1890.[18] The Yandabu treaty thus brought subsequent changes in the region, implanting the seeds of identity crisis among the people.

1. 2. 2. The British policy on Tribal people

The vulnerability of the tribal cultural identity in the face of these changes was the concern of the colonial administration. Despite suggestions to open up the hills to outsiders, the administration opted for a segregation policy[19] for the purpose of safeguarding "'customary practices' [of the tribal people], including kinship and clan-based rules of land allocation."[20] They decided to introduce an 'inner line' policy for areas now known as states,

---

16. Nirode D. Barooah, *David Scott in North-East India (1802–1831): A Study in British Paternalism* (New Delhi: Munshiram Manoharlal, 1970), 70. Intervention of the Burmese dominant was mainly the idea of David Scott, a civil commissioner in Assam who, on the occupation of Assam on 3 December 1828, was selected to be the Commissioner of Revenue and Circuit of Assam. Ibid., 8. Scott was a devout Christian and a former student of William Carey.

17. Philip Woodruff, *The Men Who Ruled India*. Vol. II. The Guardians (London: Jonathan Cape, Ltd., 1971 [Reprint]), 119.

18. Sreeradha Datta, *The Northeast Complexities and its Determinants* (Delhi: Shipra, 2004), 9.

19. Singh, *Problem of change*, 18.

20. Baruah, *Durable disorder*, 36.

like Arunachal Pradesh, Nagaland and Mizoram,[21] which prohibited free movement of non-resident Hindus of 'mainland' India without permission of district authorities. At the same time, the Christian missionaries and their works were encouraged in those areas. The continued spread of Hinduism was thus restricted while Christianity had free movement within the areas concerned.

The British policy on the segregation of the tribal people, although it continued even post-independence for states like Nagaland and Manipur, has been criticised for the difficulty it caused in promoting national integration. One example is the work of Shreeradha Datta, wherein she argues that the series of legal and administrative decisions of the colonial administration, which were meant particularly to protect the tribal peoples, are responsible for the separatist feeling in the region.[22] Viewing the British policy from the perspective of post-independence India, particularly from assimilative *Hindutva* ideology's viewpoint, the policy did keep the tribal people at a distance from the rest of India. However, looking from an insider's point of view, it was that policy of segregation that helped the people to preserve their cultural identity at that point of time, giving a Christian theology a crucial task of finding the way to preserve and enrich the people's identity in peace in a multi-cultural context such as India.

1. 2. 3. The Administration

The three annexed provinces were administered first by military officers. Captain John Butler, an assistant to the Political Agent of Upper Assam, was the first officer to be put in charge of the hill tribes.[23] He was a "[J]udge, Magistrate and Collector in one."[24] Seeing the impact of Butler's work in a gradual decline of attacks and murders among the hill tribes, such arrangement became the policy which John Shakespear took to the Lushais in the Lushai Hills, now known as Mizoram, and referred to them as 'Lushei-Kuki' (1912). Shakespear allowed the chiefs to keep

---

21. Singh, *Problem of change*, 19–20.
22. Datta, *Northeast Complexities*, 11.
23. Woodruff, *The Men*, 123.
24. Ibid., 124.

many powers and local customs which did not involve homicide.[25] Singh suggests that British policy in the region was first motivated by concern "for the maintenance of the Empire of India, as it could be threatened from the north by Czarist Russia in collusion with Burma, China and Tibet", and secondly, "the economic exploitation of Assam oil, tea and forest resources."[26]

1. 2. 4. Immediate Impact of the Annexation

The British rule in the region had both positive and negative outcomes, some of which directly or indirectly contributed to the identity crisis in the region.

Merger with India

The British administration brought the North-East region under one administration with India. Prior to this the area existed independently under the various kingdoms, chieftainships and tribal village-states.[27] The merger brought radical changes creating problems that remain unresolved. For example, shifting the centre of administration from local control to an area outside the region and thus making the region an isolated 'frontier' when viewed from the ruler's point of view had huge consequences, shifting the centre of power away from the people and beginning dependency on an administration of the region.

Demographic Change

Another immediate impact of the incorporation of these people within British India was a demographic change. The merger opened the gate for immigration, leading to immense demographic change in the region. In the first place, the British brought with them the Bengali elites as machinery of their administration and in the process they established themselves as "'second class rulers' between the alien rulers and the local population". Not only that, "[i]n their bid to establish supremacy, they

---

25. Ibid., 322.
26. Singh, *Problem of change*, 19.
27. Downs, *History of Christianity*, 6.

prevailed upon the British to declare Bengali and English as the language of administration"[28] which had far reaching consequences. Following the tea plantation work in Assam, the British also brought tribal people into the area from other parts of India, namely Chotanagpur and Orissa. The 1929 census estimated their number at 1.3 million, one-sixth of the total population of Assam.[29] The demographic change continues till the present day as we shall see under section, 1.3.3.

1. 3. The Post-Independence Experience

The socio-political and geographical changes that the colonial British rule brought into North-East India continued in the post-independent India with complex reactions some of which are yet to be resolved. This section discusses the socio-economic, religio-cultural and political context of tribal people in the post-independent India and explains why and how they responded to their new situation.

1. 3. 1. Scheduled Tribe: A Wounded Identity

The people of North-East India are not a homogenous group. As Downs rightly points out, they belong to varied cultural traditions including kinship systems which range from matrilineal to the patriarchal, and political structures from elected village headmen to powerful hereditary chieftainship.[30] The number of Scheduled Tribe groups in North-East India, B. P. Singh records, is two hundred and seventeen.[31] According to the 2001 census, the total population of Scheduled Tribes in the whole of India is 84,326,240, which is 8.2 per cent of the total population of the country.[32] They are drawn from four different groups of people spread across the

---

28. Singh, *Problem of change*, 15.
29. Ibid., 18.
30. Downs, *History of Christianity*, 5.
31. Singh, *Problem of change*, 29. Recently there were more groups being added in the Tribe list which are not included here.
32. "2001 Census of India. Office of the Registrar General & Census Commissioner, India", http://www.censusindia.gov.in/Census_Data_2001/Census_data_finder/A-Z_index/A-Z_Index.html [Accessed 14 August 2009].

country: (1) Negrito – the Great Andamanese, the Onges and the Jarawas, (2) Proto-Austroloid – the Mundas, the Oraon and the Gond, (3) the Mongoloid – tribes of the northeast and (4) the Caucasoid – the Toda, the Rabani and the Gujjas.[33] The categorization of the culturally diverse people groups was a post-independence creation.

One problem that is obvious here is the categorization of people into one social group who have no cultural affinity whatsoever. Particularly, the classification of the whole hill people groups, like the Kukis of North-East India with the tribal people of 'mainland' India, is seen to be a superficial and confusing categorization. The reason being that it obscures the significant historical, cultural and religious differences between them. Commenting on the generalization of the issue and randomness of the characteristics listed, Devalle writes, "this categorization [putting the varied cultural groups into one as tribal] turns out to be useless and, what is worse, erroneous."[34] Besides, although etymologically the term did not necessarily carry a negative meaning,[35] the adoption of the term and the manner of its use for the people concerned, during the colonial period and thereafter in India, make the labelling highly questionable. The term was first used by the colonial administration in the context of the local people's guerrilla type of resistance to their colonization process, which was considered as a form of savagery. It was in the light of a low opinion about the people, as Brightstar Jones Syiemlieh, a Khasi theologian rightly points out, that the pejorative term 'tribe' "got crystallized as a social category."[36] At first, the terms 'forest tribe' and 'primitive tribe' were used in the census of 1901 and 1931 and then 'backward tribe' was used in the Government

---

33. S. K. Singh, *The Scheduled Tribes: People of India*. National Series, Vol. 3 (Calcutta: Oxford University Press, 1994), 4.

34. Susana B. C. Devalle, *Multi-Ethnicity in India: The Adivasi Peasants of Chota Nagpur and Santal Parganas* IWGIA Document 41, Translated from Spanish by Elisabeth Soltau (Copenhegen: The Document Department of IWGIA, 1980), 22.

35. The term tribe in its original meaning refers to the three social units delineated in the ancient Roman stratification system for the purpose of "taxation, military conscription and census taking." *The New Encyclopedia Britanica*, Micropaedia, 1992 ed., s. v. "Tribe."

36. Brightstar Jones Syiemlieh, "The Viability of the term "Tribe" in the light of Postmodernity" 17–28 in *In Search of Tribal Identity and Tribal Theology* (Jorhat: Eastern Theological College, 2001), 23.

of India Act in 1935.[37] It is clear that the term was first used for the people concerned from the perspective of colonial imperialism and hence, it has a negative connotation.

The loaded nature of the term was increased when the Independent India uncritically and conveniently adopted the term, with a little modification as 'Scheduled Tribe', for the people concerned. K. S. Singh, former Director General of Anthropological Survey of India, observes two aspects of the term:

> First, it is administratively determined by the criteria of backwardness and remoteness and it is a political decision. Second, is that all tribes are not scheduled, the presumption that there are still some communities similar to the tribes which are outside the ambit of the scheduled.[38]

The problem in the identity of Scheduled Tribes includes the meaning attached to the term 'tribe' and the way in which the people are scheduled as tribes, in other words, the very use of the term is the issue in a postmodern context. This can be understood in the light of socio-economic and religio-political context of India.

First, the term 'tribe' in post-colonial India, as in the colonial time, is understood from the perspective of others, namely Aryans. In this context, both the Scheduled Tribe and Scheduled Caste, or Dalits, were put at the same level within the hierarchical structure and were constituted on a religion-based caste system, as Joseph D'souza, the International President of the Dalit Freedom Network notes: "While the Vedas set forth the theological basis for the caste system, it was Manu, the Hindu lawgiver, who codified the strict caste rules rationalizing the oppression of Dalits today."[39] In this structure, the identity 'tribal', and for that matter Dalit, is not only

---

37. Syiemlieh, "Viability", 23.
38. K. S. Singh, "Concept of Tribe: A Note" 90–98 in H. S. Saksena at al. eds., *Scheduled Tribes and Development* (New Delhi: Serial Publications, 2006), 92.
39. Joseph D'souza, *Dalit Freedom: Now and Forever. The Epic Struggle for Dalit Emancipation*. Foreword by Kancha Ilaiah and Udit Raj, two of India's major Dalit leaders (Centennial, USA: Dalit Freedom Network, 2006), 33.

a negative identity but also a religiously instituted identity which is irreversible. In light of the context in which the identity 'tribal' was imposed, Syiemlieh rightly suggests that the term 'tribe' is a euphemism among people in high castes for the fifth place in Indian social structure.[40]

It was in this context that both Dalits and tribals looked for alternatives in search of identity and liberation. While Dalits, under the leadership of B. R. Ambedkar in the middle part of the twentieth century, opted for Buddhism, which is known as Neo-Buddhism, the tribal people in North-East India embraced Christianity. The problem still continues as no system or individual could successfully break the system including Gandhi, the father of the nation, who addressed only the problem of untouchability, the symptom of caste system, and not the caste system itself. Furer-Haimendorf comments, "unless the intellectually leading sections of the Indian population develop a spirit of cultural tolerance and an appreciation for tribal values, even the most elaborate schemes for the economic improvement of tribal populations are likely to prove abortive."[41]

Second, understandably, the labelled group in this context are considered 'uncivilized', primitive and so forth, who need to 'catch up' with other groups because of the social status assigned to them. The 1952 Schedule Castes and Tribes Commission report defined tribal as:

> 1) They live far from the civilized world; 2) they belong to one of the following three groups: Negroids, Australoids or Mongoloid; 3) they speak a tribal dialect; 4) they profess the primitive religion called 'animism'; 5) they carry on primitive activities (hunting, food-gathering, etc.); 6) they are carnivorous; 7) they go naked or seminaked; 8) they have nomadic habits and like to drink and dance.[42]

In the late 1960s, these criteria were revised but the negative connotation of tribe remains. The criteria determining peoples classified as tribal

---

40. Syiemlieh, "Viability", 21–22.
41. Christoph von Furer-Haimendorf, *Tribes of India: The Struggle for Survival* (Berkeley: University of California Press, 1982), 322.
42. Quoted in Devalle, *Multi-Ethnicity*, 21–22.

includes, according to K. S. Singh, "indications of primitive traits, distinctive culture, geographical isolation, shyness of contact with communities at large and backwardness."[43] Similarly, B. K. Roy Burman, a well-known scholar on tribal issues in India, understands the term 'tribe' in two ways: first, as "a stage in the history of evolution of societies" and second, as "a society organised on the basis of kinship ties which enables it to be a multi-functional grouping."[44] While his second point may help the understanding of tribal society, his first point sounds too simplistic as he puts the labelled people at the bottom in the hierarchy of 'development' which one necessarily needs to outgrow. He writes, "A tribe can thus outgrow its primitiveness and retain its social boundary, an essential feature of its identity."[45] A careful observation of this definition shows the employment of an evolutionary frame of reference for the understanding of tribal, which is unacceptable in the post-modern time, and the vagueness of criteria, for instance, 'animism', 'drinking and dancing' as marks of being a tribal. This further indicates the lack of interest on the part of the government of India to lay down clear criteria, if there has to be one, for a social group called 'tribal'.

Third, the lack of criteria further paved the way for the politicization of the process of scheduling who should or should not be listed as a tribe. Article 342 of the constitution of India simply says that the President is empowered to specify a list of groups as 'Scheduled Tribes' by public notification and accordingly, the list is updated when required. However, in the absence of a clear guideline, the enactment of the constitutional provision can be political and causes division and confusion among the people. A clear case is the Kuki people. While the name 'Kuki' is listed as a tribe and the people are known by this name in the states, including Nagaland, Assam and Tripura in North-East India, it is by the names of their clans such as Aimol, Chiru, Gangte, Hmar, Thado and so forth that they are known as tribes in Manipur. In other words, their common name and the uniting identity 'Kuki' were dropped in Manipur and they were

---

43. Singh, "Tribe", 93.
44. B. K. Roy Burman, "Problems and Prospects of Tribal Development in North-East India", *Economic and Political Weekly*, (April 1, 1989), 693.
45. Ibid..

scheduled as tribes by the names of their respective clans. Understandably this has become one of the main factors for confusion, disintegration and the gradual weakness of the common identity Kuki. To correct the conceived destructive policy, the term 'Any Kuki' was added to the list of tribal groups in Manipur recently for those who wish to be known by it as a tribe. Considering the damage that has been caused already, it is hard to be optimistic about the effect of this act of response.

One immediate question that arises concerns the effectiveness of the Constitution of India, the world's largest democracy, for the tribal people. While Article 14 of the Constitution provides equality of all citizens, Article 15 prohibits any discrimination on the basis of religion, gender and so forth and also enjoins the state to provide special arrangements for the advancement of the socially and educationally backward people groups. Article 16 provides privileges for the tribals by means of reservation in education, employment and in politics. Although the constitutional provisions appear to be for the interests of the people concerned, the approach was assimilative and the purpose of tribal development was to 'catch up' with others. This makes it clear that even in the so-called 'tribal development plans', the goals and parameters are set by those outside the region in line with the ideology of national integration which does not take into consideration the cultural values and aspirations of the people concerned. K. Thanzauva's *Theology of Community* was an attempt to provide a response to this problem.[46]

The name '*adivasi*' in the context of the current Hindu political movement for *swadeshi*, or indigenous in India, makes the identity 'Scheduled Tribe' yet more complex. A Hindi word *adivasi* (*Adi*-first, *vasi*-people) means original inhabitants, indicating their presence in the area before the Aryan invasion around 1500 BC.[47] Despite the meaning, many tribal Christians, for instance in the state of Orissa, have suffered for being 'non-indigenous', or non-Hindus at the hands of Hindu fanatics. This clearly

---

46. K. Thanzauva, *Theology of Community: Tribal theology in the Making* (Aizawl: AICS, 2004).
47. L. P. Vidyarthi and B. K. Rai quoted in Syiemlieh, "Viability", 22.

shows that despite their being original inhabitants, the rights of the *adivasis* or tribals have not been respected.[48]

For reasons discussed above, the people classified as tribals have been critical about the use of the term. Thanzauva, one of the pioneer tribal theologians in North-East India, in his doctoral studies discusses whether the term could be redeemed. He observes difficulties involved in the usage of the term in India; however, finding no alternative he concludes that the term can be used for some time.[49] Having found Thanzauva's argument vague, Brightstar Jones Syiemlieh, a younger theologian from the same region, took up the same issue and studied it in the light of post-modern thinking. In his study, Syiemlieh argues that a name "enshrines one's honour and dignity or one's shame and disgrace."[50] Hence, he concludes, the term is no longer viable for use. In other words the term 'tribe' cannot be used for the people concerned because of its negative connotation. Syiemlieh's point is well supported, and of course it is not new. However, the problem is that he has not provided a better name to substitute 'tribal'. He uses 'labelled people' in place of 'tribe' but that is not self-explanatory. The important point here, though, is not whether or not the people are able to substitute the term but rather if the term is viable for use. In the light of what is seen above, it is clear that the term is rather dehumanizing and hence, it needs to be replaced with an appropriate term. At the same time, it should be also remembered that the infamous renaming of 'untouchables' as *Harijans*, or children of God, with no change of their living conditions did not do them much good. To put it in a question, 'what is the use of changing the name when the people are left with the same condition?' There is clearly a dilemma in the minds of the tribal people, which leads to two different approaches to the problem. While some may propose new name/s, others may consider it better to call the disease by its name until it is healed. In fact, to a great extent, the mere change of the name will not help much unless the Indian social structure itself is transformed and the people are given freedom to decide for themselves. The search for a

---

48. Syiemlieh, "Viability", 26.
49. Thanzauva, *Theology*, 19.
50. Syiemlieh, "Viability", 28.

new name will continue as an integral part of their struggle for liberation. We shall use the term 'tribe' in this work as a part of the context to which this publication attempts to respond.

1. 3. 2. Economic Situation of North-East India

Economic oppression is one of the factors that led to the identity movements in North-East India. The region is rich in mineral resources, including petroleum, natural gas and coal. However, the tribal people benefit little from these rich resources, because the region becomes only a supplier of raw materials for the wellbeing of those outside the region. The main source of income for common people is agriculture, which is largely backward in terms of modern technology.

The experiences of the people of Assam substantiate this fact, as Guha writes:

> Assam had India's most productive oil fields, yet the liquid was pumped up by public-sector firm that employed few locals (and none at the top level of management). Worse, the oil was sent to refineries located in other states. Local trade and commerce was controlled by Marwaris from Rajasthan [North-Indians]. All in all, Assam was an 'internal colony', supplying cheap raw materials for metropolitan India to process and profit from.[51]

In this regard, Nag sees a direct link between the economic situation of the people and their political movements in the region: "While subjugation of Assamese was viewed as an attack on the Assamese nationality, the employment of Bengalese was considered to be an attack on the economic rights of the Assamese . . . Economic frustration gave birth to ethnicist ideas and resentment."[52] Guha agrees with Nag at this point as he identifies

---

51. Guha, *After Gandhi*, 555.
52. Nag, *Roots*, 161.

culture, demography and economy as key factors of the Assamese ethno-political movements.[53]

Sreeradha Datta, a Research Fellow in the Institute for Defence Study and Analyses, New Delhi, in her work, *The Northeast Complexities and its Determinants*, identifies a link between British colonial and post-colonial India's approaches to the development of the people in North-East India. She argues, "To a large extent colonial interest dictated its economy and the region has become an exporter of primary raw materials. The post-colonial mode of development also seemed to endorse such a policy."[54] The examples she gives includes the way transportation and communication linkages developed in the region, which remain concentrated in the upper Brahmaputra valley leaving other areas inaccessible and backward.[55]

The economic condition of the people beyond Assam where the main source of income is Jhuming cultivation is even more pathetic. This system is also called shifting cultivation, or 'slash and burn', and it is popular among the hill people including the Kukis of Manipur. In this, one clears a forest and uses it for a rice field in the beginning of a year and then moves to another place after harvest in the end of the year. In this way, a family moves from one rice field to another in a circle within the limits of the village land. In this circle, one comes back to the same rice field a few years later. The problem in this system includes: first, as the population grows, the size of the rice fields have to be cut in order to provide rice field for all, as a result the soil becomes less fertile as the rotation goes faster due to population growth and the cultivable land becomes smaller; second, the success of rice cultivation depends on the rain water, suitable season of the year and environment which includes wild birds, animals and so forth;[56] and third, the deforestation and burning of a huge rice fields each year

---

53. Guha, *After Gandhi*, 555.
54. Datta, *Northeast Complexities,* 54.
55. Ibid., 55.
56. *Mautam* or Bamboo famine can be one example wherein the masses of rats, which are produced as the result of the death of bamboos every forty or fifty years, invade rice fields at nights and destroy the standing crops. The recent *Mautam* being during the years 2006 to 2008.

contributed to the present ecological crisis. The point is that this kind of economic system cannot be sustained in the long run.

One constitutional provision of the government of India for the development of the tribal people of North-East India is the 'Sixth Schedule' provided under Articles 214 (2) and 275 (1). Schedules are the lists in the Constitution of India that deal with different aspects of the policy of the Government and the Sixth Schedule is about the provisions for the administration of tribal areas in Assam including Meghalaya, Mizoram and Tripura. The Sixth Schedule is such that B. K. Burman equates it with the International Labour Organization (ILO)'s International Convention No.107 which makes a special provision for certain freedom for ethnic minority groups.[57]

The Sixth Schedule provides limited powers to 'Autonomous districts' and 'Autonomous regions', and accordingly constitutes District Councils and Regional Councils with certain powers, enabling them to make laws and administer their land and resources within the limits of the Indian Constitution. It also allows the people to constitute courts to deal with legal issues among the people concerned, to generate funds by imposing taxes and collecting land revenue, to establish and manage primary schools, dispensaries, roads and so forth.[58] It was under this provision that districts, for instance, the North Cachar Hills District, the Karbi Anglong District in Assam, the Khasi Hills District, or the Garo Hills District in Meghalaya and the Mara District and the Lai District in Mizoram were created. In Manipur, the Sixth Schedule is not extended to the tribal people in the hill areas for fear of further disintegration between the plains Hindu Meiteis and the so-called tribal people in the hills. This, of course, is at the expense of the latter.

Taking into consideration North-East India as a whole, the Sixth Schedule does not satisfy the aspirations of people. In fact, the Nagas of Nagaland rejected the provision when it was first introduced soon after the Independence. Burman observes three factors for this. Firstly, the financial resources are limited and functioning of development agencies in most

---

57. Burman, "Problems", 695.
58. Burman, "Problems", 695.

states make them ineffective. Secondly, the problem of articulation of the customary laws with the philosophy of legal positivism, which, according to him, is a legacy of colonial rule, has not received adequate attention. The extent of the people's dissatisfaction with the provisions, he further points out, "Even conversion of some of the Sixth Schedule areas to the status of fulfledged [full-fledged] state does not appear to have resolved the consequent problem fully."[59] Thirdly, in Burman's reading, the dissatisfaction of the people with the Sixth Schedule has to do with the integrationist approach of the Government, their own interpretation of the term and adoption of a capitalist path of development for the tribal people of North East India. For this reason, he argues for national integration wherein all, including those in the periphery, participate in the national life.[60] Burman's argument for the participation of all citizens in national life, including those in the periphery, can still rightly be regarded as integrationist and unsympathetic to the aspirations of the people. In fact, his 'constraints to tribal development' includes the presence of some of their people on the other side of the international boundaries as one of the constraints to the development of the people. He writes:

Northeast is the meeting point of South Asia, Southeast Asia. Strategic, political, economic and ideological developments in each of these subcontinents have bearing on one or the other part of Northeast India. Besides many of the tribes in Northeast India have their counterparts in the adjoining countries . . . Most of the tribal communities of Northeast India have traditions of migration from East or Southeast Asia, either directly or through stages. In post-independence period during all crisis situations, one or the other interest-groups in India and outside has tried to take up these grey areas of tradition, to weaken national cohesion.[61]

This observation is based on the perspective of a post-independence, majority Hindu understanding, which was limited in time and space. However, looking at the situation from an insider's point of view, particularly reflecting on the situation before the imposition of international

---

59. Ibid.
60. Ibid.
61. Burman, "Problems", 696.

boundaries or independence, the picture is different. For instance, the question of 'tradition of migration from East or Southeast Asia', which Burman mentioned above, did not arise before they were separated by the present international boundaries.

'Look East' policy is another and an on-going project for economic development that could benefit the people of North-East India. During the time of Prime Minister P. V. Narasimharao, 1991–1996, this policy was developed and continues to remain in discussion until this time. The aim of this policy is to foster closer relationship and cooperation with Southeast Asian nations for the purpose of security and economic growth. Taking advantage of the geographical location, the project, if successful, could have provided more opportunity for the people of North-East India to improve their economic situation. But, here again, the question is how far will the people benefit from this new scheme if the underlying structural issues, which leave them trapped in poverty, fail to be addressed. It is clear that without improving the living situation of the people in the region, the majority tribal people of North-East India will not be able to participate in and share the benefit of the 'Look East' policy.

1. 3. 3. Demographic Change

As referred to earlier, the Yandabu treaty in 1826 paved the way for the influx of immigrants into the region. After Independence, demographic change remains one of the main issues for the region. In the post-colonial era, as the result of the partition, which created the separate states of India and Pakistan, the main immigrants into the tribal areas are Bangladeshi Bengalis. The change was so great that within a short period after Independence some of the states came under the rule of the immigrants. In highlighting the case of Assam, Guha points out, "in a decade of 1970s, the number of voters in Assam jumped from 6.2 million to almost 9 million."[62]

The trend continues and as of today, the Muslims constitute 60 per cent of the population in six of Assam's 24 districts and 40 per cent in another 6 districts. Today, the Assam Assembly has 28 Muslim members out of

---

62. Guha, *After Gandhi*, 555.

126 and four ministers.⁶³ The worst case is the state of Tripura where immigrants turned the indigenous Tripuris into a minority and a politically marginal group.⁶⁴ The present tribal movements in Tripura are demanding a homeland within their own traditional land. Immigration has become increasingly a concern not only for Assam and Tripura but for all the states of the region as Nag observes, "The most serious threat to the Assamese came from the increase in the numerical strength of the Bengalese through continuous immigration."⁶⁵ He also argues that the present ethnic conflicts in the region are due to this demographic change, which gave rise to national movements within all the states so affected.⁶⁶ Similarly, Datta, in her study of the determinants for discontent and violence in North-East India observes three interrelated issues: "The psychological distance from the rest of India, limited economic development/progress and the problems associated with the economic migrants from outside the region have culminated in a number of conflicts in Northeast."⁶⁷

1. 3. 4. Politics of Containment

The North-East region is known for its political movements, insurgency and counter-insurgency activities, violation of human rights, and inter- and intra-ethnic clashes. In fact for some of these indigenous groups, the dawn of Indian Independence was the beginning of their political struggle. That is to say, the struggles within North-East India are as old as Indian Independence itself. Each decade experiences the emergence of new political movements within the region. The approach of the centre to the people of this region has been that of containment which can be explained as follows.

The Initial Attempts at Integration

The initial attempt to integrate the tribal peoples within independent India was to provide a special provision for the tribal people within the limits

---

63. Baruah, "Postfrontier", 33.
64. Ibid.
65. Nag, *Roots*, 162.
66. Ibid., 164.
67. Datta, *Northeast Complexities*, 18.

of the Constitution. The Constitution of India inaugurated in 1950 made special provisions for the tribal people in North-East India. The provisions include:

> (1) the creation of autonomous District Councils under the Sixth Schedule of the Constitution to look after social, economic and even minor criminal and civil matters of the tribal people; (2) the imposition of restrictions on the right of Indian nationals to acquire landed property within District Council areas; and (3) the constitution of Tribal Belts and Blocks in the plain areas to prevent alienation of land from the plain tribal to others.[68]

Despite these provisions some of the local people have remained opposed in principle to concessions granted by the Indian Government, pointing out, like the Nagas, for example, that they were never part of India or under Indian rule.

The Creation of States

Creating new states within the region was a further means through which the centre tried to satisfy the demands of the local people. At the time of Independence, Nagaland, Meghalaya and Mizoram were part of Assam; Manipur and Tripura were princely states; and the area now called Arunachal Pradesh was known as North East Frontier Area (NEFA). The China-India war of 1962 and the gradual rise of insurgency directly influenced the security policies and the political map of the North-East as various states were created: Nagaland in 1963, Meghalaya, Tripura and Manipur 1972, Arunachal and Mizoram in 1987. In most cases, as economist Gulshan Sachdeva observes, the reason for creating the states was "to fulfil the ethnic, political and cultural aspirations of the people" and he further argues that the question of resources to meet administrative and other non-developmental expenditures was not given adequate attention.[69]

---

68. Singh, *Problem of change*, 21–22.
69. G. Sachdeva, quoted in Baruah, *Durable disorder*, 42.

The end result is the dependence of the states on the central Government for their management and development, an outcome that fits well with India's national security goals in the region.[70]

The granting of states in order to satisfy the demand for political movements was considered by some as an act of short-sightedness and failure. Sanjib Baruah, a political scientist from Assam argues, "It was a hurried exercise in political engineering: an attempt to manage the independentist rebellions among the Nagas and the Mizos and to nip in the bud as well as pre-empt, radical political mobilization among other discontented ethnic groups."[71] What Baruah calls 'independentalist rebellions' refers to the separatist socio-political movements of the Nagas and the Mizos in the 1970s and the 1980s. While the former is currently in peace talks with the Government of India, the latter was settled through the creation of the state of Mizoram in 1986.

Baruah also observes the unsuitableness of the ethnic-based states for the local people as he says: "Political mobilization in support of homelands produces counter-mobilization by those who fear subordinate status in those homelands."[72] Another problem in the creation of such a state, particularly in the case of Mizoram, was that it further disintegrated the people by excluding those outside the state boundary.

1. 3. 5. *Hindutva*: A Self-negating Identity

Hindutva is a political ideology that does not necessarily represent the view of the majority Hindus in India. However, the element of its assimilative ideology expressed in *Hindutva*, or Hindu-ness, cannot be totally denied in the activities of many Hindu groups among the tribal people in India. Therefore, the identity crisis of the people of North-East India also needs to be viewed in the light of this imagined 'Indian identity' based on this homogenizing ideology.

Hindu nationalism under this ideology emerged in the early 1920s and was popularized in the late 1980s as the nation underwent a communal

---

70. Baruah, *Durable disorder*, 43.
71. Baruah, *Durable disorder*, 4.
72. Ibid., 11.

crisis on religious lines. The term was coined and expounded by Vinayak Damodar Savarkar in his 1923 pamphlet entitled "Hindutva: Who is a Hindu?"[73] For Savarkar, *Hindutva* is not Hinduism. Hinduism as a religion is only a part of *Hindutva*.[74] He argues that in Hinduism, 'ism' generally meant "a theory or a code more or less spiritual or religious dogmas or system."[75] *Hindutva,* for him, is not a word but a history – a history that is not only about the religious life of the people but the history of the people in full. He writes, "*Hindutva* embraces all the departments of thought and activity of the whole Being of our Hindu race."[76] The point is that *Hindutva* covers more than the religious identity of the Hindus, claiming to root identity on the teaching of the *Rigveda* itself. Savarkar continues, "Thus in the very dawn of history we find ourselves belonging to the nation of the Sindhus or Hindus and this fact was well known to our learned men even in the Puranic period."[77] It was for this reason that he regards *Hindutva* as a history that, for him, unites all the people of India.

Savarkar's understanding of the concept, *Hindutva*, is based on a presumed bond of common blood, common culture, common civilization, and common laws and rites, and includes all Indians. This is clear in his answer to the question, "Who is a Hindu?" He understands a Hindu as a person for whom "the land that extends from Sindhu to Sindu is the Fatherland, the Motherland[,] the land of his patriarchs and forefathers."[78] Secondly, a Hindu is "a descendant of Hindu parents, claims to have the blood of the ancient Sindhu and the race that sprang from them in his veins."[79] His definition of a Hindu is centred on the socio-geographical and cultural identity. Thirdly, *Hindutva* is a politico-religious movement for national identity and integration on the basis of "one nation based on one culture", meaning that "the Hindus have a special privileged position

---

73. See, V. S. Savarkar, *Hindutva,* Fifth Edition (New Delhi: Hindi Sahitya Sadan, 2005). The first edition of the book was published in 1923, a year after Veer Savarkar's release from the jail.
74. See, Savarkar, *Hindutvas*.
75. Ibid., 4.
76. Ibid.
77. Savarkar, *Hindutva*, 7.
78. Ibid., 110.
79. Ibid.

and the various multiple minority groups have to accept the so-called Hindu way of life."[80] The ideology is represented and promoted by organizations such as the *Rashtriya Swayamsevak Sangh* (RSS), the National Volunteers Association, started in 1925, the *Vishwa Hindu Parishad* (VHP), World Hindu Council, started in 1964 as an activist wing with the aim to protect Hindu culture and tradition, the *Bharatya Janata* Party (BJP) as the Indian Peoples Party, a Parliamentary front started in 1979.[81] In North-East India, the activities of such groups have been remarkable in the recent past. Jagdamba Mall's report "A Hindu Renaissance in North-east region" is one striking example. In his report, Mall recorded eighteen Hindu Sammelans [meetings] were organized in main towns and districts of Manipur in 2010 which includes Senapati, Char Hazare, Marom, Imphal Money, Tamlro (inside Myanmar), Ukhrul, and Churachandpur in order to 'regain' a 'Hindu Nation and identity'. The allegation against the Christians in Manipur ['tribals'], he writes, "These enemy forces are trying to entrench each and every individual community, big or small Janajati or non-Janajati both. They hammer at the very root of Hindutva – the umbilical cord."[82] His report also includes a large assembly of Hindus in Guwahati on 26 December 2010 wherein the VHP president Dr Pravin Togdia was said to have cautioned the Hindu society against Christian conversion, Bangladeshi Muslims infiltration, terrorism and threat from China.

What is problematic about this approach to identity is the particular form of national pride and patriotism toward the land which it promotes. For Savarkar, to a Hindu, the land not only is the father's land but also a holy land, which, he argues, is not the case with the Muslims and the Christians. He writes:

---

80. "*Hindutva* and Multi-Culturalism", *The Hindu*, Sunday, December 06, 1998, 25. Col.a. http://www.angelfire.com/al/appiuforum/hindutva.html [Accessed 27 October, 2010].
81. For details, see Lancy Lobo, *Globalization, Hindu Nationalism and Christians in India* (New Delhi: Rawat Publications, 2002), 60–74.
82. Jagdamba Mall, "A Hindu renaissance in North-east region", http://www.organiser.org/dynamic/modules.php?name=Content&pa=showpage&pid=384&page=37 [Accessed 13 April 2011].

> For though Hindusthan to them [Muslims and Christians] is Fatherland as to any other Hindu yet it is not for them a Holyland too. Their holyland is far off in Arabia or Palestine. Their mythology and Godmen, ideas and heroes are not the children of this soil. Consequently their names and their outlook smack of a foreign origin. Their love is divided. Nay, if some of them be really believing what they profess to do, then there can be no choice – they must, to a man, set their Holyland above their Fatherland in their love and allegiance. That is but natural. We are not condemning nor are we lamenting. We are simply telling facts as they stand. We have tried to determine the essentials of Hindutva and in doing so we have discovered that the Bohras and such other Mohammedan or Christian communities possess all the essential qualifications of Hindutva but one and that is that they do not look upon India as their Holyland.[83]

In short, he writes, "... he is a Hindu to whom Sindhustan is not only a *Pitribhu* [Fatherland] but also a *Punyabhu* [Holyland]."[84] In the light of Savarkar's ideology of *Hindutva*, Bhatt argues that the formation of Hindu nationalism was influenced by the nineteenth-century European primordialist-thinking which found self-expression in Aryanism.[85] In addition, it should be also mentioned that despite Salvarkar's claim of *Hindutva* as something that is more than Hinduism, the ideology is inseparably connected to the religion. In other words, there cannot be *Hindutva* without Hinduism.

The Implication for the Minority cultures

Hindutva has far-reaching implications for the minority cultures. Two of them can be mentioned here. Firstly, the problem of the ideology for the minority cultures relates to the hierarchical social structure on the

---

83. Savarkar, *Hindutva*, 113.
84. Ibid., 116.
85. Chetan Bhatt, *Hindu Nationalism: Origins, Ideologies and Modern Myths* (Oxford: Berg Publishers, 2001), 3.

basis of which the imagined identity is constructed. In his attempt to show the 'true' identity of Indian Muslims and Christians as Hindus, Savarkar points out the caste system as a common and unifying culture of the Hindus or Indians that needs to be maintained. He writes, "Many of Mohammedan community in Kashmir and other parts of India as well as the Christians in South India observe our caste rules to such an extent as to marry generally within the pale of their castes alone."[86] In the light of this, it is clear that *Hindutva* ideology promotes a national unity by following a common culture, namely a Brahmic culture that negates the human dignity of the majority population of India, namely Dalits and tribals. For that reason, it is safe to say that *Hindutva* ideology is a threat to not just minority identities but also human dignity and freedom.

Secondly, and naturally, *Hindutva* with its homogenizing and hegemonizing approach breeds the spirit of intolerance towards the minority cultures. On the basis of this ideology both Muslims and Christians are considered non-Hindus with far reaching consequences. The 1990s saw some of the ugliest forms and means of expression and promotion of *Hindutva* ideology as minority groups became the target. Lobo lists some examples, including: "the 1990 anti-reservation riots against the Mandal commission, the 1992 riots that followed Babri Masjid demolition and many atrocities against the Christians since 1998." He commented that, "underlying these events was the Brahminic communal nationalism warring against the lower castes and minorities."[87] In line with this comment, 'inter-community polarization' has been called "the reality and essence of the politics of *Hindutva*."[88] The present Christian persecutions in India, particularly among the Dalits and tribals, are the end result of this ideology. As Sathianathan Clarke, a well-known Indian theologian points out, "Christians are being persecuted because their work among the Dalits and Adivasis is perceived as an effort to thwart the homogenizing aim of Hindutva."[89] The activities of some Hindu organizations in Manipur

---

86. Savarkar, *Hindutva*, 91.
87. Lobo, *Globalization*, 72.
88. "*Hindutva* and Multi-Culturalism", *The Hindu*.
89. Sathianathan Clarke, "Hindutva, Religious and Ethnocultural Minorities, and Indian-Christian Theology", *Harvard Theological Review*, Vol. 95. No. 2 (April 2002), 208.

mentioned earlier indicate the increasing interest of the *Hindutva* propagandists in North-East India, requiring urgent reflection and response.

For these reasons, it is safe to say that *Hindutva* is a movement of the privileged group of people favoured by the Hindu social structure to transform the nation as a unified Hindu state such as has not existed before at the expense of the minority cultures.[90] In the light of this, Vinoth Ramachandra rightly observes the intention of the VHP and BJP:

> They are anti-secularist, anti-pluralist, but not anti-democratic. Their understanding of democracy is of 'majority rule' . . . They draw their political strength from those who benefitted from traditional social structures but who feel that their privileges have been restricted under the new secularist regimes.[91]

The truth is that Dalits and tribals are the products of the caste system, which is based on the Hindu scriptures, and therefore promoting an identity based on that religion is working against their own dignity and existence as equal citizens with their fellow Indians. For this reason, Gine is absolutely right when he argues that the Indian tribals are a deceived community.[92] A related implication of the rise of Hindu nationalism is a development of 'a negative identity' among the tribal peoples. Huque observes this in the experiences of the 'tribal' people in Chotanagpur in the state of Jharkhand:

> But in reality, tribal culture is facing a crisis of identity, largely due to large-scale devastation of nature in the form of deforestation and unscientific mining, the hierarchical notions of caste and class. In fact, the adivasi, out of sheer frustration and inability to cope with external pressures, is developing at

---

90. For further discussion see, Shrinivas Tilak, "*Hindutva* – the Indian Secularists' Metaphor for Illness and Perversion" in Arvind Sharma, ed., *Hinduism and Secularism After Ayodhya* (New York: Palgrave Publishers Ltd, 2001), 123–134.
91. Vinoth Ramachandra, *Faiths in Conflict?: Christian Integrity and a Multicultural World* (Leicester: IVP, 2003), 55.
92. Pratap Chandra Gine, "Doing Tribal Theology in North East Asia: A Retrospect and Prospect" in *The Journal of Theologies and Cultures in Asia*, Vol.1 (February 2002), 20.

an alarmingly increasing rate marks of a 'negative identity' for himself. He is being branded as a lazy bum, good for nothing, drunk and criminal. These are sign of cultural degradation.[93]

For tribal people of North-East India in particular, *Hindutva* ideology poses a problem for two reasons: one, the people did not share the 'history' of India as understood by Savarkar and the Rigveda on which the ideology of Hindu identity is founded. Secondly, most of the communities, particularly the Kukis, are now Christians, and so have no place in the *Hindutva* ideology. That is to say, the Kuki, and for that matter the tribal communities of North-East India, are not Hindus on account of their distinct history, culture, and religion and hence, the ideology poses a threat to their cultural identity.

1. 3. 6. Insurgency[94]: Search for Alternative

The people of North-East India, whatever their religion, Hinduism or Christianity, resisted the new and alien social structure and administration imposed on them at the time of Independence. The Nagas started their resistance movement right from Indian Independence in 1947. In fact, the Naga political movement called 'Naga National Council.' was formed in 1946 and it signed a peace accord with the Indian Government 1975 that gave birth to the succeeding political movement, the National Socialist Council of Nagaland (NSCN), which was soon divided into two factions: the National Socialist Council of Nagaland under the leadership of Khaplang, known as NSCN (K), and the National Socialist Council of Nagaland under the leadership of Isak Chishi Swu and Thuingaleng Muivah, NSCN (I-M). On 6 April 1996, the NSCN (I-M), possibly the most powerful identity movement in the region at present, amended its manifesto to constitute Nagalim into an "Independent Sovereign Christian

---

93. Mahfuzul Haque, *Ethnic Insurgency and National Integration: A Study of Selected Ethnic Problems in South Asia* (New Delhi: Lancer Books, 1997), 95.
94. The term 'insurgency', a negative term from an insider's point of view, is an official word used to describe the resistance movements.

Socialist Democratic Republic."⁹⁵ The principle of NSCN is "Nagalim belongs to the Nagas" that is, a movement for a greater Nagaland which includes some parts of Assam, Arunachal Pradesh and Manipur where Nagas live. The word, *Lim,* in Ao-Naga means land.

Then the Mizo National Movement, a movement of all the Kuki-Chin groups across the present day boundaries for self-determination, emerged in the 1970s but ended with the formation of the present state of Mizoram on 20 February 1987, excluding those in Manipur, Myanmar and Bangladesh. The Kukis of Manipur also started their own political movements in the 1940s, which will be discussed under the section on Manipur. Similar movements for protection of identity, land and culture emerged in different parts of the region and every decade since independence has seen new movements emerging. For instance in the state of Assam, the United Liberation Front of Asom (ULFA) was formed on April 7, 1979 to establish a sovereign state of Assam through an armed struggle, and the National Democratic Front of Bodoland (NDFB) in 1989 to set up an autonomous region for the Bodo people. Similar movements emerged in other states of North-East India including, Arunachal, Meghalaya, and Tripura. According to the South Asia Intelligence Review, there are 115 armed rebel groups in North-East India and Manipur tops the list with 39 organizations, while Assam has 36 groups.⁹⁶ That makes no state free from an armed movement including Mizoram, often described as the most peaceful state. Most of these movements are ethnic-based, crossing state boundaries, and committed also to identity construction. While movements from Assam and the Manipur valley are Hindu-based, others such as the Nagas and the Kukis are Christian by religion, making the role of Christianity in identity construction one of our main concerns in this publicaiton. Before we discuss further the role of Christianity in these movements, it is apt to highlight how the government of India respond to the aspiration of the people of North-East India.

---

95. See, "Preamble" of NSCN, http://www.nscnonline.org/nscn/indext-2.html [Accessed 28 October 2008].

96. "The South Asia Intelligence Review: Weekly Assessment and briefing", http://www.satp.org/satporgtp/countries/india/terroristoutfits/index.html [Accessed 28 October 2010].

To counter these responses, power counter-insurgency was one of the means adopted by the government of India. The policy became even more binding and directive to the policy makers after the Sino-India war of 1962 and the gradual rise of resistance movements in the region. An enactment of a special law, called "Armed Forces Special Power Act" (AFSPA) in 1958 explains the policy and method of the Indian government on insurgency management and national security. The AFSPA was passed by both the Houses of Parliament, and the President assented on 11 September 1958 with a single purpose to deal with resistance movements in what is called 'disturbed' areas: namely, the states of Arunachal Pradesh, Manipur, Assam, Mizoram and Tripura. The Act includes giving Armed Forces special powers: to (1) fire upon or otherwise use force, even to the causing of death, against any person who is acting in contravention of any law or assembly of any five or more persons if considered a threat to law and order or possession of deadly weapons, (2) arrest with the use of force, without warrant, any person who has committed or suspected of having done so certain offenses, (3) enter and search any premise without warrant in order to make such arrest.[97] Baruah summarizes these powers, "the power of the security forces to make preventive arrests and search premises without warrant, to shoot and kill civilians; and effective legal immunity of soldiers implicated in such actions – court proceedings being made contingent on the central government's prior approval."[98] Under this Act, the whole of Manipur was termed disturbed area since 1980.[99]

The Act was further amended to suit the varying situation of needs within the region – for the state of Mizoram in 1986, Arunachal Pradesh in 1986, and for Assam and Manipur in 1972. The Act was also extended to Jammu and Kashmir as The Armed Forces (Jammu and Kashmir) Special Powers Act 1990, in July 1990.

---

97. "The Armed Forces (Special Powers) Act, 1958", http://www.mha.nic.in/pdfs/armed_forces_special_powers_act1958.pdf [Accessed 11 September 2010].
98. 'The Armed Forces (Special Powers Acts) Act, Government of India, 1958 (with amendments in 1972 and 1986), quoted in Baruah, "Postfrontier", 2.
99. Anil Kamboj, "Manipur and Armed Forces (Special Powers) Act 1958", http://www.idsa.in/strategicanalysis/ManipurandArmedForcesSpecialPowerAct1958_akamboj_1004 [Accessed 11 September 2010].

The committee, known as the 'Reddy Commission', recommended the repeal of AFSPA but it remained in place, modified only by making the law inoperative within the city limits of Imphal, because of the opposition on the part of the Army and the Defence Ministry.[100] The Act, although a measure to maintain the public order from a ruler's viewpoint, gives to the people a picture of a 'step-motherly treatment' on the part of the Government of India. This is because of the nature of the Act as well as the way it is implemented. Arguing for the Act, Anil Kamboj, an experienced Border Security Force officer, who served both in Manipur and Kashmir, stresses that the fault is not in the Act as such but in the way it is implemented.[101] Such being the case, the AFSPA instigates public resistance in North-East region of India even to the extent of resorting to naked protest and hunger strikes in Manipur, particularly among the majority Hindu Meitei people.

Coming back to the role of Christianity in the identity movements indicated earlier, it is making the situation more complex. While Christianity helped protect the tribal people from being assimilated into Hinduism and its oppressive structure, the way it is projected needs critical reflection. The Mizo National Front (MNF) in 1960s defined its purpose as to serve the highest sovereignty to unite all the Mizo under one political boundary, to improve and develop the Mizo condition and to maintain and defend Christianity.[102] The socio-political and religious movements are indistinguishably connected as the following MNF statement indicates:

> The Indian officials chose to pay their visits to Mizoram exclusively on Sundays, thereby imposing much Sunday work and official business and making it impossible for Mizo Christians

---

100. Baruah, "Postfrontier", 4. The Committee under the leadership of B. P. Reddy, a former Supreme Court Judge was appointed by the government of India in November 2004 to review the Law.

101. Anil Kamboj, "Manipur and Armed Forces (Special Powers) Act 1958" *Strategic Analysis*, Vol. 28. No. 4 (2004), 619.

102. Tlangchhuaka, quoted in [Lalngurawna Ralte], *The Presbyterian Church of Mizoram: The Testimony of a Self-supporting, Self-governing and Self-propagating Church* (Geneva: World Alliance of Reformed Churches, 1989), 39.

to observe the Lord's Day... The Mizo people did not want to be ruled by and assimilated to 'idol worshipers' [the Hindus].[103]

Similarly, in one of the world's oldest unresolved struggles, the National Socialist Council of Nagaland (NSCN) adopts the phrase 'Nagaland for Christ' as a theme of its movement. The manifesto of the Council reads, "We stand for the faith in God and the salvation of mankind in Jesus, the Christ alone, that is 'NAGALAND FOR CHRIST'." Yet this evangelical aim is wedded to a militant policy as spelled out clearly: "We rule out the illusion of saving Nagalim through peaceful means. It is arms and arms again that will save our nation and ensures freedom to the people."[104]

The complexity of such an employment of faith identity in social identity construction lies not only in a domestication of faith in a particular cultural context but also what can be called 'ethnic conversion' in Manipur, particularly in the district of Chandel adjacent to Ukhrul, a Naga-dominated area in the state, where the first missionary worked.[105] Rizvi and Roy rightly noted that some of the tribes formerly listed in the Kuki tribe in Manipur have been assimilated into the Naga generic term.[106] And based on his empirical research, Rajat Kanti Das concludes that it was through the work of the local Christian missionaries within the state of Manipur that many disowned their identity as Kukis and gave their political allegiance to another group, namely the Nagas.[107] This shows that Christianity not only plays an important role in religious conversions but also ethnic conversions.

Ethnic conversion in this part of Manipur leads to further issues. In a situation where the identity of the people and their land are interconnected, the name of a geographical area and its boundary changes when a community within that area changes its ethnic allegiance to other groups. In

---

103. Ibid., 39.
104. See, "Preamble" of NSCN.
105. See, map 2 in chapter 1, 'Districts of Manipur'.
106. S. H. M. Rizvi and Shibani Roy, *Kuki-Chin Tribes of Mizoram and Manipur* (Delhi: B. R. Publishing Corporation, 2006), Cover page.
107. Rajat Kanti Das, *Manipur Tribal Scene: Studies in Society and Change* (New Delhi: Inter-India Publications, 1985), 18.

the case mentioned above, when some of the so-called 'Old Kuki' groups such as Anal, Lamkang, Moyong and others adopted a Naga identity, their land automatically became part of proposed *Nagalim*, recreating identity, history, and the territory of the people. Arguing for Naga domination in the hill areas in a post-ethnic conversion in the area, Jusho claims, "Even the traditionally Kuki dominated district of Chandel has become under the increasing control of the Nagas with several Naga tribes like Anal, Maring, Moyong, Lamkang etc., distributed in the area."[108] The point is that ethnic boundary lines affect the geographical boundaries, and vice versa, and when that happens, not only the notion of 'once united people' as a mark of identity becomes blurred, but also, loyalty and power get transferred to a new community creating a situation vulnerable to ethnic conflict among the people concerned.

As a movement for greater Nagaland, the *Nagalim* ideology led the Nagas into conflict with the neighbouring states and various ethnic groups within them, including Assam and Arunachal. Manipur was possibly the worst affected state because the majority Hindu Meiteis resisted the movement with great loss of lives and property, including the State Assembly, which was vandalized in 2001. The movement also led to a severe clash between the Nagas and Kukis, both Christians, living under the proposed greater Nagaland areas within Manipur with a heavy loss of lives.[109] The tension between the two communities also spread to the neighbouring states in a similar manner so that in the year 1997, a quit notice was served to the Kukis of Nagaland, one of the indigenous tribes of the state. To remember those who lost their lives during these clashes, the Kukis observe the thirteenth of September as *Sahnit*, a traditional way of showing grief at the loss of someone due to death. The date was chosen because one hundred and four innocent people, mostly women and children, lost their lives that day. In a Christian context, the day is used for prayer, sometimes

---

108. P. T. Hitson Jusho, *Politics of Ethnicity in North-East India With Special Reference to Manipur* (New Delhi: Regency Publications, 2004), 44.

109. The worst phase of the ethnic clashes was between 1992 and 1997. P. S. Haokip has listed the names of Kukis killed during these clashes as 472 and the number of villages burned down was 154. See P. S. Haokip, *Zale'n-gam: The Land of the Kukis*, First Edition (np: Kuki National Organization, 1995), 48–76.

with fasting for peace and reconciliation, which can have an unintended negative impact unless accompanied by critical theological and biblical reflection on both the inter-ethnic conflict context locally, as well as the wider situation in the region.

There is of course a disturbing irony in the way Christianity is used in these instances: by basing their identity on religion and then employing this as the justification for a culturally exclusive state, this movement adopted an ideology and policy remarkably similar to the one advancing from mainland India which it sought to oppose. In one case the religion was Hinduism, in the other, Christianity. Such naive religio-political movements blur the vision of the religion itself, in this case Christianity, when it clashes with other ethnic groups who profess the same religion. And it is precisely this use of Christianity to provide religious sanction for such movements that underlies the urgent need for the fresh theological reflection with which this publication is concerned.

1. 4. Tribal Situation in Manipur

The state of Manipur is a home to three main ethnic groups, namely the Meiteis, the Kukis and the Nagas. Including the non-tribal Meitei majority, all the groups are struggling to assert their identity and stability as people. This involves not only cultural elements but also socio-religious and political interests of the people concerned and hence it makes the nature of identity even more fluid and complex. A survey of the situation will help us understand the Kuki struggle for the recognition of their cultural identity. In this section, the land, the people and the history of Manipur as a whole, will be discussed and the social changes and issue of identity within the state.

1. 4. 1. The Land, the People and Their Settlements

The state of Manipur is a Meitei majority state with two main tribal groups: the Kukis and the Nagas. There are nine districts, five in the hills and four in the valley. While the minority tribals occupy the five hill districts, the majority Meiteis live in the smaller valley districts, which includes, Bishnupur, Thoubal, Imphal West and Imphal East.[110] The four valley districts in total cover 700 square miles, which is only ten per cent of the total land.

With the Meitei as the majority group, the valley is also populated by other minority groups, such as the Pangal (who are the Manipuri Muslim), the Loi, the Yaithibi and the Nepali. Given that the Meitei are the dominant group of the state, Manipuri or Meitei language is the *lingua franca* of the state. The remaining five hill districts make ninety per cent of the total land and are inhabited by the Nagas and the Kuki groups who form one-third of the total population.[111] In this way, the two-thirds majority Meiteis occupy only ten per cent of the total land while one-third of the population share the ninety per cent of the total land, triggering communal tensions between people in the hills and those in the plain.

In the hill areas, the people are classified into two groups: the Kukis and the Nagas. Between them the Kukis formed the majority. The census of 1881, for instance, recorded the Naga and Kuki as the two hill tribes of Manipur termed as 'clans' in the Gazetteer of Manipur in 1886.[112] The recognition of these clans as separate tribes resulted in the disintegration and separation of people sharing a common cultural heritage under the independent India. The 2001 census recorded twenty-two Scheduled Tribes created out of the Kuki community while there are only seven tribes under the identity Naga. N. Nabakumar explains the list:

> Of the twenty-nine scheduled tribes of Manipur, according to the classical classification of the earlier British ethnographers, twenty-two tribes, namely Aimol, Anal, Kom, Lamkang, Monsang, Moyon, Mizo (Lushai), Paite, Purum, Ralte, Sukte, Simte, Thadou, Vaiphei and Zou are Kukis the

---

110. See map 2 in chapter 1, 'Districts of Manipur'.
111. S. K. Singh, "Foreword" in Singh S. K. Gen. ed., *People of India: Manipur*. Vol. 31 (Calcutta: Seagull Books, 1998), xiii. See also, Guha, *After Gandhi*, 276.
112. S. H .M. Rizvi, "Introduction" in Singh S. K. Gen. ed., *People of India: Manipur*. Vol. 31 (Calcutta: Seagull Books, 1998), 5. The census was ordered by Sir Charles Elliot shortly after assuming the government office in the province and it was done among all the leading tribes of Assam.

remaining seven tribes such as Angami, Kabui, Kacha Naga, Mao, Maram, Sema and Tangkhul are Nagas.[113]

The Kukis and the Nagas lived together in the hill areas and there were no boundaries until British rule. After what the British termed the 'Kuki rebellion' in 1917–1919, a movement of resistance known locally as the 'Anglo-Kuki war', the hill areas were divided into three subdivisions, each headed by an officer from the neighbouring government of Assam, in order to prevent a future Kuki uprising.[114] The subdivisions eventually became three hill districts within Manipur: Tamenglong, Senapati and Ukhrul as seen in Map 2 earlier in the chapter. Both the Nagas and Kukis are also to be found outside the state of Manipur.[115] The Nagas are to be found in Nagaland, or the state of the Nagas, where they form the majority, Assam, Arunachal Pradesh, and some in Myanmar. In a similar way, the Kukis are to be found in Assam, Tripura, Mizoram, Nagaland and some parts of Myanmar and Bangladesh.

1. 4. 2. Political and religious context of Manipur

Broadly speaking, the people of Manipur, both the hill tribals and the valley Meiteis, belong to the Tibeto-Burman linguistic family and there are commonalities between them in terms of culture, language and religious practices that indicate their homogeneity.[116] However, in course of time, Manipur went through socio-political and cultural changes that have become reasons for the identity crisis in the present day.

---

113. W. Nabakumar, "The Inter Ethnic Relations Of The Different Communities Of Manipur: A Critical Appraisal", http://www.manipuronline.com/Features/November2005/interethnicrelationship17_2.htm [Accessed 9 October 2008].
114. The New Encyclopedia Britannica, Vol. 21. 15th Edition. (Chicago: Encyclopaedia Britannica Inc., 1992), 138.
115. The Kukis of Manipur share with those outside the sate a common myth of their origin, language, culture and so forth, but it may not necessarily be the case with the Nagas.
116. T. C. Hodson, *The Meitheis*, Reprint [first published in 1908] (Delhi: B. R. Publishing Corporation, 1975), 11. See also, M. Horam, "Foreword" in Hodson, *Meitheis, ibid.*, viii–x.

1. 4. 2. 1. *Political scenario*

Politically, Manipur as a state underwent several changes in political status. The state was an independent kingdom under the chiefs and kings until it became a princely state under British rule in 1891. At the departure of the British administration in 1947 the political status of Manipur was changed from a princely state to a constitutional monarchy until 1949 when she merged with India.[117] In the midst of these changes, the Kukis continue their traditional chieftainship practice until the present day. We shall come back to this later in chapter 3.

The British came into contact with Manipur for the first time in 1762 when the Manipur raja, Jai Sigh, sent his representative to Mr Harry Verelts, the British Resident in Sylhet (now part of Bangladesh), asking his intervention against Burmese incursions. The British became more acquainted with Manipur during the Anglo-Burma war of 1824–1826, through which the Manipur kingdom was restored and protected from the Burmese threat.[118] At the same time, the political weakness of Manipur during this time paved the way for increasing British presence in the state. Following the death of Bhagyachandra, its ruler, Manipur went through a political crisis due to constant conflicts among Bhagyachandra's sons for succession. Taking advantage of the situation, the Burmese invaded Manipur in 1819 and ruled for seven years with savage atrocities, termed the 'Seven-Year Devastation'.[119] During this period the princes of Manipur were scattered and were given shelter by other people including the Kukis. In the meantime, sensing the danger of Burmese rising in the region, the British fought with the Burmese, ending their Treaty with the Burmese signed at Yandabu in 1826, mentioned earlier. The Treaty recognized and restored Manipur state's sovereignty and paved the way for Gambir Singh to be the King of Manipur in 1926.[120] The British presence in Manipur gradually increased and in 1891 they established their administration

---

117. Jusho, *Politics*, 17.
118. Lyall, "Introduction" in Hodson, *Meitheis*, xviii.
119. Jusho, *Politics*, 5.
120. Horam, quoted in Jusho, *Politics*, 6.

by defeating the king in what was known as 'Anglo-Manipuri' war after which Manipur was made a princely state in 1892.

The British administration in Manipur was exercised through the existing traditional structure, known as the Subsidiary Alliance. Accordingly, there were two separate approaches to the administration, one for the valley Meiteis and another for the hill people, namely the Kukis and the Nagas. In 1907 an administrative system called the 'Durbar', the highest court of the state, was instituted mainly for the valley Hindu Meiteis. The President of the Durbar, the Political Agent in Manipur, was always to be a British Indian Civil Service officer whose duty was that of an ambassador and whose power included awarding the death penalty to people under the guidance of the Governor of Assam, his senior British officer.[121] In this case, the king was simply the mouthpiece of the Durbar or the British Government of India.

In the case of the hill people the president of the Durbar was the sole administrator. However, his administration was dependent on the assistance of *Lambus*, the agents employed from the valley Hindu Meitei community. *Lambus* were responsible for translating and passing orders from the President of the Durbar, or Government, to the people through the chiefs among the Kukis and the headmen among the Nagas. The hill areas were further sub-divided into two: the Kuki and Naga areas and administration was carried out through the chiefs and headmen with the help of the *Lambus*.

In this situation there was a communication gap between the people and the Government, or the President of the Durbar. This is illustrated in the following account of the Kuki administrative system by a colonial official and his underestimation of the situation prior to the Kuki uprising.

In November 1917, J. Higgins (who had 7 ½ years' service) expressed his opinion that with an escort of 150 rifles he could punish the rebel villages within 75 days. Three months have now passed in the course of which both Mr Higgins and myself have been treacherously fired on, and it has not yet been found possible to wrest any of the leading rebel chiefs

---

121. Jusho, *Politics*, 7.

although columns containing 1,070 rifles are either moving or prepared to move against the rebel Kuki villages.[122]

Contrary to the estimation of Higgins, the war lasted about three years, a fact that illustrates ignorance and underestimation due to the absence of close relationship between the ruler and the ruled that led the Kuki uprising.[123] The nature of administration of the hill areas and the gap between the ruler and the ruled further indicates the neglect of the people and lack of concern for their well being on the part of the ruler.

Seeing the administration from a different viewpoint, Gangumei Kamei, a follower of a Naga traditional religion and a well-known historian from a Naga tribe, observes that the recognition of the traditional administrative structure of the hill people was the beginning of politicizing ethnicity. Connecting the colonial administration with the present ethnic problem in the state he writes, "Politicization of ethnicity was rooted in the colonial administrative system and it is continued even later on."[124] For Kamei, the bifurcation of Manipur in administration and politicization of ethnicity contributed to the present ethnic problems in the state. The emergence of various ethnic groups and the aspiration of the tribal people for autonomy by the end of the British administration supports Kamei's argument.

At the close of the British administration in 1947, Manipur had political autonomy, although only for a short time. The Manipur State Constitution Act was framed in 1947 and provided a Constitutional monarchy with a 53-member Legislative Assembly. Thus, Manipur remained an autonomous state with complete internal independence until 1949 when Budhachandra, the Maharajah, was persuaded to sign an agreement for annexation of Manipur to India. Under that constitution an election

---

122. Letter from the Political Agent, Manipur, to the Chief of Commissioner of Assam. Foreign and Political Department. File No. 49–52, 1918, NAI, New Delhi. Quoted in S. M. A. W. Chishti, *The Kuki Uprising: 1917–1920* (Gauhati: Spectrum Publications, 2004), 22. Higgins served in Manipur in the Indian Civil Service since 1910 and later became the Political Agent of Manipur.

123. Chishti, *Kuki Uprising*, 10.

124. Gangumei Kamei, "Ethnicity And Politics In Manipur", A Speech given at the Talk on 'Ethnicity and Politics of Manipur', organized by the National Research Center, at Manipur University on 16 September 2003. http://www.manipuronline.com/Features/December2003/ethnicityand politics21_1.htm [Accessed 25 December 2008].

was held in which nine members from the Kuki-Chin groups and eight from the Naga were elected to represent the hill areas in the Legislative Assembly (MLA).[125]

On 15 October 1949, Manipur was formally annexed to India and the state underwent yet another change. The state's Constitutional Assembly was dissolved and administration was "entrusted to the President of India who ran [carried out] the administration through a Chief Commissioner appointed by him."[126] Later, in 1956, Manipur was granted a status of a Union Territory and in 1972 a full-fledged state. The merger with India, however, did not yield a positive response. The Meitei separatist element viewed the move as an unfortunate event and observes the day as a 'Dark day'.[127] Some non-separatist hill people share this view. Referring to the question of the central government's lack of recognition of the people, Kamei terms the merger as "most unfortunate" and writes:

> The Merger destroyed both autonomy and democracy of Manipur and brought a bureaucratic Central rule under a Chief Commissioner. This was, in practice, the continuance of the colonial rule, a mere replacement of the white men by the brown sahibs of the Government of India. This was a most unfortunate political development in the modern history of Manipur which was as disastrous as the British conquest of Manipur of 1891 in its consequences. Had the Government of India permitted the continuation of the working of the Manipur State Constitution within Indian Union, the people would not have felt the change from the Maharaja to the Chief Commissioner.[128]

The merger of Manipur into India raises further questions among the hill people of Manipur. Before the merger, there were two separate

---

125. Kamei, "Ethnicity".
126. Jyotimoy Roy, quoted in Jusho, *Politics*, 17.
127. Jusho, *Politics*, 17.
128. Kamei, "Ethnicity".

administrations between the hill people and valley Meiteis. Arguably the merger of Manipur, including the hill areas, into India raises the question of Maharajah's representation of the hill people. Jusho writes:

> The tribal[s] argued that the merger agreement signed by the Manipur Maharajah could not and did not cover the territory occupied by the tribal Chiefs and their subjects, because the Maharajah of Manipur was not a tribal representative who had authority to act on their behalf, and the tribals were not his subjects.[129]

The agreement signed by the Maharajah, Budhachandra, on 15 October 1949, thus merged together the valley and the hill areas, which were formerly administered separately. Both areas became part of India and functioned under its administration. Accordingly, there were efforts to infuse a sense of Indianness among the hill people on the part of the Central Government, and there have been rigorous attempts to bring together the hill areas and the valley under the same system of administration, despite the separate cultural identity of the hill people. This includes the introduction of alien political systems such as the Manipur Land Revenue and the Land Reform Act in 1960, the extension of *Panchayat* system in the hill areas, and other schemes to create the integrity of Manipur territory. Such moves were perceived by the tribals as threats to their cultural identity and as domination and further exploitation by the majority Meiteis. They opposed the introduction of the Manipur Land Revenue and Land Reform Act in 1960 fearing that the Act would alienate their lands, which cover 20,089 square kilometres out of the total area of 22,327 square kilometres.[130] Instead, they demanded the extension of Sixth Schedule district autonomy, a status with certain freedom within the Indian Constitution, which is an issue that remains unsolved until now. They also opposed the

---

129. Jusho, *Politics*, 18.
130. Sixth Schedule Demand Committee, Manipur (SDCM), Press Conference (New Delhi, International Youth Centre), September 9, 2000. Quoted in Jusho, *Politics*, 19. See also, Jusho, *Politics*..

introduction of the *Panchayat* system[131] although the pressure is increasingly high and insistent in some of the Kuki dominated hill areas such as Moreh in the southwest of the Valley and in Sadar Hill adjoining the northern part of the Valley.[132]

Movements for protection of cultural identity emerged and took different forms and expressions including demands for autonomy, statehood, cross-state border political movements and so forth. The vulnerability of the hill people on this issue can be reflected in the distribution of seats in the State Legislative Assembly. On becoming a full-fledged state in 1972, the Manipur Assembly constituencies were delimited into 60 seats, out of which 20 seats are reserved for the Scheduled Tribes, one seat for the Scheduled Caste, and the rest for the Meiteis.[133] There are nine districts in the state: five in the hills and four in the valley as shown in Map 2 earlier in the chapter. That makes 40 seats for the four districts of the valley while the remaining 20 for the five districts of the hills which covers 20,089 square kilometres out of the total area of 22,327 square kilometres as shown above. The State has two seats in the *Lok Sabha*, the lower house in the parliament of India, of which one is reserved for tribals and one seat in the *Raya Sabha*.[134] Consequently, while the larger portion of the land belongs to the tribal people, administrative power is in the hands of the valley Hindu Meiteis. Given the incomparable size of the Meitei population against that of the minority tribals, the imbalanced sharing of seats may look logical, but in a situation where land or territorial protection is crucial for the survival of the people, this is seen as oppressive and susceptible to communal tensions when viewed from a minority viewpoint.

---

131. 'Panchayat' [*panch*–five and *yat*–assembly in Hindi] means assembly of five, who, with the support of the state government, works for the development of a community in rural areas. The system is alien to the local people.

132. "Violence, strikes mark panchayat, ZP polls in Manipur" Posted: Thu Sep 20 2007, 00:00 hrs http://www.indianexpress.com/news/violence-strikes-mark-panchayat-zp-polls-i/218853/[Accessed 4 April 2011].

133. Jusho, *Politics*, 20.

134. Raya Sabha is the upper house of the Parliament of India. Membership is limited to 250 members.

1. 4. 2. 2. Religious traditions

Religiously, Manipur is a multi-religious society. The traditional religious practices were sometimes called animism[135] and were gradually substituted by missionary faiths from outside. Hinduism, the Vaishnava tradition in particular,[136] was made the official religion of the state among the Meiteis by King Garib Niwas (1709–1748). With the visit of a devout Hindu called Santidas Gosai and his continued influence on him, the king ordered Hinduism to be the religion of the people and established it, often harshly, with the help of Gosai. The impact was seen not only in the substitution of the Meitei script with Devanagiri but also in forceful imposition of Hindu religion on his subjects.[137] Since then, Hinduism remains the religion of the Meiteis in the valley, although *Sanamahi*, the name for the pre-Vaishnava religion, was incorporated into Hinduism. The revival of *Sanamahi* occupies an important place in the current Meitei identity movement. At the beginning of the twentieth century, C. J. Lyall remarked, "while Burma has accepted the mild and original animistic cult, Manipur has been taken into the pale of Hinduism, and has imposed upon itself burdensome restriction of caste and ritual from which its greater neighbour is happily free."[138] It is possible that the new religion, Hinduism, and those restrictions within it, keep the community further segregated from other communities, hence widening the gap between the communities. In fact, W. Nabakumar argues, "When the Meiteis became the followers of Vaishnavism, this historically given cultural arrogance, according to the value system of the new faith, has been expressed in the framework of a pollution-purity relationship and has alienated the non-Hindu tribals."[139] This is further supported by the fact that the hill people

---

135. Horam, "Foreword" in Hodson, *Meitheis*, viii. In this work we shall use the term "primal religion" in place of animism.
136. Vaishnavism is a Hindu tradition, which refers to the worship of Vishnu and his incarnates like Rama and Krishna. The belief and practice were based largely on the Upanishads, the Vedas and the Puranic texts, rooting the tradition into the Brahminic tradition, which is the basis of *Hindutva* ideology.
137. Lucy Zehol, *Ethnicity in Manipur: Experience, Issues and Perspectives* (New Delhi: Regency Publications, 1998), 78.
138. Lyall, "Introduction" in Hodson, *Meitheis*, xxi.
139. Nabakumar, "Inter Ethnic Relations".

are called *'Hau'* (a derogatory term), by the Meiteis. Zehol rightly puts, "The Hinduised Manipuris observed themselves in a different sense of the rules of the Hindu casteism and considered the Nagas and Kukis as rude and degraded, and later on particularly during the reign of Chandra Kirti as the 'untouchables'."[140] For this reason, it can be suggested that the new religion widened the gap between the people in the valley and those in the hill areas and hence, the latter are alienated both within and outside North-East India.

By contrast to the Meiteis, the hill people opted to embrace Christianity from their primal religion. Christianity was brought in during the early days of colonial rule. Having established an understanding with the government, William Pettigrew, who was sent by Arthington Aborigine Mission, a private agency, brought the Christian faith to the state in 1894 as the first missionary. Pettigrew's initial intention was to work among the Hindu Meiteis in the valley, which he did. But later, apprehending the risk it might involve, he was advised by the colonial authorities to go to the hill areas in the Eastern side of Manipur. On the south of Manipur, Watkin Roberts, a Welsh missionary based in the Lushai Hills, introduced the Christian faith in 1910. The work of the missionaries grew rapidly in the hills so that within a hundred years, the hill people became Christians, except a section of some Kabui Nagas living in the valley.

From a point of view of evangelization, Christianity among the hill people of Manipur may be a success story. However, viewed from the perspective of one's identity and culture and the disintegration of hill people, the Kuki people in particular, the role of Christianity has not been all positive. While the faith has transformed the peoples' lives in many ways, it also widened the gap between the culturally and linguistically allied Kuki groups through mother-tongue Bible translation, doctrinal divisions, and as the result of the unhealthy relationships among the missionaries. Also with the rise of Christianity, as Jusho observes, many have "abandoned their traditional customs and culture and adopted the life style of

---

140. Zehol, *Ethnicity*, 70. See also, Ranjit Singh, "Emergent Ethnic Processes in Manipur: A Reappraisal", in Pakem, ed., *Nationality, Ethnicity and Cultural Identity in North-East India* (Guwahati: Omsons Publications, 1990), 239.

the outside world."¹⁴¹ The work of evangelization and its impact on the Kuki people will be discussed in chapter 4.

1. 4. 3. Contesting Identities

As indicated earlier, by the end of the British administration, there were aspirations for autonomy among the people in the hills. Several ethnic-based organizations were formed such as the Kabui Naga Association (1946), the Kuki National Assembly (1946), and so forth. The same aspiration led the Mao Nagas to boycott the 1948 Manipur election for the autonomy of the hill areas. Of a different nature, the Zeliangrong movement under the leadership of Rani Gaidinliu campaigned for the protection of culture, including the primal religion. The term Zeliangrong was coined in 1947 as the common name for the movement among the Kabuis, Zemeis and the Rongmeis. The movement was against the perceived oppressors from outside the community, but also against conversion from the primal religion to Christianity. Zehol observes, "It [the Zeliangrong movement] has restored faith and pride in the traditional values and customs while forsaking superstition and 'animistic' practices which overburdened the people and prevented their social consciousness."¹⁴² However, unable to withstand pressures from other Nagas against her indigenous religion and narrow approach, Gaidinliu laid down arms in 1966 and today the Nagas of Manipur, in general, are supportive of a larger Naga movement, which was referred to earlier. One thing that stands out clearly in Gaidinliu's movement is the question of primal religion as part of an identity issue for the Zeliangrong, particularly among those who still follow the religion.

Coming to the present identity struggle of the Kuki people, their political encounter with the colonial power from 1917 to 1919 had a great impact on them. The Kukis prior to this event were known for their power and domination in the hills of Manipur. Referring to William Shaw's dismissive description of the material culture of the Kukis, J. H. Hutton wrote, "Had Mr Shaw been able to see such villages as Santing and Chongjang

---

141. Jusho, *Politics*, 3.
142. Zehol, *Ethnicity*, 76.

before they were destroyed during the rebellion he would hardly have described the Thado dwellings he does without qualification."[143]

Much more damaging than the physical oppression and destruction during the war was the destabilization of Kuki power and administration by dividing the hills areas into three subdivisions. At the end of the war, all the leading chiefs were put into jail. In the meantime, in preventing the possible future recurrence of such resistance movements, the colonial administration for the first time divided the hill areas into three subdivisions, each headed by an officer from the neighbouring government of Assam[144] so as to suppress the Kuki influence. Regarding the impact of that arrangement on the Kukis, William Shaw wrote, "by the establishment of three subdivisions in the hills of Manipur State, their prestige among other hill tribes has been much shaken."[145] For the Kukis, it was a total and sudden change and disruption of their normal life and practice that was never to be restored.

At the dawn of Indian Independence a new Kuki political movement emerged. The Kuki National Assembly (KNA), a political party, was formed on 24 October 1946. The party was active and won seats in the state's election for Members of Legislative Assembly (MLA) until the 1990s. In the meantime there was a movement for larger unification among the Kuki-Chin-Mizo groups. The Mizo National Front (MNF) was formed on 22 October 1961 and was later supported by other cognate groups including those in Manipur and Burma. In the year 1964, KNA and the erstwhile Manipur Mizo Integration Council in Manipur, passed a resolution to achieve a single administrative unit for the whole Kuki-Chin-Mizo groups. Another convention was held at Kawnpui, Churachandpur, Manipur in 1965 which was represented by all the groups within Kuki: Paite National Council, Vaiphei National Organization, Simte National Organization, Zoumi National Organization, Mizo Union, Mizo National Front, Chin

---

143. J. H. Hutton, "Introduction" in William Shaw, "Notes on the Thadou Kukis", *The Journal and Proceedings of the Asiatic Society of Bengal*, New Series, Vol. XXIV, 1928, No.1. Published by the Asiatic Society of Bengal on behalf of the Government of Assam (Calcutta: The Baptist Mission Press, 1929), 4.
144. *The New Encyclopedia Britannica*, 138.
145. Shaw, "Thadou Kukis", 50.

National Union, Mizo National Union, Hmar National Union, Kuki National Assembly, Gangte Tribal Union, Kom National Union, and Biete Convention Council.[146] The joint armed movement began in 1966 under the banner of the Mizo National Front (MNF), which was spearheaded by Laldenga from Mizoram. Laldenga was assisted by other leaders including Col. Demkhoseh Gangte, a well-known Kuki leader from Manipur. The movement persisted for two decades of long struggles with heavy loss of lives and property. However, with lasting consequences for those outside the region, the peace accord between MNF and the Government of India was signed on 30 June 1986, and the state of Mizoram was created as the result. The state covers only what was known as 'the Lushai Hills' and left the dream of the above-mentioned signatories for greater unification unfulfilled.

In the meantime, a faction of the Naga movement spearheaded by Th. Muivah, a Tangkhul from Manipur referred to earlier, came in conflict with the Kukis over the former demands for a greater Nagaland within the hill area where they live together. As the result, the later part of the twentieth century saw another resurgence of Kuki socio-political movements for the protection of cultures, land and identity. The Kuki Inpi, the traditional administration or government, was revived in 1993 by way of re-establishing and claiming their cultural and political rights as a people. As armed movements, the Kuki National Front (KNF) was formed in 1988 to be followed by the Kuki National Organization (KNO), possibly more influential than the former, with their armed wing called the Kuki National Army (KNA), promoting an ideology of *Zalengam*, in the Kuki Land, which includes part of Burma and India. Their aim is to protect the Kuki people's ethnic identity and culture by way of recognizing

---

146. Seilen Haokip, "What Price, Twenty Years of Peace in Mizoram (1986–2006): A Kuki Perspective", in the Official Website of The Director of Information and Publications, Govt. of Mizoram. http://www.dipr.mizoram.gov.in/index.php?option=com_content&task=view&id=779&Itemid=0 [Accessed 10 October 2010] Some of these names or organizations no longer exist as "Nations". Having shown their genealogical linkage, affinity in culture and dialects the author rightly argues that these are not separate tribes but groups that make a single tribe.

their ancestor's land.¹⁴⁷ They also claimed their right to enjoy the fruits of their national commitment during the struggle for Indian Independence.¹⁴⁸ Like the NSCN (I-M), mentioned earlier, the KNA also draw their sources from religion, namely, Christianity. In both the KNA and NSCN (I-M), the Bible and gun are held together at the same time.

Seeing the hill people's political movements, the valley Meiteis also started their own movements in the early 1960s. The United National Liberation Front (UNLF) was formed on 24 November 1964.¹⁴⁹ For the first two decades, the organization concentrated mainly on mobilization and recruitment but in 1990, they commenced their armed struggle.¹⁵⁰ The threat, according to the group, is the immigration and cultural influence of non-residents including those from 'mainland' India and the aim is to establish an independent socialist Manipur through cultural renaissance.¹⁵¹ The Meitei movement, in short, is a movement for a separate Meitei social-political identity through reasserting their pre-Hindu identity.

Singh makes an interesting observation, pointing out two levels at which the Meitei people reassert their cultural identity. He writes, "They [the Meiteis] have rediscovered and even reconstructed their script. Secondly, while Vaishnavism is still strong, they are restressing their pre-Vaishnava identity and reconstructing the older rituals, festivals etc."¹⁵² In this case, the Valley movement can be considered a movement for Meitei identity just as the Naga, and for that matter, the Kuki movement, but in each case what is sought concerns only a particular ethnic group. This makes the integrity of the state, which is home to three main ethnic groups, fragile, because it is impacted by the disintegrative ethnic-based movements. This

---

147. See, Seilen Haokip, *Identity, Conflict and Nationalism: the Naga and Kuki peoples of Northeast India and Northwest Burma (Myanmar)* (Unpublished Ph.D. Thesis, Liverpool University, 2001).
148. Jusho, *Politics*, 44.
149. "United Liberation Front of Asom (ULFA) – Terrorist Group of Assam", http://www.satp.org/satporgtp/countries/india/states/manipur/terrorist_outfits/Unlf.htm [Assessed 30 May 2011].
150. Ibid.
151. See, "UNLF Highlights Important Issues On Its 41ˢᵗ Birthday", http://www.manipuronline.com/Features/January2006/militancy19_1.htm [Accessed 9 October 2008].
152. Singh, *Scheduled Tribes*, xvii.

also brings inter-ethnic clashes in the state leaving the minority hill people vulnerable at the hands of the Meitei majority group. In the process, Kukis became the most vulnerable under the hands of both the majority Meiteis and the Naga movement since the early 1990s.

As the result of these competing identities, the state of Manipur has been known for conflict and violence for the last few decades. Writing in 1997, Professor B. Pakem, the Vice-Chancellor of North-Eastern Hill University, comments: "[the] ethnic situation in Manipur is undoubtedly the worst of its kind in the present decade."[153] It has been recorded that "With 4,383 militancy-related fatalities between 1992 and 2006, Manipur remains the third most violent theatre of conflict in the country, behind Jammu & Kashmir (J&K) and Assam, over this extended period."[154] With all these insurgency activities, "Manipur now has one of the most comprehensive networks of terrorist extortion in the country, affecting almost every earning citizen in the state, even as the state and its agencies remain virtually paralysed – with the exception of the Army and Central Paramilitary Forces."[155]

Conclusion

In this survey of the history of North-East India, we highlighted the socio-economic, religio-cultural and political changes brought into the region by agencies including the colonial administration, Christianization and Independent India. In that process, it was observed, political actions were ineffective in the context of North-East India, because of the lack of understanding on the part of policy makers concerning the grass root situation of the people. The issue of lack of understanding has a direct link to the question of attitude, acceptance and treatment of the people as equal citizens with other Indians. It has been observed that there are similar situations of counter-insurgency laws, travel restrictions and human right violations

---

153. B. Pakem, "Foreword" in Zehol, *Ethnicity*.
154. Bibhu Prasad Routray, "Manipur: Extortion Rules", http://www.outlookindia.com/article.aspx?234914 [Accessed 27 October 2010].
155. Ibid.

in other parts of India, notably Kashmir, but no equal level of attention has been given to North-East India. One reason for this, Tillin writes, is that "Kashmir is 'more central to the national imaginary of India' than the Northeast."[156] For this reason B. P. Singh commented on the British administration, "The pre-Independence reorganization demonstrated a lack of understanding of the social and cultural distinctiveness of the region"[157] and this still seems to be the case. If that is true, Baruah is right in saying, "So long as insurgencies are only contained, and no sustainable peace processes are in place, democracy in the North-East is likely to continue to co-exist with the use of authoritarian modes of governance."[158] It is for this reason that Yasmin Saikia emphasizes the need for New Delhi to build trust in the North-East and recognize the multiple pasts of Indian peoples. She argues, "National history has to become local, and local histories must be made national."[159] In other words, the search for identity in the North-East region of India will continue so long as there is lack of understanding, trust and acceptance between the centre and the region.

Peculiar to Manipur is that all the communities, including the majority Hindu Meiteis, are struggling for identity but in different means and expressions. While the Hindu Meiteis struggle for their identity through maintaining the present territorial integrity of the state and their pre-Hindu identity, the people in the hills including the Kukis demand political recognition of their ancestors' land and preservation of their culture. The result of these identity claims is reflected in the disintegration of the people and the vulnerability of the territorial integrity of the state. Although all the communities struggle for identity and belong to the same larger group, called Tibeto-Burman group, none of them culturally relates to Indians

---

156. Louise Tillin, quoted in Baruah, "Postfrontier", 5.
157. Singh, *Problem of change,* 19. With the British annexation in 1826, Assam was included in the Bengal Presidency, and in 1874 it became the Chief Commissioner's Province with Shillong as its capital. In 1905 it was attached to East Bengal when Bengal was partitioned. At the annulment of the partition it was reconstituted in a separate Chief Commissioner's Province in 1912, and it became Governor's Province under the Government of India Act 1919 and it remained the same until 1947 when Sylhet, a greater part of Assam, was transferred to Pakistan, now known as Bangladesh.
158. Baruah, *Durable disorder,* 70.
159. Yasmin Saikia, *Assam and India: Fragmented Memories, Cultural Identity, and the Tai-Ahoms Struggle* (Delhi: Permanent Black, 2004), 265.

outside the North-East. The divide is between the tribals and non-tribal Hindus. This was reflected in their distant relationships and feeling of fear and mistrust for one another. On account of their religious affinity, the Meiteis share the same religious identity with the majority Indians and have no threat from movements such as *Hindutva,* compared with the case of the tribals. The Kuki people, in such a situation, are alienated groups both outside and within their own state, Manipur. They are alienated as tribals in 'mainland' India by those who have no cultural link with them, and in their own state, by those who are closer historically, culturally and religiously. This double experience of alienation is not the case in the neighbouring states of the North-East, such as Mizoram and Nagaland, where tribals are dominant groups. Within the minority tribal groups in the state of Manipur, the Nagas seems to have better negotiating power as they joined a larger Naga movement, which operates across the state boundaries in North-East. In the absence of such cross-state movements, the Kukis seem to be the most vulnerable people group in the region.

We also observed that in the process of asserting identities in North-East India and Manipur in particular, Christianity is at the risk of losing its character as a faith movement, transcending any given context. Our study will seek to show that Christianity as a religion was uncritically utilized in the process of identity construction and in its promotion. This was reflected in the formation and sustenance of Christian armed movements and identity activities across ethno-cultural boundaries. Bauman, an eminent sociologist, rightly observes that ethnic identity, a social construct and fluid in nature, is constructed in the felt need for 'belongingness' or 'to relate to' others – in short, for security,[160] and unquestionably, the issue of security is a Christian concern. However, the way in which this is sought needs critical reflection and this work will show that Christianity has taken an ideological form in this context.

---

160. Zygmunt Bauman, *Identity* (Cambridge: Polity Press, 2006), 30. The same was observed in the case of Manipur by Das. See, R. K. Das, "Tribal Identity in Manipur" 253–263 in Pakem, *Nationality, Ethnicity and Cultural Identity in North-East India* (Guwahati: Omsons Publications, 1990), 263.

CHAPTER 2

Concept of Identity: A Sociological Study

In view of the complexity and seriousness of the issues surrounding identity among the tribal peoples of North-East India in general, and the Kuki in particular, it is important to reflect on the considerable body of academic work relating the topic of human identity in a post-colonial, globalized world. Issues related to themes such as 'ethnicity', 'race' and 'identity' have been discussed in depth over a considerable period of time and have constituted a major strand within the discipline of sociology since the first encounters with the peoples in the Two-Thirds World[1] presented the challenge of how to define such peoples and their struggles for recognition of identity. More recently, the migration of millions of people, which has been the outcome of globalization, has resulted in what might have previously appeared to be a rather abstract, academic debate, being propelled into the centre of public concern, as the subject of 'identity' has become a matter of almost universal concern. Manuel Castells, for example, in a volume with the title, *The Power of Identity*, refers to the "widespread surge of powerful expressions of collective identity"[2] and devotes an entire book in his trilogy dealing with the rise of the 'Information Age' to this

---

1. The term 'Two-Thirds World', synonym with other terms like 'Third World', 'Non-Western World' and 'The South' or 'Southern hemisphere', refers to discussion of theologies in the developing countries of Asia, Africa, and Latin America. It is used to avoid any connotation of 'third-rate' and points to the poverty and size of the non-western world. John Roxborogh, "Two-Thirds World" 975–976 in Moreus A. Scott, ed., *Evangelical Dictionary of World Missions* (Carlisle: Paternoster Press, 2000), 975.
2. Manuel Castells, *The Power of Identity* (Oxford: Blackwell, 1997), 2.

subject. It is clearly important that this publication, while concerned with a particular, local context in which identity issues are of critical importance, should approach the study of that situation with an awareness of the broader, theoretical debates on this subject to be found within the sociological literature. More than that, there are doubtless important insights to be gained from such a study which may be deployed in later chapters, and especially in the final section of this publication, when we come to make proposals for constructing a local theology in relation to the struggles for identity which are being played out among the Kuki.

In common parlance, minority groups such as the Kukis or the Nagas in India, or for that matter Indians in the United Kingdom, are referred to as 'ethnic groups' or 'ethnic minority groups'. At the same time, it appears, the post-colonial term 'ethnic' is not used for every minority group uniformly; hence, adoption of the term can be self-negating at times. Richard Jenkins observes that the term was used to replace 'tribe' although the underlying presumptions may not necessarily have changed.[3] In this work, a single term 'identity' is preferred and even if the term 'ethnic' is used, it is used with this consciousness.

2. 1. Defining Identity

With the disappearance of the term 'race' in sociology,[4] ethnicity or ethnic identity were popularized in the 1960s and remains a central focus for research in the 1990s.[5] Stephen Cornell and Douglas Hartmann observe

---

3. See, Richard Jenkins, *Rethinking Ethnicity: Arguments and Explorations* (London: Sage Publications, 1997), 17.

4. Some sociologists have objected to the concept 'race'. For instance, Kenneth Smith has noted three major arguments against the concept, which includes phenotypical/morphological, biological/genetic and categorical or logical objections. The main issue being the difficulty in scientific validity of the bases, that is, appearing natural difference within human population including skin color, gene and so forth on which 'race' is projected to be a static categorization of human beings. In contrary, it is argued, human population can best be modelled as a "continuum rather than a spectrum". See, Kenneth Smith, "Some Critical Observations of the Use of the Concept of 'Identity' in Modood et al., *Ethnic Minority in Britain*, 399–417" in *Sociology* Vol. 36. no. 2., 400–402.

5. Thomas H. Eriksen, *Ethnicity and Nationalism: Anthropological Perspective* (London: Pluto Press, 1993), 1.

that, "modernity, instead of doing away with ethnicity and race as bases of identity and collective action, invigorated them."⁶ The term was introduced in the context of the emergence of new nation states in the post-colonial era and the immigrant situations, referring to a complex social categorization of people in the new setting. In such a situation, a given context produces a distinct image and tone of ethnicity, making the task of defining the term extremely difficult. In this section we shall attempt to define identity, or ethnic identity, nature of identity construction and how the theory explains people's search for socio-cultural and political identity in North-East India, particularly that of the Kukis of Manipur.

The word ethnic, or ethnic identity, was developed from a Greek word, *ethnos* meaning 'nation'. The term has had different meanings in the course of its history. Cornell and Hartmann observed two major shifts in the meaning of *ethnos* or ethnicity until it entered into the field of sociology. They contended that around the fifteenth century, the adjectival form, *ethnikos* in Greek and *ethnicus* in Latin meant 'pagans' or those 'others'. Though included, belief was less important than making social boundaries.⁷ By the twentieth century, they observed, the elements of 'belief' and 'others' began to lose dominant place in the meaning and the term was used to refer to oneself. They write, "Increasingly, ethnicity referred to a particular way of defining not only others but also ourselves, and this is how it entered sociology."⁸ This general observation of the phenomenon in any way suggests that ethnicity is a simple subject. Somewhat in a definitive tone, the 1994 World Council of Churches (WCC) consultation on racism, ethnicity and indigenous people defines: "racism is based on power and privilege, while ethnicity derives from blood and belonging."⁹ However, far from being precise, the issue of ethnicity is extremely complex, while some called the phenomena in question[10], Cornell and Hartmann

---

6. Cornell and Hartmann, *Ethnicity and Race*, 250.
7. Ibid.,16.
8. Ibid.
9. Theo Tschuy, *Ethnic Conflict and Religion: Challenge to the churches* (Geneva: WCC, 1997), xi.
10. Modood et al., "'Race', Racism and Ethnicity: A Response to Ken Smith" 419–426 in *Sociology* Vol. 36. no. 2. 419.

termed ethnicity a 'puzzle' and noted four elements for this. First, the persistence of ethnicity in spite of increased blurring cultural distinctions and predictions against its survival; second, the diversity of forms that ethnicity seem to take; third, the variety of functions it apparently served; and fourth, the different kinds of attachments that claimed the ethnic label.[11] Identity being indefinite in nature, Eller considers it as the source of some of the most perplexing problems[12] and Walker Connor, "more definitionally chameleonic than nation."[13] It is precisely because of the fluidity and complexity of its nature that ethnicity is slippery and difficult to define.

The complexity is related to the empirical reality of peoples and the ways in which the phenomenon appears to observers. Ethnicity sometimes appears as a pre-existing reality, while at other times, a purpose-driven political movement reflecting the underlying fluidity of identity boundary. This has led to two opposing views: one maintains ethnic groups are based on some durable elements that cannot be easily altered; the other view sees ethnicity as a tool to gain a larger, typically material end. The two views are known as primordialism and instrumentalism, or constructionist, views. We shall attempt to explain the two views in the following and argue for a convergent approach to ethnicity in our attempt to understand the complex situation of North-East India.

2. 1. 1. Primordialist View

The concept 'primordial attachments' or 'primordialism' was conceived by Edward Shils and was developed by Clifford Geertz, an American anthropologist and a key representative of this view. Shils argues that "Ideals and beliefs can only influence conduct alongside of personal ties, primordial attachments, and responsibilities in corporate bodies and they can come into play primarily in the form of vague notions regarding the Right and

---

11. Cornell and Hartmann, *Ethnicity and Race*, 10–12. Paraphrased.
12. Jack David Eller, *From Culture to Ethnicity to Conflict: An Anthropological Perspective on International Ethnic Conflict* (Michigan: The University of Michigan Press, 2002), 7. Paraphrased.
13. Walker Connor, "A Nation is a Nation, is a State, is an Ethnic, is a . . . " 36–46 in John Hutchinson and Anthony D. Smith eds., *Nationalism* (Oxford: Oxford University Press, 1994), 43.

Good in concrete forms."[14] Geertz developed the concept of primordialism and insists that ethnicity is something that cannot be manipulated at one's own will. He argues that, "every individual is born into a particular culture that structures his beliefs and his identity."[15] Different from the instrumentalist view which we shall see later, ethnic groups for Geertz are something durable and cannot be manipulated at one's own will. He writes:

> One is bound to one's kinsman, one's neighbour, one's fellow believer, *ipso facto*; as the result not merely of personal affection, practical necessity, common interest, or incurred obligation, but at least in great part by virtue of some unaccountable absolute import attributed to the very tie itself. This attachment, he says, seems to flow more from a sense of natural – some would say spiritual – affinity than from social interaction.[16]

Rachel Beatty describes his position as follows:

> One that stems from the 'givens' or, more precisely, as culture is inevitably involved in such matters, the assumed 'givens' of social existence: immediate contiguity and kin connection mainly, but beyond them the givenness that stems from being born into a particular religious community, speaking a particular language, or even a dialect of a language, and following particular social practices. These congruities of blood, speech, custom and so on, are seen to have an ineffable, and at times overpowering, coerciveness in and of themselves.[17]

---

14. Edward Shils, "Primordial, Personal, Sacred and Civil Ties: Some Particular Observations on the Relationships of Sociological Research and Theory", *The British Journal of Sociology*, Vol. 8, No. 2 (June 1957), 130–145.
15. Sandra Fullerton Joireman, *Nationalism and Political Identity* (London: Continuum, 2003), 24.
16. Clifford Geertz, "Primordial Ties" in John Hutchinson and Anthony D. Smith eds. *Ethnicity*, (Oxford: Oxford University Press, 1996), 42.
17. Rachel Beatty, "Review Essay: Primordialism versus Constructivism", http://www.nationalismproject.org/books/bookrevs/beattyrev.htm [Accessed 13 January 2010].

Eller and Coughlan point out three components of Geertz's primordialism: First, ethnic identity as a 'given', or that which exists in a seemingly natural way before all experiences and social interactions; second, it is 'ineffable' in a sense that a member of a group necessarily feels attachment to the group concerned and its practices; and third, ethnic identity according to the primordialist approach is a question of emotion or affect, in other words, about sentiment or bonds. In summary they write, ". . . primordialism presents us with a picture of underived and socially unconstructed emotions that are unanalysable and overpowering and coercive yet varying."[18]

While this observation is true, it needs further explanation that Geertz did not argue on a biological basis. It is true that the core elements of ethnic identity for him are assumed blood ties, race, language, region and custom, in other words, culture is an important factor in forming ethnic identity but that does not mean that he is talking in terms of biological trait, nor does he endorse this as acceptable within the field of anthropology. Instead, he is referring to the way in which people *view* their cultures. The usage of the word 'assumed' makes it clear that Geertz's argument is not based on biological or genetic background. Joireman writes, "From the perspective of Geertz, people view their own cultural background as primordial, and thus it is. Culture is important insofar as people claim it to be a foundational identity."[19] Geertz's conviction, in the light of his own experience, is that "people give their ties of origin, ancestral territory or homeland, descent and kin groups a value which supersedes all others in forming their identity", but at the same time for Geertz, "it is not so much the primordial ties of birth and origin that are important, but the meaning that individuals attach to those ties and to the importance of belonging to a group,"[20] that is, the perception that identity can be objectively proven and hence it cannot be manipulated at one's own will. The consequence of such a notion is clearly stated by a Chicago sociologist,

---

18. Ibid.
19. Joireman, *Nationalism*, 24.
20. Ibid., 27.

W. I. Thomas, who says, "if men define situations as real, then they are real in their consequences."[21]

In a similar way, Manning Nash speaks of "the core elements of Ethnicity" and suggests that identity boundaries can be identified in the following two ways: first, by recognizing what he calls "basic structure of ethnic group differentiation", the most common ethnic boundary markers which include a) kinship, referring to the presumed biological and descent unity of the group which is considered to be absent in other groups; b) commensality, referring to the corporate activities, such as eating together, indicating a kind of equality that promises further kinship links; and c) common cult, implying cultural elements, including the people's value system, sacred symbols and so forth; and second, by observing what he calls 'surface pointers',[22] which includes dress, language, and physical features.[23]

Henry E. Hale compares the primordialist image of ethnic groups with that of different stones constituting of a wall that has clear-cut and enduring boundaries between each group. A 'wall' here refers to an ethnic group and its constituting stones with different features – the cultures, traditions, histories, physical traits, languages, repertoires, religion, etc. of the people concerned. In this, he rightly noted the fact that extended kinship relations are usually regarded as the critical element that holds the groups together in a primordial approach.[24]

The difficulty with primordialism, Hale argues, relates to the fact that the 'stones' are not eternal. In other words, the constituting stones, their sizes and features, the walls or ethnic groups themselves, are created.[25] Similarly, Spencer points out, "Such hard-line definitions are unable to adequately account for ethnic change and dissolution or for effects

---

21. Quoted in Bruce G. Link et al., "Real Consequences: A Sociological Approach to Understanding the Association between Psychotic Symptoms and Violence" 316–332 in *American Sociology Review*, Vol. 64 (April 1999), 316.
22. Manning Nash, "The Core Elements of Ethnicity" 24–28 in John Hutchinson and Anthony D. Smith eds., *Ethnicity*, 25.
23. Ibid., 24–27.
24. Hendry E. Hale, "Explaining Ethnicity" 458–485 in *Comparative Political Studies*, Vol. 37, No. 4 (May 2004), 460.
25. Hale, "Explaining Ethnicity", 460.

of immigration or intermarriage."[26] This view is shared by Jenkins.[27] In this regard, Joireman points out four problems with primordialism: first, although claimed to be based on blood ties, the primordialists, in reality, did not based their theory on actual biological fact, which obviously is impossible; second, if ethnicity truly is primordial then it cannot be changed; third, it cannot explain the issue of multiple ethnic identities; and fourth, it is difficult to distinguish whether primordial ethnic ties are in fact primordial and different from other types of social ties and social experiences.[28] These difficulties, including those described above, led Eller and Coughlan to conclude that primordialism is a "bankrupt concept for analysis and description of ethnicity."[29]

Nash's core elements of ethnicity are nonetheless helpful, but cannot be applied to all identities. Identity boundaries are to a great extent self-constructs in the light of a given context and hence, they are not decisive.[30] The case of Sikh ethnic identity in northern India, and that of the Mizo or Naga of North-East India, makes this clear. The fact is that the boundary of kinship, for instance, cannot be marked uniformly. Besides the markers, the 'centre', and for that matter the 'margin' of an identity for instance always moves. Take for example, the erstwhile Kuki group who now changed their ethnic allegiance to that of Naga, mentioned in chapter 1, indicating their cultural intermediary position between the two, happen to become main actors of their identity construction, so the present identity boundary will have to be redrawn from their perspective. Constructing identity, therefore, is about drawing cultural boundaries with markers that are never universally consistent. Eller is right in saying that "ethnicity is no mere reflection or reflect of culture, especially of traditional culture, but a complex reworking, remembering, sometimes reinvention."[31] Eller's statement also explains why the phenomenon was invigorated when there is

---

26. Stephen Spencer, *Race and Ethnicity: Identity, Culture and Representation* (London: Routledge, 2006), 78.
27. Jenkins, *Rethinking*, 46.
28. Joireman, *Nationalism*, 31–32. I paraphrased the arguments.
29. Eller and Coughlan, "Primordialism", 50.
30. Steve Fenton, *Ethnicity* (Cambridge: Polity Press, 2010), 180, 15.
31. Eller, *Culture*, 5.

fragmentation of culture in a globalized world in the present time. Identity understood solely as a culture-based phenomenon is unable to explain the contemporary identity phenomenon.

While it is true that the theory fails to explain the phenomenon, it cannot be denied the potency that primordial attachments have for the members of an ethnic group to sustain their attachments. Esler observes that this is more so with the group that is under threat than those who seek to use the shared values for a vested interest.[32] It is in such a situation that Geertz observes that, "Primordial discontent strives more deeply and is satisfied less easily."[33]

2. 1. 2. Instrumentalist View

The contending view against this position is an instrumentalist approach, sometimes known as constructivism. The main argument in this approach is that an ethnic identity is an instrument to achieve a common goal of a group concern. In other words, ethnic groups are not natural but are constructed so as to achieve some common interests of the members involved. It is essentially a political phenomenon. Abner Cohen expresses this view in relation to anthropological studies of the Hausa and Yoruba people of West Africa. He argues:

> Ethnicity is essentially a political phenomena, as traditional customs are used only as idioms, as mechanisms for political alignment. . . . If men do actually quarrel seriously on the grounds of cultural differences it is only because these cultural differences are associated with serious political cleavages.[34]

His basic argument is that people do not kill, for instance, because their customs are different, but custom is used as an instrument to stick

---

32. Philip F. Esler, *Conflict and Identity in Romans: The Social Setting of Paul's Letter* (Minneapolis: Fortress Press, 2003), 46.
33. Geertz, "Primordial", 43.
34. Abner Cohen, "Ethnicity and Politics" in John Hutchinson & Anthony D. Smith eds., *Ethnicity*, 84.

together as group under the contemporary situation only because of mutual interests.[35]

Taking the argument to a further extreme, Jack Eller talks of ethnic identity as one-sidedly subjective and views it rather in a negative light as he argues, "People who live their culture unproblematically tend not to be ethnic in the proper sense of the word."[36] He asks, "When is a group an ethnic group? Which part of culture is used by a particular group and why?"[37] Eller's main point is that although identity may refer to, or be based on, objective elements such as shared cultural or historical markers, it is the actors who decide which aspect of culture to use for the construction of their identities.[38]

Going back to Hale's imagery of a 'stone wall' referred to above, if the primordialists see the wall as clear-cut and enduring, for the instrumentalists it is a "façade masking a much less well defined structure."[39] For an instrumentalist, ethnic identities are formed often by the elites within the groups for a purpose of collective benefit deemed important. In the words of Hale, ethnic identities are "not holdover from ancient times but very recent phenomena."[40] Looking for examples of the two approaches in the Bible, Brett finds Paul an instrumentalist for his concept of a diverse believer community as one in Christ while he labelled Ezra and Nehemiah primordialists for their genealogical approach to history.[41]

Like primordialism, an instrumentalist approach to ethnic identity has limitations. Spencer observes, 'rational' or 'rationality' is an overriding principle in the position held by instrumentalists and this limits its advocates' ability to cope with ethnic durability, ignoring mass passions evoked by ethnic ties and cultural symbols.[42] Similarly, Veit Bader critiques the

---

35. Ibid.
36. Eller, *Culture*, 79.
37. Ibid., 8.
38. Ibid., 9.
39. Hale, "Ethnicity", 460.
40. Ibid., 461.
41. Mark G. Brett, "Interpreting Ethnicity" in Brett G. Mark ed., *Ethnicity and the Bible* (Boston: Bril Academic Publishers Inc. 2002), 13.
42. Spencer, *Race*, 79.

constructivists' stance for their failure to acknowledge the place of cultural elements and their durability in identity construction and preservation.[43] If the difficulty with primordialism is lack of mutability, the problem with the instrumentalist view is overlooking the durability of ethnic groups. The definitional debates and increasingly complex experiences of ethnicity do not march together all the time. Hale is right in saying that the primordialism-constructivism debates do not address the fundamental question 'why do people have, or feel the need to have, identities?'[44] This calls for an alternate understanding of the concept.

2. 1. 3. Ethnic Group as Social Construct

Between the two opposing views mentioned above, there is a moderate and convergent view, which is more helpful for the understanding of the complexities of the phenomenon. That is, to view identity as 'social construct' which, by taking into consideration the role of both a given context and the insiders in construction of identity, paves the way for a more flexible way to understand the phenomenon and accommodate the varied forms and natures in which identities appear. The view is built on Weber's work, which offered a classical sociological definition of ethnic group in the early twentieth century. He insisted that an ethnic group is one whose members believed that they shared common descent that need not necessarily be supported by an objective blood relationship. He writes:

> The belief in group affinity, regardless of whether it has any objective foundation, can have important consequences especially for the formation of a political community. We shall call 'ethnic groups' those human groups that entertain a subjective belief in their common descent because of similarities of physical type or of customs or both, or because of memories of colonization and migration; this belief must be important

---

43. Veit Bader, *Culture and identity: Contesting constructivism* (London: SAGE Publications, 2001).
44. Hale, "Ethnicity", 462.

for the propagation of group formation; conversely it does not matter whether or not an objective blood relationship exists.[45]

The following points stand out clearly from the statement. One, an ethnic group is characterized by the belief of the members that they belong to the same cultural group; two, that such belief must be based on physical similarities or of custom or both, or memories of the people's historical past; third, that such a belief, unlike that of kinship, does not have to be objectively proved; fourth, that such a belief must be important for the propagation of group formation; and fifth, that by being a presumed identity, ethnic membership is likely to be an outcome of political action and not the cause for a group formation. He argues, "ethnic membership does not constitute a group; it only facilitates group formation of any kind, particularly in the political sphere. . . . it is primarily the political community, no matter how artificially organized, that inspires the belief in common ethnicity."[46]

In Hutchinson and Smith's view, Weber was "concerned to combine their [ethnic groups] subjective and objective aspects and balance their cultural and political bases."[47] In order to combine the two, Weber argued that ethnic groups are founded on a 'belief in common descent' that is not necessarily a biological unity capable of being scientifically proved, but rather the way people considered themselves as being. In other words, Weber emphasized the role of the members of the group in constructing their own ethnic identity, not in biological terms, but rather based on a belief in common descent.

Another person to be mentioned here is the eminent Norwegian social anthropologist Fredrik Barth, an influential theorist in this area since the last quarter of the twentieth century. In his work, *Ethnic Groups and Boundaries,* Barth argues that ethnic distinctions persist despite social interactions. Reacting against a view that suggests that ethnic boundaries

---

45. Guenther Roth and Clause Wittich, eds. *Max Weber: Economy and Society* (Berkeley: University of California Press, 1978), 389.
46. Ibid.
47. John Hutchinson and Anthony D. Smith, "Theories of Ethnicity" 33–34 in Hutchinson and Smith eds., *Ethnicity* (Oxford: Oxford University Press, 1996), 32.

are created due to lack of social interactions, he insisted that, "categorical ethnic distinctions do not depend on an absence of mobility, contact and information, but do entail social processes of exclusion and incorporation whereby discrete categories are maintained despite changing participation and membership in the course of individual life histories."[48] For Barth, social interactions can be factors for ethnic differentiation, as he writes, "ethnic distinctions do not depend on an absence of social interaction and acceptance, but are quite to the contrary often the very foundations on which embracing social system are built".[49]

Having rejected the idea of rigid definition of the term, Barth stresses the situational, self-ascription and fluid nature of an identity. It was for this reason that he did not consider culture, cultural elements and differences as factors for identity formation; instead, he uses terms like, boundary and boundary maintenance. Ethnic boundary, for him, emerges as a result of people's interactions with each other in given socio-political, cultural and economic circumstances. In this, without denying the place of culture, identity is more of a social organization rather than a culture-based group that is closed in nature. Barth also speaks of ethnic categories as "organizational vessel that may be given varying amounts and forms of content in different sociological systems."[50] Although some still find this imagery projects the picture of ethnic categories as something constant,[51] this gives room for flexibility. It understands an ethnic group as a self-ascription and identification, reflecting a given context. Geoff Emberling, whose expertise is in Syria, notes three benefits of Barth's insights: "(1) severed the necessary links among race, culture, language, and ethnicity; (2) implied that

---

48. Fredrik Barth, *Ethnic Groups and Boundaries: The Social Organization of Cultural Difference* (Boston: Little, Brown and Company, 1969), 10–11.

49. Ibid., 11.

50. Ibid., 79. Sometimes Barth is found both in Primordial and Instrumentalist camps. See, Eriksen, *Ethnicity,* 54 and Andreas Wimmer, "The Making and Unmaking of Ethnic Boundaries: A Multilevel Process Theory", *AJS.,* Vol. 113, no. 4 (2008), 970.

51. For reason such as this Barth's position is debatable to the students of Anthropology. See Eriksen, *Ethnicity,* 56.

ethnic identity was part of a dynamic social process; and (3) introduced the possibility of change in actors' group membership."[52]

One difficulty with the self-descriptive approach to ethnicity is to ascertain which type of group is formed on the basis of the members' sense of belonging. Barth did not deal with the issue, neither did he deal with the question of why, how and who makes these boundaries. His focus was more on how the boundaries are marked and maintained hence distinguishing a particular ethnic group from others. One weakness of Barth that he over-emphasises the idea of ethnicity as 'self-ascribed' and overlooks the other side of the reality that ethnicity can be imposed from outside, one clear case of such being the emergence of 'black' as a political community in response to experiences of slavery and segregation in the United States of America.

Within the framework of the Weberian school of thought, Richard A. Schermerhorn defines ethnicity as a "collectivity within a larger society having real or putative common ancestry, memories of a shared historical past, and a cultural focus on one or more symbolic elements defined as the epitome of their peoplehood."[53] Cornell and Hartmann elaborated the definition by identifying five different points covered in the statement:

> (1) Ethnicity involves three kinds of claims – a claim of kinship, a claim to common history of some sort, and a claim that certain symbols capture the core of the group's identity, (2) as in Weber's conception, these claims need not be founded in fact, (3) the extent of actual cultural distinctiveness is irrelevant, (4) an ethnic group is a subpopulation within a larger society and an ethnic identity is self-conscious.[54]

What becomes clear from the elaborations is the aspect of 'claim' rather than facts, elasticity and not rigidity, the role of insiders and not external

---

52. Geoff Emberling, "Ethnicity in Complex Societies: Archaeological Perspective" in *Journal of Archaeological Research*, Vol. 5, no. 4 (1997), 299.
53. Richard A. Schermerhorn, quoted in Cornell and Hartmann, *Ethnicity and Race*, 19.
54. Cornell and Hartmann, *Ethnicity and Race*, 19–20. I restructured the quotation.

factors in constructing an ethnic identity, and the conclusion that the term ethnicity refers to minority groups in a given context.

In light of the quotation above, Cornell and Hartmann made three important observations regarding the nature of identity. Firstly, an assertion of some ineffable bond among group members that is believed to have been rooted ultimately in a shared and distinctive origin. This definition, they found, gives room to accommodate complex groups, classifying those groups according to their claims or the particular claims made about them. Secondly, for Cornell and Hartmann the label that is used by outsiders is of significant importance. They are convinced that although an ethnic identity is self-descriptive, the source of its self-consciousness can be the labels used by outsiders. The point is that an ethnic category can be externally defined but it becomes an ethnic identity only when the groups concerned claim it. Thirdly, they insisted that ethnicity is a matter of contrast, distinguishing some groups from others. This, however, does not necessarily mean that an ethnic population is a minority population.[55] However, they maintain the view that identity is social construct.

Possibly the strongest point, and at the same time the most blurring part, is the nature of identity as an interactive phenomenon. Eriksen expresses this well: "Ethnicity is an aspect of social relationship between agents who considered themselves as culturally distinctive from members of other groups with whom they have a minimum of regular interaction."[56] Identity, for this reason, is a product of social interactions wherein both the members and non-members of the group play a role. It is about drawing boundaries between one's own social group and others, and vice versa. It is to position oneself or a group in relation to others, for which reason Eriksen writes that in a mono-ethnic context "there is effectively no ethnicity."[57] Hale's work is helpful as he notes that ethnic identity operates like a kind of social radar whereby one sees his or her position in the social world he or she inhabits:

---

55. Ibid., 20–21.
56. Eriksen, *Ethnicity*, 13.
57. Ibid., 34.

Ethnicity is thus most usefully described as neither primordial nor constructed, neither inherently conflictual nor epiphenomenal, but as *relational* at its core. Ethnicity defines the individual in relation to the social world, a process that occurs prior to purposive action . . . it is a primary device for uncertainty reduction that precedes interest-oriented behaviour.[58]

To conclude that identity is a social construct does not solve the problem of identity boundary. The boundary of an identity, or the periphery, depends on the centre where the actors stand. This can be exemplified in the case of the Naga and the Kuki identities. The identity 'Naga' in independent India has shown itself as both a political and social movement for expansion of identity among other tribes within North-East India, making it flexible to accommodate others in the pursuit of a political goal. By contrast, an identity 'Kuki' is constructed around cultural affinity, including common language, culture and the story of origin. For this reason an identity 'Naga' could be considered a work in progress, or more politically-driven, while 'Kuki', is linguistic and culture based. In the light of the primordialism-instrumentalism distinctions referred to above, the former may be considered instrumentalist and the latter primordialist. However, viewed from Weberian school of thought described above, both of these identities are social constructs in the sense that they are self-ascriptions based not on a biological unity that is scientifically provable, but rather on assumed common descent, or belief in a common origin, commonalities of language and culture. In the case of the former, it is not even commonality of language, as the people cannot communicate with each other in their local languages.

The complexity is that in this process, the former was flexible enough to 'Nagaize' other groups, including some of historically known Kuki groups of Manipur referred to in chapter 1, making Geertz's observation of Naga identity as primordial doubly questionable.[59] Having closely observed the

---

58. Henry H. Hale, *The Foundations of Ethnic Politics: Separatism of States and Nations in Eurasia and the World* (Cambridge: Cambridge University Press, 2008), 55.
59. Geertz uses Naga identity as one of the examples for his primordialism. See Geertz, "Primordial", 43.

phenomenon, Wimmer points out the possibility of emergence of different approaches to identity when he talks about political networks, his third 'social field', wherein actors decide who should be or should not be in the groups[60] and the 'Nagaization' process among the Kuki proves his point. In this situation, it appears that while the Weberian line of argument better accommodates the varied forms' identity, it also leaves certain types of identities vulnerable in the face of others. This also implies that identity construction without dialogue with other groups in a multi-ethnic context such as North-East India can be risky to peaceful co-existence among the people.

What is helpful in the theory of ethnic groups as social construct, is that this account of ethnic identity recognizes the degree to which such an identity always involves a certain amount of contextual construction and expression, echoing the felt needs of a given context, and hence it is interactive rather than a 'given' phenomenon. Joane Nagel writes, "Ethnicity is best understood as a dynamic, constantly evolving property of both individual identity and group organization" wherein she acknowledges the fact that both the outsiders and insiders play a role. "The construction of ethnic identity and culture is the result of both structure and agency – a dialectic played out by ethnic groups and the larger society."[61] The emphasis here is the role of both a given structure and the group concerned. A given structure includes, for instance, socio-political and economic conditions that are encountered wherein the group, in the light of that context, constructs and re-constructs their identity. That includes, as noted by Beatty, negotiating boundaries, interpreting one's own past and asserting meanings and resisting the impositions of the present and claiming the future.[62] This, however, does not mean that ethnic identity can be constructed in a day, or that the emotional attachments and durability of ethnic groups are denied. Nor does it mean that an individual can change his or her own identity as

---

60. Wimmer, "Making and Unmaking", 995–997.
61. Joane Nagel, "Constructing Ethnicity: Creating and Recreating Identity Culture" 152–176 in *Social Problems*, Vo. 41, no.1 (February 1994), 152.
62. Beatty, "Review", Paraphrased.

and when he or she wishes.[63] Jenkins in *Rethinking Ethnicity* rightly argues that although ethnicity is imagined, it is not imaginary. He acknowledges the nature of fixity and plasticity, antiquity and the modernity of identity, and the role of individuals as well as groups in constructing an identity. For this reason, he emphasizes the need to strike a balanced view of the authenticity of ethnic attachments.[64]

Viewing the identity situation in North-East India in the light of above discussion, B. G. Kalsson's observation is helpful. He recalled the historical experiences of the people, particularly during and after India's Independence and writes, "the opening up of the new political space of the indigenous, participation in organizations and networks on a regional, national, and transnational level – new forms of community mobilization and ways of envisioning or imagining collective selves are bound to develop."[65] He argues that identities in North-East India are the products of the given context as he writes, "Thus, in 'pre-modern' or 'pre-colonial' India, there existed no Rabha or Naga people as they are perceived today"[66] verifying Wimmer's argument that ". . . the most prominent theories of ethnicity – from primordialism to constructivism, from instrumentalism to identity theory – are best seen as descriptions of particular ethnic constellations, rather than as general theories of ethnicity."[67] An additional question for the people of North-East India is how the concept 'ethnic' or 'ethnic identity' is different from that of 'tribal', an official identity for the people assigned by the Government of India? While accepting the fact that the two concepts overlap, Emberling suggests that we can "reserve 'tribe' for the pre-state form of political organization and to use 'ethnic group' for cultural groups that form part of complex societies."[68] His main argument

---

63. In their response to Kenneth Smith, their critique, Modood et al., rightly argued that ethnic identity cannot be manipulated by an individual subjectivity. Modood et al., "Race", 423.
64. Jenkins, *Rethinking*, 168–169.
65. Karlsson, B. G. "Indigenous Politics: Community Formation and Indigenous Peoples' Struggle for Self-Determination in Northeast India", *Identities* Vol. 8, No. 1 (March 2001), 7.
66. Ibid., 27.
67. Wimmer, "Making and Unmaking", 1011.
68. Emberling, "Ethnicity", 306.

is that the term 'tribe' is a non-hierarchical political system and is defined by cultural differences, while 'ethnic identity' is constructed by members of a group bearing political characteristics. At the same time, he insists, the two overlap in the way they use culture.[69] In India, viewed from the hierarchical social structure, the identity 'tribal' is a derogatory term. Like that of the Dalits, the term 'tribal' connotes a state of being 'uncivilized' with less human values, inferior in terms of human status and dignity. For this reason, ethnic or ethnic identity is more positive than tribe in the context of India, although this does not mean that the term 'ethnic' is perfect and, for which reason, we use it in this work cautiously.

2. 2. Context and Identity Construction

Fenton, in his attempt to re-situate ethnicity within broader sociological studies argues that the context in which ethnicity is revitalized should be given more importance than 'ethnicity' itself. There cannot be a single unitary phenomenon called 'ethnicity' because the social, economic and political contexts of ethnic groups are so different that they shape the sense, force and function of ethnic identities.[70] Fenton looks at the phenomenon in the light of late capitalism and modernity and concludes that ethnicity is not only social boundary maintenance but also sustaining inequality of power and access to social resources. For this reason, Fenton moves from Barth to include the larger issue of the context where an ethnicity is constructed and reconstructed. This is to say that identity and identity movements are not phenomena in isolation but responses to the context where they emerge. One important aspect of a study of identity is to ask, "What are the issues that a particular ethnic group is responding to?" or "What led to the formation of a particular ethnic group?"

In a more elaborate way, Wimmer identifies three 'social fields', namely, institutional order such as dictatorship, democracy and so forth, distribution of power in a given structure, and networks of political alliance

---

69. Ibid.
70. Fenton, *Ethnicity*, 180.

within which actors classify themselves and negotiate their ethnic boundaries.[71] He argues that ethnic boundaries and the ways in which they are made are influenced by the context in which actors construct their identities. Cornell and Hartmann termed these contextual factors as 'construction sites'[72] and elaborated how ethnic boundaries are created as a result of various contextual factors including politics, labour market, residential space, social institutions, cultures and daily experiences. Thus they write, "In those arenas [construction sites], various groups – some with power, some without – try to cope with the situations they encounter, pursue their objectives, make sense of the world around them, and identity themselves and others."[73]

Wimmer's, as well as Cornell and Hartmann's main point in discussing the contextual factors in ethnic boundary making, is to show how outsiders indirectly play an irresistible role in the construction of one's own identity. Wimmer, for instance, points out how, unlike in the monarchic or pre-modern era, the elite groups in the post-colonial nation-states police ethnic boundaries favouring their own interests while, at the same time, the nation-states provide incentive for the non-elite minority groups to demand state for their own groups and fair representations within an existing state.[74] Hence, the emergence of ethnic identity and the tone and nature of its existence are the product of a given context.

One example in North-East India is the emergence of the Lepcha-Bhutia identity as a resistance movement to the Nepalis' assimilation. In his study on the interethnic relationships in North-East India, Tanka B. Subba proposes what he calls, a 'negative solidarity' as a better term to explain the phenomena. For him ethnic identities are artificial, adopted and temporary: artificial because they are not natural, adopted because it is something that is used as a means to an end and temporary because it is conditioned by the given context. His example was the formation of a Lepcha-Bhutia identity, rival groups until the second half of the nineteenth

---

71. Wimmer, "Making and Unmaking", 990–997.
72. See, Cornell and Hartmann, *Ethnicity and Race*, 169–208.
73. Ibid., 208.
74. Wimmer, "Making and Unmaking", 991.

century, in order to safeguard their own identities from the threat of assimilation by the Nepalis. Should the threat from the Nepalis removed, Subba thinks, the old enmity between them would be revived and two separate identities be formed as before.[75]

Similarly, in her studies on the determinant factors for ethnic movements in North-East India, Sreeradha Datta, a South Asian security analyst and a research fellow at the Institute for Defence and Analyses, New Delhi, observes three reasons for unrest: first, the geographical isolation of the region, which includes psychological distance of the people from the rest of India; second, limited economic development or progress; and third, massive migrations, including economic migrants from outside the region. It is in such a situation, she understands, different groups sought to press their demands for autonomy, economic concessions and political representation through violent means.[76] She concludes that competition for resources, which includes property rights, employment, educational opportunities, linguistic rights, government assistance and developmental projects are at the heart of ethnic conflicts.[77]

As in any situation, a study of identity and identity constructions in North-East India confirms the fluidity of identity. At the same time, it also shows the fact that there is no uniformity of criteria, which again is due to its given context, on which one can draw an ethnic boundary line. Lipi Ghosh, for instance, observes that criteria for the Nagas and the Mizos of North-East India are the combination of descent and territory while for a Sikh, ethnicity of northern India is religion and territory combined.[78] Karlsson argues, "peoples and nations have no permanent existence in themselves, but come into being and persist as long as sufficient number of people regard themselves as a people-nation and in some ways act according to that idea."[79]

---

75. Tank B. Subba, "Interethnic Relationships in Northeast India and the 'Negative Solidarity' Thesis" in *Man In India*, 1992 (2), 153–162.
76. Datta, *Northeast Complexities*, 17–18.
77. Ibid., 38–39.
78. Lipi Ghosh, "Ethnicity and Issues of Identity Formation" 85–106 in Bonita Aleaz at.a. eds., *Ethnicity, Nation & Minorities: The South Asian Scenario* (New Delhi: Manak Publications, 2003), 89.
79. Karlsson, "Indigenous Politics", 33–34.

This, however, cannot water down the ground reality that prompted the emergence of identity movements. The North-East region of India refers not only to a geographical extremity but also to cultural isolation wherein the deemed common 'threat' is that of assimilation from Hindu majority India. Whatever form and nature they may represent themselves, it is in this situation that people of North-East India shape their 'imagined community' and dream for their future as a people with available approaches considered best at hand.

For this reason, as stated earlier, identity and identity constructions in North-East India are better understood not merely as social groupings but rather the people's socio-political movements for identity recognition, which includes culture, land and liberation. In other words, the people themselves are involved in the constructions of their own identities, and in the case of the Kuki people, as will be shown in chapter 3, it is more a socio-political movement constructed around claimed common culture, language, history and ancestors' land in search of security and survival as a group in the face of what is considered assimilative policies both within and outside the region. For this reason, Melucci is right in arguing that the revival of ethnicity is a response to a need for collective identity and demand for particular importance in complex societies in a post-modern world. In ethno-national movements, for instance, he argues, ethnic identity movement is a "weapon of revenge against centuries of discrimination and new forms of exploitation; it serves as an instrument for applying pressure in the political market; and it is a response to needs for personal and collective identity in highly complex societies."[80] Such movements are clearly political, demanding new rights and claiming autonomy and control a special living space, including geographical territory.[81] In this case, Joireman is right in saying that ethnicity is a critical part of political identity.[82]

Lipi Ghosh, specialist in the history of South East Asian studies, concludes that the purpose of ethnic identity movements is for "the protection

---

80. Alberto Melucci, "Post-Modern Revival of Ethnicity", in Hutchinson and Smith eds., *Ethnicity*, 368.
81. Melucci, "Revival of Ethnicity", 369.
82. Joireman, *Nationalism*, 17.

of and power for the identified group."[83] Similarly Burman, a well-known scholar in this field from outside of the region, points out that ethnicity is one form of assertion against the defacement of humanity.[84] Two such defacements of humanity, for him, are the people's experience of suppression under colonization, which he calls 'trauma of history' and the capitalist approach to development, which ignores the tribal integral worldview.[85]

It is true that while the works of those outside North-East India, including that of Burman, can be appreciated for their courage to voice the sociopolitical and historical factors for the identity movements in North-East India, their approach may not necessarily be liberating. Burman's critique of colonial isolation policy for tribals and his suggestion for integration of tribal people into India's mainstream is a clear example. However, despite his assimilative approach, he is right in observing that identity movements in North-East India are expressions of the people's opposition to assimilative and oppressive structures within which they found themselves.

2. 3. Indigeneity, Indigenouse or Indigenous People

Similar to ethnic identity, the term 'indigenous', or 'indigenous people' is much debated in the field of anthropology. A brief discussion on this term is apt because it will help us understand better the complexity of group identity, and since the 1960s the term 'indigenous' has been used in theological discussions in the Two-Thirds world. A study of the term in the light of anthropological literature will benefit the task of healthy indigenization of the Christian message in a given context.

The current use of the term 'indigenous' or 'indigenous people' and the subsequent debate originated on Human Rights Day in 1992 with a concern for the promotion of the rights of the people.[86] Similar to ethnic

---

83. Ghosh, "Ethnicity", 89.
84. Burman, "Problems", 693.
85. Ibid., 695.
86. Adam Kuper, "The Return of the Native" in *Current Anthropology*, Vol. 44 (June 2003), 389.

identity, the term 'indigenous', and movements for indigenous peoples' rights, are not without difficulties. The difficulties include the ideological basis of the term, the criteria, and nature in which they represented. The debate initiated by Adam Kuper shows the complexity of the issue.

Kuper in his work, "The Return of the Native", challenges the 'indigenous peoples' notion and movements for indigenous peoples' rights. Kuper's basic argument is that the reasons behind such movements are dubious. He discusses the difficulty in identifying who should be included as an indigenous group, who should decide and on the basis of what criteria. His argument is based on the fact that "over the centuries communities migrated, merged, died out, or changed their languages and altered their allegiances"[87] and he argues, "It cannot be doubted that some of the First Nations were not merely immigrants but actually colonizers."[88] There is thus ambiguity in defining who is indigenous and who is not. For this reason, he sees the 'indigenous people' notion as an euphemism for race as he writes, "A drift to racism may be inevitable where so-called cultural identity becomes the basis for rights, since any cultural test (knowledge of language, for example) will exclude some who might lay claim to an identity on ground of descent."[89]

Added to this is the problem that the right of the first settler takes precedence over the 'late'-comers who come to be regarded as less valuable. For this reason, Kuper described indigenousness as "no more a justification for claiming special rights in perpetuity than having red hair, white skin, or blue blood."[90] Similarly, James Suzman points out three important points against the 'indigenous people' notion and movement for their rights. Firstly, reflecting in the light of the San people in southern Africa, Suzman argues that it is not always possible to identify who is indigenous and who is not. Secondly, those people best placed to claim the privileges due to indigeneity are not necessarily those most in need of assistance. And

---

87. Kuper, "The Return", 392.
88. Ibid.
89. Ibid.
90. Suzman supports Kuper's view and made his own statement. See, James Suzman's comment on Kuper's work published in Adam Kuper, "The Return of the Native", 399.

thirdly, a focus on indigeneity may well reinforce the very structures of discrimination that disadvantage these peoples in the first place.[91]

Besides, Kuper also asserts that the notion 'indigenous identity' and its promotion leads to further problems and he claims, "Wherever special land and hunting rights have been extended to so-called indigenous peoples, local ethnic frictions have been exacerbated."[92] For these reasons, he argues, "Fostering essentialist ideologies of culture and identity, may have dangerous political consequences."[93] Supporting Kuper's argument, Evie Plaice, an anthropologist at the University of New Brunswick, Canada, writes, "There is no way forward from the many racially motivated points of tension that plagues current affairs except by recognizing that all humans are equal, regardless of race and ethnic background."[94]

Alcida Rita Ramos of Brazil finds Kuper's view problematic, as it does not give, in her mind, sufficient attention to an identity formation in its own context. She writes, "if the 'image of the primitive is often constructed today to suit the Greens and the anti-globalization movement' it is hardly the fault of the indigenous peoples."[95] Ramos' emphasis is on-the-ground reality, which initiates the emergence of indigenous movements and she insists, "to put Western powers of conquest on an equal footing with ethnic demands for recognition is either to ignore or to minimize the violence of Western expansion."[96] Ramos' main problem with Kuper's argument is that the given contexts in which identity movements emerge are different from one another and hence one cannot generalize identity movements, for instance, in the case of Kuper as "racist manipulations by unscrupulous opportunists."[97]

Similarly, Steve Robins, a sociologist from the University of Stellenbosch in South Africa, finds Kuper's treatment of indigenous identity claim

---

91. Ibid.
92. Kuper, "The Return", 395.
93. Kuper, "The Return", 395.
94. Evie Plaice's comments on Kuper's work published in Kuper, "The Return", 396.
95. Alcida Rita Ramos' comments on Kuper's work published in Kuper, "The Return", 397.
96. Ibid.
97. Ibid., 398.

uncomfortable because it did not take into account the voices of the indigenous people. He has no problem with Kuper's argument for the deconstruction of essentialist ideologies but is against the disrespectful attitude towards the indigenous voices. He writes, "Surely anthropology should not strive to reduce subaltern voices and histories to a sanitized and standardized version of the anthropologist's 'truth'."[98]

Robins' point is relevant for the context of identity movements in ex-colonized contexts, including North-East India. It is true that the emergence of identity movements in suppressed societies is alarming for peaceful co-existence, but arguments for the deconstruction of identities without addressing the factors that 'necessitate' the movements from an insider's viewpoint will not solve the problem. At this point, Robins sees deconstruction of essentialist ideologies of culture as a first step towards finding the solution. He writes, "Deconstructing essentialist ideologies of culture and identity should be merely a first step toward understanding and situating local construction of 'truth,' not the goal of anthropological practice."[99]

In what they claimed to be "not essentialist" and that which "does not deny the acute problems of the indigenous people", Kenrick and Lewis propose a relational approach to the issue of indigenous people and their struggle for dignity and meaning. Firstly, they acknowledge the fact that the indigenous peoples' rights movements are responses to unjust structures. They write, "We, like others, argue that the indigenous rights movement is best understood as a response to processes of severe discrimination and dispossession."[100] Secondly, they point out the fundamental truth that "equality has to be based on a recognition and negotiation of difference [including historical injustices against them] rather than upon an insistence on the creation of cultural homogeneity in a situation of ever-increasing economic inequality."[101] This led Kendrick and Lewis to suggest a relational approach to understand the issue of indigenous peoples' rights

---

98. Steven Robins' response to Kuper's work published in Kuper, "The Return", 399.
99. Robins' response to Kuper's work published in Kuper, "The Return", 399.
100. Justin Kenrick and Jerome Lewis, "Indigenous peoples' rights and the politics of the term 'indigenous'" 4–9 in *Anthropology Today*, Vol. 20, No. 2 (April 2004), 9.
101. Ibid.

and their movements. A relational understanding of the term, they argued, "focuses on the fundamental issues of power and dispossession that those calling themselves indigenous are concerned to address, and on the enduring social, economic and religious practices that constitute their relationships with land, resources and other peoples."[102] Viewing the issue of indigenous peoples' rights movements from this perspective, in contrast to Kuper who treats the movements as quintessential primitive, Kendrick and Lewis argue that they represent strategies for resisting unjust structures. They write, ". . . indigenous rights describes a strategy for resisting dispossession that employs a language understood by those wielding power."[103]

Kendrick and Lewis see the indigenous peoples, and movements for their rights, not as an end in itself, but a means to address the issues that the indigenous peoples intended to address. For this reason, they write:

> If Kuper was asking us to dispense with the term indigenous peoples in order to better focus on the particular processes of domination and dispossession experienced by such peoples then his argument could be useful. However surprisingly, it seems clear that in suggesting that we should simply dispense with the term, Kuper's argument appears blind to the suffering of indigenous peoples and serves to reinforce the processes that seek to disempower them and deny their contemporary and historical experiences of discrimination, marginalization and dispossession.[104]

They conclude that to support the indigenous people is "to restore some measure of trust and equality, rather than cynicism and superiority, . . . to support such marginalized and dispossessed peoples effectively and appropriately we must focus attention of the processes and sources of empowerment, in addition to those of disempowerment."[105] The point here

---

102. Ibid.
103. Ibid.
104. Kenrick and Lewis, "Indigenous peoples' rights", 9.
105. Ibid.

is that while addressing the negative aspects of these movements, it is also equally important to focus on the processes of dispossession and domination, which resulted in the emergence of indigenous peoples' movements, and for that matter, ethnic identity movements. To a great extent, both ethnic identity and indigenous movements are complex and at times take negative forms. However, in dealing with the phenomena one needs to take as equally important a given context that prompted the emergence of the movements as to treat the phenomena as a sign of the people's dream for liberation and equality with others.

2. 4. Challenges and Opportunities in North-East India

The basic concern behind identity construction is for the wellbeing of a community. At the same time, identity construction process is not always smooth and neutral. Challenges may come from both within and outside the group. For the latter, it being a manifestation of one's own desire for dignity and equality, the dominating group may view an identity movement negatively. For the former, Cornell and Hartmann rightly observed:

Ethnicity and race are categories invented – like other categories – by human beings, and in this they are of little distinctive importance. What makes them significant is what human beings do with them: the ways those categories are used. This is where the danger lies.[106]

Added to this, they further observed, is the issue of choice and misuse of ethnic elements as they write, "The critical issue for the 21st century is not so much whether ethnicity and race will continue to serve as categories of collective identity but what kinds of ethnic and racial stories we choose to tell and how those stories are put to use."[107] Selection and manipulation of past histories for ethno-centric purposes, for instance, are the case in point.

---

106. Cornell and Hartmann, *Ethnicity and Race*, 266.
107. Ibid.

In the multi-ethnic context of North-East India, Sanjib Baruah of Assam, a professor of Political Studies at Bard, USA, observes the problem of the constructivist approach and suggests an alternative approach to ethnic identity assertion. Baruah's argument is based on the experiences of the ethnic conflicts and Nagaization of other tribes in the process of the Pan-Naga movement. Baruah first questions the accuracy of the constellation of the Naga group itself and he points out, "Whether or not a large segment of the tribes of Manipur are Nagas has become a highly charged issue."[108] He further argues that there was no unified Naga nation in the past as is sometimes claimed. Baruah challenges the notion that identity is static and he recognizes that misrepresentation of the past may result in the formation of identity, which is at the expense of other identities. He is also sensitive to the geographical issue: "The Naga desire for a homeland that would bring together all Nagas into one political unit can come into being only at the expense of Manipur, as well as Assam and Arunachal Pradesh."[109] In this case, impact of the crisis of Naga identity creates problems for the Kukis. In addition to the imposition of new administration through colonization, and the subsequent assimilative approach of Independent India toward the minority culture, local identity movements such as that of the Nagas puts other identities in a crisis.

Added to the complexity is the role of Christianity in the formation of an identity in a post-missionary context. The role of Christianity may differ from one context to another. For example, in the context of Northern Ireland the role of religion in identity construction can be said to have been the central issue rather than merely a supporting inspiration. Mitchell writes, "In many contexts there is a two-way causal relationship between religion and ethnicity. Each can stimulate the other, rather than religion simply playing a supporting role to the ethnic centrepiece."[110] Identifying such a crucial position of religion in identity formation Mitchell emphasizes the need "to look beneath surface assumptions that identities

---

108. Sanjib Baruah, "Confronting Constructionism: Ending India's Naga War" 321–338 *Journal of Peace Research*, Vol. 40, No. 3 (May 2003), 323.
109. Ibid., 324.
110. Quoted in Claire Mitchell, "The religious content of ethnic identities", *Sociology*, Vol. 40, No. 6 (2006), 1137.

are primarily ethnic, and probe their religious foundations, expressions and implications."[111] In the context of the Kukis, and for that matter the Nagas, in relation to the majority Hindu Indians, Christianity is a common and an integral part of the identity of both groups. Christianity serves as supportive to their own respective claims. Nibedon observes how in the case of the Nagas, "They promised to achieve the objective by a revolutionary council and, at the same time, declared that they stood for individual freedom of religion and the old slogan: 'Nagaland for Christ'."[112] The missionization of identity movements with slogans including 'Nagaland for Christ' for the NSCN I-M is a clear example of religious conviction feeding into identity assertion.

The challenge as well as opportunity here concerns crystallization of the Christian message that constructively engages with the issues related to the people's identity crisis. This involves a critical outward-inward looking into issues related to ethnic identity movements. It is important because identities are products of their context/s. In other words, it is the socio-political and economic context that paves the way for emergence of identities, and shapes their nature and tone. The Kuki identity in particular is the product of colonial administration, subsequent Independent India, and the hasty Christianization of the people. Here we reach the primary focus of this research project, which involves a critical examination of the role of missionary Christianity in the current quest for identity, and the search for fresh readings of the gospel within the historical, cultural and political contexts described in this work.

In the same way, a critical inward look is needed for peaceful co-existence among the people. For instance, both the Kukis and the Nagas have a public identity as Christians and hence Christianity became part and parcel of their identities. Christianity in this case is both the foundational and inspirational factor for what people do, including their identity formation as discussed earlier. At the same time, when it comes to practical application of one's belief in an ethnic identity assertion in a multi-ethnic

---

111. Ibid., 1148.
112. Nirmal Nibedon, *North-East India: The Ethnic Explosion* (New Delhi: Lancers Publishers, 1981), 192.

context, the faith is at risk of losing its universal meaning in the hands of the actors of ethnic identity. In this context, if the concern of sociologists for the twenty-first century is not so much whether ethnicity and race will continue to serve as categories of collective identity, but rather 'what kinds' of ethnic and racial stories we choose to tell and 'how' those stories are put to use, the concern of Christian theology is to see how far such constructions of identities can be considered Christian. In other words, while identity movements are crucial to counter oppressive structures, the ways in which identity is perceived and developed needs a critical study in the light of the Christian message.

Part Two

Kuki People and Their Struggle for Identity

CHAPTER 3

The Kuki People of Manipur and Their Struggle for Identity

In chapter 1, we surveyed North-East India to locate the Kuki people's struggle for identity in a wider context. We observed that the problem of alienation, or identity crisis, is a common experience for the people of the region as a whole. That was developed in the process of change, including socio-political, demographic, religious, and economic changes under the administrations of the colonial British and the subsequent Independent India. It was in that context that we discussed the concept of 'identity' or 'ethnic identity' in the light of insights drawn from the field of sociology and argued that identity is not only a social construct, reflecting the socio-political context within which it emerges, but also the people's search for liberation. We shall now proceed to a closer examination of the Kuki people of Manipur and their struggle for identity in particular, demonstrating the urgent need for a theological response.

3. 1. An Overview of the Kuki People: The Background

The Kuki people of Manipur are part of a larger homogenous group, sometimes called 'Kuki-Chin', found throughout the region including parts of Bangladesh and Myanmar, formerly known as Burma. The exact population is difficult to ascertain due to the international boundaries that divide them. In 1904, Grierson in his *Linguistic Survey of India*, suggested the total number of people to be somewhere between 600,000 and 1,000,000.[1] An overview of the group will give us an idea about the affinity of the people in terms of their culture, language and the story of origin as well as highlight the problem of what some called 'ethnification',[2] a wider background of Kuki struggle for identity in Manipur.

3. 1. 1. The Homogeneity of the People

The homogeneity of the Kuki-Chin people is evident in their culture, language and the myth of origin. For instance, Bertram S. Carey and H. N. Tuck, two British political officers in Burma, asserted, "There can be no doubt that the Chins and the Kukis are one and the same race, for their appearance, manners, customs, and language all point to this conclusion."[3] Shakespear arrived at the same conclusion nearly two decades later: "It would be easy to fill several pages with points of resemblance between the different clans."[4] The resemblances are in their "habits, customs, and beliefs."[5] Grierson even produced a map illustrating the dialects of the Kuki-Chin groups that also gives an idea about their geographical extent, covering the areas now known as Mizoram, Manipur, parts of Assam and Tripura in North-East India and North Western part of Myanmar.

Besides external support, the homogeneity of the people is also seen in a shared story of origin called *Khul* and in their religious beliefs. Joy Lalkrawspari Pachuau from the state of Mizoram, an Associate Professor at Jawaharlal Nehru University, New Delhi, in her study of this story argues that *Khul*, also called *Chhinlung*, is an integral part of

---

1. G. A. Grierson, *Linguistic Survey of India*, Vol. III. Part III. (Calcutta: Office of the Superintendent, Government Printing, 1904), 2.
2. L. Lamkhan Piang, *Kinship, Territory and Politics: The Study of Identity Formation Amongst the Zo* (Unpublished PhD Thesis, Jawahalal Nehru University, New Delhi, 2005). The author borrowed this term from T. K. Oomen, *Citizenship, Nationality and Ethnicity: Reconciling Competing Identities* (Cambridge: Polity Press, 1997) for whom 'ethnification' is a "process through which the link between territory and culture is attenuated and the possibility of a nation sustaining its integrity is put into jeopardy." Piang, *Kinship*, 57.
3. Bertram S. Carey and H. N. Tuck, *The Chin Hills: A History of the People, Our Dealing with Them, Their Customs and Manners, and a Gazetteer of their Country* Vol.1. (Rangoon: Government Printing, 1896), 135.
4. J. Shakespear, *The Lushei Kuki Clans* (London: Macmillan and Co., Ltd 1912), ii.
5. Ibid.

the people's homogeneity, which needs to be taken seriously.[6] Similarly, Vanlalchhuanawma from the state of Mizoram argues that common belief among the people such as *mithi-khua*, places after death, *pialral*, a place of bliss beyond the shore and belief in the spirit of natural world show their cultural affinity.[7] The belief in life after death was common among the people to the extent that Lian H. Sakhong, a Chin scholar from Myanmar, even suggests that the smooth and speedy conversion of the Chin people of Burma to Christianity was because of the similarity of such a belief between Christianity and that of the Kuki-Chin groups in Myanmar.[8]

3. 1. 2. The Traditional Territory

Captain Yule, the Secretary to the Envoy to the Court of Ava in 1855, described the territory occupied by the Kuki-Chin people, unexplored by the British until then, as follows:

> Still further westward in the Naga country, between longitude 93° and 95°, a great multiple mass of mountains starts southwards from the Assam chain. Enclosing first the level alluvial valley of Manipur, at a height of 2,500 feet above the sea, it then spreads out westward of Tipperah [now known as Tripura on Bangladesh border] and the coast of Chittagong [now part of Bangladesh] and Northern Arakan [now part of Burma], a broad succession of unexplored and forest-covered spurs, inhabited by a vast variety of wild tribes of Indo-Chinese kindred known as Kukis, Nagas, Khyenes, and by many more specific names.[9]

---

6. Joy Lalkrawspari Pachuau, "*Chhinlung*: Myth and History in The Formation Of An Identity", in K. Robin, ed., *Chin History, Culture & Identity* (New Delhi: Dominant Publishers and Distributors, 2009), 159.

7. Vanlalchhuanawma, *Christianity and Subaltern Culture: Revival Movement as a Cultural Response to Westernisation in Mizoram* (New Delhi: ISPCK, 2007), 66.

8. For instance, see, Lian H. Sakhong, *Religion and Politics among the Chin People in Burma (1896–1949)* (Sweden: Uppsala University, 2000).

9. Quoted in Carey and Tuck, *Chin Hills*,1.

A description of the length and breadth of the territory is given by Grierson, Superintendent of the Linguistic Survey of India, in his *Linguistic Survey of India* in 1904, and we quote this at some length:

> *The territory inhabited by the Kuki-Chin tribes extends from the Naga Hills in the north down into the Sandoway District of Burma in the south; from Myittha River in the east, almost to the Bay of Bengal in the west. It is almost entirely filled up by hills and mountain ridges, separated by deep valleys. A great chain of mountains suddenly rises from the plains of Eastern Bengal, about 220 miles north of Calcutta, and stretches eastward in a broadening mass of spurs and ridges, called successively the Garo, Khasia, and Naga Hills. The elevation of the highest point increases towards the east, from about 3,000 feet in the Garo Hills to 8,000 and 9,000 in the region of Manipur. This chain merges, in the east, into the spurs, which the Himalayas shoot out from the north of Assam towards the south. From here a great mass of mountain ridges starts southwards, enclosing the alluvial valley of Manipur, and thence spreads out westwards to the south of Sylhet. It then runs almost due north and south, with cross-ridges of smaller elevation, through the districts known as the Chin Hills, the Lushai Hills, Hill Tipperah, and the Chittagong Hill Tracts. Farther south the mountainous region continues, through the Arakan Hill tracts, and the Arakan Yoma, until it finally sinks into the sea at Cape Negrais, the total length of the range being some seven hundred miles. The greatest elevation is found to the north of Manipur. Thence it gradually diminishes towards the south. Where the ridge enters the north of Arakan it again rises, with summit upwards of 8,000 feet high, and here a mass of spurs is thrown off in all directions. Towards the south the western offshoots diminish in length, leaving a track of alluvial land between them and the sea, while in the north the eastern offshoots of the Arakan Yoma run down to the banks of the Irawaddy. This vast mountainous region, from the Jaintia and Naga Hills in the north, is the home of the Kuki-Chin tribes. We find them, besides,*

in the valley of Manipur, and, in small settlements, in the Cachar Plains and Sylhet.[10]

Vumson, a Zo scholar, gives a general idea about the land occupied by the Kuki (Zo) people when he writes that it,

> extends from a latitude of about 25 degrees 30 minutes North in the Somra Tract facing Mt Samarati, and in Nagaland across the Namtaleik River and the North Cachar Hills, to about 20 degrees 30 minutes North. The Asho live further south of the Arakan Yomas. Irrawaddy valleys and Pegu Yamas (below Prome and Sandaway). All these areas fall between 92 degrees 20 minutes East. The North-south length about 20 degrees and 30 minutes North and falls between 92 degrees 20 minutes East. The north-south length of the Zo country is roughly 350 miles (560 km) and it is generally about 120 miles (192 km) wide.[11]

This is explained on the present political map as covering parts of different political areas as follows: a) Assam: parts of Cachar, North Cachar Hills and Mikir Hills; b) Meghalaya: Parts of the East; c) Mizoram: State; d) Nagaland: Parts of Extreme South; e) Tripura: Parts of the East; f) Manipur: State (Except parts of the extreme North); g) Myanmar: The Chin State, large group including Tiddim-Falam and Haka are to be found, and parts of the Magwe Division (Arakan Hill Tracts, Akyab, Kyakpyu and Sandaway), where various southern Chin tribes are located, and the Kabaw valley in upper Burma; h) Bangladesh: Syllhet District and Chittagong Hill Tracts.[12]

---

10. Grierson, *Linguistic Survey of India*, 1.
11. Vumson. *Zo History* (Aizawl, Published by the Author, 1986), 21.
12. Chongloi, *Indoi*, 110.

3. 1. 3. The Problem of Disintegration

It is evident that the territory concerned was divided by three different international boundaries, namely India, Myanmar and Bangladesh in the late 1940s, threatening the identity of the people through that division. The boundary demarcation was made on the basis of what was called 'Pemberton Imaginary line', the line that was drawn without studying the ground reality at the Treaty signed between the king of Burma and the British representative, Captain Pemberton in 1834.[13] Effectively, these lines divided the people without them being aware of it. Although the division of the land or the people did not make much difference during the colonial period because the administration was one and the same, the problem became more acute in the post-colonial period. L. Lam Khan Piang points out the fact that the Kuki (he uses 'Zo') people were divided by three international boundaries without their consent, the legacy of the colonial administration, and as the result they were made minority groups, or in his word, 'ethnified' in their own respective states. In such a situation, he rightly suggests, integrity and solidarity gets attenuated and existence as a nation is threatened. He also points out the problem of dual identity: ethnic national identity and citizenship-national identity constructed by the state in the Trans-border areas, creating overlapping and conflicting socio-cultural and politico-geographical identities. Further, the author also correctly points out the problem of cultural alienation of the people in the Trans-border areas by those at the 'centre'. For these reasons, Piang proposes the integration of the people.[14]

In addition to territorial division, as already evident from above, there is also a problem of a name that could include all the Kuki groups. The colonial administration made an attempt but ended up with hyphenated name, 'Kuki-Chin'. In the post-colonial era, two new names emerged, 'Mizo' and 'Zomi/Zo', thus creating a situation that is complex and confusing for outsiders, and results in the lack of any agreed term by which the various groups can be identified in the regions that now became part

---

13. Piang, *Kinship*, 65.
14. Piang, *Kinship*, 30, 68–69, 232–240.

of India, Myanmar and Bangladesh. Clearly this requires more discussion, and we shall need to justify our use of the term 'Kuki' in this publicaiton.

Prior to the colonial invasion, the homogenous Kuki groups lived in clan-based small communities, independent of each other, with no restrictions of movement within the territory mentioned above. It could have been in such a situation of freedom and the absence of common political platform, that the people developed their own smaller identities and interests as families or clans acquiring many dialects and names as the result. In such a situation, it was also possible that there were often clan feuds among the people for domination, which further worsened the problem of disintegration. Hence, the people did not have a common name of their own but called each other by the names of their respective clans. This is indicated in Carey and Tuck's Burma Census Report of 1891, in which "Chin ethnology is dismissed with the remark that the Chins or Kyins are a group of hill tribes, all talking various dialects of the same Tibeto-Burman speech and calling themselves by various names."[15] Horatia Bickerstaffe Rowney writes in *The Wild Tribes of India*, ". . . for their whole race they [Kookies or Kukis] have no common name, and are content to call one another by the names of their different clans."[16]

Different clan names emerged through the traditional practice by which people named themselves after their respective progenitors as clans, for instance, Haokip, Kipgen, Hangsing, and Chongloi. There were also groups given names in relation to others such as the *Hmar* or *Kholhang*, which means village of the south, in relation to those settled in the north. Besides traditional practices, it was possible that there were clan names that have originated from outside the community.

The colonial administration addressed this issue in their quest for a 'better' administration[17] and carried out a study of the clans including

---

15. Carey and Tuck, *Chin Hills*, 2.
16. Horatia Bickerstaffe Rowney, *The Wild Tribes of India* (Delhi: Low Price Publications, 1990), 180. The book was first printed in 1882.
17. A good example for this was the compilation of Kuki customs, Crawford, C. G. *A Hand Book of Kuki Custom* (Imphal: Printed at the State Printing Press, 1927), which was primarily intended for the assistance of the officers serving in Manipur. Crawford, President of Manipur State Darbur, published this Hand Book with the helps of the Sub-divisional Officers: William Shaw, B. C. Gasper, L. L. Peters; J. H. Hutton, director of

their culture and language, and adopted certain names by which groups were categorized into clans and tribes, including marking their territories and finding a common name for them. In the region now part of Myanmar, the Kukis or Chins are also called 'Baungshe', a name which was coined because of their traditional hair style. Carey and Tuck explained that *Paung*, in Burmese, meant wearing [a turban], and *she*, [in front] which means those who bind their hair or turban over the forehead. According to this explanation, Buangshe would mean, 'those who keep hair in their forehead' but for some reason, Carey and Tuck omitted this name for being a nickname given to the people.[18] This is one example of how the colonial rulers invented names for the people and accordingly used 'Chin' for the Kuki groups in Burma and 'Kuki' for those in the Assam, Manipur and in the Chittagong Hill Tracts. We shall show that while the contribution of the colonial administration helped preserve the history of the people and provided written sources for their later identity assertion movements, it also served as a stumbling block to their unification by perpetuating different names for the same people.

The earliest colonial writing about the people is found in works by Colonel Thomas Herbert Lewin, the superintendent of the newly established Chittagong Hill Tracks District in 1859, written after a hundred years of the occupation of Chittagong by the British East India Company in 1760. He acknowledges two different names used for the people: Dzo and Kuki. While he preferred Dzo to Kuki, which he maintained as the foreign term given by the plains people,[19] he put the two words together in his title with the former in inverted commas. Also, although he used the term 'Dzo', he noted that the Dzo language existed only in the form of speech, and the Lusei dialect, which later developed into what is now known as Mizo, was used as the *lingua franca* of the country.[20] Another

---

Ethnology; and Mr J. C. Higgins, Political Agent. The Hand Book includes customs of different tribes including, Gangte, Vaiphei and Zou.

18. Carey and Tuck, *Chin Hills*, 4.

19. Thomas Herbert Lewin, *Progressive Colloquial Exercise in the Lushai dialect of the 'Dzo' or Kuki language with Vocabularies and Popular Tales* (Calcutta: Central Press Company Limited, 1874), 2.

20. Ibid., 3. From Lushai/Lushei, the local people prefer the spelling 'Lusei'. See, B. Lalthangliana, *History and Culture of Mizo in India, Burma and Bangladesh* (Aizawl,

British civil servant who worked in the same region was C. A. Soppitt whose work was published as *A Short Account of the Kuki-Lushai Tribes on the North-Eastern Frontier with an Outline Grammar of Rangkhol-Lushai Language and A Comparison of Lushai with other Dialects* in 1887.[21] Unlike Lewin, Soppitt dropped the term 'Dzo' and used only 'Kuki' as shown in the title of his book mentioned above.

By the later part of 1890s, the term 'Kuki' seemed to have already become a common name for the people. Writing about those who settled in the region, known as Chin Hills in Burma, Carey and Tuck write, "Those of the Kuki tribes which we designated as 'Chins' do not recognize that name, which is said to be a Burmese corruption of the Chinese 'Jin,' or 'Yen', meaning 'man.'"[22] This seemed to indicate that the name Kuki was well established while Chin was not. In fact, Carey and Tuck equated the name 'Chin' with 'Naga' and 'Arbors' which were imposed names, as they write, "Some of the Assam Tribes have also been christened by names unknown to them; for instance, 'Naga,' the meaning of which is simply 'naked,' and the Arbors, who call themselves 'Padam.'"[23] Colonel John Shakespear's work *The Lushai Kuki Clans* (1912) and William Shaw's Notes on the *Thado Kukis* (1929)[24] also further indicate the fact that the name 'Kuki' was a common name used by the colonial administration outside Burma.

The statement of Carey and Tuck referred to above also indicates the fact that the term 'Chin' was imposed on those Kuki groups in Burma. The terms Kuki and Chin in this way have existed together, with the former being used for those in the northern part of the country, while the

---

Mizoram: Published by Remkungi, 2001), 102–103. Lalthangliana is the project Director of the Study Group of Mizo History and Cultural Heritage, Mizoram.

21. C. A. Soppitt, *A Short Account of Kuki-Lushai Tribes on the North-East Frontier* (In the Districts of Cachar, Sylhet, the Naga Hills, etc., and the North Cachar Hills) (Shillong: Assam Secretariat Press, 1887).

22. Carey and Tuck, *Chin Hills*, 3.

23. Ibid.

24. William Shaw, "Notes on the Thadou Kukis", *The Journal and Proceedings of the Asiatic Society of Bengal*, New Series, Vol. XXIV, No.1. Published by the Asiatic Society of Bengal on behalf of the Government of Assam, (Calcutta: The Baptist Mission Press, 1929).

latter was used for those in the southern part, Burma.²⁵ When referring to all the groups together, it was a hyphenated name 'Kuki-Chin'.²⁶ A clear example for the use of the term Kuki-Chin was Grierson's work *Linguistic Survey of India* in 1904 referred to earlier.²⁷

While they used these terms, the colonial administrators noted that they were unfamiliar to the people. C. A. Soppitt, then Assistant-Commissioner from Burma, and Lt. Colonel John Shakespear from the Lushai Hills, now called Mizoram, mentioned that the term Kuki was unknown to the people for whom it was used.²⁸ He also admits that the term is used in diverse ways:

> On the Chittagong border [now Bangladesh] the term is loosely applied to most of the inhabitants of the interior hills beyond the Chittagong Hill tracts; in Cachar [now Assam, India] it generally means some family of the Thado or Khawtlang clan, locally distinguished as New and Old Kukis. In the Lushai Hills [now Mizoram, India] nowadays the term is hardly ever employed, having been superseded by Lushai. In the Chin Hills [now Myanmar] and generally on the Burma border all these clans are called Chins.²⁹

For some colonial administrators, the term Kuki refers to the groups who are "closely allied clans, with well-marked characteristics, belonging

---

25. Shakespear, *Lushei Kuki*, xiii.
26. Sing Khaw Khai, *Zo People and Their Culture: A Historical, Cultural study and critical analysis of Zo and its ethnic tribes* (Lamphelpat, Imphal: BCPW, 1995), 1.
27. Grierson, *Linguistic Survey of India*, 1.
28. Shakespear, *Lushei Kuki*, 1; Soppitt, *Short Account*, 2. Lewin in 1869 writes, "[t]hey (Kukis) are known to the Bengalees by the name Kookie, and to the Burmese as the Lankhe." Lewin H. Thomas, *The Hill Tracts of Chittagong and Dwellers therein with Comparative Vocabularies of the Hill Dialects* (Calcutta: Bengal Printing Company Ltd., 1869), 98.
29. Ibid., i.

to the Tibeto-Burman stock"[30] while for others, it was purely a conventional designation.[31]

The main problem with the administration seemed to be lack of vision for the unity of the people by finding a common name for them. This is reflected in the works of both Shakespear and Thomas H. Lewin who were experienced officers among the Kuki groups. While the former served both in the Lushai Hills and Manipur for more than twenty years, the latter served in the Chittagong Hill Tracts and became attached to the people to the extent that he was named 'Thangliana', a Mizo name. In 1912, both Shakespear and Lewin published books, and while Lewin writes, "The generic name of the whole nation is 'Dzo'"[32], Shakespear writes, "the general population of the hills is spoken of as Mizo."[33] But interestingly enough, neither of them used those names in their books; instead, while Lewin puts the term 'Dzo' in inverted commas, Shakespear uses the term Lushei and talked of them as a clan, as indicated in his book title 'The Lushei Kuki Clans'.

In the post-colonial period in North-East India, as in many former colonies in the Two-Thirds World, the search for indigenous identity and self-governance marked the freedom of the people from colonial rule. In the context of the Kuki people, a search for identity includes the search for a common name. In that process, new names have been developed with an argument that the old names such as Kuki or Chin were foreign and derogatory terms and as the result, the generic term 'Kuki', and for that matter 'Chin', gradually lost its power to unite the people. Unfortunately the development of the new names did not involve a corporate effort. While some retain the generic names, Chin and Kuki, others promote the new terms such as Mizo, Zomi or Zo and as the result the people are further segmented. At times, it looks as though the people have a plethora of names and at other times, they seem to lack any unifying identity.

---

30. Ibid.
31. Grierson, *Linguistic Survey of India,* 1. Grierson suggests "Meitei-Chin" but he did not insist it in order to avoid further confusion.
32. T. H. Lewin, *A Fly on the Wheel or How I helped to Govern India* (Aizawl: Tribal Research Institute, 1977, first published in 1912), 246.
33. Shakespear, *Lushei Kuki,* ii.

3. 1. 4. The Use of the term 'Kuki' in this Publication

In the context of Manipur, it is better to retain the term 'Kuki'. Seilen Haokip, who claimed to be an apologist for the term Kuki,[34] uses it in a geographical sense, and is of the view that the term 'Chin' is best for those in the Chin Hills, 'Mizo' in Mizoram, and 'Kuki' for those in Manipur and the adjacent Sagang Division of Myanmar, where the majority use it for themselves.[35] By this, he meant the traditional territory of those people, who are not part of Mizoram in India or Chin Hills in Burma, and he argues that they be politically recognized as a Kuki State. Once this stage is reached, in Haokip's view, a common name for the whole Kuki groups can be coined.[36] Along the same line of thinking, Hemkhochon Chongloi, a Kuki theologian also uses the term for a particular dialect-speaking group, namely the homogenous Thadou clan and their cognate groups whom some call 'the New Kukis'.[37] Often this particular group are said to represent the identity 'Kuki' in Manipur, but the fact is that there are other clans who have also used the term for themselves, not only in Manipur but also in other states like Tripura. However, it may be noted that unlike in the colonial period when the term was used for all the Kuki groups in India, Burma and Bangladesh, the term 'Kuki' in the present-day is used in a narrow sense.

In a similar way, we shall use the term for the following reasons: First, this is one of the generic names for the people used since British rule. Second, as the term Chin was used for those in Burma, and Mizo for those in Mizoram, the term Kuki is the most widely used name among the people in Manipur where the focus of this study lies. The name in this case is identical with the territory of the people concerned. Third, the

---

34. Seilen Haokip, "Rhetorics of Kuki Nationalism", http://www.kukiforum.com/kuki-people/history/4136-rhetorics-of-kuki-nationalism.html [Accessed 6 March 2010]. Haokip is a Liverpool University graduate and is a spokesman for the Kuki National Organization (K.N.O.), which has an armed wing called Kuki National Army, one of the main revolutionary groups in India and Myanmar.

35. Seilen Haokip, "What Price", *op. cit.* Haokip developed this idea in his PhD work in the University of Liverpool in 2001.

36. Ibid.

37. Satkhokai Chongloi, *Indoi: A Study of Primal Kuki Religious Symbolism in the Hermeneutical Framework of Mircea Eliade* (New Delhi: ISPCK, 2008). This was his PhD work completed in 2004.

term is part and parcel of the people's history and identity in Manipur and to change it at this stage would only lead to further crisis. The fact is that there are socio-political movements and churches under this common name not only in Manipur but also in some of the neighbouring states including Nagaland, Assam as well as some parts of Burma. Conversely, since we will argue that identity is a social construct, it is possible that the nomenclature in question may be restored for whole groups depending on how people would envision it in a given context. In fact, there are signs of restoration of this term in the recent past, since for decades, there have been increasing signs of movement toward unification under the identity 'Kuki' in Manipur and some other states, including Tripura. The establishment of common platforms among the people including socio-political movements and cultural festivals like *Kut*, or the festival of harvest, are evidence for this. Fourth, at the height of clan or dialect consciousness and aspiration for its promotion, proposals for a common name have often ended up either being discarded as foreign or suspected of being assimilative. In other words, although there is an increasing awareness among the people about the need for unification, it is also undeniable that they are not yet prepared to sacrifice their own smaller, regional or dialect-based, group identities for this cause. Change of name will only be effective when all are convinced and prepared to come together under a single name. This will happen only when the people equally feel the need for it in the light of their given context, or what Wimmer calls 'social fields', which we have discussed in chapter 2.

For these four reasons, the term is used in a narrow sense without rejecting the existence of others and it is used with an open mind to the possibility of a better name acceptable to all. By using the term in a narrow sense with an acceptance of others, it is hoped we will be able to deal with the identity issue of the Kuki people of Manipur in a more specific way, and at the same time, remove fear of assimilation and domination within the group. Removal of such fear among the people will prepare a way for trust and confidence with one another, which is a precondition for unity under a common name. Thangkholim Haokip, a lecturer at North East Hill University, Shillong, Meghalaya, offers an important viewpoint. In his work 'Contesting Nomenclatures', Haokip stresses the importance of acceptance and respect for each other among the people groups and suggests that those in Burma may be called 'Chin', in Mizoram 'Mizo' and in other states of India including Manipur, Nagaland, Assam and others, be called 'Kuki'. Once the people can accept the names, which are common in their own respective regions, in Haokip's mind, the single name for the various groups may be easier to find.[38] Whether or not this approach can overcome the clannish spirit, or extreme dialect consciousness among the people, is still to be seen. With awareness of difficulty such as this, we shall use the term Kuki in this work.

3. 2. The Kukis of Manipur: Origin and Settlement

3. 2. 1. The Story of Origin

Some colonial writers suggested that the Kuki people came from the north of India before the Aryan invasion. To quote Carey and Tuck:

> Without pretending to speak with authority on the subject, we think we may reasonably accept the theory that the Kukis of Manipur, the Lushais of Bengal and Assam, and the Chins originally lived in what we now know as Thibet and are of one and the same stock; their form of government, method of cultivation, manners and customs, beliefs and traditions all point to one origin.[39]

The theory here is that the people, including the Chinese, once lived in the northern part of India and got dispersed as the result of the Aryan invasion. While the Chinese moved eastward, the Kuki moved southward to Burma first and then to north toward Manipur, Naga Hills and Assam. However, the theory lacks historical evidence and there is no consensus

---

38. Thangkholim T. Haokip, "Contesting Nomenclatures: The Kuki-Chin-Mizo of India and Burma" in K. Robin ed., *Chin History, Culture & Identity* (New Delhi: Dominant Publishers and Distributors, 2009), 317.
39. Carey and Tuck, *Chin Hills*, 2.

about the origin of the people. Despite this difficulty, what is clear is the mythical story that talks about their emergence from a cave or *Khul*.

3. 2. 2. The *Khul* Story

Karen Armstrong notes a positive aspect of myth as she writes, "Mythology and science both extend the scope of human beings. Like science and technology, mythology . . . is not about opting out of this world, but about enabling us to live more intensely within it."[40] Looking at the story of *Khul* from this perspective brings a new light.

According to the *Khul* story, the Kukis and their cognate groups came out of a cave, or the bowels of the earth, called *Khul*.[41] There are different versions of this story depending on the clan and region to which a person belongs. Among the Mizo-speaking group in the state of Mizoram in India, the place of origin is called 'Chhinlung', while in Manipur among the Kuki groups (including the Aimol, the Anal, the Chothe, the Chiru, the Maring, the Lamgang, the Kom, the Vaiphei, the Paite, the Gangte, the Simte, the Zo, the Thadou and their cognate groups), it is called 'Khul', or 'Khur'. The Chins and other Kuki related groups in Burma also called it 'Khul'. In a Lusei[42] or Mizo version, the cave is called *Chhinlung* and part of the story says, "as the people came out two Ralte people came out chattering so noisily that the guard of the entrance shut the opening with a stone shutter thinking too many people had come out."[43] The Hmar version (one of the clans of the Kuki-Chin group) speaks of the emergence of the people with great effort and their first meeting of a vast number of people among the human races.[44]

---

40. Karen Armstrong, *A Short History of Myth* (Edinburgh: Canongate Books Ltd., 2006), 3.
41. S. H. M. Rizvi and Shibani Roy ed., *Kuki-Chin Tribes of Mizoram and Manipur* (Delhi: B. R. Publishing Corporation, 2006), 4.
42. Lusei is a correct spelling of Lushai or Lushei used by former writers particularly the British administrators. Lusei is a sub-tribe of the Kuki-Chin-Mizo. See, Vanlalchhuanawma, *Christianity*, 22.
43. Vanlalchhuanawma, *Christianity*, 15. Ralte is another clan and much of their distinctiveness has been lost in the process of Mizo identity formation.
44. V. Lunghnema, quoted in Vanlalchhuanawma, *Christianity*, 15.

In the story among the Kukis of Manipur,[45] one Chongthu, a relative of Noimangpa, or the king of the underworld, went hunting porcupines in the jungle with his dog and discovered a large hole through which he perceived the upper earth uninhabited. Discovering the possibility of forming a village of his own there, happily he gave up his hunt, returned to his house and planned for the new village accordingly. About that time, Noimangpa was performing *Chon* festival during which Chongthu injured some people with his sword, which caused the anger of everybody, including the Noimangpa. Taking that as an excuse, Chongthu and his brother Chongja feasted in preparation for the departure and eventually moved toward the hole, although Chongja and his party were delayed and missed the chance to get across to the earth while the hole was opened. On arrival, Chongthu and his party encountered a large snake called Gullheipi, the possessor of the hole, which Chongthu managed to kill after a great loss of life. Their further struggle was to lift the stone that was used to close the hole. One of the members of Chongthu's party, called Vangalpa, lifted the stone during which only seven persons were able to get out through the hole called *Khul*. The seven persons who emerged through *Khul* were Chongthu, Vangalpa, the stone-lifter, Khupngam, the keeper of the dog, and four others who were said to have been the progenitors of the Nagas, the Burmese and the foreigners. In this way, Chongthu and his clansmen were said to have come out through the hole and settled on the surface of the earth, thus, when a Kuki talks about his or her origin, s/he says *Khul'a hung kondoh kahiuve* or 'we have come out of the cave.'

3. 2. 3. Origin in Current Research
Although this myth of origin is widespread, its interpretation is problematic and has given rise to various suggestions. For similarities in name, some Mizos suggest that the name *Chinlung* could have been a name of a person.[46] This is based on the observation that there were some Chinese kings as well as the Mizos who had similar names with Chhinlung/Sinlung –

---

45. Shaw gives a fairly well recorded version of the story and we shall reproduce it here. Shaw, "Notes on the Thadou Kukis", 24–26.
46. Vanlalchhuanawma, *Christianity*, 15.

names, such as Tonring, Tonshu, Shih Huangti, Ch'ienlung and the like.[47] But this contradicts other traditions of the *Khul* story wherein the people were said to have come through a hole. *Khul/Chhinlung* is also suggested to be a name of a place, the main proponent being Sangkima, who, in his work, *A Study of the Mizos with Reference to their Early Home*, suggests that the *Chhinlung* legend could possibly be identified with a place called Xinlong, a town in Sze-chuan province of China.[48] This view, like the one noted above, points to the northward origin of the people but again is incongruent with other accounts, which focus on the significance of emergence from a hole. This has led some modern historians to propose that *Khul* represents a hole, or a passage at the Great Wall of China through which the oppressed sections of the society, including the Kuki group, left the country in secret.[49]

Possibly the most significant scholarly work on the subject is that of the late Vumson, which suggests that the Kuki-Chin people had their origin in China and are related to the Indonesian-Malay sub-race of the Mongoloid Race. His argument is based on the similarity of physical features and language between the Kuki-Chin people and the Tibeto-Chinese.[50] According to him, the Tibeto-Chinese group are subdivided into several smaller groups of which the Kuki-Chin people, together with the Burman, Meitei (Manipuri), Naga, Kachin, Tibetans and others, formed what is known as 'Tibeto-Burman' group. How the Tibeto-Burman groups moved to their present settlement, for Vumson, can only be guessed at in the light of the history of the Ch'iang tribes, their ancestors, who were driven southward by the Chinese. The Ch'iang tribes, during the Shang dynasty (1600–1028 BC), were neighbours of the Shang people and were in constant war with them. During the Chou dynasty (722–481 BC) they were found in northwest China and it was during this time that Chinese hostility forced the Ch'iang tribes to take refuge in northeast Tibet.[51] Later, during the Han dynasty (206 BC–AD 220), the

---

47. Shakespear, quoted in Vanlalchhuanawma, *Christianity*, 16.
48. Sangkima, quoted in Vanlalchhuanawma, *Christianity*, 17.
49. Vanlalchhuanawma, *Christianity*, 16.
50. Vumson, *Zo History*, 26. Vumson uses the term Zo for the Kuki-Chin people.
51. Vumson, *Zo History*, 27.

Ch'iang tribes appeared as the Tanguts – the Tibetan Tribal Federation – and were driven southward by the Chinese.[52] Whether this was the reason for the Tibeto-Burman's southward migration, Vumson suggests, can only be imagined.[53]

Vumson concludes that present scholarship employing historical sources is limited to the conclusion that there was a settlement a few centuries ago along the Irrawady and Chindwin rivers, presently in Myanmar, from where people dispersed and moved in different directions to their present locations.[54] Beyond this, according to him, it is only a probability that the people belong to the Tibeto-Burman groups and eventually to the Ch'iang tribes, their ancestors, in the western China around 2500 BCE.[55]

Although the current research is unable to trace the origin of the people, the story that tells about their arrival on the surface of the earth through a hole, called *Khul* remains significant. Two things can be observed here. Firstly, the unavailability of information regarding the location of *Khul*, or the site or the symbol that *Khul* refers to, indicates the indigeneity of the people in the region they now live in. Secondly, as Vanlalchhuanawma, a Mizo historian from Mizoram rightly points out, this is the only living tradition that has been passed down from one generation to another and it speaks of the common origin of the people and their ethnic homogeneity.[56] Similarly, as referred to earlier, Pachuau in her study of *Chhinlung/Khul* has noted the fact that the origin myth serves as a basis for the people's construction of their common descent and provides a basis for movements for their unification. In this case, Weber's view discussed earlier is right in the sense that an ethnic group is founded on a belief of common descent that is not necessary biological unity which can be scientifically proved, but rather the way in which people consider themselves as being.

---

52. Ibid., 28.
53. Ibid.
54. Ibid., 29.
55. Ibid., 27.
56. Vanlalchhuanawma, *Christianity*, 16.

3. 2. 4. Settlement and Traditional Rule in the Hills of Manipur

We have provided a brief description of the state of Manipur and its people in chapter 1 and we now move to indicate the nature and causes of the Kuki identity crisis. Along with the Meiteis, the Nagas and other ethnic groups in the state, the Kukis came to settle in a place now known as Manipur. Some of the colonial British writers suggest that they were latecomers,[57] which later became a point of ethnic claims and conflicts.[58] However, there were both written and unwritten stories that seem to suggest otherwise. Hudson, at the dawn of the twentieth century, suggests that the Meiteis were descendants of surrounding hill tribes, namely the Kukis and the Nagas.[59] His conclusion was based on similarities in the religions, habits, organization and manner among the people concerned. Similarly, the Tangkhul Naga[60] legend speaks of the early relationship between the Meiteis and the Hill people of Manipur. The legend speaks of the origin of the people in a genealogical order: the Kukis, the Tangkhul and then the Meiteis.[61] Hudson mentioned the Mao Naga legend, which also speaks of the relationship of the three communities in the same order wherein the Kukis were spoken of not only as the first descendants, but also the stronger community over the latter two.[62] On this subject, Professor Gangumei from a Kabui Naga tribe writes, "some Kuki tribes

---

57. George Watt, for instance, says that the Kukis are the last invaders and conquerors of Manipur and they came in five phases dating some two or three centuries past. Watt, quoted in Verrier Elwin (Edited and Introduction), "The Nagas of Manipur", *The Nagas in the Nineteenth Century* (Bombay: Oxford University Press, 1969), 450.

58. Documents of the colonial rulers such as this are often used by communities to suppress one another. While this may be found purposeful by some, one may also keep in mind the fact that the colonial rulers were not friendly with the local people, most often, with the local rulers like the Kukis in the hills of Manipur.

59. Hudon, quoted in Vumson, *Zo History*, 29. Kuki influence on the Meiteis for instance was seen in Chandra Kit taking a Kuki tradition of making his eldest son his heir while the traditional practice among the Meitei was the youngest son who should be the heir.

60. Vumson, *Zo History*, 29. The Tangkhul Nagas are closer to the Kuki-Chin and Meitei groups than they are to the Nagas of Nagaland.

61. Ibid., 30.

62. Hudson, quoted in Vumson, *Zo History*, 30.

migrated to Manipur hills in the pre-historic times along with or after the Meitei advent in the Manipur valley."[63]

In the light of what is seen above, it is possible that the Kukis and the Meitei groups came together into what is now known as Manipur in the same period of time. At the same time, it is possible that in a later period the Kuki people continued to move into the same area at different times, often due to inter-clan rivalries. Shakespear mentioned how the Sailo chiefs emerged in the Lushai Hills as dominating clans, assimilating many weaker clans or driving them further in different directions. Sailos were from the lineage of Thangul or Thangura, the fourth of the six sons of their progenitor Zamuaka. Thangul lived in Tlangkua, north of Falam, now within Myanmar, possibly early in the eighteenth century. Thangul and his clansmen were said to have been driven westward by the Chin. The sons of Thangul, better known as the Thangul chiefs, slowly emerged as powerful chiefs, particularly the Sailo clans, for their ability in government. Equally well-organized clans were the Thados whom Shakespear describes, "When the Thangur had firmly established themselves, and the capable Sailo chiefs had come to the front, they felt equal to fighting the Thado clans, which were as highly organized as themselves."[64] The Sailo chiefs established themselves as rulers in the Lushai Hills, and in the process many weaker clans were assimilated while others were ejected, including the Thado clans and their cognate clans who were pushed further into Silchar in the later part of the nineteenth century.[65] Vanlalchhuanawma, in line with earlier British writers, supports a theory that the Sailos chiefs had pushed their cognate clans such as the Hmars, the Thados and others into the present day Manipur and who possibly were responsible for first driving out other clans such as the Aimol, Kom, Anal, Bete, and Hrangkhawl.[66] The Manipur Chronicles mentioned these Kuki clans in Manipur as 'Old Kukies' for the first time in 1554.[67] Stories such as this suggest that the

---

63. Quoted in Haokip, "Rhetorics".
64. Shakespear, *Lushei Kuki*, 6.
65. Ibid.
66. Vanlalchhuanawma, *Christianity*, 36. Some outsiders used terms, 'Old Kuki' and 'New Kuki' denoting the "time of their arrival" in Manipur and it is sadly divisive.
67. Quoted in Vumson, *Zo History*, 64.

Kuki groups came to their present settlements in Manipur at different times ranging possibly from the earliest period to the recent past.

In Manipur, the Kukis are also called Khongjais by the Meiteis. Some writers including Grierson[68] categorized them into two: 'Old Kukis' and 'New Kukis'. There is no satisfactory explanation about the rationale for this categorization as Ray, the General Secretary of North East council for Research, rightly pointed out, "these two types of Kukis are culturally similar with slight variations only."[69] The dissimilarity of the Kukis with other communities in Manipur is evident in the difference between the Meiteis, who lived in the valley, sanscritized and had no close cultural affinities with Kukis who traditionally lived in the hills and followed their own religion. The difference between the Kukis and the Nagas, their cohabitants in the hills were also apparent to the colonial officials. Carey and Tuck noted the differences in the nature of chieftainship, cultivation and dress. Refuting the notion of some authorities suggesting the Nagas nearly akin to the Kukis, they noted, for instance, the difference in the nature of chieftainship:

> The Government of the Naga tribes is distinctly democratic. Their chieftainships do not necessarily pass from father to son, but are practically dependent on the will of the tribesmen, and the Naga Chiefs are therefore without much individual power and their rule is based on the general approval of the clan. The Kuki Chiefs, on the other hand, invariably inherit their position by the right of birth and take the initiative in all matters concerning the administration of their clansmen, by whom they are respected and feared.[70]

With other Nagas, then known as Koupooee, temperament was said to be a difference that marked the Kukis as a distinct group of people. Colonel

---

68. Grierson, *Linguistic Survey of India*, 2–3.
69. B. Datta Ray, *Tribal Identity and Tension in North East India* (New Delhi: Omsons Publications, 1989), 33.
70. Carey and Tuck, *Chin Hills*, 3.

McCulloch, then Political Agent in Manipur for many years, in his book, *An Account of the Valley of Manipore and of the Hill Tribes*, 1859 noted:

> The Khongjai in temperament differs from the Koupooee. This is shown at their rejoicings, in their dancing, and their music. The dancing of the Koupooee is of that lively nature which is laborious to its practicers, whilst that of the Khongjai is more sober. They both enjoy their own peculiar style of amusement, but perhaps a spectator would prefer the Koupooee dance to that of the Khongjai.[71]

McCulloch's observation of the different temperament of the Kukis was also noted by Carey and Tuck in their comparison of the people with the Nagas as they write, "The Naga features are more pronounced and in many other ways the light-hearted Naga is far apart from the *solemn slow-speaking* Kuki."[72] The identity markers used here were not as strong as they appeared to these western observers, since Kukis and the Nagas are both inhabitants of the hill areas and share much in common. But what is sharp and strong is the divide between the two groups in relation to the socio-political conflicts, particularly in the 1990s. Traditionally, the Kukis were the dominant group in the hills of Manipur. William Shaw, referring only to the Thadou-Kukis, writes:

> [t]he Thadou Kukis live in a large area of hilly country bounded by the Angami Nagas of the Naga Hills District in the north, the Province of Burma in the east, the Chin Hills and Lushai Hills in the south and the District of Cachar in the west. Mainly, it may be said, they occupy the hills of the State of Manipur on all sides of the Imphal valley.[73]

---

71. Quoted in Carey and Tuck, *Chin Hills*, 159.
72. Ibid., 3. Italic, mine as an emphasis.
73. Shaw, "Notes on the Thadou Kukis", 11.

The so-called 'Kuki Rising/Rebellion (1917–1919)' was another indication of the domination of the Kukis in the hills and the fact that they were able to withstand colonial rule for three full years, which no single community in the whole region could do, shows the strength of their traditional rule. Gangte, a well-known Kuki scholar in this field, describes the power and influence of the Kukis in the hills surrounding the Imphal valley of Manipur:

> The Kukis here had been the dominant tribe spreading their authority over a wide range of hill areas surrounding the valley of Imphal during the hey-day of the Maharajah of Manipur and subsequently during the British period. The Kuki Chiefs were in supreme command over their respective domains in the hills . . . the Chahsad Haokip (Chief) . . . to the East of Imphal valley . . . extended up to the Burma Border, contiguous to the Thongdut State and part of the Somra Tract. The Doungel Kuki chief . . . the North-East of Imphal valley extending . . . to the unadministered areas of Somre which lie in between the Naga Hills of the erstwhile Assam Province and the Burmese territory, . . . the Sithou Chief, known as the Chief of Jampi, ruled the Western and North-Western part of Imphal valley bordering the Angami country. The Singson Thadou Chief ruled the areas contiguous to the Sitlhou country and the Lushai Hills of Assam. Pulverised in between the Sitlhou in the North-West and the Imphal valley in the North-East was the country of the junior of the Haokip Thadous, . . . To the South of them, bordering the Tiddim of Chin Hills of Burma, the areas were occupied by the Manluns (Zou), while the South-East of Imphal valley extending up to the areas of Kabo valley and Sukte country, were ruled by the Mangvung Haokip Thadous.[74]

---

74. T. S. Gangte, *The Kukis of Manipur: A Historical Analysis* (New Delhi: Gyan Pubishing Company, 1993), 8.

It is clear from this description that Kuki traditional rule extended not only in their present settlements but also some areas now part of Myanmar. The vastness of their territory was one of the main reasons why the colonial administration had to take three full years to suppress the Kukis: "The ultimate cause of the trouble lay in the fact that, owing to the vastness and inaccessibility of the country which they inhabit, the Kukis in the Manipur State were out of touch with the Administration and almost uncontrolled."[75]

While the 1917–19 Anglo-Kuki war was the sign of strength, it was also the beginning of the decline of the Kuki power and domination in the hills, marking the beginning of Kuki identity crisis. Noting this, J. H. Hudson commented on William Shaw's work, *Notes on the Thadou Kukis* (1929), observing how much different he would have seen the situation of the Kukis had he written about them before the war. Referring to Shaw's unawareness he says, "[t]his, I think, has caused the Thado to appear to Mr Shaw in an unduly unfavourable light."[76] The present picture of the Hills of Manipur is still different from that of Shaw's time since the whole hill area is now divided into five districts namely, Churachandpur, Chandel, Senapati, Tamenglong and Ukhrul, and the Kukis are found in all of them including Ukhrul where the Nagas are the majority.[77]

3. 3. The Kuki Traditional Society

Kuki traditional society is discussed here in order to show changes, which were brought to the people through external factors including the colonial administration, independent India and other ethnic movements in North-East India with a view to situate our research question. This is important as we seek to derive resources from cultural values in dealing with the central issue of identity. Our focus here is on selected elements belonging

---

75. 'Burma-Assam Frontier: Disturbances Among Kuki Tribesmen in Manipur', Indian Office Record (IOR) L/P,S/10/724 preserved at the British Library, London.
76. J. H. Hudson, "Introduction" in Shaw, "Notes on the Thadou Kukis", 4.
77. See map 2 in chapter 1, 'Districts of Manipur' and appendix 3 'The Five Districts of Manipur'.

to Kuki culture, which are considered to be essential marks of the people as distinct groups. This will include discussing the Patriarchy and clan system, chieftainship, system of social relationships, religion, world-view and a concept *Khankho*.

3. 3. 1. The Patriarchy, the Family Lineage and Formation of Clans

The Kuki society is both patriarchal and patrilineal. In a family, it is the sons who enjoy higher status over the daughters and among the sons, the firstborn has the birthright to enjoy the customary headship and privilege for the final say in family matters. The same is true for the children of the firstborn son when he gets married. This is a three-tier structure where the firstborn son called *Upa* is at the top, the younger son/s, or *Naupa*, in the middle, and *Numei* or daughters/women at the bottom. In this hierarchical structure, women have no equal right with male members of the society. The saying goes, "*Nemei thulah lou*" or a "word of a woman is not worth considering". The firstborn son takes the family lineage and not the daughter even if she is the oldest among the children. Having no customary right to share in the family lineage, a daughter also loses a right to own the family property at the demise of her parents even if she is the single child in the family. The property right, including her loyalty in such cases, goes to the next male kin of the family. In the case of a younger son or *naupa,* he gives loyalty to his older brother or *upa*. He has no right or authority above that of his older brother. He acknowledges this structure by giving him *sating*, or upper portion of his hunted wild animals. In turn, he is looked after and represented by his older brother in all matters including his marriage and establishment of his family until he attains a complete family by having a son. A clear example for this is *Gap*, or a paying of penalty for offence caused by a person. That is, if a person commits an offence against someone and his case is lodged to the *Haosa Inpi*, the court of the village chief, he is represented in the court and his older brother pays the penalty. In a similar way the *Naupa* gives loyalty to his older brother, and the *Upa* also gives loyalty to his next family head by giving him his *sating* and the same goes backward including for clans.

It was in this order that clans were formed and villages were set up. For instance, this researcher is a member of Songthat, which is a sub-clan of the Haokip clan. He belongs to a village called Hengjang, or a family group, who established the Hengjang village under the headship of their great-grandfather. Hengjang comes under Tingkai village, the village of their senior family group or *Upa,* Tingkai under Henglep, the village of the head of the Songthat, Henglep under Chahsat, the village of the head of the Haokip clan and Chahsat comes under the head of all the clans. Accordingly *sating,* the upper potion of the hunted animal, is given among these heads by way of acknowledgment of and submission to one's senior or *upa*. Lineage is maintained and used in this way for relationships among individuals, families, and clans and for responsibility toward one another within the society.

The clan system is expressed in terms of a Bamboo plant. A non-invasive bamboo plant formed a compact clump, or *phung,* and each single bamboo plant in that clump has nodes or *changs*. When it is used to refer to the clan systems, it is called *phung-le-chang* or a 'Bamboo plant and its nodes', referring to the genealogical order and the implied relationships among its members. In this case, it should be noted that the desire of a person in this system is the continuity of his family-line or clan. Such continuity of a family line or a life of an individual is imagined in terms of a bamboo plant that grows uninterrupted to the extent that the top of the plant bends in an arc and touches the ground. By contrast, discontinuity of the family lineage or inability to produce a son is called *Inn-gam,* or an extinction of a family, and is considered loss of worth and meaning as a person.

3. 3. 2. Chieftainship: The Administration

Of many that are considered to be elements of Kuki culture, Chieftainship is one that survives through changes as a strong element of contemporary Kuki culture. At the same time, this has become increasingly an issue for debate due to the vulnerability of the system as a source of oppression of the villagers in the hands of the chiefs. A brief description of how this was instituted and practised until the present day will reveal the complexity of this practice. Chief, or *Hausa* in Kuki, literally means 'a rich person' or a person who possesses great wealth in the form of land and bamboo, money and Mithun, also called Indian Bison, cattle, gongs, etc.[78] When it applies to a village administration, it refers to the one who owns the village and its land, or the head of a clan in whose name a village is being set up by the clansmen. The practice goes back centuries to when people were in constant feuds with other communities where a single authoritative figure was a necessity.[79] However, in the process of civilization, the practice has been discontinued by some like the Mizos in Mizoram, India.

3. 3. 2. 1. How One becomes a Chief

Traditionally, a village's chief is the senior member or *upa* of a family, or a clan. A particular clan sets up a new village and makes their *Upa*, their Chief. When felt necessary and appropriate, a chief sends off his younger brothers in age or seniority to set up a new village within his territory, or to bring about the further expansion of the village. This is in line with the *Upa-Naupa* relationship referred to earlier and it makes villages identical with one's own genealogical tree showing whom the *upa* or the *naupa* is. In rare circumstances, incongruent to the *Upa-Naupa* order, an individual can also purchase land, set up a village and become a chief there. In this way, an installation of a chief was an indication to a person's standing in clan seniority order. And in recognition of such an order, a junior chief gives *Sating* to his next senior chief. For instance, the *Hengleppa* or the chief of Henglep village in south Manipur gives his *sating* to *Chahsatpa*, the chief of Chahsat village in the West of Manipur as his senior clan and the *Chahsatpa* in the same way gives his *sating* to his immediate senior clan and it goes on.

The establishment of chiefs, or villages and village lands, not only indicates clan identities and their standings in the *Upa-Naupa* relationship order, but they also connect to the land. One example is the connection of the south and the west of Manipur hill areas through the relationship of the *Hengleppa* and the *Chahsatpa* just seen above. In other words, land becomes part of the people's identity and it regulates relationships and

---

78. These forms of wealth are traditionally taken as signs of one's wealth and they are naturally meant for the Chiefs because they are the only ones who own the lands for these.

79. This is commonly accepted theory. Thangkholim T. Haokip, *The Chieftainship among the Kukis* (Unpublished PhD Thesis, North Eastern Hills University, Shillong, 1996).

responsibility to one another in the society. That is also to say, devastation of a land or a village interrupts the social order and disrupts their relationships. In fact it was for this reason that the destructions of villages in the process of ethnic conflicts, or construction of dams in the hill areas, have a multifaceted impact on the people.

When it comes to socio-political orderliness of the society as a whole, there were layers of authorities from a *kho-hausa*, a village chief, to a *lhang-hausa,* area chief, and from a *lhang-housa* to a *gam-housa*, a country chief. This system has been revived and practiced in the form of the *Kuki Inpi*, or the supreme body of the Kukis since 1993.[80] The term *Inpi* means something like the House of Commons in the United Kingdom except that while, in the case of the latter, the members were elected through a democratic system, the former, through the virtue of being a chief of a village.

3. 3. 2. 2. Power, Nature and Function of the Chief

Each Kuki village is ruled by its supreme head, the *Hausa*, and all the villagers are bound by custom to obey him. Traditionally, the rule of the *Hausa,* as T. Thangkholim Haokip observes[81] was not autocratic but benevolent. However, the effectiveness of the system depends on the ability of the individual chief concerned. Shakespear rightly observed:

> The amount of power he wielded depended almost entirely on the personal influence of the Chief. A strong ruler, who governed mainly according to custom, could do almost anything he liked without losing his followers, but a weak man who tried petty tyrannies soon found himself without any subjects.[82]

The role of a chief was to settle disputes and provide care and protection to his villagers. His house was the shelter of the orphans, widows and the

---

80. "The Emergence of Kuki Inpi Revision", Published by Kuki Movement for Human Rights. n.d.
81. Haokip, *Chieftainship*, 99.
82. Shakespear, *Lushei Kuki*, 49.

needy persons of the community. In return, the villagers were obliged to obey and respect him.

R. N. Prasad writes of the other side of the picture, "The chief is practically independent and [the] real centre of authority in the village administration. Some of the chiefs treated the villagers as servants and reduced some to absolute slavery."[83] In the same tone Paokhothang Misao also writes, "The Chief is the sole and supreme authority in the village[,] no one else being competent to give orders to inflict punishment except through him. His words have the force of law for the particular village."[84] These two observations testified the experiences of common people under the system.

A *Hausa* is assisted by his *Semang-Pachong,* cabinets, to govern his village. The members include the village crier/courier, blacksmith, priest, village writer and the like. In relation to judicial power, the chief is the supreme judge and tries all civil and criminal cases in the village. Any dissatisfied case holder may go to another chief but only with the consent of his or her chief. The chief is also responsible to keep the custom and norms of the people. Anyone found to be guilty of disobedience of his order could be punished by the chief even to the extent of expelling him or her from the village. *Hausa* also enjoys certain privileges including receiving *Samal*, the hind leg of hunted animals, *Changseo*, an imposed tribute of certain baskets of paddy and the like. Privileges and forms of tribute differ from place to place but the principle remains the same. This shows that chieftainship is more autocratic than democratic.

By virtue of being the chief and the head of the senior family of the clan, *Hausa* has traditional rights to remain in the village as a permanent settler while others, including his own sons except the eldest, can be moved anywhere and at anytime depending on the chief. In other words, the chief in a village is the only member who can have a permanent settlement in that village. All the non-chiefs or the villagers are called *Khochagas*

---

83. R. N. Prasad, "Traditional political institution of chieftainship in Mizoram: Powers, functions, position and privileges." A paper presented at International Seminar, April 7–9, 1992, Aizawl, Mizoram, India, 50.
84. Paokhothang Misao, *History and Customs of the Thadou Kukis* (Imphal: Author, 1970), 10.

(*Kho*-village, *chaga*-orphan/poor), persons with no permanent settlement. *Chaga* is also equivalent to *Lolgeng* (*Lol*-neck, *geng*-thin), referring to a poor person without food as the saying goes, '*Chaga-lolgeng*'. The condition of a *kho-chaga* is illustrated by comparing it with a flying bird in the air: "*Chung leng vacha leh Kho-chaga*", meaning, "a flying bird in the air and a villager without a permanent settlement". In this way, the traditional land ownership divests the majority population, depriving and placing the majority of its population in a vulnerable condition.

The defects of the system can be seen in the following. First, the system of community land ownership deprives the majority. Traditionally, a village land is owned by the people through a chief, the head of a family or clan, who is put in that position by virtue of him being the head of a family or a clan. In other words, land in a traditional Kuki society belongs to a community or a clan and hence, it is a part of the identity of the people. At the same time, with the kind of chieftainship now practised in fast-fading communitarian cultural values, the people cannot have a sense of permanency in a village. The simple reason being that *khochagas* have no equal right and a sense of ownership over the village and its resources for being *khochagas*. By way of comparison, the Nagas of Manipur also have chiefs but theirs are not hereditary, hence they do not hold much authority and power in comparison to the Kukis.[85] Second, added to this is the problem that the since chief is the only stable settler in a village, and his immediate relatives are more permanent than other *Khochagas*, he and his close relatives are regarded as rightful persons to take up important leaderships in a village. This in a way is natural as the *khochagas* cannot be permanent settlers of the village in this system. However, this not only deprives the majority members of a village but also paves the way for 'necessity leadership', including in the church, without necessary gifts and skills. The system also keeps the majority of villagers under suppression, which further leads to the problem of psychological dependency and inferiority complex among them. The chief system as practised among the Kukis in this way controls not only socio-political but also religious life. If the Kuki people

---

85. S. H. M. Rizvi, "Introduction" 1–14 in K. S. Sigh. Gen. ed., *The People of India: Manipur*. Vol. XXXI (Calcutta: Anthropological Survey of India, 1998), 5.

are serious about the issues of human rights and human development, this is where it should begin. Third, chieftainship hinders a spirit of democracy and equal opportunity for all members of the community. The result of this is either suppression of one's innate will for development, or the emergence of new villages in search of opportunity for development and equality. The fourth and final problem to be noted here is commercialization of the chief system in the process of urbanization. Such corruption of the tradition includes a younger son/junior clan setting up a village of his own ignoring his senior clan and making himself a chief, but retaining the pyramid structure referred to above. The result of this is a mushrooming of new villages near the towns creating a new trend more destructive than the old as it paves the way for the rule of wealth both in the society and the church, and ignores the manipulative use of the tradition.

3. 3. 2. 3. Chieftainship in Transition

In the process of democratization, the Chin Hills in Burma experienced a successful launch against the chieftainship that succeeded in the year 1947. A similar movement, possibly an indirect impact of the colonial rule, was felt in Mizoram and also succeeded in the year 1954.[86] In those two cases the chiefs were paid compensation. The result of the abolition, as R. N. Prasad observes, was obvious: a larger number of Mizos were provided with opportunities to participate in decision-making.[87] The Kukis in Manipur, probably influenced by those in Mizoram and Chin Hills, also took up a similar movement. However their Chiefs in turn reaffirmed the status-quo, sometimes with the help of the then British administration particularly during the later part of their rule.[88]

In 1966 the Manipur Hill Area Chiefs' Acquisition Right was introduced in the Manipur Legislative Assembly along with land reform policy, which would permit a tiller to own the land. But the attempt ended in vain due to the refusal of compensation to the chiefs. The issue was taken up again in 1967 with a recommendation of abolition of hereditary

---

86. Haokip, *Chieftainship*, 177.
87. Prasad, *Chieftainship*, 55.
88. The Sub-Divisional Magistrate's (West Tamenglong) Order Misc. Case No. 66 of 1942–43, dated 23 April, 1946, quoted in Haokip, *Chieftainship*, 178.

chieftainship but once again it did not succeed. Failing in all these attempts the Government of Manipur appointed a sub-committee to look into the matter and the committee came to the consensus that the abolition of the chieftainship was not advisable until the tribal land was secured.[89]

In spite of those attempts against chieftainship, the system survives and continues till the present day projecting itself as a strong element of Kuki cultural identity. The issue of land preservation is also seen as a strong point for continuation of the chief system as it is this system through which the people own the land. At the same time, the dilemma of the common people within the system cannot be totally ignored. The chief system becomes increasingly fragile when exploited by selfish means in the age of globalization and consumerist culture by the chiefs. Haokip observes, "To the Kuki chiefs the democratization process appeared to be a sensitive issue and the pride of their tradition suddenly flared up. So they started politicizing their cultural survivability and concentrated on the point that the institution of the chief was indispensable."[90] His observation is validated as Tongkhojang Lunkim, a prominent Kuki leader, who argues that "Kuki chiefship is culture and hence nothing can replace it."[91] Shonkhothong Haokip[92] theologizes it as something that is God's blessing to the Kukis as the Israelite kings were to their people. As such there have been a number of '*Hausa* camps' conducted by the churches in the past thereby ensuring the interests of chiefs. Socio-politically, even the Kuki middle-class group and various organizations formed today, including the *Kuki Inpi*, their Supreme Body which of course is constituted mostly by the chiefs, do not dare to talk about the dehumanizing side of the chieftainship but rather vow to safeguard the interests of the chiefs.[93] The point is that chieftainship was a structure, the people's own creation and the fact that it existed long enough to become a tradition is to say that the system was working

---

89. Haokip, *Chieftainship*, 178.
90. Ibid., 187.
91. Ibid. Lunkim is a well-known Kuki leader from a Protestant church in Manipur.
92. Shonkhothong Haokip, *Thugilbu*, (Imphal: Author, 1996), 18. Haokip is a well-known chief.
93. The Constitution of Kuki National Organisation, published by the KNO Publishing Department, quoted in Haokip, 201.

well for the context where it emerged. However, in tune with the changes of time and for the sake of the majority population, it needs transformation. The issue is not about destroying the traditional practice, but rather, how to develop and transform it in the light of the Christian message. The question is, if chieftainship has to remain as part of the cultural identity of the people, it should serve the interest of all the people equally, ensuring their future as a people.

3. 3. 3. Social Relationship System

Social relationship system is another important element that can be considered as an essential mark of a Kuki cultural identity. There are systems and values that closely knit together not only the members within the community but also those outside. The practice of *Upa-Naupa*, *Becha-Tucha-Sungao* and *Jol-leh-Gol* exemplify the statement.

3. 3. 3. 1. Upa-Naupa Relationship

We have already seen the way in which an *Upa-Naupa* relationship operates in the context of family and clan relationships including that of the village chiefs and their lands. However, we shall briefly describe the institution with a view to show how some emerging theologians see the system.

Upa means older brother or senior clan, and *Naupa,* younger or junior. This relationship works not just for a family but also for the village, the clan and the whole tribe. Being a patriarchal society, the oldest male child takes the lineage of the family genealogy and thus inherits the property of the parents. This creates for him a hereditary right and first place in preferences, respect and administrative responsibilities in the family.

Upa, in the absence of the father, is the head of the family. By virtue of being the *Upa,* the oldest son has the final say on family matters and no one can bypass him. His married younger brothers recognize his status as *upa* by giving him an upper portion of hunted animals. *Upa* not only enjoys the privilege of the hereditary headship of the family, but also has the responsibility for the wellbeing of his younger brothers and all his sisters. He represents the family or clansmen in important occasions such as ritual ceremonies and traditional courts. A village chief as *upa* can also set up a village and make his young brother the chief of that village and this can go on and on.

The same principle of relationship is applied in the socio-political relationship between clans, villages and the tribe. There is *upa* of a family, *upa* of a clan, and *upa* of the whole tribe and it goes on to their cognate tribes. At family level, a younger son gives *sating*, the upper back portion of his hunted animals to the oldest son of the family. At village level, the chief, the *upa* of the village, gives his *sating* to the chief of another village, the *upa* of his village and it goes on. This order is respected and maintained even today, at least in a symbolic form, and as people 'discover' their roots new relationships are being established by giving *sating* to the people concerned. The practice of *sating*-giving is a system of acknowledging the genealogical *upa-naupa* order and the implied relationship involved. Shakespear observes how genealogy is given importance among the Kukis as he writes, "The Lusheis, in common with the Thados and other Kuki tribes, attach importance to their genealogies" and impressed by how this tradition works he writes, "pedigree, given at an interval of many years, and by persons living far apart, have been found to agree in a wonderful manner."[94] For this reason, it is possible that the elderly people and the *thempus* or a village priest are highly regarded in the Kuki society as they are the ones who keep the story of the people and their history in their memories and chantings.

3. 3. 3. 2. *Tucha-Becha-Sunggao Relationship*

Unlike the hierarchical *upa-naupa* relationship based on the genealogical tree, *Tucha-Becha-Sunggao* relationship is a horizontal relationship and it leaves no one excluded from the relationship. Tarun Goswami speaks of *Becha* and *Tucha* as "the friends, philosophers and guides of the Kuki families."[95]

Be or *Becha* is a term used to refer to a person who is nominated by a family to act as the main responsible person and spokesman on behalf of

---

94. Shakespear, *Lushei Kuki*, 3.
95. Tarun Goswami, *Kuki Life and Lore* (Haflong, Assam: North Chachar Hills District Council, 1985), 19.

the family. This is a special relationship instituted between a family and a *Becha*, giving him a status and privilege of discharging responsibilities in the family. The word '*Be*' is used when referring to a person, that is, Mr Y or Z is my *Be* and *Becha* refers to a system or the institution.

Traditionally, the eldest son inherits the parents' property and the younger sons leave to set up their new homes after marriage. It is the responsibility of the eldest son to make sure that the new family is provided with *Becha* and *Tucha*. In the case of *Becha*, the eldest son does a careful study of who should be requested to be the *Be* of his younger brother/s. Once a suitable person is found, the eldest son in a family social function formally nominates him to be the *Becha* of the family of his younger brother/s.

Becha is reciprocal. If Y is a *Be* of Z reciprocally Z becomes the *Be* of Y. If a *Be* dies his son becomes *Be* in his father's place. Thus, *Be* is essential for one to run a family. Normally a *Be* is someone who is not biologically related to the family. The responsibility of a *Be* is to act on behalf of the head of the family in all affairs, including decision-making, ritual ceremonies, and social activities. Observing the importance of his role and status Goswami writes, "the *Becha* performs the job of a general manager of the family shouldering the managerial responsibilities in all the social functions including liaison work of the family . . . Without the *Becha* performance[,] any Kuki social functions [are] unthinkable."[96] The *Be*, for this reason, is firmly attached to the family. The wife of the *Be* also plays an important role in the ritual and social ceremonies of the family concerned. She is called *Benu* while the husband is called *Bepa*. During feasting, which is an integral part of a Kuki family, *Benu*'s main role is to cook rice while the *Bepa* serves as the head of the family in consultation with the family concerned.

Normally, there are two *Bechas*: the senior *Be* called *Be-bul* and the junior, *Be-gol*. The senior *Becha*, a spokesman and overall in-charge of the family concerned, oversees matters including rituals related to births, marriages, funerals and other important ceremonies. The junior *Becha* is the one who implements with the cooperation of the *Tuchas*, who is another

---

96. Goswami, *Kuki Life*, 19.

important part of a family. He is called upon as the main *Becha* if the senior *becha* dies without having a son or leaves the village and settles in some other village. In recognition of his status and role in the concerned family, *Becha* gets the chest portion of their hunted animals.

Like *Becha*, *Tucha* is very important and central to the Kuki social system. However, unlike the former, the latter has a marital link. A nephew is called *Tu* while *cha* is a child or an offspring. *Tucha* is chosen from the sisters' offspring or someone who marries the sister or daughter of a clan. There are two *Tuchas*: the senior *Tucha* called *Tubul* and the junior, *Tuleh*. Their main responsibility includes activities such as cooking curry and fetching water during such family events as marriages, ritual ceremonies and deaths. Their roles and responsibilities are recognized by giving a back portion of hunted or sacrificed animals. That explains well the importance of *Becha-tucha* in order to set up a family. Therefore, without *Indoi* and *Tucha-Becha* a family is incomplete.

The term *Sunggao* refers to the members of the family or clan from which the wife comes. They are called *pu* or *pute*, a respectful term and they in turn call their nephews, *tu* or *tute*. The *sunggaos* enjoy respect and high regard and accordingly, their role is also different. They are not directly involved with the affairs of the family but are more of observers and they make their presence felt. The recognition of their status as *pu* or *sunggao* is shown by giving a neck portion of hunted meat and they in return give their nephew or *tu* a chicken. There are certain duties and responsibilities of a person as a *Tu* to his *pute* or *sunggaos* and vice versa. The same principle applies to *Tucha-Becha* relationship. For this reason, as indicated above, the relationship leaves no one untouched. A person is a *Be* in someone's family, a *Tu* in another and also a *Sunggau* in someone else's family. He or she discharges the responsibilities of all these *Tucha*, *Becha* and *Sunggao* depending on the family for which he or she performs his or her duty. In this way, they formed a closely knitted community.

3. 3. 3. 3. *Jol-le-gol Relationship*

The *Jol-le-gol* relationship is a Kuki traditional practice that is designed for relationship with the members of other communities including non-human beings. Technically, people who share the same name are called *Jol* and the word *gol* means friend. The term *Jol-le-gol* therefore refers to a special relationship between two individuals or families who are from different tribes or communities. The relationship is established independently between two individuals or families through close friendship and concern for the wellbeing of each other. Through this system of relationship, until the recent past, many Kukis and the Nagas made each other *jols*. In a similar way, many Kukis have *jols* among the non-tribal Meitei Hindus, as well as their cognate tribes. The bond of the *jol-le-gol* relationship is sometimes claimed to be stronger than some of those which are based on blood relations. One of the powerful resistance movements to the recent Kuki-Naga ethnic conflict was the *jol-le-gol* relationship among the people. Many of them have had a tearful departure when the militant groups forced them to part in the 1990s. Based on this practice, it can be said that the traditional Kuki social relationship system provides room for all the people and it is a communitarian culture. In fact, it has been said that some have had even the *thilhas*, or spirits of the jungles and lakes, as their *jols*. What is clear here is that one is connected to other members of the community within and outside the society. In other words, a person is connected to all other members in the society through this web of relationships.

3. 3. 4. Religion

There has been an increasingly positive attitude towards Primal religion in the recent past. It is no longer considered to be something that is unintelligent or something that is 'step one' in an evolutionary sense. Andrew Walls stresses that 'primal' is not a euphemism for 'primitive' nor does it indicate any evolutionistic understanding. What it does, he maintains, is to underlie two features of the religion of the people concerned: "their historical anteriority and their basic, elemental status in human experience."[97] With this background, let us discuss briefly the religion of the Kukis.

---

97. Andrew Walls, "Primal Religious Traditions in Today's World" 250–278 in Frank Whaling, ed., *Religion in Today's World: The Religious Situation of the world from 1945 to the Present Day* (Edinburgh: T & T Clark, 1987), 252.

3.3.4.1. The Term

Kuki Primal religion is part of their cultural identity. However, unlike the dichotomized concept of religion found in some cultures, Kuki primal religion holds together the concept of sacred and secular so that life is seen as one whole. John Mbiti, writing about African culture and philosophy, notes the inseparability between sacred, secular, spiritual and material areas of life. Mbiti writes, "Although many African languages do not have a word for religion as such, it nevertheless accompanies the individual from long before his birth to long after his physical death."[98] For this reason it is difficult to talk about one independent of the other. Our focus under this section 'Religion' is to those cultural practices that are directly related to ritual and practices in the Kuki Primal religion. As in the case of Africans, Kukis have no word that can correspond to the current English term 'religion'. The name used was '*Pu hou–Pa hou*' which means 'that which our ancestors worshipped'.

3.3.4.2. Pathen or God

The earliest written documents on the concept of God in Kuki primal religion were the work of colonial rulers. Undoubtedly, their efforts were commendable but it should be noted that they wrote from a perspective outside of the people concerned and hence the true picture of concepts often gets distorted. A clear case is the treatment given by Shakespear when, observing the external activities, he says: "Far more important to the average man are the numerous '*Huai*' or demons, who inhabit every stream, mountain, and forest, and to whom every illness and misfortune is attributed."[99] This observation is the result of narrow focus on what people did as appeasements to *thilhas* or demons, overlooking the link between the Supreme Being in the highest and the presence of God in every household in and through *Indoi*, which will be discussed below.

Looking from an insider's point of view, as Chongloi argues, God takes a central place in the life of a Kuki.[100] The word for God in Kuki

---

98. John Mbiti, *African Religion and Philosophy* (London: Heinemann, 1969), 2.
99. Shakespear, *Lushei Kuki*, 61.
100. Chongloi, *Indoi*, 134.

is *Pathen* and it literally means 'Holy Father'. The same name is used by their cognate clans, both in India and Myanmar. The Mizo spell it *Pathian* while the Paite, *Pasian* but they all mean the same. Belief in the Supreme Being called *Pathen* in Kuki Primal religion was vividly clear, even if the identity of *Pathen* was sometimes unclear to the outsiders. In the absence of a sacred book, incantation is the only important source for understanding Kuki primal religious beliefs. In the incantations, there are other names mentioned besides *Pathen* as if the people believed in many gods: *Nungzai*, believed to be a consort of *Pathen*, *Noimangpa*, one who rules the underworld and *Thennu*, the mother god. They are mentioned in the beginning of incantation as *Pathen nalhaijin, Nungzai nalhaijin* meaning, 'May *Pathen* and *Nungzai* be propitiated', or *chunga Pathen nalhaijin, noija Noimangpa*, 'May you (wine) be pleasing to *Pathen* above and *Noimangpa* below'. Incantation also mentions *thennu-thenpa,* meaning Mother *Pathen* and father *Pathen*.

The mention of these names along with *Pathen* may sound polytheistic but it is important to note that these names were never mentioned without mentioning *Pathen* and this suggests that they are not separate gods as such.[101] It is possible, rather, to suggest that these names only show the traditional concept of God and a way of expression, according to which a pair is a way of describing something in its totality. For instance, *Thi le man* 'death and loss' referring to the dead in all forms, *van leh lei* 'heavens and earth' meaning the universal, and so forth. For this reason, it is more convincing to say that Kuki Primal religion was a worship of one Supreme Being, *Pathen* or God, rather than a worship of many gods, or a male god.

The abode of God, according to this concept, is in the highest heaven. Referring to the attributes of God, God is called *Chung Pathen*. The word *chung* means 'above' hence *Chung Pathen*, 'Holy Father of above'. The concept has parallels with Christianity as it is indicated not only in the words but also the tone in prayers, '*Van chung sangpenna um Ka-Pau Pathen*', Our Holy Father in the highest heaven.

An important element often unnoticed by outsiders is the belief that God is in the highest, yet is available to each household in and through

---

101. Ibid., 135.

Indoi. The practice of *Indoi* is the expression of God's presence with the people, similar to the concept of 'Emmanuel' in Christianity, except the fact that *Indoi* or *Doibom* is installed only where a family consists of a father, a mother, son/s and daughter/s. The practice of *Indoi* is discussed below.

3. 3. 4. 3. Indoi

Indoi is symbolized by a bundle of selected articles taken from parts of animals and plants bound together by a single cord and it is hung on the front porch of a house. Each of the articles represents different virtues of God. Hemkhochon Chongloi has explained this and it can be summarized in the following ways: *Vohpi maikem* (a slanted skull of a mother pig), referring to a long life; *Kelchal kiheh* (a twisted horn of he-goat), representing maturity; *Peng* or *um* (small gourd), referring to its usefulness; *Chao* (Bangle made from *gopi* a particular kind of bamboo), symbolizing the wellbeing of the girl's family; *gopi*, smoothness and perfection; *Chemkol* (knife made from *gopi*), symbolizing defence; *Teng* (a spear made of *gopi*), durability; *Miluh/ pothul/ pocha* (a small basket made from *gopi*), symbolizing household management; *Khaopi* (a cord made from a fibre tree called *khaopi*), symbolizing perfection.[102]

The role of these articles is seen in chanting or prayer where a priest prays, for instance, *Vohpi maikem nasah bangin neisan* meaning, 'bless me as you blessed a slanted skull of a mother pig', referring to a prayer for long life.[103] It is clear that these articles are not the objects of worship. They were pointers to *Pathen* who is beyond them. In other words, these are the best instruments available at hand for the people concerned, which can lead their worship to God who is beyond the visible articles. Ironically, the missionaries and later local Christians did not notice this fundamental indigenous principle of worship. They interpreted the rituals as though the primal people worshipped *Indoi* or the bundle of those articles also called,

---

102. Chongloi, *Indoi*, 192–203.
103. A long life, under the constant threats of *thilhas*, is considered to be a blessing, victorious and a virtue that is something to dream for. For this reason, senior citizens are high regarded and respected. No one would dare to hurt the feeling of an old person in fear of his or her curse in anger. In contrast, an early death is called '*hinglhumlou*' interrupted life and is considered to be unsuccessful, a defeat.

Doibom. The object of worship and aids were mistakenly taken to be identical. On the contrary, *Indoi*, being a pointer to God who is beyond the visible things, was a medium as well as a symbol of God's presence with each household. At this point, Chongloi is right in arguing that *Indoi* is an instrument that bridges the gap between God and human beings.[104]

Indoi, being a God-made-present in one's own family and the centre of Kuki religion and cultural identity, was the most dear and valuable possession to them. For them a family without an *Indoi* was incomplete. Thus, the status of a person was discerned in terms of his eligibility and installation of *Indoi*. Being an important element of an identity and medium of worship, the abandonment of *Indoi* in the process of Christianization was not merely a change of belief but a change of way of life in its totality.

3. 3. 4. 4. *Thilha or Spirits*

Besides *Chung Pathen*, the Supreme Being, Kukis also believe in the existence of a host of *thilha*,[105] although the picture of their existence is never clearly conceived. Literally, the word *thilha* means 'spirit of dead' but it is not clear if they are conceived to be exclusively the spirits of once-living humans. The *thilhas* are feared, unfriendly and they are the main and daily concern for one's wellbeing right from birth until life after death. At the moment of birth, a child is protected from *thilha* by giving it a random name called *minchuna* (reservation of name); as the child grows there are rituals to be conducted at various stages for her or his protection known as *lhalho*[106] (imploration of spirit/soul) and at death, the living ones will do

---

104. Chongloi, *Indoi,* 314.

105. The list of *Thilhas* varies from region to region. This is reflected in the work of T. S. Gangte from Manipur and Tarun Goswami from Assam representing how the supernatural powers manifested or are apprehended in different localities. See, Chongloi, *Indoi,* 137–139.

106. *Lha* or 'soul' is in everything and they can be hurt and chased away by humans. *Lhalho* or 'prayer for persuasion' is performed for various souls, for instance, *Naolha* (a soul of a child for childless couples), *Moulha* (a soul of a bride for unmarried boys), *Changlha* (a soul of paddy), *Salha* (a soul of animals for hunters), and so forth. Letkhojam Haokip documented some of these practices. Letkhojam Haokip, *Thempu Ho Thu* (Churachandpur: Published by Author, 2000), 53–69.

the *kitom*[107] to help him pass through the way to *mithikho* without the hindrance of *thilha*. Besides *kitom*, the tomb of a deceased person is watched during the first few nights following burial by strong men who are armed with weapons such as guns and spears. It is believed that the killer/s appear in the form of some animals or insects. All sicknesses, including death, that occur in one's life are considered to be the work of *thilhas* and accordingly sacrifices were instituted. Life in the Kuki primal religion, thus, was lived under the constant fear and appeasement of the *thilhas*. Different types of sacrificial systems, rather, means of appeasement of evil spirits (*kithoina*), were instituted for the remedy of sickness caused by the *thilas*.[108] *Thempus* (the mediators or sorcerers)[109] were experts to discern the kind of illnesses and their remedies. In most cases, *kithoi* involves sacrificing one's best possessions such as animals, fowls, and so forth and that can happen to anyone at any time. Observing this Shakespear comments, "a Lushai's whole life is spent in propitiating these spirits."[110] Not all *thilhas* are necessarily malevolent – there are *thilha* which are benevolent and they can be made *jol* with humans.[111]

3. 3. 4. 5. Kithoina or Sacrifice

There are various sacrifices, however, we restrict our comments to the incantation of *Ganlhaina* (animal sacrifice) to indicate what sacrifice is like in the Kuki primal religion and its implications. In this *Ganlhaina* it can

---

107. *Kitom* is an act of showing anger and defiance at the departure of someone's soul and support for its smooth passage to the *mithikho*. When the close relatives of the deceased arrive, the women straight away enter the house and weep while the men, holding their *daos* and firearms jump and stamp vigorously on the floor of the veranda. Exclaiming his clan identity and fame one heats the forewall of the house and shouts to warn the killer not to distract the soul of the deceased "*lam ana ot in*", (give way).

108. *Gamlahlang* (sacrifice related to sickness caused by demons) and *Kholailang* (sacrifice related to sickness caused by the *kaoses*). Besides sacrifice, Kukis have religious duties and practices for different occasions and purposes. For further information, see, Letkhojam Haokip, *Thempu Ho Thu*, particularly chapter III & IV.

109. Like in Christianity, Kukis have a *Thempu* (priest) in a village called *Kho-Thempu* to cater to the spiritual needs of the people. When necessary, *Thempus* of other villages can be also summoned.

110. Shakespear, *Lushei Kuki*, 61.

111. *Jol* is a special relationship instituted between two persons who may be totally different in terms of social and religious backgrounds. In some cases, this relationship is said to have extended to *thilhas*.

be seen that the priest who performs the ritual, the animal or fowl that is to be sacrificed, and God to whom the prayer is being made, are all participants in the prayer. In other words, a priest makes prayer in dialogue and agreement with God and nature. The incantation of *Ganlhaina* goes:

> O you cock! You are the progeny of my white and black hens. Today, I am not doing this (here the priest means the action of cutting the cock) for the sake of your meat. I am not doing this like those who strike the palm trees with their axes just to try how sharp their axes are; or like the others who cut the branches of the banian tree wantonly. I am performing this job today, so that, you may call the spirits of the paddy and the spirits of *mim* seeds, and as such, may you not be sad or be regretful.[112]

Having justified the plan for sacrifice to the cock, the priest also seeks God's instruction for the actual killing of the cock. He holds the cock by its head and another person grabs its body. The priest then puts the blunt side of a sickle or Dao on the stretched neck of the cock and chants the following:

> O god of heaven! Would it be proper for me to do like this (here the priest means cutting of the cock's neck by the blunt side of the sickle. The God of heaven answers through the mouth of the priest): O man (sometimes used *Manmasi* for man), do not do like that; but cut the cock's neck with the sharp edge of the sickle. If you do like this you would be happy and healthy in body and mind and you will be successful in everything that you may do.[113]

The incantation shows that the priest acts not on his own wish but in dialogue and agreement with nature (the cock) and God. The role of a

---
112. Goswami, *Kuki Life,* 162.
113. Ibid.

priest is only a mechanism through which the act of ritual is performed. What is important to note here is the involvement of the to-be sacrificed cock itself in the ritual. The priest in justifying the plan made clear the purpose of the sacrifice to the cock. In doing so, it is imagined that the cock also agrees with the plan and joins the priest in seeking the blessings for which the ritual is being performed. In other words, the cock willingly and sacrificially gives itself up for the sake of what the priest performs in the ritual. The same is followed in other incantations where a priest speaks for various characters, for instance spear, sword, and bow in *Tol-theh* (clearing of ground incantation). Another important point to note in the incantation is the involvement of *Pathen*, God, in the sacrifice. The priest does not carry out the cutting of the chicken on his own, but seeks for God's direction lest he hurt the spirit of the sacrificial animal or fowl.[114] It is for this very reason that the priest always seeks for justification, called *Kikaona* or washing of hands, before he conducts sacrifices or rituals that might harm any individual or nature. In the case of sacrifice, a priest only acts according to the guidance of *Pathen* because in Kuki traditional belief, all creatures have souls and they can be hurt by humans. That implies respect for life and God, the creator. What is clear in the incantation is the agreement among the priest, the to-be sacrificed cock, and *Pathen* and their wholehearted involvement in rituals so that the act becomes not a mere ritual activity of an individual priest, but an act of prayer where the cock and *Pathen* are themselves involved. Sacrifice is a community affair involving not only humans, but also nature as well as *Pathen*, the creator, to whom prayers are being made.

3. 3. 5. Worldview

A worldview refers to the way in which an individual or a community views the world and interprets and relates to it. In a Kuki primal religion, the world is seen as inseparably interconnected. The reality is seen in two different realities: the visible object that can be seen and touched and the invisible reality called *lha* or soul that cannot be touched or seen. They are

---

114. There is a belief that everything has a soul/spirit that can be hurt. Care is taken that none is hurt, particularly that which are essential for living such as Rice, animals, fouls and so forth.

called, for instance, *Changlha* (soul of paddy/rice), *Salha* (soul of animals), *sumlha-selha* (soul of money/*mithun*, meaning richness) *naolha* (soul of a child), *moulha* (soul of a bride) and so on. In this worldview, human beings, creatures and God are inseparably related. It is such a framework of ideas and beliefs that shapes a traditional Kuki life.

The *lha* or soul is considered to be the main source of existence of a thing or a person. It is the *lha* of a thing or a person that makes something or someone exist. In pursuit of success and richness in life, one performs rituals such as *changlha kou* (invoking of the soul of paddy) and *salha kou* (invoking of the soul of animals), to invoke the *lhas* or souls of those he or she needed. Added to that, one takes all possible care so that no *lha* is hurt. For a farmer, for instance, paddy is sown at the beginning of the year and looked after throughout the year with care and great respect. No negative word is spoken against the paddy and other vegetables as if they have ears to hear it. The success and failure of a person was put in view in the light of this worldview. The practice of *Sa-Ai* and *Chang-Ai* well explained this.

Sa-Ai is a celebration of success in hunting, marking a complete dominance over the spirits of the hunted animals.[115] Men who hunted wild animals like tigers and elephants perform *Sa-Ai*. It is believed that a hunter who does not perform *Sa-Ai* will be inflicted by the spirits of the dead animals either during his lifetime or after death. Like *Sa-Ai*, *Chang-Ai* is an important celebration of achievement for women. The word *Chang* means paddy and *Ai* means subjugation. *Chang-Ai* therefore means 'victory over paddy'.[116] However, words like 'dominion', 'victory' or 'subjugation' used here should not be understood in terms of ruling over nature with boasting and pride. For traditional Kukis, women work in the paddy fields while the men hunt. The success of a woman is gauged in terms of harvest at the end of the year. To be qualified for the *Chang-Ai* ritual, one should have a minimum quantity of harvested paddy that can fill a basket of the circumference of three *lam*,[117] that is, harvest of paddy filling a basket of about five feet height and fifteen feet in width.

---

115. Goswami, *Kuki Life,* 115.
116. Goswami, *Kuki Life,* 157.
117. Ibid. *Lam* means a traditional measurement of both extended hands from tip to tip, which is about five feet.

Success and victory in this context seem to be more of one's achievement in 'not hurting' the *lhas*, in other words, having been able to win over the souls of those creatures through cordial relationship with them. For instance, care is taken throughout the year that no action or even attitude hurts the *Chang*. In this case, *Chang-Ai*, and for that matter, *Sa-Ai*, is more the ability to win the souls of paddy and animals. Like *Sa-Ai*, *Chang-Ai* has to do with life after death. The soul of the deceased goes to the *mithikho*, the village or place of the dead, to which reference has already been made. Neither the location nor the picture of life in the *mithikho* is clearly described. But what is clear is the journey to the *mithikho*. It is believed that *Kulsamnu*, a kind of *thilha*, obstructs the passage of the soul to the *mithikho*. For those who performed *Sa-Ai*, *Chang-Ai*[118] before death, have no problem after death. The heads of the enemies or animals killed by the person concerned escort him safely to the *mithikho*. In the case of women, those who performed the *Chang-Ai* ritual have no problem passing through the way. Goswami writes, "The Kukis believe that only after the successful observance of the *chang-ai* ritual [is] the housewife is [sic] blessed and honoured even after her death when she would be living in the world of the dead."[119] This is where the direct connection between life here and hereafter becomes clear. Hunting, taking of the heads of enemies, and performance of rituals such as *sa-ai* and *chang-ai* are not merely games or rituals. They are all important for life after death. The belief in *lha* indicates the importance of peaceful co-existence among humans, God and nature and the connection between life here and hereafter. Religious belief and activities therefore need to be seen in the light of this worldview.

3. 3. 6. *Khankho*

The binding code, and at the same time the vision of Kuki traditional life in a community, was the concept of *Khankho*. There is no precise English translation for this concept; however, we shall make an attempt to explain it in the following way. The term *Khankho* is made up of two different

---

118. *Sa-ai* and *Chan-ai* are celebrations of achievements. Men who kill animals like tigers perform *Sa-ai* as a mark of achievement or victory over animals. In a similar way, women who get a certain level of rice or paddy perform *Chang-ai*.
119. Goswami, *Kuki Life*, 158.

words, *khan* and *kho*. While the former means 'grow', 'develop', or 'behave', the latter, means 'village', 'lifetime', 'sense' and so forth. When the two words are put together, they translate as 'principle of life', or 'a way of life', or 'the way a person is expected to live'. *Khankho* refers not to a mere intellectual knowledge or an act of performing duties toward others, but rather it is about the 'being' of a person – who she or he is. Negatively put, someone who does not care about others or who does not perform his or her duty as *tucha* or *becha*, as discussed above, is called '*khankho helou*' or someone who does not know the way of life. A single word *khan* together with another word *umchan* or discipline, that is, *umchan-khanchan* means 'behaviour or way of life'. Similarly, the second part of the term *kho* with another word *helou* means a state of being ignorant, that is, *khankho-helou* literally means the one who does not have senses or someone who is lifeless. In the same way, *khankho-he* is someone who behaves in the way he or she is expected to, that is, to fear God and live in solidarity with others including nature. Solidarity with others in this context means living a life in the interest of others in the wider community of creation. In such a way, when all live a selfless life for the sake of others there is love, security, and integral harmony and peace. In this sense, *Khankho* is more than ethics and for that matter, religion. It is a combination of both. It is a principle of life that upholds the community. In comparison with *Dharma* in Hinduism, which also means 'that which upholds or supports or sustains the community',[120] *Khankho* is transforming since it is not part of a hierarchical and rigid duty imposed on others.

In a village context, it was on the basis of and for the sake of *khankho* that a chief was made a chief and he in turn discharges his responsibilities selflessly for the wellbeing of his villagers or vice versa. In a similar way, a person is related to all the members of the society through the social institutions and formalities. *Tucha-Becha* and *Jol leh Gol*, referred to earlier, are some of the ways in which one relates to other members of the society. *Tucha* is a relationship earned through marriage, that is, a husband and his children are *tucha* to his father-in-law's family. And by being so, the

---

120. William K. Mahony, "Hindu Dharma" 329–332 in Mircea Eliade, ed., *The Encyclopedia of Religion*. Vol. 4. (London: MacMillan Publishing Company, 1987), 329.

in-laws became *Sunggao* to them. And as *Tucha-Sunggao*, they both have their own responsibilities to each other. *Becha* and *Jol leh Gol* are special relationship systems beyond and outside of the marital relationship. While one makes a person of his choice as *Becha* who would act as a second person to the head of the family in times of family activities, *Jol* can be anyone within or outside the family circle including even a person from another community.[121] In short, life and its activities are inspired and guided by the concept of *Khankho*. Stages of life, including both before birth and after death, were marked by ritual ceremonies showing concern for the wellbeing of the person concerned. One example can be *kitom*, referred to above, which refers to an act of showing anger at the death of someone by hitting the door posts and shouting '*Lam ana ot in*', or 'give way'. The same was performed at the death of the mother of this researcher.

A traditional Kuki believes that evil spirits block the soul of the dead on the way to heaven and *Kitom* is performed in order to help the soul get a safe passage to that place. Another good example was the legal system. With regard to the traditional way of punishment, there never was capital punishment. The highest punishment was called *Bultuh*, or stocks, a wooden structure with holes for the feet in which the criminals were locked as a punishment outside of the village where food was provided until death. This reflects the high ethics of the Kuki people grounded in the concept *Khankho*. In this way, *Khankho* is the foundation, the inspiration and the guiding principle of a traditional Kuki life.

The limit of the concern of *Khankho* extended beyond human community. *Kikaona* or self-justification in the sacrifices of animals or fowls referred to earlier, for instance, makes this point clear. When a priest is to cut a fowl or an animal for sacrifice, he makes sure first to clarify that the act of killing is not as an act of cruelty or for selfish purpose, but for a reasonable cause. Similarly, when clearing a forest for a rice field that includes a pond, the cultivator first offers an offering of appeasement called *twi-lut*. It was believed that ponds are the dwelling place of spirits who should not be offended by cultivating around the place. For this reason, one is careful in speech and behaviour so that no spirit is infuriated. Behind this conviction

---

121. Detailed information is given by Gangte. Gangte, *The Kukis*, 46-77.

and practice was the belief that there is an integral harmony and peace that no one should disturb.

3. 4. The New Administrations and Kuki Identity

The introductions of the British administration and the subsequent Independent India have made a lasting impact on the Kuki people. Under this section, we shall show how the new administrations brought abrupt changes to the Kuki way of life paving the way for the present Kuki identity struggle.

3. 4. 1. The British Rule

As was the case for many in the Two-Thirds World, British rule had a lasting impact on every aspect of the people's lives. This section attempts to discuss the political impact of the British rule on traditional Kuki life.

3. 4. 1. 1. The Initial Encounter

British India, through the East India Company, established their political presence in the region in the 1820s. There were four main reasons why the colonial administration was extended in North-East India: resource exploitation, commercial expansion, territorial spread and peacekeeping.[122] The Anglo-Burmese war (1824–1826) that ended with the British emerging victorious and the Yandabu peace treaty signed on 24 February 1826, paved the way for the British annexation of the whole of lower Assam and parts of upper Assam now known as Arunachal Pradesh.[123] This historical event was significant as the whole region for the first time was brought into one single administration with India and was confirmed when India became independent in the year 1947. For the Kukis, as well as other ethnic groups in the region, this change undermined their traditional way of

---

122. Basudeb Dutta Ray and Asok Kumar Ray, "Editorial Notes" 11–45 in Basudeb Dutta Ray and Asok Kumar Ray, eds, *Dynamics of Power Relations in Tribal Societies of North-East India* (New Delhi: OM Publications, 2006), 11.

123. Ramtanu Maitra and Susan Maitra "Northeast India: Target of British apartheid", http://www.hvk.org/articles/1002/113.html [Accessed 11 March 2010].

administration, changing the centre of power from their hands to people outside of their own region. It was, of course, a change of their national identity, as they became Indians, causing the people of the region as a whole to react negatively in their own ways.

In the case of Kukis, their relationship with the new rulers was often unfriendly. The main reason for this was the issue of political and cultural invasion of a 'foreign' culture. The military encounters between them and the colonial power are recorded to have begun from 1777 during the time of Warren Hastings, the then Governor General of India.[124] The threat was felt with all its seriousness when in 1907 the British administration was imposed in the hill areas and new rules were introduced for the local people. One such was confiscation of unlicensed guns, which were mostly used for hunting. This interrupted the system of the people for whom hunting was not only a trophy but also achievement to be honoured after death. For Kuki men, the killing of animals was the criterion to scale their achievements and respect in the society. And as such, their ambition in life was to kill more animals, including tigers, in order to perform *Sa-Ai* (*Sa*-animal, *Ai*-triumph, celebration of being able to dominate the animals killed). A row of three *Sa-Ai's* was considered to be complete stages of the scale of one's achievements in life. Similarly, for women, it was *Chang-Ai* (*Chang*-paddy, *Ai*-triumph, celebration of a great harvest). Kukis believed that the souls of those who performed such triumphal ceremonies are safely guarded to the *mithikho* or the place of dead by virtue of their achievements, whereas those who couldn't achieve would have to make their way to heaven after death by enduring the obstacles that may come on their way. Not seeing this interconnectivity of the people's life, possibly only for administrative interests justified by their own cultural worldview, the orders of the alien government, such as the confiscation of the guns, was a direct disruption of the cultural life and belief of the people.

---

124. A. Mackenzie, *The North-East Frontier of Bengal* [first published in 1884 as History of the Relations of the Government with the Hill Tribes of the North-East Frontier of Bengal] (New Delhi: Mittal Publications, 2005), 271

3. 4. 1. 2. The Anglo-Kuki war: The Beginning of Kuki Identity Decline

The ill relationship between the Kukis and the colonial administration resulted in what the administration termed 'Kuki Rising'[125] or 'Kuki Revolt'/'Kuki Rebellion'.[126] For the missionaries, this was regarded as a mere local problem between the Kukis and the Nagas.[127] Whereas, for the Kukis the event was an occasion[128] to raise their voice against the colonizing power that posed them a threat, hence it was called the War of Independence.[129] The immediate context of the conflict had to do with the recruitment of the local people for labour work in France during the World War I.

The Telegram message from Viceroy to Secretary of State on 10 December 1917 includes the internal condition of India which reads: "Temporary disturbances occurred among Kuki tribes, Manipur State, in connection with recruitment for Labour Corps in France. Recruitment being held in abeyance until Political Agent is satisfied that it is not likely to provoke opposition."[130] A later telegram, sent on 22 December 1917 includes a tougher warning against the Kukis:

Kuki chiefs are being summoned to Manipur and informed that recruits for labour corps will not be demanded, and that immediate attendance and submission of Chiefs will save them from drastic punishment. If summons is disobey(ed), Political Agent with escort of 150 rifles will

---

125. This is according to the official records preserved at the British Library, London; file: IOR L/P,S/10/724. This file includes 358 pages of documents of the Political and Secrete Department including, the Minute Papers, Resolution on the Kuki Rising, Plans of operation against the Kuki Rebels, Composition of the Column, Warrants, and Telegraph messages until 1918.

126. Hudson, "Introduction" in Shaw, "Notes on the Thadou Kukis", 4.

127. William Pettigrew's pamphlet "Twenty-five Years, 1897–1922" quoted in Dena, *Christian Missions and Colonialism*, 39.

128. Lal Dena, *Christian Missions and Colonialism: A Study of Missionary Movement in North East India With Special Reference to Manipur and Lushai Hills 1894–1947* (Shillong: Vendrame Institute, 1988), 39.

129. Looking from a Kuki perspective, this historical event was called a 'Kuki War of Independence'. T. S. Gangte, *Anglo-Kuki Relation from 1849–1937* (Churachandpur: Author, 1980), 12 & 18; P. S. Haokip, *Zale'n-gam, op. cit.*

130. Indian Bulletin, no.20, Preserved at the National Archives, London.

visit villages and burn them, provided this will not interfere with co-operation from Lushai hills in connection with Chin rising reported separately.[131]

Having failed to bring the Kukis to submission through political means, the colonial administration resorted to use force to suppress the Kukis in Manipur and in that they were concerned that none of the Kuki brethren in the Lusei Hills and the Chin Hills were provoked by their action. In other words, care was taken so that the whole Kuki-Chin people as a group was not provoked to rise against them. The operations against the Kukis in Assam and Burma, under the control of the Burma and Assam Governments, were carried out by columns of Military Police from Burma and Assam, with a company of Sappers and Miners, and some loyalists, including the eight hundred Nagas recruited for France, who were directed to the operation. While the Lieutenant-General Sir H. D'Urban Keary, the General Officer Commanding Burma Division, directed the operations, Mr Higgins, the Political Agent in Manipur, was set free to deal with the Kukis of Manipur in particular.[132]

The ultimate purpose of the colonial administration in the conflict was to 'crush' the morale of the Kukis or 'break their spirit' as a people in order to rule their country. This is clearly stated by Keary, who by the end of the war in 1919, wrote to the Chief of the General Staff, Army Headquarters, India, Simla, dated Maymyo, June 1919 about the war:

> I considered that in view of (1) the acceptance by both local Governments of the need for subduing the Kukis; (2) the heavy responsibility which we had towards the Maharajah of Manipur; (3) the fact that we were not asking the Army for any men; and (4) the opportunity which had now arisen of pacifying the Kukis once and for all, that the operations for the punishment and disarmament of the rebel Kuki tribes should be undertaken without delay.

---

131. Ibid., no.21.
132. "Burma-Assam Frontier", IOR:/L/MIL/17/19/42 preserved at the British Library, London, IOR:/L/MIL/17/19/42

His continues by outlining his plan:

> I therefore decided to put an end to the Kuki revolt by force of arms, break the Kuki spirit, disarm the Kukis, exact reparation and pave the way for an effective administration of their country. To do this, my plan was to divide the hostile Kuki country into suitable areas, to enclose these areas by a chain of posts, and by movable columns and active patrols so [to] harass the enemy, as to crush his 'morale' and force him to submission.[133]

It was according to this plan that Longja village, or Mombi as it was called, a centre of opposition, was destroyed in 1917 and thus the war began. The war against the Kuki tribes, as it was called, was underestimated by the British, and it did not end with an easy victory. It took more than five hundred armed men and three long years to suppress the Kukis under the traditional leadership of their chiefs. A. W. Botham, the Chief Secretary to the Chief Commissioner of Assam in his post-conflict report, titled, "Resolution of the late Kuki Rising", has a full account. He divided the Kuki Rising history into five periods:

---

133. File No: 4895 Field Operations: 'Despatch on the Operations Against the Kuki Tribes of Assam and Burma. November 1917–1919' preserved at the British Library, London, IOR:/L/MIL/17/19/42.

1. April to December 1917: During which the trouble was brewing
2. December 1917 to mid-April 1918: During which the first attempt at the suppression of the rebellion was made
3. April to October 1918: During which the Kuki raided and harried loyal tribesmen and interrupted traffic
4. November 1918 to April 1919: When operations under military direction were in progress and the rebels were systematically attacked and disarmed
5. (May 1919–?): The stage of punishment and reconstructions.[134]

The magnitude of the clash was remarked by Botham as the most formidable which Assam faced for at least a generation. He writes, "The Kuki rising of 1917–1919, which is the most formidable with which Assam has been faced for at least a generation, was confined almost entirely to the Thado Kukis, who with few exceptions were implicated, and to the Manhlun and Mangvung."[135]

As the result of the war, all the able chiefs were taken captive to the Andamans in 1919, while more than sixteen different British officers were honoured with various awards,[136] and the Kuki territory was divided and put under different administration: "[a]fter an uprising of the Kuki hill tribes in 1917, a new system of government was adopted; the region was divided into three subdivisions, each headed by an officer from the

---

134. 'Burma-Assam Frontier Rising', 4. IOR L/P,S/10/724, preserved at the British Library, London. For Troops employed, number of casualties, their achievements including arrest of Kuki chiefs, see appendix 2 'Operation Against Kuki Tribes'. Further details of the operations are given in 'Summary of Operations', IOR: L/MIL/7/16899, British library, London.
135. Ibid.
136. 1 CIE, 1 OBE, 14 IDSMs, 1 King's Police Medal, etc. quoted in P. S. Haokip, *Zale'n Gam: The Kuki Nation* (np. Published by Kuki National Organization, 1988). 166–167.

neighbouring government of Assam."[137] In his post-conflict report in September 1920 referred to earlier, Botham made a triumphant statement:

> On the 15th November the operations were commenced by the Assam Force; owing to delay, due to epidemics of influenza and surra which broke out, the Burma Force was not able to co-operate in the southern areas until the beginning of December. Nevertheless by the 31st March I had achieved all my objects more effectually than I had ever hoped for.[138]

Botham's claim of success needs to be understood in the light of the purpose for which the 'punitive measures' were carried out, that was, to 'crush' the morale of the Kukis or to 'break the Kuki spirit' as noted earlier,[139] and the plan of operations was to "prevent a combination of the Kuki tribes by dividing the area into sub-areas and enclosing the latter by chains of small fortified posts, and to overrun the country and harass the enemy by small mobile columns and active patrols based on these posts."[140]

Understandably, post-war life was a sudden, day-night experience of change for the Kukis as their traditional administrative power was snatched away and they found themselves like sheep without a shepherd under the alien rulers. In order to prevent a similar Kuki uprising in the future, the government strategically divided the Kuki country and ruled over them by setting up sub-headquarters with movable columns as planned by Lieutenant-General Sir H. D'Urban Keary mentioned earlier. As Kuki rule gradually weakened in that process and Manipur fully merged with India in 1949, that administrative arrangement was ended but the division of the territory remained unchanged and later became District Headquarters, continuing the legacy of the colonial wrath on the people.

---

137. *The New Encylopaedia Britannica*, Vol. 21. 15th Edition. (Chicago: Encyclopaedia Britannica Inc.,) 1992, 138.
138. Operation Against Kuki Tribes, IOR L/P,S/10/724 preserved at the British Library, London.
139. For further detail of the Operation and the achievements, see appendix 2. Operation Against Kuki Tribes.
140. IOR L/P,S/10/724 preserved at the British Library, London.

Gangte writes about the significance of this political outcome: "The most permanent and lasting effect of this war of Independence by the Kukis was not only the suppression of the Kukis, but marking of permanent boundaries of Manipur, which still exists till today."[141] The Anglo-Kuki war was a major drawback for the Kuki people, eroding their traditional identity as a group. At the same time, to the missionaries, it was a defeat of the old way of life, the dawn of the gospel light.[142] When viewed from an identity perspective, the oppression had far-reaching implications as it widened gaps between the communities, affecting their relationships. As it is clear from above, while the administration restrained the cooperation of the Kukis of Manipur with their cognate groups outside state by a careful strategy of not provoking the anger of the latter, they employed the Nagas, who were recruited for the war in France, in the operation, hence widening the gap between the two communities. It is in this light that we need to understand the present day problem with nomenclature for the larger Kuki groups and the ethnic conflicts in the hills of Manipur. In 1942, the Kukis again rose to fight for their ancestral territory by joining hands with the Indian National Army (INA) under the leadership of Subhas Chandra Bose who was supported by the Japanese, but these efforts were in vain. In the case of tribal people of India in general, A. Wati Longchar, noted that the identity of a tribal is an identity of a 'defeated' community[143] and this is particularly so in the case of the Kukis.

3. 4. 2. Independent India: Contradiction in Terms?

We have discussed in chapter 1 the challenges for the people's identity under Independent India. We argued that the issue of identity crisis in North-East India has to be understood in the light of the colonial administration

---

141. Gangte, *The Kukis*, 9–10. See the demarcation of districts in map 2 'Districts of Manipur' in chapter 1.

142. For instance, Downs sees the defeat as an opportunity for evangelization of the people. See, Downs, *The Mighty Works of God: A Brief History of the Council of Baptist Churches in North East India: The Mission Period 1836–1950* (Gauhati: Christian Literature Centre, 1971), 169–170.

143. A. Wati Longchar, quoted in Pratap Chandra Gine, "Doing Tribal Theology in North East Asia: A Retrospect and Prospect" 17–32 in *The Journal of Theologies and Cultures in Asia*, Vol. 1 (2002), 20.

and the subsequent socio-economic and religio-political context of India. In that, the problem of the new identity of 'Scheduled Tribe', the economic situation of North-East India, the demographic change in the region, the political dealings and the ideology of *Hindutva* were discussed, which need not be repeated here.

However, in order to show how the impact has been felt on the Kukis in particular, we shall first discuss briefly the assimilative approach of Hindus expressed in and through *Hindutva*, creating a feeling of alienation among the people; secondly, the introduction of a new category, 'Scheduled Tribe', which has played a role in the disintegration of the people; and thirdly, we shall also look at the issue of land and identity movements within Manipur with a view to showing the multifaceted dimension of Kuki identity crisis.

3. 4. 2. 1. Hindutva ideology and its implication for the Kukis

Hindutva as an ideology may not necessarily represent the majority Hindus in India. Also, being the movement of Hindu fundamentalists of central India, often this may not be seen as immediate threat to the people of North-East India in general and the Kuki in particular. However, the increasing interest of its propagandists in the region since the recent past and their activities of spreading Hinduism among the tribal people, as referred to earlier, indicate that the threat of this ideology cannot be totally ruled out. Basic to this ideology is an argument that the primal religions were part of Hinduism and hence they were once Hindus and they need to 'come back home'.

An attempt to homogenize the people of India on the basis of the assimilative *Hindutva* ideology detaches non-Hindu peoples, including the Kukis, from the rest of India. The fact is that the Kuki people have their own history and religion. We have discussed their religious background, which has no indication to suggest that it was part of Hinduism. The absence of polytheistic practice, for instance, is clear evidence for this. Kuki Primal religion, rather, was similar to that of the biblical Hebrews in many ways. There was a belief in one God, practice of sacrifices similar to that of the biblical Hebrews, and so forth. Another evidence for their dissimilarity with Hindus is the absence of the caste system among the Kukis. All of this makes it clear that the Kukis, and for that matter many tribal people of North-East India, cannot be part of India according to the scheme of *Hindutva* ideology. In other words, the identity of the Kukis and other tribal people of North-East India has not been recognized and respected as equal with that of others in the 'mainland' India.

3. 4. 2. 2. Scheduled Tribe Recognition: 'The Last Nail In the Coffin.'

Under the new status as Scheduled Tribe, the Government of India has provided certain benefits such as quota for education, jobs and so forth. The arrangement for tribal development later turned out to be a factor for further disintegration of the people, particularly the Kukis. Two years after India's Independence, in 1949, Manipur was merged with India as Part C States. In its Schedule Tribe list in 1951, Manipur has only three tribes: Any Kuki Tribe, Any Naga Tribe and Any Lushei Tribe.[144] With a huge change in its modification order in 1956, Manipur increases its tribe list from three to twenty-nine tribes.[145] Out of the twenty-nine tribes the Nagas listed only four tribes, namely Angami, Kabui, Kacha Naga, and Tangkhul, the rest were the different clans of what was categorized earlier as 'Any Kuki or Any Lushei' who are of the same cultural group. For their immediate need and in their inability to see the greater implication of it, each clan demanded their recognition as a separate tribe. Gangte rightly observes, "When . . . the Government of India started preparing the list of Scheduled Tribes in Manipur, every imaginable group or clan aspired to get the recognition by inclusion in the list as a separate tribe."[146]

The end result of this trend is the further disintegration of the people. The people are known as a tribe by the names of their respective clans, so much so that the district of Churachandpur in south Manipur, traditionally a place of a single tribe, is now known as "A Land Mosaics of Tribes".[147] In other words, the Kukis were segregated more than others in

---

144. Quoted in Haokip, *Identity*, 429.
145. See appendix 1. The Tribal Population of Manipur in 2001.
146. Gangte, *The Kukis*, 26.
147. See appendix 3. The Five Hill District of Manipur and the population.

the modification order. In pre-Independence, most of the names of the tribes mentioned in each district could have been put under one single name, 'Kuki'. In fact, the district of Chandel could have been known as a district of one single tribe, 'Kuki'. What is considered still worse was the fact that the common and unifying name 'Any Kuki' was removed from the list of the Scheduled Tribe in Manipur, hence, the common identity 'Kuki' was removed with a stroke of the pen. Added to the confusion, in other states like Nagaland, Mizoram, Meghalaya and so forth, the name 'Kuki' is recognized as a tribe and the same people are still listed as Kuki tribe.[148] The incongruity of Tribe lists in the different states, or better put, the politicization of scheduling the people as referred to earlier, led to further confusion and often conflict among the people.[149] The 'development system' for the so-called tribals under the new administration led to further disintegration of and confusion among the people. It was for this reason that Seilen Haokip terms the scheduled tribe modification of 1956 as the "last nail on [in] the coffin".[150]

3. 4. 2. 3. Vulnerability of Land and Its People

We have noted earlier that the larger part of Manipur is hilly and is inhabited by tribals, namely the Nagas and the Kukis. Also, we have mentioned the fact that the hill areas were demarcated during the colonial time in order to prevent the Kuki uprising, which continues to disfavour the Kukis in one way or the other. In spite of this, the status and administration of the hills have been different and independent from that of the valley Meiteis, right from the beginning. It was exactly because of this that the colonial officer had to deal with the hill people separately when they invaded Manipur. It was for the same reason that the merger of the hill areas into India by the signing of the King of Manipur in 1949 was rightly

---

148. See appendix 4. Lists of Schedule Tribe in Different states of North-East India.
149. By 1981 all the different Kuki groups in Manipur were recognized as tribes by their respective clan names whereas in others states like Nagaland, Assam and Mizoram, they are recognised as Kuki tribe. See, Gangte, *The Kukis*, 26–27.
150. Haokip, *Identity*, 309.

questioned as the representation of the hill people and their land.[151] The point is that the tribal people inhabited the hill areas of Manipur and in fact, even in the present day, the lands remain in the names of the chiefs and not the government.

The traditional status of the hills has become increasingly vulnerable in the post independence context. This is seen in the light of the government schemes and projects such as the Manipur Land Revenue and Land Reforms Act introduced in the 1960s. Under this Act, the government of Manipur seeks to bring the whole of Manipur including the hills under some form of uniformity.[152] The Act, however, was not implemented due to the strong opposition of the chiefs but that does not mean that the attempt has been given up. The issue has been very much alive under the ideology of the 'territorial integrity of Manipur'. But, the ideology of integration in such a manner practically means change at the expense of the traditional life and practice of the hill people including chieftainship, their traditional administrative system that upholds the community as a people. In fact, the regulation known as the Manipur (Hill Peoples' Administration) Regulation was introduced in 1956 for the administration of the hill areas. Contrary to the autocratic chief system, the regulation makes the members of village governance elective and democratizes the village administration. Similarly in 1967, after a decade, the Manipur Hill Areas Acquisition of Chiefs' Right Act was passed in an attempt to abolish the institution of chieftainship.

The introduction of new policies, however, alarmed the authoritarian chiefs and hence, the policies could not be implemented.[153] The vulnerability of chief system in the hands of selfish individuals has been pointed out earlier; in fact, if such selfish misuse of the system continues unchecked, the future of the society as well as their land is uncertain. At the same time, the importance of the system cannot be ignored. It is fact that the lands of the Kukis are protected through the rights of the respective chiefs.

---

151. T. Lunkim, "Tribal Land and Heritage in the North East India Context", *National Workshop on Theologizing Tribal Heritage: A Critical Re-look, Aizawl Theological College* (Aizawl, Mizoram, India, January 15–19, 2008), 7.
152. MLR & LR Act in http://manipurrev.nic./Default.htm [Accessed 6 December 2010].
153. Ray and Ray, "Editorial Notes" in Ray and Ray, eds., *Dynamics of Power*, 18–19.

In other words, if the chief's right is removed then the Kukis will lose their traditional right of land ownership in the hills, with the probability that this will result in the poor tribal people of the hills being uprooted from their ancestors and passing it to the rich valley people. The point is that the change should be brought about in the interest of the people concerned and not at their expense. For this reason, C. Doungel, one of the Kuki politicians, with regard to Tribal Forest Acts 2006 rightly suggests, "either a Committee or Commission be set up to go into these issues and to come up with sound and acceptable recommendations on which the law should be based."[154]

The threat also comes in the name of the so-called 'development'. A common experience of the tribal people of India as a whole is the loss of lands for the construction of dams. One clear example is the construction of the Khuga Dam in a Kuki area of Manipur. The dam is a multi-purpose project 38 metres high and 230 metres long. It was started in 1983 and completed in 2009 by displacing many tribals and their rice fields. Moreover, having constructed the dam there, the government has restricted the people's access to the area, thus making the displaced people's search for livelihood in that forest area very difficult. Such alienation of tribals from their land is common in India. G. Prakash Reddy, a non-tribal of North-East India, in his study of the native tribal people of Utnoor Taluka in Andra Pradesh in south India, rightly observes that the tribal people of India are 'victims of progress.' Having highlighted the miserable situation of the native tribal people in the district due to factors including unchecked immigration and domination of the non-tribal people, the policies and programmes of both the central and state government in the name of 'national integration' and 'national politics', he accurately writes, "After looking at the tribal scene in the country and the attitude and actions of the government, one gets doubt whether the country has a tribal policy at all."[155] His point is the irrelevance of the government's policies for the people. For such reasons, he also pointed out the fact that the govern-

---

154. C. Doungel, "Applicability of Tribal Forest Act 2006 in Manipur" posted at kukiforum@yahoogroups.com [Accessed 26 January 2010].
155. G. Prakash Reddy, *Politics of Tribal Exploitation* (Delhi: Mittal Publications, 1987), 138.

ment policies and programmes for the 'development' of the tribal people become a source of anxiety among the people.[156] This is not different for the tribal people of Manipur in general and for the Kukis in particular. Reddy's main observation is that the land and forest cannot be taken away from the tribal people even if it is to develop people because, as he says, "Improvement in technology and adoption of better agricultural practices cannot help any agrarian society if it is deprived of access to the basic traditional resources on which they depended, in the present context land and forest."[157]

Alienation from traditional land for the hill people, particularly the Kukis, is not merely a loss of land but it is also a loss of identity and meaning. As referred to earlier, villages and village lands are set up in such a way that they are indicative to clans, where one stands in an *upa-naupa* relationship order and his responsibility toward others. Losing village or village land, in this case, is considered as losing their cultural rights.

3. 4. 3. The Kuki Identity, Kuki Identity Movement and a Task for Theology

Kuki identity concerns become clear in the light of the above discussion. British rule and the subsequent administration have put the traditional Kuki cultural identity under a great deal of pressure. Under the colonial administration, the negative impact was felt mostly in the areas of traditional life and political administration. A wider issue was the division of their territory generally known as 'Pemberton Imaginary lines' into three different countries – India, Myanmar and Bangladesh – which remains until today, ignoring the ethnic component in the region. Having divided their territory into three different countries, the people became minority groups in their own land. At the same time, this was a shifting of centre of administration or power from their land to a distance place, for instance, Delhi, for those Kukis within Indian borders. The division of the territory also created trans-border identity problems.

---

156. Ibid., 136.
157. Reddy, *Politics*, 126.

Like the Kurds in the region known as Kurdistan, the Kuki people have overlapping identities in which in their own traditional territory they are Kuki, and in the new states they are Indian, or Burmese, or Bangladeshi, depending on which side of the border one lives. The overlapping identity becomes detrimental to one's own cultural tradition when a nation-state also imagines and imposes a common identity based on a majority culture onto the minorities within its borders. The *Hindutva* ideology is a clear example of this. The dilemma for the minority groups in such a situation is whether to maintain their own cultural identity and take the risk of being considered anti-national, or to submit to assimilation. This is the situation of the Kukis and their cognate groups on all sides of the international border and it is the context of the Kukis of Manipur.

In the state of Manipur where our focus lies, the Kukis were once the 'monarchs of the hills'. Chieftainship was the political system of administration as well as the indication of one's own lineage and responsibility toward others in the community. The concept of *Khankho*, the binding code, was the foundation, the guiding principle and vision for the communitarian society. There was an inseparable human-nature-God relationship, which was part of one's own integral identity.

The invasion of the colonial administration in the hills of Manipur side by side with the work of the missionaries developed negative attitudes toward one's own culture and its gradual decline in the process of colonial rule and Christianization among the Kukis. Conversion to Christianity for Kukis was not only a change of heart but also a change of worldview, considering the pre-Christian culture was totally dark and evil.

In post-Independent India, the hierarchical social structure of India and the Brahminic Hindu nationalism alienated the people as 'tribals'. Lack of recognition and acceptance of the cultural identity of the people being the root cause, the 'development' projects of the Independent India for the 'tribal' people, including tribe recognition, had negative impact on the society in the long run. It was in this situation that Seilen Haokip describes the situation:

> Authority of the chieftains had considerably declined and there was no cohesive agency to harness the reigns of the

Kuki community. The absence of visionary leadership and lack of acknowledgement by the Government of India concerning Kuki's historical opposition to colonialism fell short of realising an honourable political status for the people. Consequently, the socio-political condition of the Kukis in the post-independent era was extremely vulnerable. The existing circumstances prompted clannishness to assert itself to the detriment of the entire community.[158]

Having suffered setbacks under the two administrations mentioned above, Kuki identity experiences increasing challenges in the face of local identity politics. One of them is the Naga movement for *Nagalim*, which began from Indian Independence in 1947. This being a movement which is a cross-ethnic and cross-border in operation, it has a direct impact on other communities including the Kukis. The ideology of *Nagalim*, or a Naga homeland, which includes some parts of other states including Manipur, and the assimilation of smaller communities into the movement, has become a contentious issue and a source of communal tension. Lipi Ghosh observes this in his study of ethnicity and identity issues in the context of North-East India. He writes:

> In Manipur again, militant Nagas are trying to drive out the Kukis and carve out the southern part of the state to form an independent sovereign state of Nagaland. Thus, ethnic groups with long history of co-existing with each other for years may get communalised and go on a killing spree as evident in n[N]aga-k[K]uki Naga-Meitey[i] clashes.[159]

In this process, as pointed out earlier, the Kuki people of Manipur suffered drawbacks to the extent of witnessing some clans changing their allegiance and becoming Naga under various pressures in the absence of common political platform among the allied Kuki groups.

---

158. Haokip, "Rhetorics".
159. Ghosh, "Ethnicity and Issues".

Another movement for identity within the state of Manipur is that of the majority Hindu Meiteis in the valley of Manipur. Again, we have already discussed this in the previous chapter, however, it can be mentioned that the Meitei movement has added another dimension to the Kuki identity crisis. Unlike that of the Nagas, the Meitei movement aims to keep the geographical boundary of Manipur intact and the approach obviously is an assimilative one.

The end result of this process was that including their traditional land, history and culture, the common name 'Kuki' itself has been threatened. In search of security and stability as a people, there have emerged various socio-political movements among the Kukis in Manipur since the Independence of India as attempts to restore the common identity 'Kuki'. In other words, there has been a longing for identity as a people with their own cultural identity and meaning. The last three decades or so have witnessed a resurgence of socio-political and 'revolutionary' movements for the restoration of a common identity Kuki in response to the situation. Seilen Haokip, the spokesman of Kuki National Organization (K.N.O.) aptly explained the present Kuki identity movement in the following way:

> In regard to Kuki, 'nation' stands for the people and nationalism is referred to 'conceive' identity, except when referring to the era prior to, and during British colonialism. In other words, the concept of nationlsim [nationalism] is emphasised in relation to unification under a common identity. Identity, as a basis of nationalism is stressed because drawing on Smith's observation 'they add to one's psychological sense of security.['] Nationalism is also important because 'it is about 'land', both in terms of possession and rebuilding, and of belonging where forefathers live and where history demarcates a 'homeland.'['][160]

This statement clearly shows Kuki identity movement as a movement for common identity – reconstructing the past and the present history of the people – the need for security and stability as a people in the given

---

160. Haokip, "Rhetorics".

context, which means preservation of traditional identity and culture that includes land and its resources and the demand for a political solution. In 1998, the Kuki National Organization (KNO) was formed on the principles of federalism with a view to restore Kuki identity based on its pre-British status. Haokip, who is the spokesperson for the organization, writes, "KNO's inclusive and unified ideology established a firm base for the clans to return to their roots and embrace their birthright identity."[161] Accordingly, the organization has identified twenty-seven names of tribes, out of twenty-nine, under a common Kuki identity and has twelve different armed groups within the community as its constituent members.[162] On 10 August 2005, 'Suspension of Operations' (SoO) was signed between the Indian Army and KNO, followed by another agreement on 22 August 2008 between KNO and both the State and the Central Government.[163] The United People's Front (UPF) is another umbrella organization and comprises seven other different armed groups from the same ethnic group.[164] On 26 February 2010, the Union home secretary G. K. Pillai visited the official designated camp of Kuki National Front (KNF), one of the seven constituent members of UPF who also signed the SoO with the Indian Government, and he was said to have promised to discuss their demand for a separate homeland for the Kuki people.[165] It is too early to speculate the results of these movements.

One important point to note here is that unlike in the 'Kuki Revolt' 1917–1919, this time, it is a 'Christian response' in the sense that it is 'Christians' who are involved in the movement. In other words, the people drew inspiration for their identity movements from Christianity, or better put, the way they understand what Christianity is. However, there is a concern that there are no critical theological reflections on these responses.

The problem is reflected in the naïve use of the Bible and guns or violence in the identity movements, seen in ethnic conflicts and the disruption of peaceful co-existence among different ethnic groups and the

---

161. Haokip, "Rhetorics".
162. Ibid.
163. Ibid.
164. Ibid.
165. *The Telegraph*, Calcutta, India, Saturday 27 February 2010.

increasing rule of force in the newly formed 'Christian society'. At the site of the KNO camp on India-Myanmar border, V. S. Shashikumar in his CNN-IBN News report says, "At all K.N.O. camps, the Bible and the Gun stay side by side." The reason, according to a cadet cited in the report is: "We are doing this to gain God's blessing."[166] A similar case is a Naga movement with the motto 'Nagaland for Christ', referred to earlier, which, including this one may be termed 'missionization of identity movement'. The complexity of the situation is reflected in the identity and role of the armed groups in a 'Christian society' like that of the Kukis. One example was the recent church conference the researcher attended wherein the first three prizes for the missionary fund contributions for the year went to three leaders of the armed groups. Besides, in some cases, the armed groups get involved in solving church disputes. These are indications of increasing acceptance of the movement in the church, including the way in which it is carried out, and hence risking the credibility of the Christian message of love. In other words, there is a lack of critical reflection and articulation of the Christian message in the context of identity movements among the Kukis.

Besides the absence of critical articulation of theology, there were no cultural values that the people can fall back upon. In the process of Christianization, the cultural identity and values, including the concept of *Khankho,* gradually declined. The foundation of the society is weak without a theology which is liberating yet self-critiquing and is rooted in a local culture. In other words, in their search for socio-political identity in response to the oppressive structures with the absence of a sound Christian theology rooted in culture, and yet also transcending culture, they put themselves at risk of distorting both their own Christian identity and traditional culture, which they seek to protect. This leads us to examine the Christian faith as understood and practiced among the Kuki people with a view to unearth what went wrong and with a view to propose a relevant, contextual theological response in the context of Kuki struggle for identity.

---

166. V. S. Shashikumar "Kuki outfit demands statehood" CNN-IBN News published on October 8, 2006 http://ibnlive.in.com/news/kuki-outfit-demands-statehood/23463-3.html [Accessed 11 March 2010].

CHAPTER 4

History of Evangelization: A Study of Christianity among the Kukis of Manipur in Relation to Their Identity Crisis

Conversion from traditional religion to Christianity has been termed as 'Darkness to Light' and the lifestyle of the people after the conversion, 'from head-hunting to soul-hunting'.[1] The meanings of these triumphant claims have become increasingly vague in the light of the people's struggle for identity, and the way in which the people responded to their situation discussed in the preceding chapters, questioning the relevance of theology in the context of the people's struggle for identity. Therefore, it is important to examine the history of evangelization.

The aim of this chapter is to determine Christian concerns for and commitment to issues related to the people's identity, which includes culture or way of life, history, language and territory with a view to showing the role of Christianity in the present identity crisis of the people. This involves an overview of the background of the late nineteenth- and early twentieth-century missionary movements and the work of evangelization in North-East India, a study of the work of evangelization in Manipur and its impact on Kuki identity.

---

1. These are popular claims among the Christians in North-East India including the Kukis. One example for this is the theme of the Southern Manipur Gospel Centenary Celebration, February 11–15, 2010, 'Darkness to Light', organized by the Evangelical Churches Association, at Tuiboung, Churachandpur, Manipur, India.

The study is important for three reasons: (1) replacing the local Primal traditions, Christianity became the one dominant and influential religion among the people concerned; (2) being the dominant religion, naturally, Christianity has become the source either for transformation or oppression of the people; and (3) the study is important in order to find what could be considered as a better or more relevant theological approach to the issue of identity in a context of North-East India, particularly that of the Kukis of Manipur. This part of the publication is based upon original research which makes use of materials in the archives of the National Library of Wales in Aberystwyth, Regent's College in Oxford, the British Library in London and the Council of Baptist Churches of North-East India in Guwahati, Assam, India.

4. 1. The Background

The period to which the missionaries of North-East India belonged, particularly that of the Kukis, was marked by the peaks of colonization and missionary movement based on a concept of racial and cultural superiority and religious optimism in the West. The dominant strands of evangelical enthusiasm during this period, Andrew Porter noted, were those associated with the Keswick Convention, the North American Student Volunteer Movement, its British arm – the Students Volunteer Missionary Union – and the Young Men's Christian Association; they fed directly into bodies as diverse as the Church Mission Society (CMS), China Inland Mission (CIM), and the Salvation Army.[2] In the case of the Kukis, particularly in the southern part of Manipur, the influence was from the Keswick Convention.

In recent years, there has been interest among both colonial and mission historians in the West on the question of 'culture' and 'identity' of the native people in the process of colonization and movements for religious conversion. This has resulted in a number of consultations and publications

---

2. Andrew Porter "Introduction" 1–13 in Andrew Porter, ed. *The Imperial Horizons of British Protestant Missions, 1880–1914* (Cambridge: William B. Eerdmans Publishing Company, 2003), 4.

on the issue including *The Imperial Horizons of British Protestant Missions, 1880–1914: The Interplay of Representation and Experience* published in 2003.[3] Some of the articles in this volume were revisions of papers presented at a consultation around the theme of missions and empire organized earlier. Other studies of British imperialism and protestant missionary movements include Brian Stanley's work *The Bible and the Flag*[4] and Andrew Porter's *British Protestant missionaries and overseas expansion*.[5] It is not the purpose of this work to enter the broad debate on mission and imperialism, but rather to investigate the theological presuppositions of the particular British missionaries whose work was to have a profound impact on the tribal peoples of North-East India in general, and the Kuki in particular.

4. 1. 1. The Catholic Missionaries in North-East India

The earliest Christian missionaries known to have contacts with North-East India were the Catholics in the seventeenth and eighteenth centuries. The first missionaries were Reverends Stephen Cacells and J. Gabral who belonged to the Jesuit order. The purpose of their visit was to explore the possibility of finding a route to China and Tibet, but it resulted in the establishment and growth of two Catholic churches in lower Assam, one dedicated to Our Lady of the Rosary and the other to Lady Guadolope at Rangamati, Nowgong, Assam in 1696.[6] The community soon disappeared but Downs points out that later other small Catholic communities were said to have existed in Bondashil in the Cachar district of Assam, and at Mariamnagar in Agartala. He is of the opinion that the Christian community was preoccupied with its own affairs and took no initiative in the later spread of Catholic Christianity in North-East India.[7] The Catholic missionary work in North-East India was continued in 1889 with

---

3. Porter, ed. *Imperial Horizons*.
4. Brian Stanley, *The Bible and the Flag: Protestant missionaries & British imperialism in the nineteenth & twentieth centuries* (Leicester: Apollos, 1990).
5. Andrew Porter, *Religion versus Empire? British Protestant missionaries and overseas expansion, 1700–1914* (Manchester: Manchester University Press, 2004).
6. Lal Dena, *Christian Missions and Colonialism*, 18.
7. Downs, *History of Christianity*, 65.

the creation of the Prefecture Apostolic of Assam, Bhutan and Manipur.[8] However, in the hill areas of Manipur, particularly among the Kukis, the church is still small in comparison with other denominations.

4. 1. 2. The Serampore Mission

After a gap of one full century, Christianity was re-introduced in the region in the early part of the nineteenth century by the Serampore Mission. Following the death of Joshua Marshman in 1837, the last surviving member of the three pioneering missionaries to India, the mission was integrated within the Baptist Missionary Society (BMS) and it was during that period that they officially extended the work to North-East India, particularly in the areas which are now called Assam and Meghalaya.

Interestingly enough, during this time, 'the faith' came with the initiation of colonial power. In his assessment of the early Christian mission activities in Naga Hills, S. K. Barpujari pointed out that, having realized the futility of military expeditions, the colonial officers used the Christian missionaries for their political interests.[9] The Serampore mission of the British Baptist Missionary Society was the first agency to be invited to work in North-East India by the colonial administration with a conviction that "what could not be achieved by the military power could be gained by the power of the gospel"[10] and in that manner, the colonial officers, including James Johnstone, the then Political Agent of Manipur, functioned.[11]

In 1813, the mission sent Krishna Chandra Pal to the Khasi Hills, now called Meghalaya. This native missionary was the first convert of the Serampore Mission and he went to the Khasi Hills at the invitation and under the protection of the British administration of Sylhet.[12] Later, with the defeat of Burma in 1826, Assam came under British control and this opened the way for the missionaries. At the initiation of David Scott, then Commissioner, the mission was enabled to open a school in Gauhati in 1829 and began a more substantial work in North-East India. Scott was

---

8. Ibid., 93.
9. S. K. Barpujari quoted in Dena, *Christian Missions and Colonialism*, 19.
10. Dena, *Missions and Colonialism*, 19.
11. Ibid.
12. Downs, *History of Christianity*, 66.

even willing to support the missionaries at his own expense;[13] however, the mission did not last long. There were four factors: the death of Joshua Marshman, the lack of manpower, the financial constraints, and the amalgamation of the activities with the BMS as mentioned earlier. Hence, the work was discontinued and was handed over to the American Baptist Mission in 1837. The contributions of the Serampore mission in North-East India include the publication of Assamese New Testament in 1819 and the entire Bible in 1933. Both the Roman Catholics and the Serampore Mission did not have direct impact in Manipur among the Kukis.

4. 1. 3. The American Baptist and Welsh Presbyterian Missions

One of the main mission agencies in North-East India to have a lasting impact in Manipur, particularly into the northern part of the state, was the American Baptist Missionary Union.[14] The group came in contact with North-East India at the invitation of a colonial officer, Francis Jenkins. The first American missionaries arrived at Sadiya at the eastern extremity of the Brahmaputra valley in March 1836[15] and Jenkins himself supported their work. Finding the situation opportune, the American missionaries established their station in North-East India not with the intention of evangelizing the people in that area, but as a strategic base for reaching the Shan tribes of northern Burma and southern China. When this was unsuccessful due to poor planning,[16] the attention of the missionaries shifted to the people in the plain areas of Assam. The first convert was made in 1841, the first church organised in 1845 and a more structured organization called the Baptist Association of Assam was formed in 1851. However, the progress was not satisfactory to the missionaries – instead they were attracted by the warm responses from the hill people, particu-

---

13. Barooah, *David Scott*, 177. There are some observers who suggest that Scott was interested not in spreading the Christian faith as such but in using it as a means for "taming" the unruly. See, Dena, *Missions and Colonialism*, 20

14. American Baptist Missionary Union (ABMU) was later changed to American Baptist Foreign Mission Society (ABFMS). In this work, we shall use 'American Baptist Mission'.

15. Downs, *History of Christianity*, 69.

16. William Cammel quoted in Dena, *Missions and Colonialism*, 19.

larly by the Garos and the Nagas. They then focused their attention more on the hill tribes of Assam. In 1871, the work among the Nagas was revived and this time, F. W. Clarke was given permission at his own risk, without the assurance of protection from the British, to work among the Nagas.[17] In 1896, the American Baptist Mission entered into Manipur in the person of William Pettigrew[18] and became an official mission agency in the state. Pettigrew had come to Manipur in 1894 with the support of the Arthington Aborigines Mission; however, he had to leave this agency because of the inflexibility of the organization's mission principles.

Another mission agency that came to North-East India and later had much influence in Manipur, particularly in the southern part of the state, was the Welsh Presbyterian Mission. Unlike the American Baptist Mission, the Welsh did not have links with the colonial administration in the beginning. The initial discussion of the mission in 1840 was whether to go to Gujarat, the northern part of India or to the Khasi Hills in the North-East. The decision favoured the latter and Thomas Jones was sent by the mission, arriving at Cherrapunji in Meghalaya on 2 June 1841. By this time the Welsh Calvinistic Methodist Foreign Mission Society (WCMFMS) and the London Missionary Society (LMS) had disagreements over the issue of administration resulting in the separation of the WCMFMS from the LMS.

Although the mission and the colonial government had no formal link in the initial stage, they later cooperated with each other through education. The first Khasi converts were baptised in March 1846, the first theological training institute was established in 1887, and the first four Khasis were ordained in 1890. By the end of the century, Downs points out that the church was well established with a rapidly growing Christian community solidly based on an extensive educational system and a comprehensive church structure.[19]

---

17. Dena, *Missions and Colonialism*, 26.
18. Pettigrew came to Manipur in 1894 with the Arthington Aborigines Mission. However, like his fellow missionaries from the same mission working in Mizoram, he had to leave his agency because of the inflexibility of the Arthington's mission principles.
19. Downs, *History of Christianity*, 77.

By the end of the century, the missionaries from the Welsh Presbyterian Mission in the Khasi Hills paid a visit to the Lushai Hills, now called Mizoram, adjacent to the southern part of Manipur. The first missionary to visit Mizoram was Rev William Williams. Williams arrived at Aizawl on 20 March 1891 but was not permitted to stay for long as fighting continued between the Luseis and the invading colonial power. He returned to the Khasi Hills in mid-April with a heart for Mizoram and persuaded his church back home to adopt Mizoram as one of its mission fields in June 1892.

With the ground well prepared, Rev D. E. Jones was the first Welsh Presbyterian missionary to work in Mizoram. He arrived on 31 August 1897 and stayed with Savidge and Lorrain, missionaries of Arthington Aborigines Mission until they left on 31 December 1897. A year later, on 31 December 1898, Rev Edwin Rowlands, another Welsh Presbyterian Church missionary, joined Jones and they continued their work in Mizoram, witnessing the first two native converts who were baptized on 25 June 1899. In 1907, the Welsh Calvinistic Foreign Mission Society at Liverpool deputed a medical doctor, Dr Peter Fraser, to join D. E. Jones in Mizoram. Fraser and his wife, joined by another private missionary called Watkin Roberts, who later became the first missionary to the Kukis in southern part of Manipur in 1910, arrived in Mizoram on 14 October 1908. Both Fraser and Roberts worked together closely in the missionary work in Mizoram.

About the same time, the revival which began in 1904 in Wales arrived in Mizoram via the Khasi Hills. The year 1906 was considered to be the first revival in Mizoram.[20] Waves of revivals in Mizoram influenced the people's lives so much that they became instrumental in shaping the form and nature of Christianity in Mizoram and subsequently in other regions including the neighbouring state of Manipur, particularly among the Kuki groups in the south. This was possible because of cultural similarities between the Mizos and the Kukis of Manipur as discussed in chapter 3.

---

20. [Ralte], *The Presbyterian Church of Mizoram*, 9.

4. 1. 4. The Arthington Aborigines Mission

As already indicated the first mission agency to send missionaries to Manipur and Mizoram was 'The Arthington Aborigines Mission', named after its founder, Robert Arthington. The mission as an agency did not survive long due to its rigid policies, but its missionaries continued to work in the region by joining other agencies. Arthington learned about the 'untamed' hill-men, the Lushais of Assam from St. John Dalmas, a missionary on a furlough from Bengal. As a result he got interested and sent three of his missionaries to India: William Pettigrew, Rev F. W. Savidge and the Rev J. H. Lorrain. While Pettigrew became the pioneer missionary to Manipur and soon abandoned the mission and joined the American Baptist Mission, Savidge and Lorrain went to the Lushai Hills now called Mizoram, and they too abandoned the mission after three years of work and joined the Baptist mission from Britain. Savidge and Lorrain arrived on 11 January 1894 and they stayed until 1897. During this time they reduced the Mizo language to writing in Roman script and did literature work including translations of John, Luke and Acts of the Apostles into Mizo and produced a Mizo Dictionary, catechism and a hymnbook. However, they did not have any converts during the first four years of their ministry. To add to their disappointment, they had to leave their work in 1897 because Arthington's mission policy did not allow his missionaries to remain in one place, or work with one tribe, more than three years. However, to their delight, Savidge and Lorrain got another chance to return to the same place as Baptist missionaries and became popular missionaries in southern part of Mizoram. Similarly, in Manipur, William Pettigrew left the Arthington Aborigines Mission for the same reason and joined the American Baptist Mission. Pettigrew continued his work in Manipur under his new mission agency and became the official and influential missionary in the state. With the loss of its three missionaries the Arthington Aborigines Mission in North-East India came to an end; however, Arthington's theological convictions continued to be reflected in mission as his missionaries continued their works though under different agencies.

Arthington's theological convictions, particularly on the issue of the elect, were Calvinistic. Stanley observes this when he writes, "Arthington's pessimism about the numbers of heathen who would be converted was matched by a sound Calvinistic optimism about how they would be converted and then nurtured in Christian discipleship."[21] Stanley also points out Arthington's deep conviction about the nearness of the second coming of Christ and the conversion of the 'heathens'.[22] The second coming of Christ, for Arthington, can be delayed or hastened depending on how soon the whole world could be reached with the Christian message. According to him, the event is delayed on account of many people still not having heard the Christian message and it is hastened when that message is spread among all nations.[23]

With such a conviction, his single desire was the spreading of the Christian message. This is clear in his statement, "Let us assume that we all have one object distinctively in view, viz; to forward the reign of our Lord Jesus on the earth, fully and universally, whether by His Spirit in us simply, or also by Himself in person, and the present saving of souls – of them who shall be heirs of salvation."[24] In spreading the faith, Christian traditions hardly matter as he writes, "I greatly desire that we, whether we be Independents, Epi-copaleans [Episcopalians], or Presbyterians – Baptists, Calvinistic Methodists, or Moravians, etc., should make the best use of our resources."[25] The inscription placed upon his grave described his contribution as "His life and his wealth were devoted to the spread of the gospel among the Heathen."[26] In doing so, Dena observes, "The sole motivating force for organizing such a private mission society was an unusual dream that 'every tribe in every land shall have the gospel.'"[27]

Arthington's missionary principle was an itinerant preaching, or mobile missionary movement. His conviction resulted in a method by which

---

21. Brian Stanley, " 'The Miser of Headingley': Robert Arthington and the Baptist Missionary Society" 371–382 in *Studies in Church History*, Vol. 24 (1987), 374.
22. Ibid.
23. A. M. Chirgwin, *Arthington's Million* (London: The Livingstone Press, 1936), 30
24. R. Arthington, "To the Church of Christ Jesus" a small booklet found in Box H/31 at Regent's Park College, Oxford.
25. Ibid.
26. Samuel Southall, "An Uncommon Life in Friends" 277–286, *Quarterly Examiner*, Vol. 35 (1901), 277.
27. Dena, *Missions and Colonialism*, 32.

"if a Christian foothold was gained in any country, that was enough for him; he would press on to the next country and the Christian there must, according to him, be urged to press on too."[28] It was based on his conviction that the will of God was not to plant the church in every land, but to offer the gospel to all people without delay. Chirgwin comments: "The slogan, 'Preach and pass on' practically summed up his [Arthington's] view."[29] Arthington required a survey of the world with a view to discovering the unreached areas and then he would supply people with the gospels of Luke and John and the Acts of the Apostles, training ten to a dozen people in a tribe, teaching them how to read the gospels, and urging these converts to evangelize other groups. All tribes and populations were to be reached promptly, the actual heathen first, Muslims being left to Bible agencies, and finally, a tribe should be visited until a church was established.[30] He was confident that once the gospels of Luke and John and the Acts of the Apostles had been translated into a particular native tongue the Word of God and the Holy Spirit would do the job of witnessing of Jesus and enabling the missionaries to move on to the new territories.[31] Accordingly, Arthington sent his missionaries with an instruction not to stay for long in one place, but to move from one place to another. This policy, which missionaries on the ground discovered to be impracticable and ineffective, let to a situation in which all of his missionaries in North-East India left him. Arthington also sent his missionaries with the principles of abstention from marriage when going as a missionary the first time and preparedness to endure hardness as good soldiers of Jesus Christ.[32]

In his evaluation of Arthington, Stanley writes, "The 'miser' who devoted his ample share of the mammon of unrighteousness to constructing habitations in eternity contributed more to habitations of a temporal kind than he bargained for." The failure of his mission resulted from

---

28. Chirgwin, *Arthington's Million*, 35.
29. Ibid., 30.
30. Ibid., 34.
31. Arthington to BMS Committee, 21 Jan.1881; Arthington to Baynes, 12 Oct. 1885 in Stanley, "'The Miser of Headingley'", 374.
32. Chirgwin, *Arthington's Million*, 76.

"his lack of first-hand knowledge of the realities of the field."[33] Besides this, Arthington's limitation included his narrow understanding of the Christian message and lack of an integral approach to Christian service. Also, as a product of his day, his mission work functioned within the dualistic worldview of mission agencies that viewed the 'mission field' as dark or heathen and 'only the missionary' as a bearer of Truth.

4. 2. The Coming of Christianity to Manipur

Being the first missionary to work in Manipur, William Pettigrew became the lone recognized missionary in the state and apart from him no other mission organizations were allowed to enter the area. The impact of such arrangement on the diverse ethnic groups of Manipur was that while Pettigrew's community benefited from his work, others remained lesser priority in his programme of Christianization or 'civilization', paving the way for later 'tribalization' of Christianity in the state. The next missionary in Manipur, whom some called an 'intruder', was the untrained and private missionary, Watkin Roberts, who did a tremendous work for the spiritual conversion of the Kuki people but was limited in his approach to theology and mission as we shall show later in this chapter.

4. 2. 1. Northern Manipur: The American Baptist Union

Hearing of the massacre in 1890 when some British officers were killed in Manipur, Pettigrew wanted to come to the region. The princely state was sanskritized and Hinduism officially declared the state religion in 1705. The then British Indian policy for the State was 'non-interference' or 'strict neutrality';[34] for that reason, the government was apprehensive about the missionaries. Pettigrew was already in Dhaka, now in Bangladesh, as early as 1890 and took a believer's baptism and learned Manipuri, the language of the Meitei people of Manipur. In the meantime there was a tempo-

---

33. Stanley, "The Miser of Headingley", 382.
34. L. Jeyaseelan, *Impact of Missionary Movement in Manipur* (New Delhi: Scholar Publishing House (p) Ltd., 1996), 52.

rary change of officials in Manipur. Major Maxwell, the Political Agent and the President of the State went on his furlough and in his absence a debate took place among the colonial administrators as to whether or not Manipur should be annexed as a result of the massacre referred to earlier. While some supported the annexation based on the fact that the native people waged war against the Queen, others felt guilty because of the attack which they first carried out. In the end it was decided that Manipur be given local government under a minor raja Churachand Singh. It was in that context that Pettigrew approached and got permission from A. Porteous, the Acting Political Agent, for his work in Manipur.[35]

On his return, Maxwell was disturbed to discover the strength of opposition of the native Meitei Hindus toward Pettigrew's work and revoked the permission of the Officiating Agent as invalid. At the same time, he also suggested that Pettigrew should work in the hill areas.[36] Having left the Arthington Aborigines Mission and joined 'forces' with the American Baptist Mission in 1896,[37] Pettigrew was recognized as the official missionary in Manipur and the government refused access to any other missionary to Manipur besides him, giving a hard time to other missionaries, including Watkin Roberts in the southern part of the state.

There is a theory suggesting that on his being refused permission to work in the valley, William Pettigrew first went to a Kuki village called Senvon in the southern part of Manipur. According to the theory, Kamkholun Singson, the chief of the village, refused him entry into the village[38] and as a result, Pettigrew travelled through the Songsang hill range on foot, but all in vain. He then went to the Mao Naga people in the northern part of Manipur but still was not successful. It was after all such failures that he went to Ukhrul and was accepted by the chiefs to

---

35. Dena, *Christian Missions and Colonialism*, 32–33.
36. Pettigrew's letter, December 1894 in *Rev William Pettigrew's Mission Reports and Letters 1891–1932*, compiled and reproduced by Rev Champhang Jajo (Chandan Press, Gauhati: n.d), 9.
37. "Report on Christian Work in Manipur" in *125 Anniversary Jubilee Reports of Baptist Work in North East India 1836–1961* preserved at CBCNEI, Gauhati, Assam, India.
38. T. Jamthang Haokip, *Manipur a Gospel leh Kuki ho Thusim* (The Gospel in Manipur and the Story of the Kukis) (Churachandpur, Manipur: Published by the Author, 1984), 3; Downs, *History of Christianity*, 84–85.

establish his work. Although we have no missionary records to confirm this theory, there are four reasons to support the claim. The first reason is the geographical location of Senvon in the southwest of Manipur, which is close to the Silchar-Manipur link road in the northwest of Manipur that Pettigrew took when he first came to Manipur. Prior to that Pettigrew stayed in Silchar while waiting for a chance to enter into Manipur, and it was possible that he went west to Senvon, the region which was already familiar to him. Second, on his failure to secure permission to work among the valley Hindu Meiteis, his first choice, Pettigrew must have chosen to the Kuki people, a dominant group in the hills in those days. In fact, centres like Senvon, Mombi, Chasad and others were popular on the colonial map in those days. Third, Senvon is close to the Lushai Hills where other Arthington missionaries, the missionary colleagues of Pettigrew, worked. Fourth, in the light of their experiences as a community, which will be seen later in this chapter, there is a general feeling among the Kuki people that Pettigrew's work in some ways disadvantaged them more than others. This creates room to ask if Pettigrew's activities were somehow affected by his past painful experience of refusal in Senvon, if he had visited the place as claimed in the theory. These remain an issue for further investigation.

What we know for sure is that Pettigrew established his mission station at Ukhrul in the north and had lasting impact on the Tangkhuls. He believed that work in Ukhrul would act as a kind of bridgehead and, if successful, could eventually make possible evangelization among the Manipuries. Beyond this he also envisaged his work as a step towards occupying the ground between Assam and Burma.[39]

This clearly shows that the work among the tribal people was not the first priority for Pettigrew, whose original plan was to work among the valley Meitei Hindus. He writes,

> The Manipuri Hindus of the valley was the first missionary objective, but objection being raised by the British authorities on account of their administering the State at that time on

---

39. E. G. Phillips "Missionary Conference in Assam" 72–75 in *Baptist Missionary Magazine*, Vol. LXXVI, no.12 (1896), 75.

behalf of the young Rajah, then a minor, led the way in the providence of God for the opening of mission work among these mountains surrounding the valley.[40]

Despite his desire to work among the Meitei Hindus in the valley, Pettigrew established his work in Ukhrul focusing mainly on the Tangkhul Nagas. It was true that he later extended his work among the Kukis in that region, but initially his mission was directed to the Tangkhul Naga, so that it might be said that the Kukis were the last in the line in respect of the missionary priorities.

4. 2. 2. Southern Manipur: The Thado-Kuki Pioneer Mission

In the southern part of Manipur dominated by the Kukis, Christianity was brought 'through the back door' by Watkin Roberts in 1910, marking a sixteen year gap from the time Pettigrew first arrived in Manipur in 1894. Born in 1886 at Carnarvon, North Wales, Roberts was a successful slate miner and merchandiser. He was a product of the 1904–1906 revival in Wales and the particular point that led him to his missionary work in India was through the Keswick Convention in 1907. At that convention, Roberts heard the appeal of Peter Fraser: "Hundreds of tribes in Assam and North India are in utter darkness. They need the gospel. They need Jesus to save them from their heathen darkness." Roberts felt God's call and responded by deciding to go to the tribals of then Assam.[41] He came to India as an independent missionary and assisted the work of Fraser, a medical missionary sent by Welsh Missionary Society Mizoram.[42] Roberts was never on the staff of the Welsh Presbyterian Mission nor the Baptist Mission. Rather he was a self-appointed, unpaid, unordained, and untrained missionary working as an assistant to Fraser at his own expense.

---

40. William Pettigrew, "My Twenty-Five Years 1897–1922 at Ukhrul Mission School", appendix 1, in *Rev William Pettigrew (a pioneer missionary of Manipur)* Published by Pettigrew Centenary Celebration Committee (Imphal: Fraternal Green Cross, 1996), i.
41. Jeyaseelan, *Impact*, 84; Lal Dena, *In Search of Identity: Hmars of North-East India* (New Delhi: Akansha Publishing House, 2008), 46.
42. Jeyaseelan, *Impact*, 84.

Fraser's letter to Rev R. J. Williams, the Secretary of Calvinist Methodist Mission Society shows Roberts' commitment for mission among the tribal people and the extent to which he was committed:

He [Roberts] has made it a matter of prayer and believes he would be disobeying our Lord if he stayed at home now for a number of years. He feels sure all the time that our Lord wishes him to go out with me. I asked him this question, 'Supposing you go out and only live a week out there, do you feel you ought to go?' His reply was that even then he would have to go.

About his missionary status and arrangement for teamwork, including his behaviour, Fraser assured,

> It is my duty and privilege to pray that the Lord will send out labourers into His harvest. Mr Roberts seems to be an answer to that prayer. He does not wish to be considered a missionary but would act as dispenser and private helper. He is willing to pay his own passage out, and does not ask for anything even towards his maintenance. My wife and I would be very glad to provide lodging accommodation for him wherever we might be living, and also trusting in the Lord, would venture to be responsible for his behaviour.[43]

Being a product of the Revival in Wales and subsequently Keswick, Roberts' commitment was to spread the message of Christianity. One thing to note here is that, besides evangelistic works, both Fraser and Roberts unswervingly fought for the abolition of *Bawi*, a local slavery system. It was part of the local culture which the colonial rulers did not interfere with for administrative reasons. Local chiefs kept the poor people as slaves, and seeing the condition of these people and the evil of the system, Fraser and Roberts fought against the structure, which included the colonial administration and the mission agencies, until it was finally abolished. The rationales for their fight included the issue of justice, the abolition of

---

43. A Letter from Peter Fraser to Rev R. J. Williams, Secretary, Calvinistic Methodist Mission Society, dated 14 September 1908. CM Archives, 27, 314 preserved at the National Library of Wales in Aberystwyth, UK.

slavery in Britain and the Indian anti-slavery law, which were an integral part of their understanding of Christ's work for salvation.[44]

Roberts learned Lusei dialect and did evangelism while he assisted Fraser in the clinic. It was during that time he received a gift of £5 through a minister in Wales with which he bought some copies of John's gospel that he distributed among the surrounding chiefs. As a result, he got an invitation from the chief of Senvon, Mr Kamkholun Singson, to come and explain the message of the book, and he saw this his 'Macedonian call.' The invitation reads: "Sir, come yourself, and tell us about this book and your God."[45] Roberts immediately responded by visiting Singson at his village in 1910 and preached in the surrounding villages too. As a result, within two months, a school was started at Senvon with the arrival of three Bible students from Mizoram namely, Savawma, Vanzika and Thangchhingpuia. The three students arrived on 7 May 1910 and started a mission school and did the work of evangelism at the same time.[46] There was no mission work among the Kuki of southern Manipur prior to this, both the American Baptist mission and the Welsh Calvinistic Methodist Mission having earlier made plans to work among the Thado Kukis but later abandoning the project in order to pursue other fields.[47]

Roberts made converts in South Manipur and later formed an independent mission called, 'Thado-Kuki Pioneer Mission' (TKPM) which became the gateway of Christianity into the region. The main concern of the mission was the evangelization of those who did not yet have a missionary namely, the non-Naga groups in the hill areas of Manipur. The print on the official letterhead reads, 'An undenominational and thoroughly Evangelical Mission, formed with the express desire of preaching

---

44. Sources, including 72 pages of document file called 'Doctor Fraser's Case', are kept in the National Library of Wales in Aberystwyth, UK, CMA 27,318, Letter File V; Loyd George Correspondence, NLM MS 22522, 204–212; and A Report on Slavery in Lushai, CMA 27, 316 File III.
45. S. T. Henpu, "*Kum 50 Jubilee Thu Belh* (The Jubilee Year)" 9–11, *Rest: Christian Magazine Issued by the Association of N.E.I.G. Mission Christian Workers*, Published Quarterly (March 1960), 9.
46. D. Hluothang quoted in Jeyaseelan, *Impact*, 85.
47. An official letter of Watkin Roberts to Rev Lloyd Jones in England dated 2nd June 1912, preserved in the National Library of Wales in Aberystwyth, UK.

the gospel among the Thado-Kookies in the State of Manipur, India. "Go ye into *all the world* and preach the gospel to every creature . . . Lo, I am with you always . . . "[48] This shows that Roberts' mission was nonconformist, evangelistic and was committed to the Kuki people. It was named after one of the Kuki clans, 'Thado', possibly due to the influence of a particular dialect-speaking group called 'Thados' at that time, but the scope of the mission included all the Kuki groups now known by different names, recognized as separate tribes. Here, a clan identity like Thado needs to be understood as social construct, as also was Lusei in the Lusei Hills. Both of the terms were popular in their respective regions at that time. However, while the latter was replaced by Mizo as a signifier of common identity for the people in Mizoram, the former was deconstructed in the process of tribe recognition mentioned in chapter 3.

The exact date of Roberts' arrival in Manipur is not clear. It is possible that as an unofficial and private missionary Roberts had no one to make a record of his activities. Dena suggests 12 February as the day on which Roberts arrived in Senvon, basing this on the unpublished official statement of the Thado-Kuki Pioneer Mission signed by Rev D. Lloyd Jones and Watkin R. Roberts, issued on 20 February 1914, which reads:

> About the end of January 1910 Mr Roberts and a few of the Lushai Christians and others started for Manipur. The Sunday evening before they left, Mr Jones kindly drew the Church's attention to the fact that they were leaving on the morrow to Manipur, and prayers were offered for the safety of the party and God's blessing on the undertaking . . . On February 4th 1910 – a few days after Mr Roberts' party had started, Dr Fraser wrote to the Rev R J Williams informing him that 'Mr Roberts and several of the school-boys' had gone to a Thado village about 13 days journey from Aizawl in response to the Chief's appeal. About the end of February 1910, Mr Roberts returned from Manipur and at a reception meeting

---

48. An official letter of TKPM, CM Archives, 27, 318 preserved in the National Library of Wales in Aberystwyth, UK.

under the presidency of Mr Jones held at Aijal Church, Mr Roberts and others of the party gave a report of their journey to this previously untouched field.[49]

With the arrival of Roberts in 1910, Manipur had two missionaries: William Pettigrew and Watkin Roberts. Pettigrew, an Anglican turned Baptist, was an officially recognized missionary in Manipur while Roberts, a young man from a working class background in north Wales, with no formal training and link with any mission agencies, was considered an 'intruder' by the colonial powers. Although Pettigrew later on extended his work among the Kuki in northern part of Manipur, his work concentrated more on the Tangkhul Nagas while Roberts' vision was to work among the Kukis since there was no missionary among them. That led to conflict between the two missionaries, leaving the local converts, particularly the Kukis, innocent victims.

4. 2. 3. Conflict between Missions and the Implications for Kukis

Dena observes two kinds of rivalries in mission enterprise: first, intra-mission or personal differences resulting from personality clash, and second, inter-mission rivalry, usually stemming from denominational differences. Of the two, he observes that intra-mission rivalry was the most common in mission among the Kuki[50] and that had a lasting impact on the relationship between the people they worked with.

In the initial stage, the relationship between the American Baptist Mission and the Thado-Kuki Pioneer Mission was cordial, except for some minor conditions, which later appeared as purely official. K. M. Singh writes:

> The conflict first started when the Superintendent of the Lushai Hills sent a telegraphic message to the Political Agent

---

49. 'The Thado-Kookie Pioneer Mission Official Statement.' Preserved at the National Library of Wales, Aberystwyth, UK. CMA 27, 318 (Hereafter cited as Official Statement).
50. Dena, *In Search of Identity*, 58.

of Manipur requesting for a permission in favour of Watkin Roberts to visit Senvong [Senvon] on the Lushai border. The vice President of Manipur State Darbar did not object to Mr Robert's short visit to Senvon, but he informed that a permanent location he would require the Darbar's approval. Three months later Mr Roberts again asked for a permission to settle and work with some Lushai teachers at Senvon. His Highness the Raja of Manipur agreed to this but he had a wish to see Mr Roberts before granting him the final permission to settle and authorising the establishment of a Mission station at Senvon.[51]

The issue deteriorated when in October 1911, the Political Agent of Manipur, William Shakespear, sent a telegraph to the Superintendent of the Lushai Hills directing him to stop Watkin Roberts from entering Manipur. In December 1910 and in September 1911, Roberts wrote to Shakespear indicating his desire to work in Manipur. However, in both cases, he was denied permission.

Although the matter appeared purely political and administrative, there was a deep-seated mission organizational issue. Pettigrew being the only officially recognized missionary of the state, was informed of all the developments either by the Political Agent or the Vice-President of the Darbar.[52] In his interview with Colonel Shakespear in November 1911 regarding Roberts, Pettigrew made a case saying,

> if the Welsh Mission from the Aijal [Aizawl, the capital of then Lushai Hills] asked to extend its operations over the village in the State in which Lushai was understood, it would have been just and wise to grant the permission but that was quite a different matter to granting strangers permission to work wherever any Thados were found.[53]

---

51. K. M. Singh, *History of Christian Missions in Manipur and the Neighbouring States* (New Delhi: Mittal Publications, 1991), 111.
52. Singh, *History of Christian*, 114.
53. Ibid., 115.

T. W. Reese mentioned a receipt of Pettigrew's letter, enquiring if the Calvinistic Methodist mission, particularly Fraser, was intending to work among other hill tribes of Manipur adjacent to the Lushai Hills.[54] Pettigrew seems to have had no problem in allowing the Welsh Presbyterian Mission in Manipur on the ground of dialect but at the same time, objected to allowing Roberts to work on the same ground. Also, it is interesting to observe that Pettigrew himself was working on the same ground: on ethnic lines. His first missionary priority was the Hindu Meiteis of Imphal valley and when that failed he chose to work among the Tangkhul Nagas in the hills.

D. Khaizalian suggests that the growth of the Thado-Kuki Pioneer Mission caused antagonistic feeling among other missionaries, including Pettigrew, who utilised the government machineries to protect and defend a privileged position. He observes that in the year 1911, some fifty households of Letzakai, a village in Lushai Hills migrated to Tuithaphai and subsequently another group of nearly one hundred and fifty families from the same region came to settle in Khopibung in the south Manipur where Watkin Roberts gave them a school which helped them to grow numerically.[55] Having learned about the situation, Pettigrew got alarmed and "recalled the agreement with the Manipur Maharaja that in the State of Manipur no one but ABM could preach the Christian faith."[56] Unable to stop the work of Watkin Roberts in the southern part of Manipur, Pettigrew took the help of government to further restrain the movement of the mission in the south.

In 1914, during the Annual Conference of the Presbytery of the Thado-Kuki Pioneer Mission, the President of Manipur State Darbar under the incessant pressure of Pettigrew gave an order through Lambu Housoi which reads, "Quit Manipur State."[57] Seeing Roberts remaining in the

---

54. Rev T. W. Reese's letter (nd), CM Archives, 27, 314 preserved in the National Library of Wales in Aberystwyth, UK.
55. Khaizalian quoted in Jeyaseelan, *Impact*, 87.
56. Ibid., 88.
57. Khaizalian quoted in Jeyaseelan, *Impact*, 89. See also D. Ruolngul, *Chanchintha Kalchawi* (The Gospel's Onward Movement) (Churachandpur, Manipur: Published by Author, 1982), 45.

state, Major Cole, the Political Agent, who was directly in charge of the hills areas, wrote to Rev H. Dala, the native in charge of the mission. But, despite this attempt at suppression, within a short period five villages had embraced Christianity namely, Kailam, Kangkap, Selbu, Singngat and Beheng.[58] This prompted the government to issue an even stronger order demanding all the Christians to leave their villages even to the extent of saying to the Christians of Sialbu [Selbu], "If you do not want to go away, you should stop being Christian."[59]

The fact was that earlier in 1912, Pettigrew visited Senvon and found out that Roberts had already sent five native missionaries from Lushai Hills even after instructing him not to. In reaction to this, the permission given on 30 May 1910 for Roberts to send the local missionaries was cancelled. Pettigrew and Mr U. M. Fox, another American missionary, were asked to study the situation of Manipur by the Board of Managers of the American Baptist Mission. The main issue discussed was that no more than one missionary should be allowed in Manipur in order to maintain the policy of the British administration in the state of 'non-interference'.

Roberts' status as a private missionary and an adherent of nondenominational mission credited him less acceptance by other missionaries and their agencies. While in Mizoram, D. E. Jones, one of the missionaries of the Welsh Mission, objected to Fraser's appointment of Watkin Roberts as interim-editor of the *Kristian Tlangau*, a Christian magazine in local dialect that was part of the activities of the mission;[60] in Manipur, he was not accepted as an equal missionary with others. In the same way, both the American Baptist Mission and the Welsh Mission denounced him and his work as unrecognized. On hearing the conflict between his work and that of the American Baptist Mission in Manipur, the Executive Committee of the Directors of Welsh Mission in Wales took a strong action against Roberts, disproving him and his work in Manipur,[61] indicating that the politico-religious structure of his day had no room for Watkin Roberts,

---

58. Khaizalian quoted in Jeyaseelan, *Impact*, 89.
59. Ibid.
60. Lloyd quoted in Vanlalchhuanawma, *Christianity*, 228.
61. Letter of the Directors to Revs. D. E. Jones and Dr Fraser, appendix 5.

a private and unrecognized missionary in the region. Worse still, having learned that the Manipur District Committee was discussing his work in Manipur, Roberts wrote to Fraser explaining his case and urged him to speak for him in the committee meeting concerned.[62] Fraser forwarded Roberts' letter to Rev W. T. Reese with his recommendation for the continuation of Roberts' work.[63] However, when asked if Roberts started his work in Manipur with his consent, Fraser replied,

> I knew he was going, and I did not think it was my place to stop him. I let him do as he liked. He did not understand the field was in the B.M.S. territory. Mr Pettigrew he thought worked some hundreds of miles to the north. We felt it was a great victory to get the gospel into the country at all.[64]

Fraser was appreciative of the extension of the Christian mission among the Kukis on Manipur, however, possibly for political reasons he did not support Roberts openly. When it comes to his involvement of the work in Manipur, the 'territory' of the American Baptist Mission, despite his promise to venture Roberts' behaviour referred to earlier, Fraser washed his hands and said, "I did not think it was my place to stop him." Although he wholeheartedly supported Roberts in the beginning, he did not continue the same kind of support in tough times, leaving him, whom he once thought was the answer to his prayer, to face the challenges alone. At the same time, Fraser did not support the conformist position of his mission. In fact, quoting the Edinburgh International Missionary Conference in 1910, he appealed for a nonconformist stand on mission and government on 14 September 1911.[65]

---

62. Letter of Roberts to Fraser, appendix 6.
63. Letter of Fraser to Reese. CM Archives, 27, 314 preserved in the National Library of Wales in Aberystwyth, UK.
64. 'The Thado-Kuki Mission', CM Archives, 27, 314; A Letter of P. Fraser to Rev R. J. Williams on 3 January, 1914 as an answer to the questions put forth by the Directors on 18 November 1913. CM Archives, 27, 318.
65. Included in 'Dr Fraser's case and Letter, File V.' CM Archives 27, 318 preserved in the National Library of Wales in Aberystwyth, UK.

In this situation, some scholars feel that Roberts' work was unnecessary.⁶⁶ Dena, a local scholar also alleges,

> While one cannot deny Roberts' genuine missionary zeal, his modus operandi and the manner in which the work of his mission was extended from its very inception, into the state of Tripura and into the province of Assam were wrapped up with evidences that he had little or no regard for rights of other missions.⁶⁷

It was true that Roberts did not allow the rules and structures of mission organizations to interfere with what he thought was the will of God. However, it is important to note that despite his limitations and the conflict, it was Roberts who could see the situation of Kuki people without a missionary and took the challenge to start his work among them. In other words, if it were not for such a radical mission approach of Roberts, the Kuki people of southern Manipur would not have had the chance to hear the Christian message in the way they did in 1910. It was possible that the Welshman Roberts was able to see the Kuki with sympathetic eyes because of his own experiences in Britain and for his contribution in the abolition of slavery among the Lusei Hills, he can be called a daring missionary who sided with the less advantaged people despite the politico-cultural structures.

In his letter to the Treasurers of the 'The Thado-Kookie Pioneer Mission', Rev D. Lloyd Jones, England and F. Kehl, Esq, Calcutta, India, in 1912, Roberts writes:

> If the fact that the gospel has been preached to a people so long neglected, and in whose language not a single missionary could preach the gospel, previous to our entering the territory, has been the cause of any 'ill-feeling', I am extremely

---

66. Singh, *History of Christian Mission*, 116.
67. Letter addressed to Mr Cole from Berar, Central Province on 27 February 1929 quoted in Dena, *Christian Missions*, 53.

sorry. Sorry, not that the lord has given us the honour of being the first to take the gospel to this important tribe, but <u>sorry</u> for those who are decidedly working on lines which are not Scriptural. The heathen are perishing, and no one can afford to be 'annoyed' and 'Upset' over these matters when we have His very own command to 'go . . . into all the world'. Praise God, even the Thado-Kookies are included in His programme![68]

In the official statement of the 'Thado Kookie Pioneer Mission', signed by D. Lloyd Jones, the Treasurer, and Watkin Roberts Hon. Secretary on 20 February 1914 it was argued:

> The American Baptists . . . had not done any work at all among the Thados . . . who were in utter darkness . . . Heathen are perishing and have a right to know of their Saviour who died for them, and Mr Roberts felt, after being invited by the Chief . . . that he had to go . . . After seeing the terrible darkness of the people and how they were going into Eternity without having heard of Jesus and His love, (he) pledged himself to God that he would do all (in his power) to help to save these precious souls for whom Jesus died. Is this considered a crime by the Church of Christ, the carrying of the gospel to perishing souls? If so, is there not something wrong somewhere?[69]

Based on this argument, Roberts continued his work, which flourished beyond the region as far as North Cachar Hills, Tripura, Burma, and Chittagong Hill Tracts which is now a part of Bangladesh. To include all these areas, Roberts later changed the name of his mission from Thado-Kuki Pioneer Mission to North-East India General Mission (NEIGM).[70] In spite of the positive developments, the extension of his work, which was the very sign of the success of his mission, turned out to be the reason for

---

68. Roberts' letter dated 22 June 1912 preserved in the National Library of Wales in Aberystwyth, UK.
69. 'Official Statement.'
70. Ruolngul, *Chanchintha*, 20.

his fate. The comity of Protestant Foreign Missions in Bengal and Assam suspended his mission in December 1922 for breaching the comity.[71] The point is that while Pettigrew had little concern for the work among the Kukis in the southern part of Manipur, Roberts saw the need and was committed to serve.[72] For Pettigrew, rules and structures were more important than the needs of the people, in this case, other tribes including the Kukis. In contrast, Roberts looked beyond the colonial political structures and worked on the basis of need which, for him, was in part a justice call. When there was no missionary to reach the Kukis, it was Roberts who brought them the good news of Christ and in standing for them he even became an opponent of both the government and the missionary.

In the process of the conflict, the converts were the innocent victims. Worse still, when the missionary work was community-based, the effect of mission conflicts becomes communal. Christians in the south suffered atrocities and persecutions such as expulsion from their villages, dismantling houses and so forth, and while the Assam Governor made enquiry, the responsible officers escaped because the order was given orally and hence there was no written record.[73] They were even regarded by some of the missionaries as 'nominal Christians' or second-class Christians as was reflected in Crozier's writing:

> In the southwest subdivision of the State the so-called Thado-Kuki Pioneer Mission has several hundred members and a nominal Christian community of about 2,000 where the door was open to us ten years ago and then closed because our Society could not at that time send a missionary for that work.[74]

---

71. Dena, *Missions and Colonialism*, 53.
72. Henpu, "*Kum 50 Jubilee*" 9–11 in *Rest*, 9. Henpu was one of the first leaders of the church.
73. Khaizalian quoted in Jeyaseelan, *Impact*, 89
74. A Report of Dr G. G. Crozier (cyclostyled) found in CBCNEI Office, Gauhati, Assam in *History of Christianity in Manipur*, 76–77.

The innocent converts suffered a stigma of being 'nominal' or inferior under a new form of hierarchical spiritual structure in their new religion, Christianity. Being a non-official missionary, Roberts and his converts were regarded as inferior to Pettigrew's, the 'true' missionary of the state.

In addition, they were deprived of support during the calamity called *Mautam,* or Bamboo famine, which occurs every forty or fifty years until the present time. Bamboo famine is considered a natural calamity as masses of rats, produced as a result of the death of bamboos, destroy the standing crops at night and cause famine. During *Mautam* in 1913, Pettigrew came to see the condition of the people in the southern part of Manipur but returned without completing his visit. As a result the people suffered much with no support from mission. However, after the *Mautam* they restarted their life and church and with the arrival of R. Dala, a native worker from the Lushai Hills in 1913, they increased in number to about two hundred members and twenty workers. At the same time, the government warned them that they would be imprisoned if they did not leave the place within a month. On their refusal of the order, the government finally arrested the group and took them to Imphal where they were asked to join the American Baptist Mission.[75]

4. 3. The Work of Evangelization

The work of Christian mission is often understood within western Christianity in a positive and non-critical manner. The spread of the gospel of Christ, and with it the introduction of education and science, are seen as beneficial to 'tribal' peoples, bringing religious hope and enabling them to make the transition into the modern world. However, this process of conversion needs to be viewed from the 'inside', from the perspective of the people who received missions and discovered that the consequence was a mixed blessing. It is a central concern of this publication to attempt to offer such a perspective with regard to the Kuki people of Manipur.

---

75. Savoma, "*Pathian Thu Lo Luh Dan* (How the Word of God came)" 5–7, *Rest: Christian Magazine Issued by the Association of N.E.I.G. Mission Christian Workers,* Published Quarterly (March 1960), 6.

4. 3. 1. Mission Approach

The missionaries came to North-East India with a negative view of the people's culture in mind. In that situation, their approach to the native people in Manipur was one-way traffic in the sense that there was no room given for local culture in theological formulation. The following experiences explain this observation.

After about six years of experience in Manipur, Pettigrew in his annual report of 1910, writes: "My many years' experience of heathen teachers has taught me that they are absolutely unworthy, and unreliable . . . I wish to repeat that I do not believe in heathen teachers in any school under Mission supervision."[76] Consequently the religion of the tribal people was regarded as less developed and primitive. Lloyd comments on the missionary perception of the religion of the Mizos in Mizoram: "In those days the people were animists. Animism has been described as the faith of pre-literate people. It depends on tribal memory and oral traditions more than on sacred literature and it is inarticulate in comparison with the great religions of the world."[77] Based on that supposition, in the sight of the missionaries, the local people were untamed and uncivilized with an inferior religion.

Viewing the people and their condition in this light, the aim of the missionaries was to convert them to Christianity. The fundamental objective for the American Baptist Mission was "winning of the world to the obedience of Christ" which meant, the "planting of self-sustaining, self-governing and self-propagating churches, the developing of Christian communities with all that this implies."[78] After the World Wars, the attitude toward other religions seemed to be softened but the aim remained the same, that is, to convert others. The Foreign Mission Policies of the ABFMS under the heading "The Work of the foreign missionary in the light of changed conditions" adds new policies that include "attitude toward other faiths".

---

76. Ukhrul Field Report for 1910 in ABMC of the American Baptist Mission Union, 1910, 74–84 in *History of Christianity in Manipur: Source Materials*, Compiled by Elungkiebe Zeliang (Imphal: Manipur Baptist Convention, 2005), 26.

77. J. Meirion Lloyd, *History of the Church in Mizoram: Harvest in the Hills* (Aizawl: Synod Publication Board, 1991), 9.

78. *Foreign Mission Policies: American Baptist Foreign Mission Society & Women's American Baptist Foreign Mission Society*, Massachusetts (1917), 5.

The statement reads: "The missionary should sympathetically study the religions of the people among whom he labours that he may be able to realize their religious background and more effectively to lead them into the fullness of Christian truth."[79]

It is clear that although there was some importance given to the understanding of local religions, the ultimate purpose was not to learn from them but to convert them. In other words, despite some respect given to them, the native cultural values were still considered incapable of revealing the truth of God. Converts were considered new creations needing to be totally cut off from their culture and society. In some cases, they were kept in a compact area away from their own villages, a policy of isolation or segregation intended to ensure that anything practiced before conversion, now considered evil or devilish, would be discarded completely. That included traditional practice of social relationships, worship of God, and traditional songs and instruments. In this case, a convert was alienated from his or her own culture and therefore, the mission approach was detrimental to the people's identity.

4. 3. 2. Methods of Evangelism

The American Baptist Mission under its foreign mission policies on 'Missionary Objectives and forms of work' laid down guidelines that clearly showed shifts of emphasis in the process of evangelization. In the earlier stage, the emphasis was on evangelization and as they grew in number, education was given more importance. It reads:

> In the earlier stages of our mission work the strictly evangelistic side has been the more prominent. As the work has advanced and churches have been established and converts have multiplied, the educational side has assumed a greater relative importance. We are now coming to see that, in certain fields especially, it is essential that we lay yet greater emphasis on education, still considered as a means to the great end, and

---

79. *Foreign Mission Policies*, ABFMS, New York (1925), 12 preserved at CBCNEI, Gauhati, Assam, India.

there are cases in which it proves to be the key that unlocks the door of opportunity for the work of the evangelist.[80]

Similarly in the Lusei Hills, now called Mizoram on the southern border of Manipur, they concentrated on preaching tours and then schools. Teachers trained and appointed by the mission were evangelists in the villages and wherever there was a school a church was also planted.[81] Possibly due to the different political situation in the Manipur valley, Pettigrew's first emphasis was on schools. He started his first school in the valley and later moved to Ukhrul in the hill area in 1896 due to the refusal of the government to allow him to remain.[82]

4. 3. 2. 1. Education Programmes

The main objective of education in the mission fields according to the Foreign Mission Policies adopted by the Board of Managers, ABFMS, in New York 1925 reads:

> In the program of evangelizing the world Christian education occupies an indispensable place. While the schools are a direct and conscious evangelistic agency, bringing to their students the challenge of the Christian gospel, their primary educational aim is to develop a strong Christian community with an adequately trained leadership and an intelligent and responsible laity.[83]

---

80. *Foreign Mission Policies: American Baptist Foreign Mission Society & Women's American Baptist Foreign Mission Society*, Massachusetts (1917), 5.
81. [Ralte], *The Presbyterian Church of Mizoram*, 12.
82. "Report on Christian work in Manipur" 49–52 in *125th Anniversary: Jubilee Reports of Baptist work in North East India 1836–1961*, 49 preserved at CBCNEI Library, Gauhati, Assam, India.
83. *Foreign Mission Policies*, ABFMS, New York, 1925. The American Baptist Foreign Mission Society and the Women's American Baptist Foreign Mission Society jointly discussed and adopted their foreign mission policies according to the needs of the 'mission fields'. The policies adopted in the 1912 conference were made more comprehensive in the 1917 conference and from there, particularly due to the needs as the result of the war, the 1925 conference made still further comprehensive policies.

Three things stand out clearly from the statement: schools were started, first, as means to convert the local people; second, to develop a strong Christian community; and third, to make the local people 'civilized'. Besides, the other purpose of the schools was to send converts to convert others. This was the case in Mizoram[84] and in Manipur among the Tangkhuls and the Kukis alike. Reporting from the North-East India General Mission, formerly known as Thado-Kuki Pioneer Mission, Vungthawn writes how the school children during the vacation evangelized their own parents: "Class 7 and the lower classes are now on vacation. . . . When they are on vacation, they often witness for the Lord to their own parents and relatives who want them to give up their faith and live as they did before they became Christians."[85]

Pettigrew in his report makes clear the context in which such aims and activities were carried out and the rationale for the programme of elementary education:

> The rigid clannishness of the people, their great ignorance coupled with gross superstition and their fatalistic beliefs in their animistic worship, the environment and shut-offness of the whole country, valley included, from the world outside, decided us on a policy of an elementary education.[86]

In the case of the Lushai Hills, Savidge writes in his 1910 report:

> The Lushai mind is a mixture of disorder and untidiness. Education has to begin here with 'A place for everything & everything in its place' for the text. Every square inch of the wide world is regarded as a suitable dumping ground for

---

84. BMS Report of 1910 written by Savidge in the absence of Lorrain entitled "London Baptist Missionary Society, Lushai Hills" 57 in Box IN/113 in Regent's Park College, Oxford.
85. Vungthawn, "Children Evangelize Their Parents" in *North East India Tidings*, Issued Monthly by the North East India General Missions, Inc, Philadelphia, PA (October 1953), 6.
86. Pettigrew, "My Twenty-Five Years', xvii; 'Report on Christian work in Manipur" 49–52 in *125th Anniversary: Jubilee Reports of Baptist Work in North East India 1836–1961*, 49.

Lushai movable property. The first item on our educational programme is to disillusion them of that idea.[87]

Three years later in his decadal report of achievements the India Secretary of the mission continued to confirm the purpose of education: "The aim of the School is to make character."[88]

At this point, we should note that the interest of the colonial administration in education was both paternalistic and imperialistic.[89] The administration realised that through educational programmes the native people might be not only 'civilized' but also made 'peaceful and loyal subjects.'[90] Schools were influential instruments in winning the loyalty of the native people for the colonial power as well as capturing their hearts for the Christian faith. For this reason, mission schools were run in collaboration with the government as this served the interests of both. In the early days of work it was said that, "Most of the pupils came because the Government threatened to levy fines on villages which did not send boys to school."[91] And later, "With the help and encouragement of the Political Agent, Colonel J. Shakespear, village schools were opened on a three years basis in about a dozen villages of the tribe, and manned by young men of 6th class from these schools, whose salaries were paid by the State."[92] Education was thus an avenue for the collaboration of the missionaries and the colonial administration as it served the interests of both. In other words, it was a means for double conversion: one, for spiritual conversion from traditional religion to Christianity, and two, political conversion, that is, change of political loyalty from local rulers to that of the colonial administration.

---

87. BMS Report of 1910 written by Savidge in the absence of Lorrain entitled "London Baptist Missionary Society, Lushai Hills", 55 in Box IN/113 in Regent's Park College, Oxford.

88. "The South Lushai Mission" BMS India's Secretary's Report in 1913, 70 preserved at Regent's Park College, Oxford.

89. Dena, *Missions and Colonialism*, 90.

90. John Shakespear to J. H. Lorrain, as cited by P. H. Jones quoted in Dena, *Missions and Colonialism*, 90.

91. "Report on Christian Work in Manipur" in *125th Anniversary Jubilee Reports of Baptist Work in North East India 1836–1961, op. cit.*

92. Pettigrew, "My Twenty-Five Years", vi.

With that, background schools were run in Manipur. From 1894 to 1908 for instance, there were already two English schools and fifty-five primary schools established in the valley, which had only one girls' school. There were nine village schools and one station school in the hills, that is, among the Tangkhul Nagas. With the installation of Chura Chand Singh as the King of the state in February 1908, permission was sought afresh to work among the valley Meitei Hindus, which was the main interest of the pioneer missionary, Pettigrew. However, the petition was not successful; instead, work was allowed among the hill tribes surrounding the valley which paved the way for missionary activities among other hill tribes, particularly among the Kukis.[93] In Mizoram, schools were started by the Arthington missionaries and reopened by Jones. Three primary schools were started in 1903 and the first examination was held in the same year. The first middle grade English examination was held in 1909[94] and it was during this period that two students from Manipur also attended the schools, namely Thangkai and Lungpao, who later became two of the first converts from southern Manipur.

The inseparability of educational activities from evangelization was clear, although as far as the missionaries were concerned, the primary purpose of schools was to impart the Christian message. For that reason Dena asserts, "the missionary who preached the gospel could not be distinguished from the missionary who taught in educational institutions."[95] The link between evangelization and education was the belief in the primacy of the Scriptures and the need to ensure literacy in order that the converts might be able to read the Bible for themselves. It was the conviction of the missionaries that if the individual was to worship God aright, he [or she] must be able to read.[96] In other words, the primary purpose of education was to impart the spiritual message to the local people through helping them learn how to read and write. Schools were more for religious purposes than for learning knowledge and skills. Dena rightly asserts, "the

---

93. *William Pettigrew's Mission Reports and Letters*, 27.
94. [Ralte], *The Presbyterian Church of Mizoram*, 16.
95. Dena, *Missions and Colonialism*, 98.
96. Laird quoted in Dena, *Missions and Colonialism*, 90.

involvement of missionaries in educational programmes was to be viewed as supplementary to the primary task of communicating the 'spiritual' message to the people."[97] Literacy was thus made a pre-condition for spirituality and the rich oral traditions of traditional peoples were set aside assuming they have no real values.

The by-product of such an educational programme was the rise of elite groups against the traditional administration within the community. Generally the elite groups were Christians, non-chiefs who were influenced by democratic ideas through mission education. In the context of chieftainship, an autocratic traditional practice of the people, the new elite groups were often seen as rivals of the tradition. Ngulhao Thomsong, the first convert and interpreter during the war, was one clear example. Against the will of the chiefs, he supported the government for the Labour Force. He was in France as an interpreter for the Kuki Labour Corps, or manual labourers, and returned to India in 1919 and then he was appointed as the Head Clerk in Tamenglong Sub-Division after the Kuki-Anglo war and then went as an evangelist among the Anals.[98] In a similar way, all the interpreters of the Labour Force were Christians[99] who were the products of the mission schools. In some ways, schools were the primary agents of change, and so played a key role against the local cultural practices and identity. It was a powerful means for 'winning' the hearts and minds of the people into the way of life of the missionaries, but the system did not contribute to the overall development of the people. This is clear from the fact that there were no institutions for higher training because once the narrow evangelistic objective had been achieved, the education programme of the missionaries had completed its purpose.

4. 3. 2. 2. Literature Work

Once people became literate, the mission priority became one which sought to provide edifying literature. This included translation of English literature like Pilgrim's Progress, Primer and so forth. The Kukis of Manipur

---

97. Dena, *Missions and Colonialism*, 90.
98. Haokip, *Manipur a Gospel*, 12.
99. Singh, *History of Christian Missions*, 158.

did not have literature until 1912 when two primers were prepared in Thado, a dialect of one dominant clan, by Ngulhao Thomsong with the help of Pettigrew.[100] The next literary work after the two primers was the publication of a hymnbook of 216 hymns, which was sometimes used as a kind of substitute Bible in the absence of the Bible in that particular language. Pettigrew records what the people said: "This is our Bible until you can give us the Word of God in our own tongue."[101] *Lecherous Patna*, or *The First Primer*, was published in Ukhrul by the School Library in 1916. Luke, John and Acts of the Apostles were published in 1925 by the British and Foreign Bible Society, Calcutta, and were followed by the publication of *Thadou Thusim*, Thadou Kuki stories compiled and edited by William Pettigrew and published by D. N. Banerjee, Calcutta in 1926. By way of contrast, it is interesting to see that the New Testament was translated in a Meitei language in 1827 although that had no association with any missionary work in Manipur.[102]

The priority given to spiritual conversion in mission is paralleled by the fact that the missionaries depended mostly on the New Testament and neglected the Old Testament. Accordingly there was a general practice to first translate the gospels according to Luke, John and the Acts of the Apostles, which conveyed the impression that the four gospels were somehow more important than other parts of the Bible. These books were translated into various similar dialects so that, at the end, the Bible translation became a dividing factor in the society. Hminga, discussing the Lakhers in Mizoram writes, "Had not the Lakher Pioneer Mission reduced one of the Lakher dialects and used it for translation of the Bible and hymns in that dialect, Duhlian dialect would have become the one dialect spoken by all in Mizoram."[103] Hminga is not against the development of Lakher dialect as such, but he highlights the fact that the Duhlian dialect was popular enough to communicate the gospel to most of the tribes in Mizoram. However, his statement brings out the fact that Bible translation was in one

---

100. Pettigrew, "My Twenty-Five Years", x.
101. Quoted by Pettigrew in Pettigrew, "My Twenty-Five Years", xii.
102. Downs, *History of Christianity*, 67.
103. C. L. Hminga, *The Life and Witness of the Churches in Mizoram* (Serkawn, Mizoram: Baptist Church of Mizoram, 1987), 44.

way or the other instrumental in the division of the people. The same is the experience of the Kukis in Manipur, where Thado dialect was common to the Kuki groups, but despite the opportunity for formation of a common language, people were segregated through the Bible translations. Khupzago in his work, *A Critical Historical Study of Bible Translations among the Zo People in North East India,* beautifully brought out this fact. According to his findings, in the southern part of Manipur, Bible translation began when Watkin Roberts translated the gospel of John into Vaiphei, one of the Kuki clans, in 1917. The next was the gospel of Mark translated in Hmar dialect in 1920, gospel of John in Thado-Kuki in 1924 and in Paite in 1951, gospel of Matthew in Gangte in 1952 and in Kom Rem in 1954, gospel of John in Simte in 1957 and the New Testament in Zou in 1967.[104] The floodgate of the Bible translation was opened and within the first half of the twentieth century, the foundation was already laid for the inevitable divisions in the church. At the same time, it was interesting to observe that the North East India General Mission (NEIGM) had its own publications such as, the *Kristian,* the *North East India Tidings,* the *Rest* and the *Herald of Truth* where all the dialects were used and were understood by all. Some of these publications were done as late as the early 1950s.

This raises a question as to why the Bible translations into those dialects of the Kuki groups were felt a necessity when they could use a common literature. This reflects both the clannish spirit and short-sightedness of Christian mission which in the long term exacerbated division on the basis of clan and dialect which resulted in the problem of finding a common nomenclature until the present day. In this light, it is possible that while Bible translation was a means to hear the Word of God in one's own dialect, it was also considered as a means to assert or construct one's own identity. Peter Chiru, who is currently translating the Bible in a Chiru dialect, observes how in Bible translation, often words are recreated in order to make the tribe concerned look different from others.[105] We conclude

---

104. Khupzago, *A Critical Historical Study of Bible Translations Among the Zo People in North East India* (Churachandpur: Chin Baptist Literature Board, 1996), 73–88.

105. Peter Chiru is currently translating a Bible in Chiru dialect. He was interviewed by the researcher on 22 February 2008, on the way to Choroi Kholen in Churachandpur, Manipur.

that in a hasty process of Christianization, the translation of the Bible for dialect groups contributed to further disintegration among the people, so preventing them from lasting unity under one platform.

4. 4. The Role of Colonial Rule in Mission

The nineteenth-century experiences painted the picture of Christianity identically with the European colonial imperialism in Asia and Africa and hence distorted not only the image of Christianity as a cross-cultural faith movement but also the identity of the native people. The nature of the interaction between Christian missions and colonial powers differed from situation to situation. Dena suggests three broad categories of missionary relationship with colonial power: total collaborationists, as in Spain and Portugal; partial collaborationists, as in the British colonial politics in Asia; and non-collaborationists in Fiji, Burma and elsewhere where the Christian missions existed long before the colonial power arrived.[106] In the case of Manipur, while Roberts in the southern part of Manipur did not have an official link, Pettigrew in the north had close links with the colonial administration.

4. 4. 1. The Rationales for Relationship

The coming and success of Christianity in North-East India, except the Thado-Kuki Pioneer Mission, owed much to the cooperation of the government officials and, vice versa, the success of the colonial administration owed much to the work of the missionaries. This is clear in the history of mission both in Manipur and in the Lushai Hills, now called Mizoram, where the help of the colonial officials facilitated mission, while the support of the missionaries for the political administration of the region was clear in various ways, including military actions. One of the officials whose name appeared very often in this regard was Lieutenant-Colonel Shakespear. He lived for twenty years among the 'wild tribes' both in the Lushai Hills and Manipur and showed great interest in the work of

---

106. Dena, *Missions and Colonialism*, 1–7.

the missionaries. He even wrote to the American Baptist mission urging that assistance be afforded to Mr Pettigrew.[107] He pressed the authorities concerned for missionary work to be permitted in the valley, asking for this in 1894 and 1901. It was refused both times on the basis that the Raja was still a minor. Again, in 1908, the request was made and refused and for the fourth time; but Shakespear took the initiative, and the case was reopened.[108] The colonial government provided the mission with a Bengali teacher and published the school primer, catechism, and grammar.[109] Similarly, in Mizoram, while the government carried out what was known as 'disarmament policy', that is, collecting of guns from the chiefs, the missionaries did their philanthropic works, which benefited both the administration and the missionaries. In Manipur, Pettigrew was appointed by the government as superintendent of the first real census of the hill tribes (1910–11) because the missionary was the only one who knew the language of the people.

The reasons for their collaborations were varied. Shakespear writes how the work of the missionaries served the interest of the administration in Mizoram: "their [the missionaries'] valuable work had materially assisted in the pacification of the Lushais."[110] He was observed to have "had all the time wooed the missionaries and supported them without any least hesitancy and slackening of enthusiasm."[111] The colonial authority took advantage of the close relationship established between the local people and the missionaries through selfless services to them.[112] Th. Lamboi Vaiphei suggests: "It may be true to assume that British supreme priority was political stability rather than any other recognition in the state" and he goes on to say, "the colonial officials looked to missionary work

---

107. "Mission in Assam" 71–83 in the *Ninety-Sixth Annual Report of the 1910 American Baptist Foreign Mission Society* Presented at the Annual Meeting held in Chicago, Illinois, May 6–13, 1910, 72.
108. "Ukhrul: Report of Rev Wm. Pettigrew", 56–59 in *ABMC of the ABMFMS* Report of the Twelfth Biennial Session, 1913, 57.
109. Dena, *Missions and Colonialism*, 44.
110. J. Shakespear's letter to the Secretary to the Chief Commissioner of Assam quoted in Dena *Missions and Colonialism*, 44.
111. Lloyd quoted in Dena, *Missions and Colonialism*, 45.
112. Dena, *Missions and Colonialism*, 3.

particularly in Manipur in terms of the stabilization of colonial occupation only."[113] For the missionaries, this relationship provided security and material assistance.

Secondly, the nationalistic feelings of the missionaries and the theological justification of colonial rule as 'divine willed' were observed to be one of the reasons for the interlinking of the Christian missions and the colonial power.[114] In fact, the official policy of the American Baptist Foreign Mission on cooperation with Government was derived from the Scriptures. The statement reads:

> The charge of the Master, "Render therefore unto Caesar the things that are Caesar's", is authority for the missionary in seeking to work in harmony with the government under which he labours. . . . The Conference reaffirms the time-honoured policy of our missions in British India in their cooperation with the government in education.

This cooperation with the government in education was justified by the following reasons: first, such cooperation enables the mission to serve the people among whom they are working by providing education under decidedly Christian influences; second, the cooperation would make mission school students eligible to get government jobs and the cooperation under the policy of 'religious neutrality' permits the Christian teaching in mission school.[115] In addition, for some there seemed to be a hidden political agenda in the work of evangelization as Rev William Ashmore wrote,

---

113. Th. Lamboi Vaiphei, *Advent of Christian Mission and Its Impact on the Hill-Tribes in Manipur* (Imphal: Published by Author, 1997), 63.

114. Dena, *Missions and Colonialism*, 4 & 5. Dena points out how the nationalistic feelings among the missionaries, including people like David Livingston, had confused the interests of the Kingdom of God with the interests of the colonizers who share the same nationality with them. It has been noted that claiming to be both a missionary and a nationalist at the same time, some missionaries even carried with them their national prejudices and took up the work of spreading the gospel as a matter of "patriotic honour" and "national duty" as well; Bengt Sundkler, *The World of Mission* (Michigan: 1965) quoted in Dena, *Missions and Colonialism*, 9.

115. *Foreign Mission Policies of American Baptist Foreign Mission Society & Women's American Baptist Foreign Mission Society*, Massachusetts, 1917, 10–11.

"we must evangelize other countries in order to save our own country."[116] Ashmore's view was shared by J. Johnstone, a British colonial officer in *My Experiences in Manipur and the Naga Hills*, in 1896, wherein he insisted that the people should be given both education and Christianity to ensure that they did not become Hindus or Mussalman, which would make them a constant source of trouble and annoyance.[117]

It is important to recognize, however, that missionary attitudes were not uniform and there were prophetic voices which were clearly critical of such cooperation. Fraser and Roberts were two such missionaries. Upon their arrival in Mizoram, they saw the cruelty of the institution of *Bawi* (*Soh* in Thado-Kuki) or slavery. *Soh* was a traditional practice both in the Lushai Hills as well as among the Kukis in Manipur. Fraser took up the issue with the authority concerned and Roberts wholeheartedly supported Fraser in his fight against the institution. Dena calls him "the most daring missionary among all the Welsh missionaries who came to North East India." Fraser fought against the institution of *Bawi* even to the extent of sending a memorandum to King George V demanding the liberation of the slaves.[118] In doing so he stood against the will not only of the Lushai chiefs but also the British officials and the missionaries both 'at home' and in the 'mission field.' As a result Fraser was sent out of the 'mission field' and later allowed to return to Mizoram by the government on the condition that he would not interfere in politics.[119] According to D. E. Jones, Fraser was accorded a royal welcome by the Mizo Christians,[120] which showed how much he was appreciated by the people. Fraser and his wife continued their medical work in Lakhimpur, north Assam, until he died in 1920. All through this critical period, including signing the memorandum sent to the king, Roberts solidly stood behind Fraser. Undoubtedly, as Lloyd rightly says,

---

116. William Ashmore "Evangelize the Heathen in order to save America", 567–568 in *Baptist Missionary Magazine*, Vol. LXXVI, No.12 (1896), 567.
117. Quoted in Verrier Elwin, ed., *The Nagas in the Nineteenth Century* (Bombay: Oxford University Press, 1969), 598.
118. Dena, *In Search of Identity*, 46.
119. A Letter of Major Cole to Fraser on 19 December 1910 in a File 'The Bawi System in Lushai. Dr Fraser's Case and Letters – 1909–1910'. CMA 27, 315 preserved at the National Library of Walse, Aberystwyth, UK.
120. Quoted in Lloyd, *History of the Church*, 169.

"The departure of Dr Fraser from Aizawl signalled also Watkin Roberts's departure."[121] It may be inferred from this that Roberts was concerned with the situation of the less-privileged people within the society for which very reason he also went to evangelize the neglected Kukis in Manipur despite the stiff opposition both from the government and the American Baptist Mission in the person of a British missionary, William Pettigrew.

4. 4. 2. Cooperation for the War in France

The linkage between colonialism and mission, and the resulting confusion as to the real nature of the gospel, is further illustrated by the fact that converts were persuaded to join France on the side of the allies in World War I. Manipur being under their administration, the British government demanded that local people go to France during the war, but this met with strong resistance from the Kukis. The failure of J. Higgins, the president of the Manipur state Durbar, to recruit the local people led to a request that Pettigrew, at that time in Assam, come back to persuade and recruit the local people for Labour Force in France. He was successful in this task, which without his help the government could not do. He recruited two thousand local people out of whom one thousand and two hundred were Tangkhul Naga Christians, among whom he had already worked about twenty years.[122] In recruiting the local people as manual labourers, it was not Pettigrew alone, but also his own converts, who were actively involved. Ngulhao Thomsong, one of the first Kuki converts, was one of such who "persuaded a number of the Christian Kukis to go with him to France, and by his action was the direct means of influencing about 500 of the non-Christian Kukis to volunteer for that service."[123] For them, change of belief involves a change of political loyalty and administration, an alienation from the community. The cooperation between the colonial administration and mission continued after the labour service as Dena writes: "On return from the war, the Tangkhul Nagas were again enlisted in the coolie sections of the Kuki Punitive Measures which was unleashed for the sole

---

121. Lloyd, *History of the Church*, 158.
122. Dena, *Missions and Colonialism*, 39.
123. Pettigrew, "My Twenty-Five Years", xi.

purpose of suppressing the Kuki uprising."[124] The above incidences show that conversion to Christianity included giving loyalty to the missionaries and their government.

The significance of cooperation for mission can be seen in the reaction contained in the ABFMS report in 1918. It highlights two prominent happenings of the year, first of which was the numerical growth of converts, and second, the recruitment of local Christians for labour force in France. The report states: "The first to volunteer have been the Christians in every case. Is not this a hopeful sign, pointing to the unity and solidarity of Christianity throughout the world?"[125] The cooperation between colonial power and mission was not exceptional to the missionaries of the tribal people but there are "bishops, clergy, doctors, nurses, and members of the House staff [which] have joined the forces, and many of them are in the Front."[126] In April 1918, Pettigrew was given a commission in the India Army Reserve, and was demobilized in September 1919.[127] For this reason, Dena states: "The missionary took it [cooperation in the war] as a hopeful sign pointing to the unity and solidarity of Christians as if the war were for the defence of Christian faith."[128]

The impact of the war in France on those who left their village homes and crossed the borders to engage in a European conflict was narrated by Pettigrew in untroubled language:

> There was great opposition and only when the writer and his wife, who were stationed temporarily at Gauhati at the time doing Mission Treasurer's work, were asked by the Political Agent to come to Ukhrul and help in the work of persuasion did these people finally agree to go, and now they are back once more and have related their experiences of travel, and

---

124. Dena, *Missions and Colonialism*, 39.
125. "The Assam Mission" 93–95 in the *Report of the American Baptist Foreign Mission Society*, 1918, 94.
126. "The Missionary Aspect of the War" in *The Church Missionary Gleaner*, 1 February 1916, 18.
127. William Pettigrew, "The Year in Manipur" in *ABFMS*, 1922, 93.
128. Dena, *Missions and Colonialism*, 39.

on the battle fields of France. All are ready to go again on a similar adventure if occasion should demand it . . .[129]

Similarly, the Karens in Burma were persuaded to be fully supportive of the war as an English official said: "Karens, under the influence of Dr C. A. Nichols of the American Baptist Mission in Bassein, have come to regard it as their duty and privilege to take part in the present struggle."[130] Pettigrew also recalls what the labourers themselves said: "We had little faith in your stories of lands across seas and oceans, people with beings who believed in the Christ you preached to us, but we have seen with our own eyes the emblem of the cross over thousands of graves on the battlefields, and the beautiful grave stones on the cemeteries of France." Pettigrew hailed this as a sign of progress, "The message of the Cross is being listened to now, by these Tangkhul Naga young men and young women."[131] Religious conversion appeared to mean the same thing as change of political loyalty to the colonial rule. Even more remarkable is the fact that while the war was eroding the faith of vast numbers of British people, the missionary could treat it as an agent of progress in far-off India. The cooperation in France was a useful means for the work of evangelization and it was said that it raised 'the prestige of the Christians' and enhanced the 'confidence of the State'.[132]

Another element in helping to bring many to decision for the Christian religion was the large company of young men who had been to France and had come back with new ideas and new aspirations, and the rigid belief in a ceremony of this kind did not appeal to them any more, and they were ready to give it up, and many other things besides.[133]

The irony is that the adventure in France did appear to trigger church growth. As Downs says: "The Tangkhul church did not really begin to

---

129. Pettigrew, "My Twenty-Five Years", ix.
130. "The Contribution of Mission Fields to the War" in the *Report of the American Baptist Foreign Mission Society*, 1918, 15.
131. *Rev William Pettigrew's Mission Reports and Letters*, Compiled and Reproduced by Revd Champhang Jajo (Gauhati: n.d. Chandan Press), 40.
132. T. Luikham, *A Short History of the Manipur Baptist Christian Golden Jubilee, 1948* (Ukhrul, Manipur: North East Christian Association, 1975), 27.
133. Pettigrew, "My Twenty-Five Years", xix.

grow until after 1920. Then it grew rapidly. By 1922 there were 2,000 Tangkhul Christians."[134] In this case, the war in France turned out to be a missional tour and hence, sadly, Christianity was mistakenly identified with the colonial identity and was an enemy's force to those who were not yet in support of the colonial power.

The cooperation not only served the purpose of evangelization but also boosted the image of the missionaries. For Pettigrew, in recognition of his successful recruitment of the local people for the labour work in France, the government allowed his long pending petition to tour in the western part of the state and permitted another missionary, Dr Crozier, as well, although with a condition that no attempts should be made to convert the Meiteis but only the hill people.[135] Earlier, Crozier volunteered as a Medical Officer during the Kuki Punitive Measure from June 1918 to 1919 in order to gain favour and confidence.[136] In recognition of his service as a commission in the Indian Army Reserve from April 1918 to October 1919, Pettigrew was given permission to open a mission headquarters at Kangpokpi in October 1919.[137] In addition, he was awarded the *Kaisar-i-Hind* silver medal for his public service in 1918, a war medal in 1920 for his military service as a commissioned officer of the British army during the Great War and in 1928 he was made an honorary member of the British and Foreign Bible Society in recognition of his Scripture translation work in Manipuri, Tangkhul Naga, and Thadou Kuki.[138] Pettigrew retired in 1933.

The above facts show that for these missionaries, their national and religious identities were inseparably identical. Their religious identity was 'tamed' in order to suit the interest of the national identity. And for the local converts, religious conversion, which included a change of political loyalty to the colonial rule, was considered as a change for betterment.

---

134. Downs, *Mighty Works of God*, 164.
135. Memo No. 507–P, dated Imphal, 22 September 1917, from His Highness the Raja of Manipur to the Manipur State Darbar quoted in Singh, *History of Christian Mission*, 155.
136. Annual Report of the ABMC, (Indiana, 14 June–20 June, 1922), 93 quoted in Dena, *Missions and Colonialism*, 40
137. Pettigrew, "The Year in Manipur", 93.
138. Luikham, *A Short History*, 41.

Cooperation for the War in France, for instance, was seen as the reflection of the success of the missionaries as well as the sign of 'Christian commitment' for the converts. In the process, colonial administration played an important role in terms of preparing the ground and rendering support for mission work when necessary. For this reason, it would be incorrect to assume that Christianization of the people was only the result of the work of the missionaries. At the same time such cooperation created enormous problems for local people who remained loyal to their own culture, while in the long term it distorted Christianity and laid the foundation for the confusion surrounding identity and the tragic conflicts around this issue with which this work is concerned.

4. 5. The Work of Evangelization Among the Kukis

Christianity came to the Kukis of Manipur like a crumb fallen from a rich man's table in the north, and in the south, it came through a back door. In both cases, the faith came as one-way traffic for the sole purpose of the conversion of souls. Despite the ways in which Christianity was presented and the resistance movement against the faith at the initial stage, the evangelization of the Kukis was a success story, if 'success' is measured in terms of statistics and quantity.

4. 5. 1. Inception and Growth

On the installation of Chura Chand Singh to his throne in 1907, the mission work was extended to other hill tribes of Manipur, particularly the Kukis[139] and that paved the way for them to come to the Christian faith. Under the American Baptist Mission in the northern part of Manipur, the work commenced in 1912, eighteen years after Pettigrew's arrival in Manipur. The Kukis were strong opponents of both the colonial rule and Christianity, however, once the work began among them it grew very fast, except during the 1917–1919 Kuki Rising. In his report of 1913, Pettigrew

---

139. William Pettigrew, "Ukhrul Field Report for 1910" 74–84 in *ABMC of the ABMU*, 1910 in *History of Christianity in Manipur: Source Materials*, compiled by Elungkiebe Zeliang (Imphal: Manipur Baptist Convention, 2005), 31.

writes with hope, "Four or more Kuki boys are now in the school and it is hoped that in the next three years, or probably before, they will be ready to act as teachers and preachers for this great and promising tribe."[140] Comparing his own experiences with both the tribes Pettigrew was impressed to write, "These people of this clan [the Kukis] are on the whole more open-minded and hospitable, and evidently, from information gathered from the Kuki Christians, are more susceptible to the truth than the Naga tribes."[141]

Once the work began, it grew rapidly. Reporting how it had happened Pettigrew writes:

> These Kuki tribes are very susceptible to the gospel, and the majority of those who have attended this school have left as Christian boys eager to tell the story to their own villagers scattered in every area of the State. From 1914 on there have been voluntary workers and paid mission workers travelling in all parts proclaiming the truth.[142]

Consequently, a large number of baptisms took place in 1914, which continued until 1917 when the work was disrupted because of the Anglo-Kuki war. The year 1915 in particular was a great year for the Kukis with regard to conversions for reasons yet to be discovered. According to the Ukhrul field report in 1916, the nineteen people who had been baptized in that year were all Kukis, and the first Kuki boy received a medal for his All India Sunday School examination. Another hundred Kukis were baptized in the western hills and a church was organised.[143] A. J. Tuttle in his Assam Mission Secretarial report in 1916 shows the continued progress of work among the Kukis: "Our work among the Kukis has developed so rapidly

---

140. "A Survey of the Field", *ABMC of the ABFMS*, 1913 in *History of Christianity in Manipur*, 37.
141. "Ukhrul Field Report for 1913" by William Pettigrew, *ABMC of the ABFMS*, 1913, 56–59 in *History of Christianity in Manipur*, 40.
142. *Rev William Pettigrew's Mission Reports and Letters,* 41.
143. "Ukhrul Field Report for 1916" in *ABMC of the ABFMS*, 1916 in *History of Christianity in Manipur*, 49 & 50.

within the last year that our station must be so placed that we care for this work, and adequately staff our station while at the same time guarding against undue isolation of our missionaries."[144] U. M. Fox in his report writes, "Three stages out from Imphal toward Kohima, I baptized twenty-six Thado Kukis from one village, there being only three families who had not accepted Christianity. This sees the beginning of a great awakening among this tribe."[145] The growth continued until 1917 as it was reported, "In Manipur State the Kukis have manifested a very encouraging desire to become Christians even though no aggressive work has been done among them."[146]

The growth of Christianity among the Kukis in the northern part of Manipur was disrupted by the 1917–1919 Kuki Rising, during which the missionaries and their converts, both the Kukis and Nagas, turned against them by supporting their 'enemy'. In September 1918, Pettigrew, their missionary, was given a commission in the India Army Reserve, and the would-be second missionary, Dr G. G. Crozier, served as a special medical officer for the war against them. For this reason, 1917–1919 could be termed as 'Kuki Three-Year crisis of faith'.[147] The growth of Christianity among the Kukis, however, took up even faster in the post-conflict situation, which some credited to the colonial's suppression of local way of life.[148] More will be said in the next section, 'Mission and the Chieftainship.'

In the southern part of Manipur, the work of Roberts, which began in 1910, was responded to very well. Seeing the sufferings of the people and the opportunity to begin work among the Kukis in the southern part of Manipur, Roberts started his ministry, having been informed that no

---

144. "Report of the Secretary for 1916, Supplement to the Minutes of the American Baptist Missionary Conference", 12, in *History of Christianity in Manipur*, 51.
145. U. M. Fox, "Ukhrul" *ABMC of the ABFMS Report of the Fourteenth Session*, 1915, 53–54.
146. *ABFMS 1917: One-Hundred-Third Annual Report*, 89, in *History of Christianity in Manipur*, 52.
147. By 'crisis of faith' I mean the dilemma of Christians caused by the oppression of those claimed to be Christians like the suffering of the Black Christians under Apartheid in South Africa. See, *Evangelical Witness in South Africa: Evangelical Critique their own Theology and Practice*, published by Concerned Evangelicals, Dobsonville, 1865, 4–5.
148. Downs, *History of Christianity*, 142.

missionary was working in the region[149] among the Kukis. Accordingly upon the receipt of his 'Macedonian call' referred to earlier, Roberts went to the region. It was mentioned earlier that Roberts was someone who was always concerned with the situation of the less privileged and it could have been that such convictions drove him to work among the Kukis who were not yet reached with the Christian message. Other missionaries with Roberts in the southern part of the State were five young converts from Mizoram: Vanzika, Savawma, Taitea, Luaia and Thanglura.[150] Besides spiritual commitment, it was possible that the people had concern for each other because they belonged to the same cultural background.

In the midst of the tension referred to above, Roberts organized the congregation of the Mission's converts on Presbyterian principles,[151] and he went to Imphal to inform the administration about the development of the work. Fearing the negative reaction of the Manipur Rajah against the British administration the Political Agent refused to grant permission to Roberts to remain in the area. However, against the will of the government, the work progressed and within two years they also employed local people, namely Thangkai and Awmtaia, as evangelist teachers. The nature of Roberts' mission, including his emphasis on the importance of rebirth, prayer, and literature are reflected in 'Sunrise of Manipur.'[152] Within five years the Christian message spread throughout the entire hill region in the south of Manipur. The missionary work carried out by the local people soon went beyond the region, and in order to include the entire region, the name of Thado-Kuki Pioneer Mission was changed to North East India General Mission (NEIGM) in 1923.[153] Regarding the new name Roberts writes, "As every parents named the name of their children, so I give the name of field that God gives me. I call it as, North East India General Mission, which sounds pleasant as the parents feel good when they call the

---

149. Singh, *History of Christian Mission*, 111.
150. A Letter of P. Fraser from Aijal to Rev R. J. Williams. CM Archives, 27, 314 preserved at National Library of Walse, Aberystwyth, UK.
151. Vanlalchhuanawma, *Christianity*, 229.
152. *Yr Efengyglydd*. For the text in English, see appendix 6.
153. Khaineng quoted in Jeyaseelan, *Impact*, 88. Hereafter refer to as NEIGM.

name of the child."¹⁵⁴ In his appreciative note of the NEIGM's work in the Chittagong Hill Tracts, a local ordained minister Buiting writes, "Thus Christianity was spread among the Bâwm people and today the Bâwm are 100 per cent Christian. The first adopted denomination Evangelical Christian Church continues its mission till today."¹⁵⁵

The growth of mission, reported in *Khristian,* or Christian, a monthly journal of the mission, in November 1929 shows not only the numerical growth but also how the mission grew as a uniting organization among the Kuki people in Lakhipur, now in Assam, Tripura, now dominated by migrants, Chittagong Hills Tracts, now Bangladesh, Upper Chindwin and Upper Burma, now Myanmar.¹⁵⁶ By the year 1954, there were 27,824 converts with 134 national pastors, evangelists and teachers, 341 chapels in Manipur, and 1,762 enrolled in Sunday School and 50 teachers in Chittagong Hill Tracts¹⁵⁷ and by 1960, the number of converts grew to 29,678 with the remark, "From our Mission Compound at Churachandpur men and women go forth to preach, to teach and to baptize, not only within the confines of the North East India General Mission field, but in other areas as well."¹⁵⁸ S. T. Henpu, one of the pioneer local leaders, recorded the growth of the mission in this way: From 1909–1927, 19 years, The Thado Kookie Pioneer Mission started by Watkin Roberts from Aizawl; from 1928–1950, 22 years, NEIGM under Paul Rostad and Coleman as the General Secretary; from 1951–1960, 10 years, Royal C. Paddock; from 1954–1960, there were no missionaries but the church was managed by the local people themselves.¹⁵⁹ The NEIGM now called 'E.C.C.I.' claims to be one of the largest evangelical denominations in North-East India.¹⁶⁰

---

154. Thimkhup Buiting, "The Advent of Christianity Among the Bawms", http://bawm.info/bawmchristianity.htm [Accessed 8 April 2010].
155. Ibid.
156. *Kristian,* November, 1926. The names of workers and their place of origin, date of joining, place and nature of work are given in this report.
157. Census Report from Manipur State, India and Chittagong Hill Tracts, Pakistan, *North East India Tidings,* December 31, 1954.
158. Thangkai, "How The Light First Pierced Into the Darkness" *North East India Tidings,* [Monthly Magazine of NEIGM] May 1960, 3.
159. Henpu, *"Kum 50 Jubilee",* 9.
160. "ECCI: Who Are We" http://www.ecchurchindia.com/index_files/ecci.htm [Accessed 26 March 208].

Two things can be observed: first, the work of evangelism among the Kukis was carried out by the people themselves. While in the north, the mission work among the Kukis began after nearly two decades of missionary activities in the state; in the south, restrictions placed on the missionary and his marginalization by the colonial authorities, as well as by other missionaries, resulted in a situation in which evangelization was carried out by the people themselves, first among their own people, and then to other tribes across the region. Related to this was the cooperation among all the groups now known as Kuki, Mizo, and Zomi discussed in chapter 3. In those days there were no divisions of clan or tribe or denomination as we have in the present day.

Second, being a private mission, the NEIGM did not follow the Comity arrangements. In other words, Roberts looked beyond the boundaries and structures and worked according to his understanding of justice and fairness. This is clear in the way his work extended beyond Manipur and spread even to areas which are now part of Bangladesh and Burma. This indicates both the traditional territory of the people as well as his concern for the disfavoured wherever they were. Robert's commitment for tribal people, particularly those who were neglected, was evident in his unwavering fight for the abolition of the local slavery system in Mizoram referred to earlier. In the case of Kukis, although his mission had some missionaries to non-Kukis, his initial aim and main target was to work among the Kuki groups wherever they were found based on the fact that they were neglected by other missionaries. For that reason it can be said that Roberts was a man for the Kukis and that is to say, at the same time, the disruption of his activities was an interference of vision for the Kuki people as a group.

4. 5. 2. Mission and the Chieftainship

Chieftainship is fundamental to Kuki traditional identity and is one of the main surviving elements of a Kuki traditional culture in the present day. Therefore, we shall take the system as a representative of the people's culture and show its condition in the process of evangelization. It will be shown that although chieftainship has to be viewed as the strong point of Kuki culture, it needs reformation in the light of the Christian message.

Except in the case of Senvon village in the southern part of Manipur where the chief himself was the initiator, the first converts came not from the chiefs and their counsellors called *Semang-Pachongs* but from people of 'low' social status and young people. Why the chiefs were more difficult to convert than their ordinary villagers is important to mention. At a superficial level, the firmness of the chiefs and their counsellors may seem self-centred and power-hungry. However, looking from the perspective of the local culture, the chiefs, supported by their counsellors, were the custodians of the local culture and practices. It was the symbol of the people's identity and hence, giving up the practice was like assassinating their own socio-political identity and the future of their society. As shown earlier, traditionally chiefs are the rulers of Kuki villages and hence the society. In fact it was with that system that the Kukis stood against colonial imperialism. At the same time, a one-man ruling system of chieftainship was a weak point for the Kukis as both the missionaries and the colonial administration took advantage of the pyramid structure of the system to win the people to their side.

In Mizoram, among their cognate groups during the period in which the chief of Senvon was evangelized in 1910, the missionary strategy was to target the chiefs, the top of the pyramid structure of the society, and that ended with great success. It was said that by 1913, twenty-two chiefs[161] in the Lushai Hills were converted, including Vanphunga's brothers, the fiercest persecutors of Christians.[162] In those situations, "The conversion of the chiefs and other leading men led to conversion of whole villages."[163] The missionary activities continued in a same manner and according to the Welsh Calvinistic Methodist Foreign Mission report, the year 1922 tops the conversion of the local people when 7795 joined the church.[164]

---

161. Eight Sailo chiefs in the North and fourteen chiefs in the south of Lushai Hills. *Krista Tlangau*, March 1912, 47, quoted in Vanlalchhuanawma, *Christianity*, 212.

162. D.E. Jones' letter to AB, dt. 13.8.1915, quoted in Vanlalchhuanawma, *Christianity*, 212.

163. Sandy, *Some Difficulties and Triumphs*, not dated, quoted in Vanlalchhuanawma, *Christianity*, 212.

164. *Report of WCMFMS*, 1922, quoted in Vanlalchhuanawma, *Christianity*, 261.

With such a mass movement the evangelization of the North Lushai Hill was said to have been completed within a decade.[165]

In Manipur, the circumstance in which the chiefs came to Christianity was different. At their refusal to send their men for the Labour Force in France, the government resorted to suppressing the Kuki chiefs, which took them three full years as discussed earlier. The post-conflict period saw a mass movement among the Kuki chiefs and their subjects toward Christianity. For Downs, the defeat of the Kuki chiefs was "more than a defeat at arms. It was a defeat of the old way of life" the result of which, he triumphantly writes, was "large numbers of Kukis began to turn towards Christianity."[166] The growth of Christianity among the Kukis in the aftermath of their suppression was further recorded by Downs: "From 1920 onwards the Kuki Church grew rapidly. Most of the evangelistic work was done by Kuki Christians."[167] The growth continued and they became the second major group in Manipur by 1950s.[168]

Downs has given five reasons for the rapid growth of Christianity among the Kukis: first, the gospel of Christ brought a welcome word of peace and brotherhood to a people so recently ravaged by war; second, they were influenced by the fact that Christianity was the religion of their conquerors; third, the establishment of the centre at Kangpokpi; fourth, appointment of a missionary primarily for the Kuki work; and fifth, the Manipur Revival which further stimulated the movement.[169]

Although Downs' points are credible whether or not the people embraced the Christian faith in the way he suggests is open to discussion. The 'enemies' of the people were both the colonial rulers and their religion, and in their attempt to resist those forces they were destabilized as a people. For that reason, Downs' first two points sound rather unrealistic because the bringers of the gospel, the welcome word of peace, and the agents of armed force were indistinguishable. In addition, Downs seems to regard the

---

165. *Glad Tidings*, June 1923, 24, quoted in Vanlalchhuanawma, *Christianity*, 202.
166. Downs, *Mighty Works of God*, 169.
167. Ibid., 170.
168. Kim Vaiphei, *The Coming of Christianity in Manipur: With Special Reference to the Kukis* (Imphal: Published by the Joint Women's Programme, New Delhi, 1995), 32.
169. Downs, *Mighty Works of God*, 169–170.

1917–1919 Kuki Rising as merely a local conflict to which the gospel was a message of peace and brotherhood. The truth of the matter was that those communities were recruited by the colonial administration in their attempt to suppress the Kuki, thereby widening the gap between them. With regards to Downs' suggestion that the people had accepted Christianity because it was the religion of their conquerors, this ignores wider reality. Under colonial rule advancement of 'civilization' was intertwined with the Christian message, which could possibly be an added reason for embracing Christianity. The primary schools and literature being popular methods of evangelization, the young people who were the hope for future generations had abandoned their traditional ways and followed the new faith, Christianity. In such a situation, the chief system that once resisted colonial culture now became instrumental in the hands of the colonial rulers and their religion. Pettigrew writes, "the fact that the Thados [are] having a chief in each village with absolute authority is a great advantage compared to the democratic Nagas, where every Tom, Dick and Harry of the village has his say in matters that come before the village court."[170] In this case, the suppression of Kuki chiefs through Kuki punitive measures 1917–1919 was one important factor for this change. Added to this, possibly most important of all, was freedom from fear of evil spirits under whom they constantly lived. There were then many complex reasons why the people, the chiefs and their counsellors including the village priests in particular, embraced Christianity. And once the chiefs who were the custodians and symbols of the culture were converted, they became instrumental in the conversions of the common people on a large scale.

4. 5. 3. What does a Christian Kuki look like?

Conversion to Christianity was not only a change of heart but also a change of the traditional way of life of the people. In Thado-Kuki, the word for 'Christian' is *Pathen oi* or *Pathen hou*, which means 'one who accepts the Word of God,' or the 'one who worships God.' In outer appearance, the converts were made to remove their *tuhcha* or traditional

---

170. "Ukhrul Field Report for 1913" by Pettigrew *ABMC of the ABFMS*, 1913, 56–59 in *History of Christianity in Manipur*, 40.

hairstyle, to replace their *pheichom,* a traditional dress with trousers and so forth. In social life, they were restricted from participating in the traditional festivals, family ceremonies and community activities, like *Sa-Ai,* and *Chang-Ai* discussed in an earlier chapter. Another example, which the researcher himself experienced, was abstention from eating meat that was used for rituals and traditional festivals. In this way, the social system of relationships and responsibility such as *Tucha-Becha, Jol-le-Gol* and other practices referred to earlier were devalued and the cultural values attached to them were also discarded. One such was the concept of *Khankho,* the underlying conceptual value with which all outward practices were articulated. Recalling his own experiences, Mr Thangkhothong Haokip laments the abandonment of a cultural system of relationship – concern for the wellbeing of each other in the society. In other words, *Khankho* was gone.[171] Similarly, T. Lunkim, one of the eminent church leaders regretfully says, *"Min ama ama chonna a Pathen ahou thei ahin, ana mahet lang katuhcha kaki tan louding ahi".* (Translation: Had I known that people do worship God in their own cultural ways, I would not have cut my *tucha,* traditional hair style for me).[172] What had gone with conversion was not only the outward appearance but also an understanding of one's own worth and dignity as a person including his or her worldview. In other words, converts were uprooted from their culture.

On the issue of the wellbeing of converts, the approach of the missionaries was segregationist. Hawlngam Haokip, a senior leader of the Kuki Baptist Convention, records the incidence of persecution of the early Kuki converts under the American Baptist Mission: ". . . William Pettigrew intervened with the authorities, securing permission for the Kuki Christians to settle on a new site only about a quarter of a mile from the old village Kaihao."[173] In other words, new converts were physically separated, the communities in which they had lived being isolated in ghetto-like condi-

---

171. Mr Thangkhothong Haokip was interviewed on 22 January 2008 at the residence of the researcher at K. Salbung, Churachandpur, Manipur. Haokip was a convert. He is now in his 60s.
172. Dr T. Lunkim is currently the Administrative Secretary of the Kuki Christian Church, Manipur, India. He was interviewed in his office, Imphal, on 15 February 2008.
173. Hawlngam Haokip, *Good News for Manipur* (Imphal: Kuki Baptist Convention, 1995), 32.

tion. Dena points out, "the American Baptists resorted, in most cases, to the separation of Christians from the adherents of traditional animism and secluded them in a separate village by careful control of the social atmosphere and prevention of external contamination."[174] These evidences show that the early converts were completely separated from the society. Denunciation of the traditional way of life pointed out earlier substantiates this point.

In separating the converts from the society, the missionaries wanted them to be a Self-supporting, Self-governing and Self-propagating church. In his decadal report of achievement the Secretary of the Baptist Missionary Society, India had twelve points in which this was mentioned in the first place.[175] Although it was the aim, it however appeared that the actual realization of the policy was not easy and the way in which the indigenous leaders were prepared was more directive than participatory. The difficulty of implementing the policy is reflected in a critique of 'Self-supporting' method as it appeared in 'Notes on Findings':

> There have been two lines that have been mentioned for our work to take as we have sat here yesterday and today. Working *for* the native Christians and working *with* them. I suppose that we all feel the working with them is the right thing and yet in most of our discussions it seems to me that we are taking the line of working *for* them. . . . Can we not set them to work in our administration field and work with them and get behind them?[176]

The nature of missionary-native relationship is expressed even clearer in the words of William Wynd:

---

174. Annual Report of *ABFMS*, 23 November–1 December 1927, quoted in Dena, *Missions and Colonialism*, 101.

175. "The South Lushai Mission" BMS India's Secretary's Report in 1913, 69 preserved at the Regent's Park College, Oxford, UK.

176. "Notes on Findings", Note 1. in *Foreign Mission Policies of American Baptist Foreign Mission Society & Women's American Baptist Foreign Mission Society*, Massachusetts, 1917, 25.

> The missionary is the centre of authority. He alone is responsible for the opening and development of the work, and the native workers who gather around him are the mission employees, who take the foreigner as their model and are content to work under him in a subordinate position.[177]

What is clear from the above is that conversion to Christianity uproots a person from his or her own cultural identity and values.

In the case of chieftainship, it is one of the few cultural practices that remain until the present day but the way in which it is preserved is a problem. We have already discussed this issue in the previous chapter. The point here is that while it is regarded as a fundamental element of a Kuki cultural identity, the autocratic system in a pyramid structure becomes increasingly vulnerable for exploitation and abuse in a society like that of the contemporary Kukis, fast becoming eroded from communitarian cultural values. This is an indication of the absence of *Khankho*, an upholding cultural value of the people. Presumably this happens due to the fact that no chief would prefer to risk his own privileges and no *khochaga* dares to upset the structure by addressing this issue. In the light of these evidences, it can be said that through conversion, a Kuki is uprooted from his or her own cultural identity and even if there is any cultural element that is continued, it is vulnerable for exploitation and abuse in the absence of transformative theology.

4. 6. Christianity from Kuki Identity Viewpoint

Our question at the beginning of this chapter was whether or not the Christian missions among the Kukis had concern for and were committed to issues related to the people's identity? Our study shows that the process of Christianization did not helped the reconstruction of Kuki identity as it did for some other groups. For instance, the construction of a common

---

177. William Wynd, "The Status of Native leaders" 47–50 in *Foreign Mission Policies of American Baptist Foreign Mission Society* & *Women's American Baptist Foreign Mission Society*, Massachusetts, 1917, 47.

language for the Tangkhul Nagas in Manipur further contributed to the formation of a Pan-Naga Identity and similarly, Christianity played a positive role in the reconstruction of what is now known as Mizo in the state of Mizoram. Lalsangkima Pachuau, for instance, in his study of the place and role of religious identity (Christianity) in the Mizo political struggles for recognition concludes that the new religion became a defining factor of the normative structure of Mizo society.[178]

Unlike these two experiences, it was clear that the impact of Christianity on the Kuki identity is rather negative from the people's identity viewpoint. Christianity brought an abrupt end to the traditional life of the people and introduced a new way of life with modern education, which is a common experience of the people in the whole of North-East India, including that of the Nagas and the Mizos. However, what was different in the context of the Kukis, and hence became part of the factor contributing to the present identity struggle, is that Christianity did not help reconstruct their identity in the new setting, as it did for other groups highlighted above. Conversion, understood within a Western worldview as involving individuals embracing faith without reference to the traditional bonds of kinship and community, resulted in new forms of spirituality and theology which do not take into consideration issues of the people's identity and existence as a group in a multi-ethnic context. There are two possible reasons for this and we shall discuss them briefly.

4. 6. 1. The Way in which Christianity Came

The work of evangelization among the Kukis, if not unplanned, was certainly not the top priority of the missionaries. In the northern part of Manipur, it came to them like crumbs fallen from a rich man's table and Kukis as a people group had not been the mission focus until the early part of the twentieth century. Moreover, when Christianity and its consequent changes first came, it came through ordinary villagers including the youth converts through the schools and not the chiefs and their counsellors, which disrupted the social order. In addition, after the suppression of their chiefs, the Kukis did not have an equal share of benefits from the

---

178. Pachuau, *Ethnic Identity*.

missionaries with their fellow hill tribes. Crozier, the newly recruited missionary, was assigned to work among the Kukis while Pettigrew remained among the Tangkhuls with the responsibility for education. The misfortune of the Kukis soon came when Crozier left Manipur in 1932 due to the conflict between him and Pettigrew. The presence of Crozier for the people was crucial so that his leaving, in Downs' opinion, could be interpreted as "the victory of anti-Kuki forces within the church."[179] In Crozier's leaving the people lost a leader for their newly-founded Christian society. Crozier, a medical officer during the Kuki Punitive Measures turned a missionary among the Kukis, learned the language and with the help of Ngulhao Thomsong, one of the first converts, translated the New Testament in Thado-Kuki. Earlier, in the southern part of Manipur, Crozier worked with the NEIGM.[180]

Like those in the north, Christianity came to the Kukis in the southern part of Manipur accidentally. The people in this region were the neglected group. Culturally they were closer to those in Mizoram, their neighbouring state, but they were not part of Mizoram and the missionaries in that region could not help them. Politically they were part of Manipur but they were not part of the tribal group for whom the official missionary, Pettigrew, worked. Having observed their situation in that setting, Watkin Roberts came to the Kukis in the southern part of Manipur with the justification that there was no work among them. It can be said that in the southern part of Manipur, Christianity came through the back door. This caused conflict between Roberts and the American Baptist Mission, the official mission in Manipur, in the person of a British missionary, Pettigrew. Roberts was regarded as an intruder, unrecognized and his work unnecessary. Consequently his converts were not well accepted either by the government or the missionaries and he was removed. As a result, the people did not have proper shepherding as did the Naga Christians in the northern part of Manipur under Pettigrew who enjoyed the support of the government.

---

179. Quoted in Vaiphei, *Coming of Christianity*, 32.
180. Vaiphei, *Advent of Christian Mission*, 115.

In such a crucial time of transition from traditional to modern, one of the drawbacks for having a missionary late, or not having well-organized mission activities, was the absence of proper guidance for the newly-founded Christian society. The intensification of clannish spirit through the Bible translation referred to earlier was one good example. In contrary, for instance, Duhlian or Lushai dialect in the Lushai Hills was developed for those in the region to what is now called Mizo. For the Tangkhul Nagas, the missionaries have created a common dialect out of unintelligible diverse dialects spoken in the region. U. M. Fox in his report writes, "Nearly all the villages differ in dialect and have difficulty in understanding each other. Ukhrul through its Mission tends to unify the language by making its dialect universal for the tribe."[181]

The possibility of forming a common language for the Kuki groups in Manipur is seen in the fact that they all understand each other, particularly the dialect that was then called Thado-Kuki dialect. This is indicated in the report of the editor of Assam Baptist Mission Conference of the Assam Baptist Foreign Mission Society 1913: "By means of the Thado dialect not only the Kuki Naga but many other tribes can be reached."[182] The same was observed by Pettigrew when he said:

> The extraordinary thing that strikes one is the predominance of the Thado language among all these many and varied branches. Even the Kabui Nagas who occupy a good number of the villages to the north and south of the Cachar road, and whose population is estimated at about 6000, use the Thado language in intercourse with village and village. Thado is no doubt the *lingua franca* for all these branches of Kukis and Lushai who occupy this region, and there is no doubt that whenever mission work is established in these sections, Thado should be the medium of instruction for all. Whoever reduces

---

181. "Ukhrul Field Report 1913" Presented to the 12th Biennial Session. *ABMC of the ABFMS*, 1913, 59–61 in *History of Christianity in Manipur*, 45.
182. "Report About Mission in Manipur (1913)", Abstract from the editor's 'A Survey of the Field' *ABMC of the ABFMS*, 1913, 5–6; 16–17 in *History of Christianity in Manipur*, 37.

the language to writing, and produces literature, will not only reach the Thado clan, but the many and varied clans that cover the southern and western hills of Manipur.[183]

Despite such a possibility of developing a common language out of the different dialects, which are intelligible to each other, the gaps between the dialects were widened by the Bible translation into those dialects. In the absence of a far-sighted leader who could look far into the future of the people and prepare them accordingly in a multi-ethnic context such as the hills of Manipur, the Kuki people got trapped under the problem of disintegration in their search for the Word of God. In other words, the work of evangelization, which was carried out solely for conversion of the soul did not prepare the people for the questions with regard to their identity. Dena, a historian from the local community, asks if the present state of church disunity could be attributed to Roberts' activities. He asks, "Could this [Roberts' background and way of working] be the reason why the mission and churches he planted have been suffering from internal contradictions and splits even till today?"[184] Roberts was adventurous but lacked management skill.

A second problem with regard to the way in which Christianity came was the uncritical relationship between the colonial administration and Christianity, making spiritual conversion often a change of loyalty to that of the rulers at the same time. Dena observes this in the case of the Kukis during the World War I.

It is interesting to note that all through the uprising the Christian Kukis had not only sided with the government but also acted as the means of influencing the non-Christian Kukis to volunteer for the war service. In fact, one leading Kuki evangelist, Ngulhao, the native evangelist, had mobilized as many as 500 non-Christian Kukis for the first Labour Corps.[185]

---

183. "Ukhrul Field Report for 1913" 56–59 by William Pettigrew, *ABMC of the ABFMS*, 1913, 58.
184. Dena, *In Search of Identity*, 57.
185. William Pettigrew's pamphlet "Twenty-five Years, 1897–1922", Ukhrul Mission School (1922), 14 quoted in Dena, *Missions and Colonialism*, 40.

Having converted through the missionaries, the local converts considered the war of the colonial administration as their own, and fully supported and cooperated with the warfare while the non-Christians, led by the Kuki chiefs, showed an indifferent attitude towards the movement and this finally resulted in the 'Anglo-Kuki war.' The local converts began to look with disgust at their traditional values through the glasses of their new masters. They acted and even preached that their ancestors were 'savages', 'head-hunters', so as to make their fellow tribesmen ashamed of their past.[186] The early Christian experiences had painted the picture of Christianity identical with the European colonial imperialism among the Kukis and hence paved the way for the development of negative attitude toward their own cultural identity. Sadly, in spite of Stanley's observation that the "Western culture had lost its self-confidence, and as a result missionary thinking entered the period of profound re-evaluation which has continued to the present day"[187] such notion still is a reality among the Kuki people. The danger of this is explained by George E. Tinker in the context of the American Indians when he talks in terms of participating in one's own cultural genocide by accepting what he calls 'new cultural model' or internalizing the illusion that whites are superior to the American Indians.[188]

4. 6. 2. Lack of Integral Approach to Theology

With due recognition of the importance of spiritual conversion and its transforming impact on the people in the past, present and the future, the absence of an integral approach to theology was one weakness for the missionaries. This is well spelled out by Franklin when he, prompted by the conviction that the Second Coming of Christ was soon, writes, "In all our planning let us constantly remember that our task is essentially

---

186. Lal Dena, "Patterns of Leadership in a Changing Hmar (Mizo) Society" quoted in Lal Dena, *Missions and Colonialism*, 110.
187. Stanley, *The Bible and the Flag*, 167.
188. George E. Tinker, *Missionary Conquest: The Gospel and Native American Cultural Genocide* (Minneapolis: Fortress Press, 1993), 2.

spiritual."[189] This kind of theology, particularly in the southern part of Manipur, can be regarded as an echo of the Welsh Revival in 1904 which came via Meghalaya and Mizoram. For instance, Vanlalchuanawma observes the theme of the second stirring revival in Mizoram as "combining in it the Cross of Christ, Christian Love, the Holy Spirit and the End Time or the Second Coming."[190] And accordingly he observes the most popular hymns were those referring to the time of Christ's Return such as, 'The Lord is coming by and by: Be ready when He comes,' 'Lo! He comes with clouds descending' and 'Oh my comrades, see the signal waving in the sky!'[191] The theme of the Second Coming of Christ and expectation of the nearness of the event was influenced by the missionaries, Fraser in the north[192] and Lorrain in the south of the Lushai Hills. Katie Jones observes, "The Second Coming is the subject of greatest interest in these hills now and it seems Mr Lorrain of Lungleh has preached a lot about it."[193] A direct influence of such theology on the people was reported as follows; "Many people disposed of their clothes except those they were wearing and of their tools for cultivation, stopped working in their jhums [shifting cultivation], resorted to continuous meetings, singing and dancing, awaiting the coming King."[194]

The belief in the nearness of the Second Coming of Christ promoted the practical work of evangelization. The Assam Mission report in 1923 writes, "The near approach of the Lord's coming as indicated in the dreams and visions related by many from each area led to an earnest desire

---

189. J. H. Franklin, "Missionary Objectives as seen by the societies" 40–43 in *Foreign Mission Policies of American Baptist Foreign Mission Society and Women's American Baptist Foreign Mission Society*, Massachusetts, 1917, 41.

190. Vanlalchhuanawma, *Christianity*, 200.

191. Vanlalchhuanawma, refers to *Kristian Hlabu* (Church Hymn), 1986, Nos. 202, 204, & 376 respectively translated from SSS, Nos. 182, 161 & 669. Vanlalchhuanawma, *Christianity*, 201.

192. Fraser's reply to the Director's questionnaire dt. 9.10.1907 explaining why he preferred working abroad to ministering at home, reads, 'a distinct and powerful conviction that I am disobeying Jesus by not offering myself for service among the heathen. If I disobey Him in this I know I shall not be able to stand before Him and hear Him say, "Why didn't you go?"' quoted in Vanlalchhuanawma, *Christianity*, 201.

193. Katie Jones' letter to Mr Williams dt. 15.4.1913, quoted in Vanlalchhuanawma, *Christianity*, 202.

194. Vanlalchhuanawma, *Christianity*, 207.

to form themselves into parties, and sometimes one only would feel a call to go alone to a village or a group of villages and preach the gospel of God's grace."[195] Thangkai, one of the first native converts writes about his own experience:

> Ka Pathian thugen haw chu zia hi ahi deupen hi. John 3:16 kasimua, Pathian thu awi un thawi le kithawi takiun. Thitha le ho diak kiu. Pathian thu la awi u chun, van gam lam a khin kumkhawtuang hinna a um ding la hiu, tin ka gen ka gen mai sek ui. Chule kuale cha thu awi tapoh chu hingzingin tin kuale Cha thu awi lo chu thin a, tin le ka gen ui.[196]

> [Translation: What we preach was mainly this. We read John 3:16 and preached to them to obey (or worship) God and to stop performing sacrifices. Also, we preached to them to stop appeasing evil spirits and said if you obey the word of God you will have everlasting life. Whosoever believes in the Son will live forever but whoever does not believe in Him will die].

T. Jamthang rightly pointed out that the concept of lost soul and the emphasis on its vital importance came with the coming of Christianity.[197] This observation was well supported by the testimony of Rev Ngamjalhun Baite, one of the first converts at Loikhai Village, southern part of Manipur, when he says, "I used to stand on high raised platforms in the village and shout 'stop sacrificing to the evil spirits, it will be like the days of Noah'."[198] The above experiences reflect the dominant belief among the people that spiritual conversion was the prime concern of theology even to the present day. It may be remembered at this point that the missionaries, particularly

---

195. Katie Jones' letter to Mr Williams dt. 15.4. 1913, quoted in Vanlalchhuanawma, *Christianity*, 202.
196. Thangkai, '*Bagnti'n a hung kipandawk em* (How did it happened)' 7–8 in *Rest*, 7. Thangkai was the first local convert from South Manipur.
197. Haokip, *Manipur a Gospel*, 1.
198. Rev Ngamjalhun Baite also added to say that he recited those words without knowing what they actually meant. He was interviewed at the residence of the researcher, K. Salbung, Churachandpur, Manipur on 22nd February, 2008.

Roberts and Fraser were connected to the Keswick Convention one way or another. Keswick emphasizes more on personal holiness, evangelism that paved the way for faith-mission movements, non defilement with the concerns of the world such as politics. Unlike the earlier type of premillennialism during the nineteenth century where afterlife was understood in terms of 'restitution of all things' or a belief in an establishment of God's kingdom on a renovated earth populated by resurrected human beings rather than for the soul to go to heaven after an individual's death[199], this kind of theology makes the people inactive and non-participatory in the societal life of a person and makes them only to wait for the *Parousia*. It was true that Roberts unswervingly worked against a form of slavery in Mizoram; however, it was also true that in the early twentieth-century evangelical theology, the soul of a person was taken to be more important than his or her physical body.

Related to this was the teaching of the church, promoting a Christian passivist attitude toward political administration. A monthly publication of the North East India General Mission, *The Herald of Truth*, October 1942 includes a well-articulated article on a Christian understanding of war called, *Kristian leh indona,* or a Christian and War. There were three main points that the article argued: (1) God is a warrior or God is the God who fights in a war. This point was drawn from the story of God's deliverance of Israel recorded in Exodus 15:3; (2) one could be at the will of God in a war situation by seeking and following God's leading. This point was drawn from 2 Samuel 5:19 wherein David asked for God's direction in a war and this was further exemplified by the fact that in the New Testament, Matthew 8:5ff, Jesus did not refuse to accept the faith of the Roman Centurion nor did he stop being a soldier after his confession of faith in Him; and finally (3) government is an instrument in God's hands to punish wrong doers. The point is based on Romans 13:3–4 wherein rulers are said to have represented God in punishing the wrong doings and the example used for this was a conviction that God used Great Britain to punish Hitler. Having followed the three points, the application of this

---

199. Martin Spence, "The Restitution of all Things in Nineteenth-century Evangelical Premillennialism" 349–359 in Peter Clarke and Tony Claydon eds., *The church, the afterlife and the fate of the soul* (Suffolk: The Boydell Press, 2009), 349.

article was clear: to accept the given structure. This was done by uncritically reaffirming, "give to Caesar what is Caesar's, and to God what is God's (Matt 22:21)" and "submit yourselves for the Lord's sake to every authority instituted among men (1 Pet 2:14–15)."[200]

The problems with this kind of theology can be seen in the fact that there is a dichotomy between the Old and the New Testament – that was why the gospels were translated into many local dialects and by being so, it often neglects a prophetic role in theology in relation to issues of justice, social evils, structural sins, and so forth. Secondly, it was a ready-made theology that was developed by those outside the region in response to their own contextual questions, and thirdly, it was not a theology that was developed by and for the people in response to their contextual questions.

The question which this chapter attempts to answer is whether or not Christianity, as understood and practiced among the Kuki people, was concern about and committed to the people's identity which includes their culture, history, ancestors' land and territory. Our studies show that these concerns were not included in the missionary agenda, and hence, they were not taken into consideration in the articulation of a Christian theology. To put it simply, the Kukis do not yet have a relevant Christian theology that will help them respond to their identity issues. The uncritical application of the Christian message for ethnocentric purposes, for instance, is one example of this situation as an eminent Kuki Church leader, Hawlngam Haokip, observes: "The Christianity which had been a persecuted religion has become the official religion of the hill tribals. However, in the plain areas, especially among the Meiteis, Christianity is still treated as a low caste or tribal religion and not yet welcome by the plain people."[201]

4. 6. 3. Opportunities and Scopes

Our evaluation of Christianity from the people's identity viewpoint was more negative than positive in terms of harm it has done to the people's cultural practices. However, in the post conversion, Christianity also provides an opportunity and means for the people to reconstruct and preserve their

---

200. *The Herald of Truth*, October 1942, 5–6.
201. Haokip, *Good News for Manipur*, 33.

identity that have yet to be utilized. First, Christianity enables the people to belong to a global Christian community. If it was not for Christianity, the people might not have had a chance to be known to the outside world, especially if they happened to be Sanskritized with the assimilative ideology of *Hindutva*. The truth is that Christianity brings the good news in Christ, which liberates the people and makes them equal members of the universal community. The problem is the way in which the missionaries, and for that matter their converts, understood the message and communicated it to the people.

Second, although not their priority, in their attempts to propagate their faith, the missionaries reduced the local language to a written form for the Kuki people. At first, they translated the four gospels, Christian pamphlets, songs and finally the whole Bible. It was true that the Bible translation works among the similar dialect speaking groups had unintended negative impact on their unity, the written language itself was an irreplaceable gift from the missionaries for the people. For this reason, Downs is right in observing, "the missionaries provided the vehicle of the new identity, a written language and literature, and the means of acquiring the skills necessary to accommodate themselves to the new situation, education."[202] The need is to articulate theology in the light of contextual resources, using 'the vehicle' provided by the missionaries, which would give room to the people's culture and values without detaching them from the global church. A pioneer in developing such a local theology in the Indian sub-continent is Dalit theology with which we shall now turn to interact in the next chapter.

---

202. Frederick Downs, "Administrators, Missionaries and a World Turned Upside Down: Christianity as a Tribal Response to change in North-East India," in his book, *Essays in Christianity in North-East India* (New Delhi: Indus Publishing Company, 1994), 180.

Part Three

A Theological Response

CHAPTER 5

Dalit Theology in Response to Dalit Struggle for Identity

The tribal people of North-East India accepted Christianity in the form presented to them by western missionaries and, as a result, have suffered the loss of their own culture, and struggle to discover a sense of dignity and identity. In this situation there is an urgent need for a critical evaluation of the theological foundations of Christianity among the tribal people as well as the development of local theology, which will draw on aspects of both the Kuki heritage and the Bible. In this task, there are significant lessons to be learned from the struggle of Dalit Christians in India who have found themselves in a similar situation and have provided an innovative and creative theological response.

With the initiation of A. P. Nirmal in the late 1960s, Dalit theology began to take its shape and grew as an ecumenical movement. One significant development in this movement was the establishment of the Centre for Dalit/Sabaltern Studies in Delhi (CDS) under the leadership of James Massey, a prominent Dalit theologian, which is devoted to research and publications including Bible commentaries from Dalit perspective.

A study of Dalit theology is important for this study for three reasons. Firstly, both Dalits and tribals suffer oppression under the same hierarchical social structure of the Indian caste system. However, their experiences have not been taken into consideration in the articulation of theology in India. Secondly, it was in response to this situation that Dalit theology emerged as an alternative theology to both traditional Indian Christian theology and Western theology. Dalit theology has pioneered the construction of theology from the perspective of the marginalized in India. Thirdly, in a search for relevant theology for the people concerned, Dalit theology, like other liberation theologies, takes the socio-political and religio-economic context very seriously in theological reflection. We shall first present the context within which Dalit theology emerged and then discuss the methodology, which is an integral part of the theology itself. The final section will be an evaluation from a tribal perspective with a view to identify ways in which a tribal theology can be enriched by and differ from Dalit theology in response to the issue of identity in the tribal context of North-East India.

5. 1. The Context of Dalit Theology

5. 1. 1. The Caste System and Dalit Oppression

In order to understand Dalit theology and its methodological issues, it is important to highlight the context in which the theology emerges, as it is a given context that shapes the nature of theology, its method, and the tone of its expression.

The emergence of Dalit theology has to do with both the caste system and 'Christianity' as understood and practised in India. Caste system, the 'hidden apartheid',[1] possibly the longest surviving social system in the world, was the background from which Dalit theology emerged in the later part of the twentieth century. The term 'caste', which appeared first in Spanish and later in Portuguese, denotes 'rigid social divisions in India.'[2] It is called *jati* in Sanskrit and that literally means 'birth' denoting communities and sub-communities in India. The caste system, or *varna* which means 'arrangement' in Sanskrit, is a hierarchical structure consisting of four castes which is said to have originated through the writings of the Aryans some three thousand or a little more years ago in what is known as the oldest Scriptures, the Rig Vedas.[3]

The second source is the *Manusmriti*, or 'Laws of Manu', a Hindu holy legal code that outlined the social hierarchical order governing Hindu society into four castes as referred to above. The division is based on one's birth and occupation. Brahmins who were said to have been born from the head

---

1. The report of Human Rights Watch, "Hidden Apartheid: Caste Discrimination against India's 'Untouchability'" to the UN Committeee on the Elimination of Racial Discrimination in 2007. http://www.hrw.org/reports/2007/india0207/ [Accessed 9 October 2008].
2. *The Oxford Reference Dictionary* (Oxford: Clarendon Press, 1986), 137.
3. *India's Broken People: Three Documentary films*, DVD, dir. Michael Lawson, marketed and distributed by Authentic Media, 2005.

of Brahman, or God, are responsible for religious duties; the Kshatriyas, from the chest of Brahman, are the warriors and their duty is to protect the people; the Vaishya, from the thigh of Brahman, are the merchants or money lenders; and the Sudras, from the feet of God, are the manual labourers who are to provide service.[4] The groups which are not included in these four castes are called outcaste Dalits and tribals. The caste system is theologically defined by the Hindu Scriptures, the *Vedas,* and they are codified and legalized by Manu, the Hindu law giver, and effectively justify the oppression of the so-called outcaste Dalits and tribals.[5] Pacifying the gravity of its oppression, some from within Hindu religion, argue that the caste system is not hereditary nor is *Manusmriti* a primary scripture.[6] Whatever may be the argument, the fact is that in this structure, Dalits, and for that matter the tribals, are incessant victims of the system.

As far as the four castes of Hinduism are concerned, Dalits and for that matter tribals are not created from the body of God and hence they are nameless groups. The term 'untouchable' was a common name used to refer to them. Reacting against the practice of untouchability Gandhiji proposed a new term, *Harijan,* 'children of God' for Dalits, the term which was already used by Narasimha Mehta to refer to the children born from Dalit women used by the Hindu priests in the temples,[7] often uncritically called 'temple prostitutes'.[8] In his attempt to remove untouchability Gandhi's target was to change the hearts of the people and not the system. Critique of Gandhiji's approach to untouchability will be shown later. At this point, we can note the fact that by not changing the system, Dalits remained outside the Indian socio-religious order hence,

---

4. V. Jayaram, "The Hindu Caste System" in http://www.hinduwebsite.com/hinduism/h_caste.asp [Accessed 18 November 2008]; D'souza, *Dalit Freedom,* 33–34.

5. D'souza, *Dalit Freedom,* 33.

6. "Hindu and Caste System", www://vhp.org.uk/vhpcms/index.php?Itemid=44&id=27&option=com_content&task=view [Accessed 14 November 2008].

7. V. Devasahayam, "Identity in Theology" 13–19 in Devasahayam, ed. *Frontiers of Dalit Theology* (New Delhi: ISPCK/Gurukul, 1997), 13.

8. A prostitute according to the Oxford Reference Dictionary is "a woman who engages in sexual intercourse for payment" indicating one's own willingness to use her or his body for payment. See, Joyce M. Hawkins, ed. *The Oxford Reference Dictionary* (Oxford: Clarendon Press, 1986), 666. To the contrary, the condition of Dalit women in the temples is neither for payment nor of their own choice.

instead of liberating them, the new name showed contempt for Dalits. Devasahayam rightly puts it: "They are called children of God without the right to enter into the House of God [the Hindu temples]."[9] During the British Colonial period, the phrase 'depressed classes' was used, later 'Scheduled Caste' for the first time in 1935, and the same was adopted by the Indian Constitution in 1950. The term Dalit is a recent name, against all the imposed names, accepted and used by the people themselves. The exact number of Dalits is difficult to ascertain. Sometimes, it is used to include other oppressed groups including the Scheduled Tribes (STs) and Other Backward Castes (OBCs); however, in political usage, it refers to the Scheduled Castes numbering about 138 million people, which is 15.8 per cent of the Indian population.[10]

Dalits have been denied of their rights and equality with others in India. At the Second Round Table Conference in London in 1931, B. R. Ambedkar proposed a separate electorate for Dalits to elect their own representative to the legislature, which was granted by the British Government. His argument was based on the fact that only the 'Untouchables' can represent the 'Untouchables'. However, the attempt ended in vain in 1932 as a result of Gandhi's opposition based on his [Gandhi] assumption that such a provision would weaken the vision of Indian union between the Muslims and the Hindus which he was aiming to achieve.[11] Hence, instead of a separate electorate, they were given 148 seats against 78 with no assurance of reservations in services. Because of this, although some people praise him,[12] Gandhi's commitment for the cause of Dalits, from

---

9. Devasahayam, "Identity in Theology", 13.

10. Ghanshyam Shah, "Introduction: Dalit Politics" 17–43 in Ghanshyam Shah, ed. *Dalit Identity and Politics* (New Delhi: Sage Publications, 2001), 17–18. D'Souza estimated the population of Sudras 50–52 per cent, and of 'Untouchable' 16–25 per cent of India's total population. See, D'souza, *Dalit Freedom*, 34. The issue is discussed further under the "Sources of Dalit Theology".

11. Bhagwan Das, "Reservations Today and Tomorrow" 234–275 in Walter Fernandes, ed. *The Emerging Dalit Identity: The Re-Assertion of the Subalterns* (New Delhi: Indian Social Institute, 1996), 234. Das served as the Director of Asian Centre for Human Rights and an Advocate at the Supreme Court of India.

12. For instance, see Bindeshwar Pathak, "Gandhi, Ambedkar and Sulabh" 198–208 in Walter Fernandes, ed. *The Emerging Dalit Identity: The Re-Assertion of the Subalterns* (New Delhi: Indian Social Institute, 1996), 198–208.

a Dalit viewpoint, has been debatable. Ambedkar felt that Gandhi "did not give as much importance to the removal of Untouchability as he did to the propagation of Khadi and Hindu-Muslim unity."[13] Webster makes it clearer when he writes, "Gandhi sought these [removal of untouchability and its accompanying disabilities] largely by changing the hearts of caste Hindus without destroying the prevailing socio-religious order."[14] Unlike Ambedkar's political approach to the problem of untouchability, Gandhi's was more in tune with the traditional concept of *varna* system wherein he sought to make the duties of Dalits more honourable, rather than changing the caste structure.[15] This is the point where Gandhi appears to have addressed the problem of Dalit oppression without tackling it at its root, which is the oppressive caste structure. In fact, although Gandhi worked tirelessly toward abolition of untouchability, his attitude toward Dalits appears rather derogatory. In his conversation with John Mott, a well-known leader in mission movements, he asked: "Would you preach the gospel to a cow? Well, some of the Untouchables are worse than cows in understanding. I mean they can no more distinguish between the relative merits of Islam and Hinduism and Christianity than a cow."[16]

Another instance is the so-called reservation. The Constitution of India provided reservations or quotas for the Scheduled Caste and Scheduled Tribes for education and jobs. There were 429 castes included in that category in the Government of India Act, 1935. The Constitution (Scheduled Caste) Order of 1950, which includes the 'untouchables' professing Hinduism and another four castes from Sikh community, was extended to all 'untouchables' professing Sikhism in 1956. In 1990, it was further amended to include those professing Buddhism. There was no further amendment to include in the Scheduled Caste Order the Dalits who are

---

13. Eleanor Zelliot, *From Untouchable to Dalit: Essays on the Ambedkar Movement* (New Delhi: Manohar, 1992), 103.
14. John C. B. Webster, *Religion and Dalit Liberation: An Examination of Perspectives* (New Delhi: Manohar, 2002), 57.
15. Babara Joshi, quoted in Sudha Pai, "From Harijans to Dalit: Identity Formation, Political Consciousness and Electoral Mobilisation of the Scheduled Castes in Uttar Pradesh" 258–287 in Ghanshyam Shah, ed. *Dalit Identity and Politics* (New Delhi: Sage Publications, 2001), 261.
16. Quoted in Webster, *Religion and Dalit*, 57.

professing Christianity.[17] It is also interesting to note that the practice of 'untouchability' was legally abolished by Article 17 of the Constitution of India however, nowhere in the Constitution or in the Protection of Civil Rights Acts, 1955 is the term defined.[18]

In this setting, the experience of Dalits has been that of a denial of basic human rights and dignity. For Ambedkar, the main problem for Dalits under this structure was that of misery which operates at three levels: physical misery caused by poverty, mental misery caused by the disregard of human dignity, and finally, spiritual misery caused by guilt and sin.[19] James Massey points out the impact of the system on the Dalit psyche. He quotes the first report of the Commissioner:

> By the force of habit the Harijan (Dalit) has lost his self-respect to such an extent that he regards his work to which his caste is condemned not as a curse from which he should extricate himself, but as a privilege . . . , which he must protect. He has not much courage to seek another job in a field or a factory. He has thus become lazy in mind and body and callous to his own condition; and he will not educate his children.[20]

This report reveals the fact that the system has been internalized and accepted even by the Dalits themselves and by accepting the status quo they work against their own life and dignity as human beings. For this reason Massey concludes, "This system [caste system] is capable of drawing

---

17. Das, "Reservations", 236.
18. Ibid., 235.
19. Webster, *Religion and Dalit*, 67.
20. The Indian Constitution empowers the government to appoint a special officer to investigate all matters relating to the safeguards provided for the Scheduled Castes and Scheduled Tribes who would report to the President for further action. The first officer was L. M. Shrikant appointed in November 1950 and he reported his investigation in 1951. Quoted in James Massey, *Down Trodden: The Struggle of India's Dalits for identity, solidarity and liberation* (Geneva: WCC Publications, 1997), 25. Webster discusses in more detail the psychological impact of the Caste system on Dalits and argues that religion plays a healing role in that situation. See, Webster, *Religion and Dalit*, 120–146.

persons into a kind of self-captivity, a slavery from which it seems almost impossible to be liberated."[21]

It was in such a situation of oppression that Dalits had a new vision for equality[22] and sought for liberation from the system through various means. George Oommen, a well-known Indian church historian observes three different ways in which the Dalits have sought for liberation: one, by integrating themselves into the colonial system by joining the army or by serving as labourers in British colonies; two, by choosing Sanskritization as a means of upward mobility; and three, and the most prominent means, was mass conversion to non-Hindu religions which began during the second half the nineteenth century.[23]

Similarly, Webster observes three ways in which Dalits have sought for liberation from caste oppression. One, a strategy of Sanskritization wherein, as Oommen points out, some Dalits integrated themselves and worked for social justice within the structure but with no satisfying result; two, strategy of resistance by which he meant those who sought to preserve Dalit culture within Hinduism; and three, a strategy of self-redefinition, that is, those who reject the Brahminic definition of who they are and their place in the social order.[24] It is here that Dalit scholars including Kancha Ilaiah argue that Dalits, and for that matter, tribals, are not Hindus.[25] The main mass conversion to a non-Hindu religion during the mid-twentieth century has been the Neo-Buddhist movement wherein Bhimrao Ramji Ambedkar, in search of dignity as humans, led his people into Buddhism

---

21. Massey, *Down Trodden*, 25. Massey explains the oppression as four layers of colonization, that is, the Aryan, the Muslims, the British and the high caste colonization. See, Massey, *Down Trodden*, 12–28.

22. The vision was to dismantle the oppressive and hierarchical caste system and bring about equality among all people. See, Gail Omvedt, *Dalit Visions: The anti-caste movement and the construction of an Indian identity* (Hyderabad: Orient Longman Limited, 1995); S. M. Michael, "Dalit Vision of a Just Society in India" 99–117 in S. M. Michael ed. *Dalits in Modern India: Vision and Values* (New Delhi: Vistaar Publications, 1999).

23. George Oommen, "The Emerging Dalit Theology: A Historical Appraisal" 19–37 *Indian Church History Review*, Vol. XXXIV, Number 1 (June 2000), 22 & 23. Paraphrased.

24. Webster, *Religion and Dalit*, 82.

25. See, Kancha Ilaiah, *Why I am Not a Hindu: A Sudra Critique of Hindutva Philosophy, Culture and Political Economy*. Second Edition. (Kolkata: Mandira Sen for Samya, 2005).

in the 1950s.²⁶ In Zelliot's view, this move was motivated by a desire to reject Hinduism and consequently, the status of Untouchables and to establish a religion, that is, Buddhism, which would serve as a bulwark against [for] communism, and to which all Indians could eventually turn.²⁷ For Ambedkar, "religion is not just ideals but also the actual living practice of religion [social equality or *dharma*²⁸] that are important to Dalits."²⁹ Having analyzed the movement, Omvedt rightly defines the Dalit struggle against caste discriminations as 'valued-oriented.'³⁰

5. 1. 2. The Neglect of Dalit Experience in Indian Christian Theology

As already indicated, the emergence of Dalit theology also has to do with 'Christianity' itself. Similar to the Neo-Buddhist movement, there were mass movements or conversions to Christianity in the nineteenth century in order to escape from the oppressive caste structure. George Oommen's study of the Travancore Pulaya mass conversion movement to Anglicanism in the latter half of nineteenth century, concludes, "For thousands, conversion was an act of social protest heralding exit from the inhumanity of the caste system."³¹ Conversion of Dalits to Christianity has continued so that they now make up 65 to 75 per cent of the Christian population in India.³²

---

26. In 1961, Ambedkar led 3,200,333 Dalits, mostly the Mahars of Maharasthra, into Buddhism and as a result, they formed 87.16 per cent of the entire Buddhist population of India. Census of India 1971 quoted in Webster, *Religion and Dalit*, 83. Ambedkar was converted into Buddhism in Nagpur on 14 October 1956 along with other Dalits estimating 300,000 to 600,000. Zelliot, *From Untouchable to Dalit*, 126.

27. Zelliot, *From Untouchable to Dalit*, 137. Ambedkar already had an interest in Buddhism when a Bombay teacher gave him a copy of the life of Buddha at the occasion of his passing matriculation examination in 1908. The problem with Hinduism is that it has been equated with Brahmanic tradition by using Hindu Scriptures namely, Rigveda. See, Omvedt, *Dalit Visions*; Savarkar, *Hindutva*.

28. Ambedkar's writings and speeches quoted in Webster, *Religion and Dalit*, 50.

29. Webster, *Religion and Dalit*, 52.

30. Gail Omvedt, *Dalits and the Democratic Revolution: Dr Ambedkar and the Dalit Movement in Colonial India* (New Delhi: Sage Publications, 1994), 13.

31. George Oommen, "Dalit Conversion and Social Protest in Travancore, 1854–1890" 69–84 in *Bangalore Theological Forum*, Vol. XXVII, Nos. 3 and 4 (Sept–Dec. 1996), 84.

32. Lancy Lobo, "Dalit Religious Movements and Dalit Identity" 166–183 in Walter Fernandes ed. *The Emerging Dalit Identity: The Re-Assertion of the Subalterns* (New Delhi:

Within Christianity, the problem is that despite the dominant presence of Dalits in the church, traditional Indian Christian theology has not considered the experiences of Dalits in its articulation and expression of theology. Theology in India was dominated by Western Christianity and when it was contextualized, it was done in the light of the Brahminic tradition. Robin Boyd points out how Western Christianity dominated the church in India, a domination reflected not only in external aspects, such as architecture and liturgies, but also in attitudes, modes of thought and theology.[33] He argues, "In church architecture, church organisation, church services, church music and church publications, western forms and attitudes still seem to predominate"[34] His observation on the syllabus of theological colleges in India is more interesting:

The teaching given in theological colleges throughout India has been, and still is, dominated by western theology, as a glance at any syllabus will show. The result is that the preaching of the average Indian minister or evangelist reflects the western theological categories in which he has been trained.[35]

Added to this was, when theology was contextualized, that it was done in the light of Brahminic tradition. A cursory look at traditional Indian Christian theology will make this point clearer. To begin with, a theological reflection in India from an Indian perspective as such was initiated not by the Christians but by the Hindus, like Ram Mohan Roy and Keshub Chunder Sen, the leaders of the Hindu cultural renaissance in the nineteenth century. While Roy incorporated the moral teaching of Jesus, Sen interpreted the Christian trinity in terms of the Vedantic understanding of God, *Brahman* as *sat-chit-ananda* (truth-consciousness-bliss). Taking their clue from them, Indian Christian theologians began their

---

Indian Social Institute, 1996), 166. It is not possible to know the exact number of Dalit Christians for two reasons: firstly, there are many believers who have not professed their faith openly for fear of losing the government quotas in children's education or jobs and secondly, calling the movement as 'home coming' some Hindu groups converted Dalits Christians, often by force, to Hinduism.

33. Robin Boyd, *Indian Christian Theology* (New Delhi: ISPCK, 1969). Boyd's book has been reprinted nine times.

34. Boyd, *Indian Christian Theology*, Reprint., 1.

35. Ibid., 1–2.

work of theologizing. Brahmandhav Upadhyaya developed Sen's work and argued for the possibility of being a Christian in India without changing one's cultural identity; that is, a Christian yet remaining a Hindu.[36] The following concepts, including Vengal Chakkarai's 'Christhood of God', Pandipeddi Chenchiah's *'Adi Purusha'*, or Jesus as the original man, and A. J. Appasamy's 'Bhakti', or devotion, were all formulated within the framework of the Hindu Brahminic tradition.[37] Lancy Lobo observes three reasons why Brahminic tradition is glorified: first, a 'downward filtration' theory that suggests if the tip of the pyramid is changed, the rest of the pyramid is changed; second, that "nationalism and patriotism were expressed in Hindu idiom and the church was keen to throw off the colonial baggage and show itself as Indian;" and third, "non-Sanskritic tradition is looked down upon as mumbo-jumbo, low, uncouth, rural, illiterate, backward, superstitious and inferior."[38]

Dalit theology emerged in the later part of 1960s in response to the irrelevance of both Western and traditional Indian Christian theology. The limitations of these theologies are, James Massey observes, while the former is systematic theology and the latter was an effort made by the so-called upper caste converts in response to their faith, Massey contends that both theologies followed the Greek connotation of expression, that is, theology as a study of God, Pure Being or *Brahman*. He quoted John Macquarrie's book, *Christian Theology*, in which Macquarrie mentioned six formative factors of classical (European) Christian theology: experience, revelation, Scripture, tradition, culture and reason. Similarly, the traditional Indian Christian theologians, he observes, have followed classical Hinduism: *pramanas* (authorities), *Sruti* (inspired Scriptures), *anubhava*

---

36. Kirsteen Kim, "India" 44–73 in John Parratt ed. *An Introduction to Third World Theologies* (Cambridge: Cambridge University Press, 2004), 48–49.

37. For detailed discussion of these concepts, see Boyd, *Indian Christian Theology*, Reprint., 110–184.

38. Lancy Lobo, "Visions, Illusions and Dilemmas of Dalit Christians in India" 242–257 in Ghanshyam Shah ed., *Dalit Identity and Politics. Cultural Subordination and the Dalit Challenge*, Vol. 2. (New Delhi: Sage Publications, 2001), 256. I paraphrased. David Smith rightly observes that Indian nationalism arose from the need to drive out the British and Hindu nationalism, in that case, was an important part of the growth of Indian nationalism. David Smith, *Hinduism and Modernity* (Oxford: Blackwell Publishing, 2003), 182–183.

(personal experience of God), and *anumana* (inference or reason). Neither of the two, he argues, has directly to do with human history, which is an important issue for Dalits.[39] Clarke made another interesting observation in his study of the works of two Indian theologians – Khrishna Mohan Banerjea of Bengal (1813–1885) and Bramabandav Upadhyaya (1861–1907) – wherein he observes that the theologians have missed out the historical locatedness of Jesus, which is of a paramount importance for non-Brahmins.[40] In the light of the grassroot experiences of the people, Clarke also asks if it was the caste bias in the minds of those 'high caste' converts that they did not emphasize the historical experiences of Jesus, neglecting the experiences of the majority Indian Christians.[41]

In this situation, the continued experience of oppression in the church was observed by George Oommen who writes, "Although Christianity is an egalitarian religion, the caste system found its way into it in India. Dalit Christians within the church were discriminated and were denied powers within the ecclesiastical structure."[42] Walter Fernandes, a well-known Catholic historian, in his study of Dalit conversion to Christianity in Tamil Nadu in South India observed a similar situation. He writes, "They ['untouchables'] had entered the Church in search of equality. But the upper castes who were already in control of the churches would not grant it to them. In some cases upper castes' refusal prevented conversions."[43] Lobo, another Catholic scholar, observes a clear case in the Pondicherry archdiocese, Tamil Nadu, in South India:

---

39. Massey, *Down Trodden*, 50. For further detail on the castes of the so-called Indian Christian theologians and discussion on the absence of Dalit experience in traditional Indian Christian theology, see James Massey, "Ingredients for a Dalit Theology" 152–157 in R. S. Sugirtharajah and Cecil Hargreaves, eds. *Reading in Indian Christian Theology*. Vol. 1. (London: SPCK, 1993), 152–154.

40. Sathianathan Clarke, "The Jesus of Nineteenth Century Indian Christian Theology: An Indian Inculturation with Continuing Problems and Prospects" 32–46 182 in *Studies in World Christianity*, Vol. 5 Part 1 (1996).

41. Ibid., 40.

42. Oommen, "The Emerging Dalit Theology", 20–21.

43. Walter Fernandes, "Conversion to Christianity, Caste Tension and Search for a New Identity in Tamil Nadu" 140–165 in Walter Fernandes, ed. *The Emerging Dalit Identity: The Re-Assertion of the Subalterns* (New Delhi: Indian Social Institute, 1996), 161.

Dalit Catholics comprise 80 per cent of the population [in the Pondicherry archdiocese] whereas only 10 per cent of the priests are Dalit, and none of them occupy any important post in the archdiocese. In contrast, priests from the other minority upper castes comprise 90 per cent and most of the higher posts in the archdiocesan hierarchy are held by them.[44]

The problem of the caste system is found also in many non-Catholic churches in the 'mainland' India. The experience of Dalit Christians in Guntur District of the state of Andra Pradesh in South India is one example as T. Swami Raju writes:

> Originally the oppressed sections have joined the Church with the hope to get out of this caste structure, but after joining the upper castes in the Church, perhaps they were/are allowed into the church with their caste identity hence this problem still continues troubling the oppressed people.[45]

In this case, Dalit Christians are doubly discriminated: firstly, in conversion to Christianity they lose reservation of jobs or quotas for Dalits, and secondly, they continue to experience unequal treatment in the church because of their background.[46]

The experience of Dalit Christian women is even more complex and pathetic. Webster and others observed that Dalit women were thrice handicapped or thrice alienated: first, on the basis of their gender; second, because of caste; and third, on account of religion. The reason being Christianity remains a religious minority group within the context of Hindu India. Further complexity for a Dalit woman, they observed, lies in the difficulty of functioning at the intersection of three traditions. While both Dalit tradition and the dominant Indian tradition are patriarchal, the men in both the traditions treated women similarly and they, the Dalit women, have to react to them similarly. At the same time, being Dalits,

---

44. Lobo, "Visions, Illusions and Dilemmas", 247.
45. T. Swami Raju, *Vira Cult in Fold Religion of Guntur District: A Dalit Perspective* (New Delhi: ISPCK, 2005), 328.
46. Fernandes, "Conversion to Christianity", 140.

the way in which the dominant Indian tradition defines their identity may not be acceptable to Dalits as a whole and they, as Dalit men and Dalit women, have to react to it together. This is a further complexity, according to Webster et al, which a Dalit woman experiences as a Dalit woman.[47] In such a situation, Dalit women's experience is more complex than that of Dalit men.

At this point, it may be noted that Asian theologians, including those in India, are proud of the cultural plurality of the context and emphasize the need for recognition of the same. For instance, in his attempts to show the divergence of Asian Christian theology from that of Latin America, Tissa Balasuriya asserts that religious plurality is one of the main points of divergence between the two. The births of some of the major world religions, including, Hinduism, Buddhism, and Sikhism are proof of his observation. Balasuriya argues for mutual religious dialogue with no claim of uniqueness of tradition. His conviction is that we know the manifestation of God better through such inter-religious dialogues.[48] This is one reality that is specific to the Asian context. However, here again, the religions of Dalits, and for that matter that of the primal people, are not given equal recognition. Lobo's observation fits well here:

> Religion calls for internal transformation leading to societal transformation. But, unfortunately, religion mostly brings in cultural change once the initial spurt of inner transformation is over. Most sects, cults and denominations that preached equality ended up institutionalising inequality, be it in the form of caste or class.[49]

It was in such a situation of exclusion that Dalit theology emerged as an alternative theology for the marginalized in the latter part of the twentieth

---

47. C. B. Webster et al. *From Role to Identity: Dalit Christian Women in Transition* (New Delhi: ISPCK, 1998), 1.
48. Tissa Balasuriya, "Divergence: An Asian Perspective" 113–119 in *Third World Theologies: Commonalities & Divergence*, K. C. Abraham, ed. (Maryknoll: Orbis Books, 1990), 115.
49. Lobo, "Visions, Illusions and Dilemmas", 257.

century with the efforts made by Dalit theologians including, Arvind P. Nirmal, M. E. Prabhakar, Bishop M. Azariah, K. Wilson, D. Devasahayam and James Massey. There have been different opinions about the nature of Dalit theology. While some, like Devasahayam, argue that it emerges as a counter-ideology,[50] others, like James Massey, do not share this position. Massey's argument is that traditional Indian Christian theology, or systematic theology of the Europeans, was not developed to address the issue of Dalits.[51] Whichever way it may be seen, Dalit theology emerges as the result of the failure on the part of the Indian church to include Dalit experiences in the articulation and expression of theology in India. This is well expressed in Devasahayam's work: "The failure of the caste Christians, to recognise the identity of Dalits in their theological formulations, has occasioned the emergence of Dalit Theology."[52] What the church failed to recognize, for Devasahayam, is the oppression of the caste system, the 'wounded psyche', and articulation of salvation in that context. According to him, in failing to explicate the salvation of Jesus Christ in the context of caste oppression, theology has failed "to arouse in Dalits the consciousness of being in bondage and an urge for liberative struggles."[53] With the same conviction, Massey also points out the situation of Dalit oppression, poverty, suffering, injustice, illiteracy and denial of human dignity and identity, which requires the formulation of Dalit theology.[54] Contrary to this reality, he argues, the theologies of western missionaries and traditional Indian Christian theology are "centred around the ideas, not on actions."[55]

---

50. See, V. Devasahayam, "The Nature of Dalit theology as Counter Ideology" 53–67 in Devasahayam, ed. *Frontiers of Dalit Theology* (New Delhi: ISPCK/Gurukul, 1997), 53–67.
51. Massey, *Down Trodden*, 62.
52. Devasahayam, "Identity in Theology", 15–16.
53. Ibid., 18.
54. Massey, *Down Trodden*, 49.
55. James Massey, "History and Dalit Theology" in Devasahayam, ed. *Frontiers of Dalit Theology* (New Delhi: ISPCK/Gurukul, 1997), 173.

5. 2. Methodological Concerns of Dalit Theology

In Dalit theology, methodology and theology are interrelated. Dalit theology, as an alternative to the traditional Indian Christian theology, attempts to articulate God-experience or theology from the perspective of the marginalized. This means re-imagining God and God's dealings with people, history and the future hope. It is a reversal of the usual approach in theology because, unlike traditional Indian Christian theology, Dalit theology adopts an approach 'from below' and employs sociology rather than philosophy as a methodological tool. Finally, like any other theologies, Dalit theology is a biased theology.

5. 2. 1. Definition of Theology

Dalit theology is a critical reflection of God-experience in the light of Dalit experience of suffering and pain. It draws insights from Liberation theology in Latin America, Black theology of America, Minjung theology of Korea, and so forth. Massey calls them 'sisters'[56] of Dalit theology. The difference between Liberation theology as developed in Latin America and Dalit theology is that while the former attempts to respond to the economic situation of Latin America, the latter relates to the caste system which is peculiar to India. That being the case, Dalit theology has inspiration from Ambedkar, a critic of both Hinduism and Christianity.[57] Secondly, although both the Liberation and the Dalit theologies employed Marxist analysis of society, the immediate context within which Dalit theology emerges was that of the enduring caste oppression. The issue that Dalit theology seeks to address is much older than those of many of the current liberation theologies.

Dalit theology, in this sense, is different from liberation theologies as well as traditional Indian Christian theology. It is a theology from the perspective of those oppressed by the caste system. For this reason, A. P.

---

56. Ibid., 169.
57. See, P. Arokiadoss, "The Significance of Dr Ambedkar for Theologising in India" 290–313 in Devasahayam, ed. *Frontiers of Dalit Theology* (New Delhi: ISPCK/Gurukul, 1997), 290–313. Ambedkar rejected both Hinduism and Christianity on account of caste influence.

Nirmal, a pioneer Dalit theologian understands Dalit theology as a radical discontinuity from, or a counter-theology to, that of traditional Indian Christian theology, arguing, "It [Dalit theology] will represent a radical discontinuity with classical Indian Christian Theology (in) the Brahmin i.e. tradition . . . which needs to be challenged by the emerging Dalit theology. This also means that a Christian Dalit theology will be a counter-theology."[58] The imagery given here is that of a protest.

Different from Nirmal's view, Massey sees Dalit theology as not necessarily a counter-theology. His line of argument is that the traditional Indian Christian theology was not constructed to address the situation of Dalits. For this reason, he would not consider himself an opponent of the traditional Indian Christian theology as long as it does not pretend to be the normative theology for all Indians. For him theology is a "critical reflection on the relation of God and human beings in different historical circumstances."[59] In other words, theology is articulated in the light of people's experience of God in a given context.

The emphases are threefold: the context or environment in which one articulates his or her experience of God; the experience of the people which is the people's history; and the medium or the language through which they speak about that experience in a given context.[60] For Dalits, the context is the caste oppression, history is that of suffering and pain under that oppression, and the medium is the vernacular language of Dalits, which is the first medium to express their faith in God. Massey's theological basis for the definition is the way in which God deals with and makes promises to the down trodden and oppressed people in the Scriptures.

In support of this conviction, Devasahayam emphasizes the importance of the role of Dalits in articulating theology in their own context. He understands Dalit ideology as a counter ideology, which he explains in the light of the Cross where Jesus suffered and died in order to save others. For him, it is that act of love that inspires and empowers Dalits to strive for their liberation. Accordingly he emphasizes the need for Dalits

---

58. Quoted in M. E. Prabhakar, "Christology in Dalit Perspective" 402–432 in V. Devasahayam, ed. *Frontiers of Dalit Theology* (New Delhi: ISPCK/Gurukul, 1997), 410.
59. Massey, *Down Trodden*, 48.
60. Massey, "Ingredients for a Dalit Theology", 154.

to regain their self-worth and construct theology out of their own experiences. He writes, "Traditional theologies have reduced humans to utter incapacity and encouraged people to look for a saviour from outside, sometimes even looking to heaven. Jesus' call and example should particularly inspire Dalits to take on [up] their historical task on their shoulder and strive to achieve it trusting in their potential."[61] In short, Dalit theology may be defined as a critical reflection and articulation of the people's God-experience and the expression of it for liberation in the context of the caste oppressions in India.

5. 2. 2. The Understanding of God

Dalit theology identifies God as the God of the oppressed. In other words, God is a Dalit God. Reflecting on the nature of God, K. P. Kuruvila argues, "This God is a Dalit God, a servant God, who does not create others to do servile work, but does work himself. . . . hence we the Indian Dalits are this God's people."[62] The difference of the Dalit understanding of God from that of the traditional theology is that while the latter sees God like a "ruthless judge demanding a pound of flesh from the sinner", the former perceives God as someone who is "participating in the agony along with the agonizing people."[63] This is articulated in the light of the Christ-Event which explains the fact that Christology takes the central place in Dalit theology.

Dalit theology sees Jesus as a historical figure rather than a dogmatic figure,[64] and Dalits relate their own experiences to him in a dialectical manner. They see in Jesus their own experiences of suffering injustice, oppression, pain and death. In doing so, like Black theology, Dalit theology affirms the identity of Jesus as Dalit.

Nirmal's statement makes this clear:

---

61. Devasahayam, "Nature of Dalit Theology", 67.
62. K. P. Kuruvila, "Dalit Theology: An Indian Christian Attempt to give voice to the voiceless", http://www.csichurch.com/article/dalit.htm [Accessed 18 November 2008].
63. Devasahayam, "Nature of Dalit theology", 54.
64. Kuruvila, "Dalit Theology".

> Our exodus from Hinduism which was imposed on us, to Christianity or rather to Jesus Christ is a valuable experience. It has enabled us to recognize our dalitness and also the dalitness of Jesus of Nazareth and the dalitness of his Father and our Father, our God. The dalit theology, therefore, should also be doxological in character. Our struggle is not over yet, but we ought to be thankful for our exodus experience.[65]

The inclusion of the 'sinners' and the 'foreigners', including Tamar, Rahab and Ruth in the genealogy of Jesus supports the dalitness of Jesus and that further indicates the importance of accepting a Dalit identity. Devasahayam puts it beautifully: "Matthew in the presentation of Jesus' genealogy, does not try to cover up the shadow of a stained past, but includes those considered sinners and foreigners."[66] Devasahayam's point is that by having in common such a genealogy of 'scornful' lineage, Jesus himself was like a Dalit and that this was not hidden from the public shows the dalitness of Jesus and the boldness of that identity in the process of his work of salvation.

From a Dalit viewpoint, Jesus was not only born with a Dalit identity but also lived as a Dalit. This is seen in his total identification with the poor, the downtrodden, and the oppressed, who were the Dalits of his time. The cleansing of the temple, for instance, directly links to their own experiences of denial of temple worship. Manodeep Daniel in his answer to the question 'What kind of Messiah are we looking for?' asserts, "We are beholding God who is not quite clean. Furthermore in Jesus we see yet more of this God. As Messiah Jesus suffered the pain of rejection because he rendered himself dirty. He became dirty because he was busy serving others."[67] The dalitness of Jesus was culminated at the cross as Kuruvilla argues, "Above all, Jesus' dalitness is symbolized at its best on the cross.

---

65. Quoted in Webster, *Religion and Dalit*, 68.
66. Devasahayam, "Identity in Theology", 17.
67. Manodeep Daniel, "Eyes that can See: A way of reading the Bible from Dalit perspective", CDS Pamphlet, No. 7, Published by CDS, New Delhi, 2004, 45.

On the cross he was broken, the crushed, the split, the torn, the driven – the dalit, in the fullest possible etymological meaning of the term."[68]

The cross is not a defeat but rather the symbol of hope for Dalits. It was the cross that precedes the resurrection of Jesus, which is the victory and hope of Dalits. It was Jesus of Nazareth, the prototype of Dalit suffering and hope, that gives hope and inspiration. For instance, M. E. Prabhakar argues, "For the Indian Christian Dalits, to know Jesus Christ is to realise that the God of Jesus Christ will save them from inhumanity, social oppression, economic exploitation and cultural subjugation."[69]

5. 2. 3. Hermeneutics: A Dalit Reading of the Bible

The Bible is very important for Dalits and at the same time they insist that it must be read in context. Thus, hermeneutics is a key issue for developing Dalit theology as a theology for and by marginalized people. Jesurathnam, in his pioneering work in this field, observes that biblical interpretation in India is based on the Western use of the historical critical method and is considered 'the correct' method. In reaction to this he proposes that Dalit hermeneutics should be: firstly, a hermeneutics of suspicion; secondly, in exposing social reality, Dalit hermeneutics proceeds to work out hermeneutics based on equality; thirdly, like other liberation theologies, Dalit hermeneutics also attempts to connect the loving action of God in the light of the Israelites' past experience and the present socio-economic and cultural reality of the people. In this way, the biblical text becomes a tool for Dalit emancipation.[70] The importance of Dalit historical experience – their becoming the subjects of the hermeneutics and their liberation as the goal of Dalit hermeneutics – have been pointed out by others.[71]

Jesurathnam uses this hermeneutics in his work, "Towards a Dalit Liberative Hermeneutics: Re-reading the Psalms of Lament." Here, he

---

68. Kuruvila, "Dalit Theology".
69. Prabhakar, "Christology in Dalit Perspective", 409.
70. K. Jesurathnam, "Towards a Dalit Liberative Hermeneutics: Re-reading The Psalms of Lament", http://www.religion-online.org/showarticle.asp?title=2452 [Accessed 2 Sept 2008].
71. For instance, M. Gnanavaram, "Some Reflections on Dalit Hermeneutics" 329–335 in V. Devasahayam ed. *Frontiers of Dalit Theology* (New Delhi: ISPCK/Gurukul, 1997), 333.

takes the Psalms of Lament and tries first to "situate the Psalms of Lament in their original setting for a meaningful appropriation of their message", and then "appropriates the interpretative keys available with the Psalms to resonate and to discover the liberation potential that is in convergence with the Dalit liberation."[72] In doing so, he argues that Dalit hermeneutics is scientific and praxis-oriented and the Psalms of Lament being resonated to their own situation help Dalits in their struggle for liberation.[73] In a more elaborate way he proposes the following five aspects of Dalit hermeneutics: first, hermeneutics of liberative transformation; second, hermeneutics of protest and action; third, hermeneutics of suspicion; fourth, hermeneutics of identity; and fifth, hermeneutics of empowerment.[74] Thus, for example, Psalm 22 provides Dalits, according to him, "an opportunity to find [*sic*] God's solidarity in their distress situation and at the same time hope and victory."[75] That makes it clear that in Dalit theology the text is read in and through the eyes of Dalits and in doing so, Dalits discover their own experiences in the Scriptures.

Still different from this, as a groundbreaking experience in the current exploration of Dalit hermeneutics, Y. T. Vinaya Raj argues for the physical body as a hermeneutical tool for Dalit theology. Raj draws his insights from postmodern theories including Seidman's *Contested Knowledge*[76] and Derrida's deconstructionist model, which advocate for the silenced voice of the marginalized who see the world differently.[77] He does this in opposition to the prevailing spirituality in the dominant Brahminic tradition, which neglected the significance of the body in knowledge. The dominant Brahminic epistemology conceives knowledge as "situated in the soul and

---

72. K. Jesurathnam, "Towards a Dalit Liberative Hermeneutics: Re-reading The Psalms of Lament" 1–34 *Bangalore Theological Forum*, Volume 34, Number 1 (June 2002), 2.

73. Ibid., 23–24.

74. J. Jesurathnam, *Contextual Reading of Psalm 22 with Special Reference to Indian Christian Dalit Interpretation* (Unpublished PhD Thesis, University of Edinburgh, 2006), 233–238.

75. Ibid., iv.

76. Steven Seidman, *Contested Knowledge: Social Theory Today*. Third Edition (Oxford: Blackwell Publishing, 2004).

77. Derrida's 'deconstruction' is explained in James K. A. Smith *Who's Afraid of Postmodernism? Talking Derrida, Lyotard, and Foucault to Church* (Michigan: Baker Academic, 2006), 51.

disseminated through ritualistic practices."[78] This can be understood in the light of the concept of *Maya* wherein the physical body is perceived negatively. Added to this, Raj points out, modernity "desacralized nature and marginalized people who lived in a symbiotic relationship with nature and ridiculed their knowledge as irrational and unscientific."[79] Raj's argument is that spirituality is fundamentally "relational and communal commitment" wherein he sees "body becomes the locus and anti-caste social practice becomes an act of worship and forms its liturgy."[80] Raj's argument for the role of the body in knowledge promises Dalit participation in knowledge and theology, which in itself is a part of the Dalit liberation process. This is a promising insight that needs to be seen in reality.

5. 2. 4. The Goal of Dalit Theology

The goal of Dalit theology is Dalit liberation from the socio-economic and religio-cultural domination created by the caste system. This is expressed in different ways. While Webster observes Dalit theology as an activist theology which aims at change rather than upholding the status of the church and society as well as to heal the wounded psyche of the Dalit people,[81] Devasahayam explains it in terms of identity as a people. He explains the goal of Dalit theology as "the daring act of recognizing oppressed people as subjects of theology, and providing these subjects with a name and face, which have been hitherto denied to them."[82] For M. E. Prabhakar, it is realization of Dalit full humanness – the image of God – as he writes, "For a Christian Dalit theology it cannot be simply the gaining of rights, the reservations and privileges. The goal is the realisation of our full humanness or conversely, our full divinity, the ideal of *Imago*

---

78. Quoted in Jacthanni's review of Raj's work. Y. T. Vinay Raj, '*Re-Imagining Dalit Theology – Postmodern Readings* (Tiruvalla: Christava Sahitya Samithi: 2008). http://www.shvoong.com/books/1822256-re-imagining-dalit-theology-postmodern/ [Accessed 2 Sept 2008].
79. Ibid.
80. Ibid.
81. Webster, *Religion and Dalit*, 65.
82. Devasahayam, "Identity in Theology", 16.

Dei (Gen 1:26, 27)."[83] Webster et al find the importance of the biblical concept of *Imago Dei* for a self-understanding of Dalit Christian women. They further linked this to the Pauline concept of freedom in Christ found in Galatians and 1 Corinthians where they discovered freedom of an individual, not individualism, but a person-in-community, with reference to the analogy of the body.[84]

The ultimate function of Dalit theology, for Massey, is two fold: to act in solidarity and to act for liberation. Liberation would release Dalits from the historically oppressive structures, both religio-cultural and socio-economic. In this, theological articulation is not only a faith expression but also a means for liberation. In other words, the vertical relationship affects the horizontal relationship at the same time. Here, solidarity is understood in the light of the Christian values of sacrifice, charity and commitment to others exemplified in the works of God in the history of humankind, particularly in the Christ-Event. Thus, incarnational theology for Massey is the basis of such a two-sided solidarity with God and with fellow Dalits. This is clear in in his statement:

> The model of solidarity we find in God's incarnational act in history challenges us Dalit Christians to follow it, so that the experiences we share with the Dalits in general should become the basis of an authentic Dalit theology. . . . Being in solidarity with our fellow Dalits of different faiths and ideologies is a demand which the God of the Bible, through his own act of incarnation, places on Dalit Christians. This is an important factor for the authenticity of Dalit theology, enabling it to become an instrument of destroying the social and religious structures responsible for the Dalits' historical captivity.[85]

In the light of the above discussion, the goal of Dalit theology can be understood as the liberation of Dalit identity as people. It is a realization of

---

83. Prabhakar, "Christology in Dalit Perspective", 413; Webster, et al. *From Role to Identity*, 120.
84. Webster, et al. *From Role to Identity*, 124.
85. Massey, *Down Trodden*, 61.

Dalit humanity in the light of the *Imago Dei,* which speaks for their dignity, freedom and equality with others and the application of the meaning to their concrete day-to-day life.

5. 2. 5. Sources of Dalit Theology

The phrase 'Dalit theology' refers to two things: 'Dalit', the situation of oppression, and 'theology', an articulation of God-experience in the light of that situation. It is an experience of oppression and discrimination where theology begins as well as takes its shape. Having drawn insights from the incarnational act of God, Massey argues that Dalits' historical experiences need to be the basis for an authentic Dalit theology. Experience and history being like the two sides of the same coin, Dalit experience and history are equally important for developing Dalit theology. He asserts, "It is in God's act in history we see the roots of Dalit theology as well as its theological task."[86] We shall briefly discuss Dalit experience, the name 'Dalit' and Dalit history as sources of Dalit theology.

5. 2. 5. 1. Dalit Experience: The Starting Point for Theology

Dalit experience is the experience of oppression, discrimination, suffering and pain. This is the starting point for Dalit theology. A. P. Nirmal, one of the pioneers of Dalit theology argues for this when he writes, "It is in and through this pain-pathos the sufferer knows God. This is because the sufferer in and through his/her pain-pathos knows that God participates in human pain."[87] For him, the experiences of suffering and pain are the reality of Dalit life and it is there where theology has to begin. He uses the term 'pain-pathos' to describe the Dalit experiences of suffering and pain. The nature of people's experience includes, Kuruvila writes, "absurdity, inconsistency, incoherence, unsystematicness."[88]

The emphasis on Dalit experience is important not only for a critique of the caste system but also for strength in the process of Dalit emancipation. A. Maria Arul Raja, who specializes in Dalit Contextual Theology,

---

86. Massey, "History and Dalit Theology", 181.
87. A. P. Nirmal, quoted in K. P. Kuruvila, "Dalit Theology", http://www.csichurch.com/article/dalit.htm [Assessed 2 Sept 2008].
88. Ibid.

vehemently argues for this. He stresses that Dalit emancipation has to evolve from the depth of their roots. By 'their roots' he means their history of oppression under the caste system, which he called the "Dalit experience of Thrown-away-ness."[89] Rajas' main point is that Dalit experiences are both for the critique of the unjust structure within which they find themselves and at the same time the source of strength to combat the evil structure. How this would happen, he writes, "It [Dalit emancipation] has to be consciously evolved from the depth of their roots by themselves as the subjects of their own history."[90]

5. 2. 5. 2. *The Name 'Dalit': Accepting the Reality by Way of Resisting the Structure*

Like the tribal people, the Kukis in particular, the Dalit struggle is a struggle for a finding a name. A name includes identity and equality as a human being. In the words of Devasahayam, "Dalits are people who are robbed of their identity and their quest for identity is actively resisted by the caste people."[91] The struggle for a name needs to be understood in the light of the Indian hierarchical caste system referred to earlier.

The term Dalit had already appeared in literature in the 1930s. In 1930 there was a newspaper published in Pune in central India called, '*Dalit Bandu*', meaning "Friends of Dalits."[92] In their 1973 manifesto, the Dalit Panther Movement, which was the post-Independent Dalit emancipation movement, had expanded and popularized the term.[93] The term Dalit comes from the root word '*dal*', which means oppressed, broken

---

89. A. Maria Arul Raja, "Inner Powers with Emancipation Agenda: A Probe into Dalit Roots" 151–160 in James Massey et al., *Breaking Theoretical Grounds for Dalit Studies* (New Delhi: Centre for Dalit/Subaltern Studies, 2006), 151–152.
90. Ibid., 151.
91. Devasahayam, "Identity in Theology", 15.
92. Quoted in Webster, "Who is a Dalit?" 68–79 in S. M. Michael, ed. *Dalits in Modern India: Vision and Values* (New Delhi: Vistaar Publications, 1999), 68.
93. It is debated who exactly are included in the category 'Dalit'. Some include in the category 'members of the Scheduled Castes and tribes, neo-Buddhists, the working people, the landless and poor peasants, women and all those who are being exploited politically, economically and in the name of religion.' See, Omvedt, *Dalit Visions*, 72. Convincingly, Webster argues that caste alone can determine who a Dalit is, and not class or religion. See, Webster, "Who is a Dalit?", 77.

and crushed. In Sanskrit, it means 'broken' and 'downtrodden'.[94] As such, the term is a negative term, however, it was found relevant by the Dalit activists and writers for two reasons: firstly, it recovers their past experience of oppression and, secondly, the term refers to them collectively.[95] The term Dalit also incorporates elements of a positive expression of pride and a resistive surge for combating oppression. For Dalit theologians like Devasahayam, "attempts to change the terms because they are of reproach is only an exercise in evading the problem."[96] His argument being that the suffering hard realities of Dalits, the end result of the caste system, needed to be called by its name 'Dalit' so that people could be conscientized of the reality.[97] For Devasahayam, the term Dalit is a term of protest against caste name, and Dalit identity is an anti-caste identity.[98] Massey captures the wide usage of the term Dalit as follows:

'Dalit' is thus not a mere descriptive name or title, but an expression of hope for the recovery of their past identity. The struggle of these 'outcastes' has given the term *dalit* a positive meaning. The very realisation of themselves as Dalit, the very acceptance of the state of 'dalitness', is the first step on the way towards their transformation into full and liberated human beings.[99]

Thus, for Dalits, choosing 'Dalit' as their name itself is a part of their search for identity and liberation as S. M. Michael rightly points out, "[t]he name Dalit is not merely a rejection of the very idea of pollution or impurity or untouchability, it reveals a sense of a unified class, or a movement towards equality."[100] In the same line of thought, Vinaya Raj argues that Dalit is not a caste category as generally understood but rather a means

---

94. Michael, "Dalit Vision", 99; Webster, "Who is a Dalit?" 68–79.
95. Gopal Guru, quoted in Sathianathan Clarke, "Viewing The Bible Through The Eyes And Ears of Subalterns In India" http://www.religion-online.org/showarticle.asp?title=2450 [Accessed 2 Sept 2008].
96. Devasahayam, "Identity in Theology", 18.
97. Ibid., 19.
98. Ibid.
99. Massey, *Down Trodden,* 3.
100. S. M. Michael, "Introduction" 11–35 in Michael, ed. *Dalits in Modern India,* 28. Michael has elaborated a presentation on the history of and issues related to 'untouchability' in India which resulted in the emergence of the identity 'Dalit'.

to resist the oppressive structure. Having drawn insights from Seidman's *Contested Knowledge* as mentioned earlier, Raj concludes that Dalit is a "category through which the Dalits reject the notions of caste and its formation of casteist subjectivity. It is a category by which Dalits envision a renewed social status and social space."[101]

5. 2. 5. 3. Dalit History: The Source of Identity and Liberation

Dalit history is the source from which the people find their original identity and dignity as human beings. For Massey, past history reveals that once Dalits were ". . . full human beings, enjoying all the benefits of a normal human being which includes land, property, human dignity, natural resources, and human freedom."[102] It was for this reason that Dalit theologians like him argued for the need to take the history of the people as one whole, accepting with honesty and boldly all that this entails.

Massey points out three categories of people who avoid talking about Dalit past history – the non-church thinkers, the so-called upper caste converts and some Dalit converts who have been brainwashed by the old missionary theological thinking that all that existed before Christianity was evil.[103] In Massey's view, this is a crucial issue for Dalits as far as their search for identity is concerned. For when their history is destroyed their identity is also destroyed at the same time. Equally crucial on the part of Dalits is to accept their inferior status assigned to them by their opponents as he writes "ultimately it was not oppression, which destroyed the Dalits, but acceptance of the superiority which destroyed them."[104]

Similarly, contrary to the Hindu concept of *maya*, George Oommen stresses that the realization of Dalits as subjects of history is essential towards recovery and recapture of their lost dignity. Secondly, unlike the traditional Indian Christian theology which is based on the transcendental

---

101. Quoted in Jacthanni's review of Raj's work.
102. Massey, "History and Dalit Theology", 174.
103. Ibid.
104. Massey, "History and Dalit Theology", 177. For the importance of Dalit History for Dalit theology, see also, James Massey, "Dalit Roots of Christianity, Theology and Spirituality (Revised)", C.D.S. Pamphlet 11, Published by C.D.S. New Delhi, 2008.

nature of the Ultimate Reality, and for that matter the Hindu cyclical view of history, he also argues that the understanding of human experience and ultimate liberation as integral parts of the 'here and now' is primary to Dalit theology.[105]

5. 2. 6. The Subject of Dalit Theology

The Dalit struggle for liberation is a struggle to become a subject of theology. Indian theology so far has been done by the so-called high caste Christians; hence, Dalit participation and their experiences were marginalized in the articulation and expression of theology in India. By taking the people's experience as a starting point for theology, the emergence of Dalit theology paves the way for Dalits to become subjects of their theology. Indeed if Dalit theology has to be an articulation of God-experience in the light of Dalit experience of pain and suffering, unquestionably the people themselves have to be the subjects of their theology. That makes Dalit theology exclusive. Accordingly Nirmal argues for "Dalit theology for Dalits and by Dalits."[106] The question, however, is whether Dalits should be the only subjects of Dalit theology. The issue here is the limitation of Dalit experience, like any other experiences, without the contribution of others.

With this regard to the participation of others in Dalit theology, Sathianathan Clarke argues that non-Dalits can be facilitators of the process of developing Dalit theology. For him, a non-Dalit theologian can write about Dalit theology but not do the theology *per se*. His point is that Dalits should articulate and express their God-experience in their own vocabulary and terms. He even stresses that Dalits should not become spokespersons in the hands of the caste Christians to tell the world what Dalit theology is all about.[107]

It is absolutely important that Dalits, in the light of their own God-experiences, initiate a God-talk or theology. At the same time, it is equally

---

105. Oommen, "The Emerging Dalit Theology", http://www.religion-online.org/showarticle.asp?title=1121 [Accessed 2 Sept 2008].

106. See, R.S. Sugirtharajah, ed. *Frontiers in Asian Christian Theology: Emerging Trends* (Maryknoll, New York: Orbis Books, 1994), 31.

107. Sathianathan Clarke was interviewed by the Countercurrents.org on 7 October 2007. http://www.countercurrents.org/sikand071007.htm [Accessed 2Sept 2008].

important to recognize that the God-experience of Dalits is one of the many human experiences of God and hence, their God-talk is local in nature. On that account, Dalit theology, and for that matter, Tribal theology, should articulate theology by way of learning from, and acting as corrective to other theologies, particularly the missionary theology in the cradle where they were nourished. Balasundaram, another Dalit theologian stresses this point when he says, "Dalit theology is not and can't be exclusive. A [t]heology that is exclusive can't be Christian."[108]

5. 3. An Evaluation from a Tribal Perspective

A critique of Dalit theology from a Tribal perspective focuses around the issue of methodology, that is, the ways in which a theology was formulated. The pioneers of Dalit theology formulated an alternative theology to that of traditional Indian Christian theology which is Brahminic in essence because their voices were not represented in the articulation and expression of theology in what is usually known as Indian Christian theology. This is a right trend in a multi-cultural context such as India; however, that needs to be done without domesticating the Christian message.

Second, Dalit theology is an articulation of theology from the perspective of the victims of oppression. In this, not ignoring others, the main actors are Dalits themselves. The simple reason being they are the ones who experienced the 'Dalit experience' as oppressed people and also experienced God in that situation. It was right that Dalit theology was and has been formulated by and for the Dalits themselves. In this case, local theology includes reformulation of theological concepts, adoption of a different approach to theology, and employment of methodology suited to a given context. This, however, does not seek to usurp the place of the Brahminic Indian Christian theology. It only corrects the mistake of considering that theology as normative and thus showing the possibility of doing theology in a different way. In that sense, Dalit theology is merely one theology among many theologies. Dalit theology, and for that matter, Tribal

---

108. Balasundaram quoted in Oommen, "The Emerging Dalit Theology," 28.

theology do not necessarily become counter theologies to the traditional Indian Christian theology. They should rather be honest in their commitment to search and rediscover God's heart for the people in their given context showing the translatability of the Christian message.

Third, the role of history in Dalit theology is another dimension that Dalit theology contributed to the task of formulating theology in India. History for Dalits is the foundation for their present and future life as a people. It is there that they discover their past experiences of oppression and suffering preserved in the forms of stories, songs, arts and oral tradition. And by asserting the importance of these experiences, Dalit theology helps the people to re-discover who they are. The Brahminic Christian theology, by contrast, does not emphasize a place for history in theology and as a result Dalits are denied their historical right of land and dignity. This dimension of Dalit theology is vital for tribal people of India, particularly the Kukis of Manipur, whose history is regarded as dark and inferior.

Fourth, by taking the context as a whole, Dalit theology is more integral in nature than the theology which was brought by the late nineteenth- and early twentieth-century missionaries. In this, the concern of theology is not only for the conversion of the soul and life after death, but also for those that relate to the physical body here and now. For this reason, Dalit theology enriches the existing theologies by broadening the theological vision to include the marginalized. The danger of Dalit theology, though, is the tendency to disregard totally the missionary theology while pointing out its limitations. The belief in and emphasis on spiritual transformation of a person, the concept of life after death and the need for the work of evangelization should be understood as an integral part of the Christian message of liberation or else one will make the same mistake which many missionaries made in the past.

Fifth, theologians from Dalit and Tribal communities need to work together for mutual critique and enrichment with a clear conviction and commitment to construct a local theology that would finally lead to the transformation of the society as a whole. A local theology needs to be linked with other local theologies, but also recognize the global community. As

Andrew Walls has said, "The church must be diverse because humanity is diverse; it must be one because Christ is one."[109]

The difference between Dalits and tribals, however, is that while the former lived together with the oppressor and suffered discrimination by their neighbours, the latter suffered oppression without seeing their oppressors. An additional issue for the people of North-East India in general and the Kukis in particular is alienation of the people from their own culture, which includes their ancestors' land and administration. While, for the former, the objective is to reclaim the lost identity with human dignity and value which was destroyed by the Hindu Brahminic tradition and integrate within mainstream Indian culture, the latter is concerned to protect their identity from outside forces, including that of the hegemonic Hindu nationalism. What a local theology in North-East India in general, and among the Kukis of Manipur in particular, needs to take further is the issue of cultural and geographical distance from those outside North-East India, and at the same time, find a peaceful way to articulate and preserve their particular identity in a multi-ethnic context. The task involves asserting identity without affecting other identities. Put differently, the need is to construct a local theology which is genuinely local and yet transcends one's own local identity for peaceful co-existence.

---

109. Andrew Walls, *The Cross-Cultural Process in Christian History* (Edinburgh: T & T Clark, 2002), 77.

CHAPTER 6

Toward a Theology of Identity in Kuki Context

This work investigated the history of traditional or primal peoples in North-East India, particularly the Kuki people of Manipur, with a view to propose a theological response to their struggle for identity. It explored the cultural and religious traditions of the people and noticed the enormous changes resulting from the impact of Western, especially British, colonialism creating multiple crises for the people. The arrival of missionary agents of a particular form of western, Protestant Christianity, had contributed to the alienation of the people from their own cultural past. We have examined how the combination of an alien political power and Christianity shaped by the modernity of western culture created a grave identity crisis across North-East India in general and for the Kuki of Manipur in particular. Subsequently, the tribal people found themselves incorporated within the modern states which emerged in the era of political independence, an outcome which left them both divided by newly defined state boundaries – India, Burma and Bangladesh – and within India, became members of a nation-state whose political culture is geographically remote, and whose dominant religious and cultural traditions are strikingly different from their own.

The problem posed by this research now becomes clear. Among the tribal peoples, and especially the Kuki of Manipur, the forgetfulness of ancient communal beliefs and values, the adoption of a highly individualist form of Christianity and the sense of geographical and political alienation all combine to create a profound social and cultural crisis. It was shown that there are other groups within India that have experienced a similar kind of alienation and oppression, and the emergence of Dalit theology offers both an example and a sign of hope to tribal Christians in North-East India. At the same time, the two situations are not identical. While much can be learned from Dalit theology, the challenges confronting the Kukis are the ones that require giving attention to the primal religious past as well as the difficult and complex socio-political realities of the present day. Our study of the concept of identity in chapter 2 helped us understand that identity is social construct, reflecting the socio-political and cultural and religious context within which it emerges. In the context of North-East India, we argued, identity and identity constructions are not merely social groupings but rather the people's socio-political movement for recognition of identity, which includes culture, land and political rights.

6. 1. Theology and Cultural Identity in North-East India: Current Scenario

A brief outline of previous approaches to contextual theology within the wider context of North-East India will be helpful. We shall take some examples from Mizoram and Nagaland, the neighbouring states of Manipur. On the issue of 'continuity and discontinuity' of Christianity in North-East India, a Mizo pioneer theologian, K. Thanzauva, highlights two views prominent in the region - what he calls the transplantation and fulfilment models. The transplantation model concerns the traditional missionary approach in which converts regarded the message communicated through traditions associated with the Western cultural context as unchanging and culture-free. At the same time, the local context was viewed as primitive, pagan, heathen and savage and needed to be abandoned. This approach provided little or no incentive to recognize local culture in articulating theology. Similarly, the fulfilment model maintained that Christianity was superior to all other cultures because of Jesus Christ, seen as the culmination of all the values of cultures. J. N. Farquhar's work, *The Crown of Hinduism*, is a clear example of this model. As we have seen, Farquhar argued that Christ provides the fulfilment of the highest aspiration of

Hinduism; in other words, Christ is the crown of the faith of India.[1] This model functioned in the framework of social Darwinism, so influential in the West at the time, and deeply influenced missionary perceptions of other religions, resulting in a particularly negative evaluation of primal traditions.

An important example of the 'transplantation' model is found in the work of the Dutch missionary theologian Hendrik Kraemer. In the 1938 Tambaram conference, Kraemer took seriously the issue of religious plurality in India but maintained that there was no connection between Christianity and other religions. Kraemer recognized the presence of truth in other cultures but did not believe this was the same as the gospel truth. In Kraemer's view, Thanzauva observes, "There is no link between the two, and certainly no continuity."[2] About the position of theologians in North-East India, Zauva observed that many Christian leaders subscribed to Kraemer's view whether or not they actually knew of his work. They recognized good things in their culture but could not treat them as compatible with the gospel in substance. He identified leaders, like, C. L. Hminga, a Mizo, and O. Alem, a Naga Christian leader, as having supported Kraemer's view.[3] The problem with this model is that it takes the imported tradition as the only valid articulation and expression of faith, ignoring the cultural and historical context of the church in the West in which the view emerged. At the same time, when a local culture is treated merely a preparatory to the reception of a theology wholly developed in other cultural contexts, God's revelation and involvement in a local culture is limited and often denied. For these reasons, Thanzauva proposes what he calls a Synthetic-Praxis Model, which he developed for a given context by synthesizing the concerns of traditional theological models such as 'Transplantation', 'Fulfilment Model' and so forth.[4]

In his attempt to bridge the cultures before and after Christianization, Lalsangkima Pachuau, another Mizo theologian, argues that the present

---

1. Quoted in Thanzauva, *Theology*, 85.
2. Ibid., 86.
3. Ibid.
4. Ibid., 104.

appearance of charismatic Christianity among the Mizos is rooted in their pre-Christian culture where belief in spirits was fundamentally important. He concludes that the Mizo pre-Christian era continues to mark their religiosity even in the present day. In this case, the primal world-view as a subculture provides a medium to communicate the Christian message and the concept of *Pathian*, spirits, and *tlawmngaihna* are the bridge already available in the local culture for the transmission of the Christian message.[5] This is an important insight, but we must enquire how far the primal cultural resources were used in the articulation of the Christian message. Must the cultural resources be limited to being merely mediums through which theology is expressed, or can the cultural resources be incorporated in the substance of theology itself? An equally important question is how far such an indigenous theology may be crucial to the identity struggle of the marginalized people.

Ezamo Murry, a Naga theologian, shares a similar view with Pachuau when he writes, "Almost all the Nagas and the Mizos are Christians today but their Christianity is still influenced by the tribal culture and religion much like the early church being influenced by the Jewish and Hellenistic cultures."[6] Murry highlights the perceived communitarian culture among Christians, arguing that "though educated and being in touch with modernity [the Naga people] have not been captured by ideas like individualism and private ownership."[7] He notes the continuing importance of village community identity, writing, "The individual's identity is found in the village community and in the age group. The village is the guardian of the individual. To be banished from the village, therefore, is the greatest punishment and humiliation for any individual."[8] Murry's main argument is that it was the communitarian existence which prepared

---

5. Lalsangkima Pachuau, "Primal Spirituality as the substructure of Christian Spirituality: The Case of Mizo Christianity in India" 9–14 in *Journal of African Christian Thought*, Vol, 11, No.2 (2008), 12–13.

6. Ezamo Murry, "Bible and Culture – A Model of Christian Acculturation of Tribal culture", *The Third Theological Educators' Symposium on Constructing a Relevant/Contextual Theology for the People of North East India, Eastern Theological College* (Jorhat, Assam, India, 17–23 November 2008).

7. Ibid.

8. Ibid.

the tribal people to switch to the church smoothly. There is truth in this observation but the communitarian existence in the traditional culture and that evident in Christianity are not one and the same. As he rightly points out, an identity in the traditional culture was a common identity, in other words, there was no individual identity independent of others, whereas in Christianity as inherited from the missionaries, community is understood in terms of a gathering of different individuals, who are individually 'saved' by God.

While accepting the positive contribution of Christianity, Takatemjen, another Naga theologian, observes deficiency in the way the Christian message was presented. He argues that Christianity has transformed the habits and the character of the Naga people through bringing them a new philosophy of life, a status of equality with the rest of the world and a new social consciousness for which, he says, the Nagas are eternally grateful.[9] At the same time, he observes the limitation of Christianity in the form in which it entered the region:

> The churches in the North East India remain to be still western. By that, I mean to say that we have not been able to make use of all the rich resources available in our socio-cultural traditions in the theologizing process. Until the gospel is reinterpreted and present in the light of the thought patterns of the people, it would remain superficial and irrelevant.[10]

Takatemjen seeks to revitalize cultural resources like the practice of *Morung,* or *Som-Inn* in Kuki, which is a traditional and integral learning centre for young people, through which they gain an understanding of ethics, the concept of God, and so forth, in order to preserve their distinct identity as a people. He is convinced that re-reading of such tradition would provide an answer to the present predicament of the people. For instance, in the concept of God, *Lijaba,* he finds liberation for the poor, justice to the outcasts, and sharing in community. He writes, "Such a

---

9. Takatemjen, *Studies on Theology and Culture* (Delhi: ISPCK, 1998), 1. Paraphrased.
10. Ibid., x.

discovery is crucial even for the present Naga context in which a lot of men and women have been demoralized and dehumanized as a result of rapid modernization. The traditional spirituality holds an answer to our present predicament."[11] Takatemjen's main dissatisfaction with Christianity among the Nagas has to do with the way in which the faith is presented without the local cultural resources. A similar position among the Nagas is taken by Ruho, who stresses the importance of conceptual clarity on God, spiritual living, the use of the Bible, and on civilization. Ruho argues that Christ is not against culture and therefore cultural concepts need to be re-articulated and redefined. If the content of belief is deep enough and appealing, he contends, what we have come to believe would make more sense to our heart and minds. To do this, Ruho emphasizes the need to redefine these concepts biblically and contextually. The history of the people should be rewritten, he uses the word 're-right', with a conviction that the west does not have monopoly over 'truth' and Christ is not against culture.[12]

What is clear from this discussion is the absence of an authentic articulation and expression of faith employing local cultural resources. The local culture is taken only as a medium through which faith, articulated in the West, is expressed. If this is the situation with those communities who were much advanced in embracing the Christian faith and developing theology in their cultural contexts, the late-comers such as the Kukis, are far behind in this task. Moreover, all the works cited above were found to be limited to groups who are confined to their particular cultural and geographical boundaries. The implication of this for other groups can be understood in the light of the fact that Christianity, while contributing to their identity crisis, did at least bring the skills of literacy and enable the people to get exposed to a wider world as noted earlier. The first comers to Christianity were the first ones to be introduced to modernity with all its benefits and opportunities including imagination and construction of

---

11. Ibid., 66.
12. Rukuzo Ruho, "Concepts and Tribal Christian Theology", *The Third Theological Educators' Symposium on Constructing a Relevant/Contextual Theology for the People of North East India, held at Eastern Theological College* (Jorhat, Assam, India, 17–23 November 2008). Paraphrased.

group identity and articulation of the Christian message within that context, leaving other ethnic groups behind.

This brings us back to the specifically Kuki context with which this publication is concerned. The particular circumstances in which Christianity took root among the Kukis, as described earlier, has created problems and challenges in the state of Manipur which demand a specific locally contextual response. A critical theological response to the continuing Kuki struggle for identity in fact requires a new paradigm. While retaining many elements from the traditions received from the missionary past, theology should move beyond them to listen afresh to the Bible and the gospel in the light of this particular cultural and historical context. The people's cultural values and the gospel need to be revisited in search of better grounding for identity formation and preservation. At the same time, a theology that is an articulation of God and God's love for human beings should aim for peaceful coexistence among all people. What we seek for, and the contribution this publication endeavours to make, is a theology that inseparably links the local and the global, thus affirming the validity of an oppressed and marginalized people's quest for identity and dignity, within the broader context of North-East India of the sub-continent as a whole, and the total ecumenical, global situation. That is, a local theology that affirms what is local and at the same time enriches a wider community of God's people. The element of the Biblical narrative which is of particular significance to this quest is precisely the tension between the particular, represented by the election of the people of Israel, and the universal, which is from the very beginning the ultimate end, or *telos*, of all God's action in history. We observe, for example, that the account of God's call to Abraham in Genesis 12:1–3, long identified as a seminal text from which later developments can be traced across both Testaments, is preceded by the much neglected "Table of the Nations" in Genesis 10, which clearly signals the divine concern for all peoples on earth. There is the balance between the particular and the universal at the very beginning of the biblical story, and the object of Yahweh's laws and care, this election has a purpose, a *telos*, in the ultimate blessing of all nations and people.

6. 2. Biblical Basis for a Theology of Identity

The Biblical and theological basis for local theology for identity is rooted in the fact that God desires for all people on earth to exist. This is clear from the first book of the Old Testament to the last book of the New Testament. Gerhard von Rad, for instance, argues that the significance of the Table of the Nations referred to above, first of all, is the fact that it shows the fulfilment of God's blessing for Noah and his sons for physical multiplication recorded in Genesis 9:1.[13] The point is that it is God's will that nations exist. Westermann develops this insight further and stresses the equality of all people as God's creation. He writes, "It [the creation of the nations] means that all peoples existing in the present, all of them, belong to the human race that God created."[14] He quotes A. Dillmann as saying, "all individuals and peoples are of the same race, the same dignity and the same character."[15] In the same line of thinking, Gordon J. Wenham, another Old Testament commentator, puts the table of the nations together with the genealogy in Luke 3:34–36 and observes that the significance of these two passages is seen in the fact that they were forefathers of the one who is going to bring salvation to all humankind. He writes:

Though we may find names like Serug or Reu quite irrelevant, this genealogy states that they were most significant, for they were forefathers of the one who was to bring salvation to Israel and ultimately blessing to all mankind, a point Luke makes later by including these men in the genealogy of our Lord.[16]

It was in the light of such an understanding of multicultural community that the election of Israel is understood. That is, God chooses the people of Israel not for their own benefit but rather to become a channel of God's blessing to all nations of the earth. This includes the view that

---

13. Gerhard von Rad, *Genesis: Old Testament Library* (London: SCM Press Ltd., 1970), Third Impression, 140.
14. Claus Westermann, *Genesis 1–11 A Continental Commentary* (Minneapolis: Fortress Press, 1994), 529.
15. Ibid.
16. Gordon J. Wenham, *Word Biblical Commentary, Genesis 1–15* (Texas: Word Books, 1987), 254.

even God's actions against other nations on Israel's behalf serve for the good of all people, including those who are the objects of God's action. Westermann writes, "what is peculiar to the Old Testament is that God's history with his people went on through the centuries so that his action on Israel's behalf was of positive significance for other peoples, for humanity, as indicated in Genesis 12:3."[17] The point here is that it is God's own desire that a nation exists but not for her own benefit but for the benefit of all, declaring God's goodness in their differences.

The theme of multicultural community, or the need for the existence of all people on earth, runs through the whole of the New Testament. In line with the divine allotment of periods and boundaries for an individual nation to flourish in Deuteronomy 32:8, the Song of Moses, Paul affirms in his Areopagus evangelistic address in Acts 17:26 that the God who created humankind has "made all nations to inhabit the whole earth, and he allotted the times for their existence and the boundaries of the places where they should live."[18] Many Old Testament commentators directly connect the table of the nations with this passage, contending that the nations are under the sovereign rule of God. Similarly, most New Testament commentators, particularly those in the affluent global north, conclude that the point being made in this passage is to say that all the affairs of human beings and nations are in the hand of God.[19] However, none of these commentators reflect the passage from the perspective of the marginalized people. A more relevant reading of the passage for the marginalized group is Gonzalez's commentary on Acts. Reading the passage in the context of land discrimination among the poor in the global south, and recognizing its direct significance for the quest of the people under study, Gonzalez argues, "God is not only interested in our religion. God is also interested in our dwelling on earth. . . . God is offended when idolatry is committed, . . . God is also offended when the land is hoarded, and when for that reason

---

17. Westermann, *Genesis*, 530.

18. Acts 17:26. NRSV.

19. For instance, I. Howard Marshall, *The Acts of the Apostles: An Introduction and Commentary* (Leicester: IVP, 1980), 288; C.K. Barrett, *A Critical and Exegetical Commentary on the Acts of the Apostles*, Vol. II (Edinburgh: T&T Clark, 1998), 844.

some do not have land on which to dwell."[20] Gonzalez's point implies that possession of land, or recognition of ancestors' territory in the context of the Kukis of Manipur, is part of God's concern for the people so that this text has special significance for this study as land is a part of the people's identity as explained in chapter 3.

Perhaps of even greater significance for this study is the contemporary re-reading of Paul, especially the letter to the Romans, in the light of social science insights into issues related to ethnicity and ethnic conflicts. For example, Phillip F. Esler in his work *Conflict and Identity in Romans*[21] shows how Paul, without erasing the people's ethnic identities, dealt with their differences by affirming a primary identity, which resulted from the fact that they all were one in Christ. Having in mind the present day ethnic conflicts around the world, Esler employs insights from recent social science and makes it clear that Paul recognized and accepted the socio-cultural reality of ethnic tensions between the Romans and the Greeks, and their common dislike of the Judeans.[22] However, according to Esler, Paul did not erase the differences but puts them under the same condition of sin and salvation through Christ. He argues that Paul's letter focuses on "one righteous God who righteouses [all] those who have faith in his son, Jesus Christ [without distinction], who has laid down his own life to break the power of sin in the world."[23] This, for Esler, is the basis for one's own identity and the reason to transcend it. He continues, "Paul regards the unity that they must achieve as a direct expression of the oneness of God. It is a unity also capable of visual expression as the body of Christ [transcending particular identities within one body]."[24] In this vision of unity, Esler also contends that Paul did not discourage the formation of new identities, although he insists that agaph was Paul's norm for the community life.

---

20. Justo L. Gonzalez, *ACTS: The Gospel of the Spirit* (Maryknoll, NY: Orbis Books, 2001), 204.

21. Philip F. Esler, *Conflict and Identity in Romans: The Social Setting of Paul's Letter* (Minneapolis: Fortress Press, 2003).

22. Ibid., 358.

23. Esler, *Conflict and Identity*, 358.

24. Ibid., 360.

He [Paul] wants Judean and non-Judean to unite in praise of God. If, as seems possible, the 'weak' continued to have some form of association with the Judean communities in Rome meeting in their impressive *proseuchai*, there is no sign here that Paul is interested in discouraging them from doing so.[25]

Esler's position on this point is even clearer when he writes:

> While it is probably going too far to say that Paul retains all existing social differences between the two groups and only advocates unity on a theological level, since the thrust of his thought undermines the cultural distinctiveness of Israel by its assertion that the Mosaic law is unnecessary for righteousness, Paul does not tell the Judean members of the Christ-movement to stop being Judeans. . . . While one may admit that Paul's is a compromise position that was unlikely to last, it is nevertheless inaccurate to attribute to him the positive aim of destroying the differences between Judeans and non-Judeans.[26]

God's will for the existence and equal dignity of all people on earth, or a multicultural community, is further reflected in the book of Revelation. Gonzalez observes this theme being repeated seven times in the book through a vision of the gathering of a great and countless multitude drawn from every nation, tribe, people and languages, glorifying God. The significance of the eschatological vision of God's people in the book of Revelation is that it gives room for all cultures, languages and peoples including the minority groups, and offers them opportunity to participate in the new community God is making. Gonzalez in a book with the significant title, *For the Healing of the Nations*,[27] rereads the multicultural situation of the present time through the lens of the book of Revelation and argues that it provides a paradigm for the present day church through its

---

25. Ibid., 364.
26. Ibid., 364–365.
27. Justo L. Gonzalez, *For the Healing of the Nations: The Book of Revelation in an Age of Cultural Conflict* (Maryknoll, NY: Orbis Books, 2003, Third Printing).

eschatological vision wherein the people of God will be drawn out of every tribe, nation and language. Gonzalez argues that for John, who probably was a Jew, cultural differences are very important since he saw and took seriously his own culture while being convinced of the fact that other cultures were equally important. In Gonzalez's words,

> If he [John of Patmos] did not care for his own culture and tradition, he might convince himself that cultures after all make no difference, that their variety is not important, that they can simply be ignored or assimilated. In a way, it is precisely because he is a Jew, and conscious of his own culture, that John has to come to grips with the variety of people included in this new people that God is creating.[28]

Gonzalez observes, however, that the prophetic task of John in a context of ethnic diversity and tension is a bittersweet one. The 'sweetness' described in the vision of 10:9–11, is the result of the beauty of the dream of a multi-cultural community characterized by mutual respect and harmony, while the bitterness arises from the difficulty of challenging ethnocentric views currently operating within the writer's own community. He explains:

> That is a vision sweet as honey, for it shows the fullness of the mercy of God; but it is also a vision bitter to the stomach, because it shows that no people, no tribe, no language, no nation, can claim a place of particular honor in that fullness. And it is bittersweet, because it involves radical change in the very congregations where John has served and which he loves.[29]

The biblical narratives briefly studied here show that cultural difference is not an evil in itself, and enable us to clarify theologically the nature and purpose of identity within God's own plan.

---

28. Gonzalez, *Healing of the Nations*, 69.
29. Ibid., 92.

6. 3. Proposals for doing Theology in Kuki Context of Identity Struggle

6. 3. 1. The Theological Vision

The theological vision for Kuki context is recognition of the people's identity as part of the eschatological multicultural community God is making. Recognition of identity here means neither an idealization of culture, nor does it presume that culture can exist in isolation. It means giving room for the people to participate in the decision-making process which affects their life as a people, including matters pertaining to political, social, and economic and cultural life, and the recognition of the validity of their aspirations for human equality and dignity. A Kuki theology will allow freedom for the people to reflect on contextual issues in the articulation of faith in response to the divine encounter and the outworking of it. In other words, it is to give room for theology to emerge in a Kuki context.

To recognize the people's identity is to correct the negative view that the so-called tribal culture is of lesser value to others – needing to catch up with others. The vision is founded in the biblical truth that different cultures, languages, and peoples are the divine will and purpose. As it is asserted in this work, while there are negative elements as it is true with all cultures, there is much to learn from tribal culture such as a God-human-nature related worldview, the concept of *Khankho* and so forth, and hence, recognizing the people's culture is to give them a chance to contribute for the wellbeing of a wider human society. It is both a theological and missiological imperative. That makes it clear that the ultimate purpose for the recognition of tribal culture and cultural identity is for peace as well as to give them freedom to take part in God's work of transformation.

6. 3. 2. Preference for the Term 'Local Theology'.

An articulation and expression of the Christian message in the light of a given context is the very nature of theology and hence, all theologies, including the classical theologies, are contextual. What makes a theology different from others is the context in which it emerges and the purpose for which it is done. In the context of mission, different terms were coined for instance, indigenization and contextualization. While each of these terms has important elements that cannot be rejected, they have limitations. The term 'indigenization' has more of a colonialist ring in the ex-colonized nations[30] and also creates the difficulty of discerning who is indigenous and who is not, as discussed in chapter 2. In a more inclusive way, the term 'contextualization' takes into account not only the Christian message and its hearers but also the context in which theology is articulated.

The members of the Theological Education Fund of the World Council of Churches, who coined the term in 1972, asserted that the term 'contextualization' includes all that is implied in the older indigenization or inculturation, or incarnation, but seeks also to include the realities of contemporary secularity, technology, and the struggle for human justice. William P. Russell observes that the document included three aspects of content and four tensions in the term. The three aspects of content were: (1) understanding of contextual issues in the widespread crisis of faith and search for meaning in life, the urgent issues of human development and social justice; (2) the dialectic between a universal technological civilization and local culture; and (3) religious situations. Four tensions include: those tensions between (i) continuity and change; (ii) local perceptions of the needs of a given context and initiatives for reform arising beyond that context; (iii) being critical of whatever is deficient while remaining appreciative of the good things that are already happening; and between (iv) study and action.[31] The point here is that the term contextualization emphasizes the understanding of the context in its totality prior to the articulation of theology and having included wider contextual issues along with culture it is also prophetic rather than accommodative in its approach.

The term, which emerged in the context of missiological discussion, has become a popular concept in other fields. Dean Flemming's work

---

30. Robert J. Schreiter, *Constructing Local Theologies* (London: SCM, 1985), 5.
31. William P. Russell, "Contextualization: Origins, Meaning, and Implications: A Study of What the Theological Education Fund of the World Council of Churches Originally Understood by the Term 'Contextualization,' with Special Reference to the Period 1970–1972", http://web.ebscohost.com/ehost/pdfviewer/pdfviewer?vid=7&bk=1&hid=15&sid=75a5a071-5e98-4dcd-9e5a-a8153c96e6a9%40sessionmgr4 (Assessed 8 October 2010). I rearranged the quote.

Contextualization in the New Testament is a good example.³² In this work, Flemming broadens the scope of the meaning and shows how the New Testament writers, including John of Patmos, have contextualized the gospel in their own settings, indicating the relevance of the concept for other fields of Christian ministry including preaching, apologetics, theological education, evangelism and church growth, worship, leadership style, organizational structure, social and political witness, and spiritual formation.³³ In a more elaborate way, Young states:

> Contextualization includes ecological, social, political and economic conditions, views culture more dynamically as interactive, begins with the forms of context which must be understood before Christian faith can be 'good news', and emphasizes local Christian responsibilities.³⁴

With a view to include in this concept an aspect of connectivity between theology that is articulated in a given context and that of a wider church, Schreiter prefers 'local theology' to contextual theology. He argues that while the latter focuses more on the present and hence neglects the past, the former implies the importance of a wider church.³⁵ Schreiter also observes two kinds of approaches – liberation, which concentrates especially on the dynamics of social change in human societies, and ethnographic, which looks to issues of identity and continuity.³⁶

For our purpose, without rejecting concerns included in the terms mentioned above, the term 'local theology' is preferred for the following reasons. The term contextual theology being a missionary invention emphasizes an external element that needs to be contextualized in a given context. In one sense, this needs to be the case because the Christian message

---

32. Dean Flemming, *Contextualization in the New Testament: Patterns for Theology and Mission* (Leicester: IVP, 2005).
33. Ibid., 321.
34. A. Young, "Culture" 82–87 in John Corrie ed., *Dictionary of Mission Theology: Evangelical Foundations* (Nottingham: IVP, 2007), 86.
35. Schreiter, *Local Theologies*, 6.
36. Schreiter, *Local Theologies*, 14–15.

is the 'external element' that is contextualized in all cultural contexts. However, the limitation of the term is that often this external element is treated as meaning the supposedly culture-free articulation of the gospel in the western churches. The difficulty lies with the mystery of the gospel, which is comprehensible yet transcends all human comprehensions. The term 'local theology' emphasizes the local without ignoring the place of those outside a given context. We used this term not in the sense that we elevate local culture and articulation of theology with its resources as yardsticks in theology but rather, it is used as a background in which we attempt to understand theology afresh from this particular viewpoint. In the context of Asia, and an articulation of theology with Asian cultural resources, a Taiwanese theologian C. S. Song coined the term 'A Third-Eye Theology' by way for differentiating such a theology in Asia from that of the West.[37] Following Song's style of expression, a theology that emerges from a Kuki context of identity struggle contributes to this 'Third-Eye' perspective, adding to previously developed Asian and Indian Christian Theologies, while also contributing its own insights.

Paul Hiebert's idea of 'critical contextualization' gives more room for local culture. Hiebert, who had a long missionary experience in India, develops and proposes what he calls 'critical contextualization' by which he meant neither to reject nor accept the old but that which "critically evaluates cultural issues in relation to function and meaning in society and coherence with biblical norms."[38] Hiebert's positive attitude toward local culture came from his own experiences in India where Christianity was regarded as a foreign religion because of the negative attitudes of the missionaries toward the local culture. Although Hiebert was positive toward local culture, he stresses the importance of transcending a local culture. Hence, critical contextualization, he writes, "seeks to find metacultural and metatheological frameworks that enable people in one culture to understand messages and ritual practices from another culture with a

---

37. C. S. Song, *Third-Eye Theology: Theology in Formation in Asian Settings* (Maryknoll, NY: Orbis Books, 1979).
38. Eunhye Chang et al. "Paul G. Hiebert and Critical Contextualization" 199–207 in *Trinity Journal*, Vol. 30, No. 2. (2009), 202.

minimum of distortion"[39] and that, he hopes, will be achieved through conversation among diverse Christian communities. Chang et al. writes, "Hiebert stresses that theologizing done by Christians from diverse cultural communities in conversation with each other will bring consensus on core theological understandings."[40]

A pioneer tribal Christian theologian, Thanzauva of Mizoram, argues that the core of the gospel is found in all cultures in an imperfect form, which needs to be interacted with one's faith in Jesus Christ. Unfortunately, he asserts, that was not the case with the tribal people of North-East India. He laments, "The tragedy is that in the process of interaction, the hidden gospel in the tribal culture was ignored, dominated and not theologically articulated."[41] In this light, for Thanzauva, contextualization is an interaction of one's faith in Jesus Christ with his or her re-discovered transformative element of culture. He writes, "The articulation of faith in Jesus Christ with the help of that hidden gospel often makes theology more meaningful and effective. This is nothing but contextualization."[42]

Theology in the context of the Kuki identity struggle needs to take seriously the people's identity without disconnecting themselves from others. To express this in terms of biblical imagery, it is like joining the voice of the uncountable multitudes drawn from every tribe and nation in praising the Lamb, the vision of John recorded in Revelation. As Richard Bauckham beautifully puts it, "If the Bible offers a metanarrative, a story of all stories, then we should be able to place our own stories within that grand narrative and find our own perception and experience of the world transformed by the connexion."[43]

Theology needs to emerge in the light of the people's experience. In other words, it is an attempt to affirm and express the lordship of Christ in the context of the people's struggle for identity. We will have to wait

---

39. Paul G. Hiebert, "Critical Contextualization" 104–111, *International Bulletin of Missionary Research*, Vol. 11, No. 3. (1987), 111.

40. Chang et al. "Paul G. Hiebert", 203.

41. Thanzauva, *Theology*, p. 82.

42. Ibid.

43. Richard Bauckham, *Bible and Mission: Christian Witness in a Postmodern World* (Grand Rapids, Michigan: Baker, 2003), 12.

and see what such a theology will produce, knowing that even if there is any element of heresy committed in this process, it is because of a genuine attempt to express the lordship of Christ in a given context, which will always be ready for correction for the sake of, and under the lordship of the same Christ.

6. 3. 3. Re-visiting Kuki History and Culture

6. 3. 3. 1. Was God Totally Absent in Kuki History?

In chapter 3, we pointed out that the colonial writers and missionaries were the first to write the history and culture of the Kuki people. While the works of the former were stimulated by the need for their smooth administration and hence often divisive studies but the latter were mostly motivated by their aim for conversion, and the history of the people was considered dark and filled with evils. Later attempts were made by Indian anthropologists, historians and scholars from outside of the community, but while these were motivated by a need to understand tribal culture, they viewed the people and their culture from the writers' perspectives and often put them in a negative light. In response to such views in the recent past, there has been an increasing interest among local scholars in researching and writing their own histories, which can be termed as 'the third phase' of writing Kuki history. However, being influenced by the views and structures inherited from the colonial and the subsequent Indian administrations, they tend to be limited to a particular clan or tribe.

In doing a local theology in Kuki context, and to find a more balanced picture of their history for theological reflection, there is a need for a fresh look at the people's history, enabling people to tell their own stories, both their successes and failures as a people, from their own perspectives. In doing so, a more balanced view of the people's history will emerge. A fresh look at the history of the people should also include looking beyond the boundaries and structures of communities created by the colonial administration and the subsequent independent India as discussed in chapter 3, in order to re-visualize their future as a people. A history devoid of the people's voice is an incomplete history and hence it is limited to providing a fuller story to reflect God's involvement in the history of the people.

A theological task here is to reflect and infer God's involvement in their history, both for an affirmation of what was good and a critique of what was evil, making their history an inspiration as well as a caution. The conviction is that God, in some way, got involved with the people from their earliest origins, as described in the myth of *Khul,* rather than the idea that God began to get involved in the people's lives only after their conversion to Christianity, as if the Western missionaries brought God to them. It is in this view that we need to look at the history of the people and discern God's involvements in their history.

This aspect of theology is prominent in many liberation theologies in Asia. Koyama, for instance, attempts to show this truth in the light of the circular and linear images of history in a Thai context. He writes, "We see the glory of God both in history and in nature. Circular nature shows God's glory as much as linear history. Both are purposeful. Yet, as we have seen, circular nature finds its proper place within linear history. In this proper location, circular nature finds its purpose."[44] In a more specific way in his section on 'Interpreting History', Koyama discusses the issue of the diverse cultural worldviews as well as changes brought about by agents such as colonization, modernization and technology asking, "If God is thus involved, isn't this involvement a challenge *to all Christians?* How should we make the theological insights of the efficiency of the Crucified One the powerful leaven in the universal technologically efficient civilization?"[45] Koyama's view of history can further be seen in his writing, "In all the immense complexities of the histories of Egypt, Assyria, Babylon, Persia, Rome . . . God experiences history."[46]

Similarly in the context of Africa where ancestors are highly respected and given an important place in the society, Bediako writes:

> The constant message of the Scriptures is that the lives and careers of the 'ancestors' (that is, Adam, Eve, Noah, Abraham, Isaac, Jacob, Moses, David and the rest of them) have an

---

44. Kosuke Koyama, *Water Buffalo Theology* (Maryknoll, NY: Orbis Books, 1999), 31.
45. Ibid., 49.
46. Ibid., 152.

abiding relevance for every succeeding generation. If so, we too must have our ancestors, our fathers and mothers, who like the biblical ancestors, made choices at critical points in their lives, choices that shaped their destinies of our traditions, till, in the fullness of time, they became merged, in Christ, with the history of all people of God.[47]

The benefit of such a change of understanding and attitude, Hwa Yung rightly envisions, is a dual discovery of confidence both in the gospel and in one's own culture. He writes:

> The overwhelming predominance of Western culture in the modern world, and its consequent effect on the development of Christianity in the non-Western world in the last two hundred years are generally accepted facts today. As a result non-Western Christians in general and Asian Christians in particular, lost confidence in their own cultures and histories. Partly because of this, some Asian Christians have embraced Enlightenment categories which deny objective truth to religious beliefs. Consequently, as the pluralism debate and other trends indicate, they have lost confidence in the gospel of Christ as well. Authentic contextualization that takes seriously both of Wall's pilgrim principle and indigenizing principle demands a *dual recovery of confidence*, both in the gospel and in one's own culture and history.[48]

In the Indian sub-continent, Dalit theology is committed to do the same thing, that is, to re-discover confidence both in the gospel and in their culture and history. We have pointed out in the preceding chapter that Dalit history is crucial to Dalit liberation and identity. It was for that reason that the people have started writing their own history. We also

---
47. Kwame Bediako, *Christianity in Africa, The Renewal of a Non-Western Religion* (Edinburgh/Maryknoll, NY: Edinburgh University Press/Orbis Books, 1995), 227–228.
48. Yung, *Mangoes or Bananas*, 241. Emphasis, mine.

pointed out that Dalits could easily identify their lives with the historical Jesus and read their stories in the biblical narratives, as part of their story. Even closer to home is the emerging Khasi cultural theology in Meghalaya in which theologians relate their experiences to the God of the Bible. For instance, arguing the divine revelation in Khasi tradition, T. Nongsiej writes:

> As Indian citizens in a secular state we should not have a negative view against either Christianity based from Palestine, or Hinduism based from Mesopotamia or even Islam which originated in Arabia or Khasi religion handed over by God at the bottom of *Lum Makashang* (Himalaya mountain) because all these respective places are in one land (World) under one supreme God.[49]

The Kuki people need to abandon the idea that their past was devoid of God and therefore their history has no significance for theology. Instead, they need to identify God in their past history, both in their joy and suffering, rise and fall, and be proud of the fact that they have seen an aspect of God which no one ever has seen. Through identifying God's involvement in the people's history, not to propose a writing of a sacred history and the danger this involves as in the case of South Africa's Apartheid, the third phase of writing of the history would bridge the gap of the people's history before and after Christianization and reaffirm the cultural affinity of the Kuki people across the geographical boundaries, paving the way for mutual enrichments in doing theology with culture. This is one important part of the solution to the present day Kuki identity struggle.

6. 3. 3. 2. Should Culture be only a Medium in Theology?

Like history, it is important to revisit the people's culture in constructing a local theology. Despite being part of human fallen nature, culture is a way of life which helps the community to cope with changes. In other words, a given context necessitates a particular way of life or a culture for a smooth

---

49. T. Nongsiej, *Khasi Cultural Theology* (New Delhi: ISPCK, 2002), 76.

and peaceful co-existence. For this reason, it serves not only as a mark of one's own identity but also enables the people to survive in a given context. It was because of this that Cone argues for the affirmation of culture before one begins to construct a theology: "Because the starting point of black and Third World theologies is defined by a prior cultural affirmation and political commitment to be in solidarity with the poor, our theologies bear the names that reflect our affirmations and commitments."[50] What Cone is saying is that theology being an answer to the questions arising from a given context, we need to first understand the question or context before an attempt is made to provide the answer to the perceived problems arising within it. It is a non-controversial view among the contextual theologians that in the post-colonial context, cultural identity is a prime locus for developing a theology.[51]

Therefore, in revisiting culture for doing theology in a Kuki context, we consider culture not just an instrument through which the Christian message was communicated, but rather, our hope is to discover a new way which will allow theology to emerge from and grow in the soil of Kuki culture. Having noted a primal worldview being operated in varying degrees in different periods of time and cultural situations, Taylor envisages, "It is now apparent that the dialogue we seek in the primal area may occur across a wide front ranging from worshippers in a continuing primal religious system to Christian believers."[52] This line of thinking has already started to emerge in the minds of some Kuki theologians. Peter Haokip, a Kuki Catholic priest for instance, talks about three stages of his own theological journey:

> Converted to Christianity as a boy in the early 1950s, I had to give up everything that was considered to be traditional, customary and cultural because these were considered to be

---

50. James H. Cone, *For my People: Black Theology and the Black Church* (Maryknoll, NY: Orbis Books, 1984), 148.
51. Stephen B. Bevans, *Models of Contextual Theology: Faith and Cultures* (NY: Orbis Books, 1999), 20.
52. John B. Taylor, *Primal World Views: Christian Dialogue with Traditional Thought Forms* (Ibadan: Daystar Press, 1976), 4.

of the pagan past and diabolic. In the second stage of my Christian journey, I thought the right thing was to baptize the good things of my culture and discard its negative elements. However, during my theological formation in the 1970s, especially during my MTh studies, I realized that many aspects of Christianity are historically and culturally conditioned and Christianity needs to be liberated from these conditions and allow it to grow in the soil of any culture and traditions as it is meant to be.[53]

The same will be the experiences of younger Kuki theologians. The question now is "where and how do we discern God and God's work in the people's culture?" Our task here is to identify avenues in the people's culture and suggest how they can serve as resources for a theology of identity, which, in turn served as instruments to transform the culture itself. We shall look at the concept of *Khankho* and suggest in what way this can serve as a resource for doing a local theology.

6. 3. 4. *Khankho*: An Avenue for Local Theology

The concept of *Khankho* lies close to the heart of traditional Kuki cultural identity and this concept can serve as a local resource for a theology of identity, providing a valuable means to critique deviations from the tradition, as well as offering a positive goal for the community to pursue. In chapter 3, we discussed the traditional Kuki society and pointed out that the reality of the natural world is interrelated and interdependent with the social world. *Khankho* was a life of integral harmony with God, with creation and with fellow human beings as the reflection of this worldview. As such, this element of culture served as the foundation, inspiration and guiding principle of a traditional Kuki life. In this section, we shall show how *Khankho*, the local version of *Shalom*, can be a fertile ground for theology of identity by exploring select aspects of *Khankho*, namely, the *Indoi* and the *Tol-theh* incantations and the practice of *Lha-kou* and then suggest

---

53. Peter Haokip, *Kuki Culture and the Christian Message: Theologizing in the Context of Kuki Culture* (Unpublished MTh Thesis, Jnana Deepa Vidyapeeth, Pune, 1979), vi.

their theological potential in the Kuki traditional view of life in the light of the biblical concept of *Shalom*. Our conviction is one with Bediako's when he writes, "Far from constituting a prison that inhibits our human development and from which we are to break free in order to experience salvation in a so-called 'Christian culture' brought in from outside, our primal cultural heritage is in fact the very place where Christ desires to meet us in order to transform us into his own image."[54]

6. 3. 4. 1. *The Concept of God and Nature in the Incantation of Indoi Institution*

In chapter 3, we discussed the practice of *Indoi* as a culture and will not repeat the detailed information, including the incantation and its translation, given there. Here, we shall show how the practice reflects the concept of God and nature and offers resources to enrich the Christian theology inherited through the western missionaries.

Chongloi, a pioneer in studying *Indoi* from a Christian point of view, notes how each element selected in *Indoi* in the worship represents a specific aspect of God's attribute and blessing. For instance, a pig with a slanted forehead refers to a long life or 'full life', a *se* tree, a healthy life and so forth, and prayer using these terms was for such blessings seen in those elements. This reveals the fact that the traditional Kukis did not worship nature, as often claimed, but God, the creator of nature, who is beyond nature and by doing so, they transcend space and time in worship. Second, the people understood and talked of God in terms of their own day to day life as reflected in the incantation, "Throughout the year may I provide you with meat and wine" as if, like humans, God survives through eating and drinking. Third, with regards to the way in which the people address God as *Pathennu-Pathenpa*, or 'the Mother-God, Father-God', and for that matter the different names and imageries used for God, Chongloi argues that they are not to be understood as referring to many individual gods but rather it was a cultural expression about God in God's totality. T. Nongsiej observes a similar tradition among the Khasis of Meghalaya, where there

---

54. Kwame Bediako, "Why has the summer ended and we are not saved? Encountering the Real Challenge of Christian Engagement in Primal Contexts", 5–8 in *Journal of African Christian Thought*, Vol. 11, No.2 (2008), 7.

are five different names for God: *Mei, Bei, Bablei, Balehei* and *Baleh-synei*, and he argues that these are but the traditional expression of one supreme God.[55] Fourth, is the prayer for a long life reflected in the incantation, "Deal graciously with me till such a time when my skin shrink with age as is the case with the gourd". Chongloi is right in saying that for the primal Kuki people, living a long life without deformity, in peace and harmony with others, in itself was a religious act.[56] Having pointed out the role of *Indoi* and the way in which it was preserved, Chongloi also suggests that the presence of *Indoi* in every family home can be used as a medium to present the concept of God as Immanuel as mentioned in chapter 3. This is one creative and helpful insight to understand God with the help of Kuki culture, except that *Indoi* was installed only in the families that have sons and daughters with both parents alive or 'full-fledged families' and not in the homes of single parents or that of childless couples.

The *Indoi* tradition as described by Chongloi suggests that with such a view of God, the traditional Kukis did not divide themselves on the basis of doctrines as they do today. Using the instrument, *Indoi*, each family, including that of the researcher, used to worship God who was beyond the instrument and there was no argument about who knew God better than others. This is not to thrust aside the importance of a Christocentric approach, however, it is to make a point that they articulated theology and made meanings with whatever resources were available to them and were silent about the things of God which lay beyond human comprehension. In other words, there was a place for 'silence' in talking about God, and this is an important aspect of theology often neglected in Christian theological enterprises. In fact, it was true that Jesus himself was God incarnated, fully God and fully human, who chose to be conditioned by time and space in order that we might accept him as Lord. In the words of Paul, we now see in a mirror, dimly, but then we will see face to face (1 Cor 13:12). Giving room for silence, an important part of theology, is one important insight that can be found in *Indoi* tradition.

---

55. Nongsiej, *Khasi*, 22.
56. Chongloi, *Indoi*, 237–243.

6. 3. 4. 2. An Integral Understanding of Sin and Salvation in the Tol-theh Incantation

Tol (ground), *theh* (clean/clear) literally translates 'clearing of the ground', which means clearing of the elements of sins from the community. This is performed when a person, either intentionally or unintentionally causes harm to others in the community, such as shedding of blood, making someone pregnant outside marriage, and so forth.

> The ritual of *Tol-theh* is performed in the following way. Before the ritual which involves cutting of the pig into halves, the priest tries to find out the culprit by calling out all the characters mentioned in the incantation, like the Sword, the Spear and so forth and justifies his act by seeking direction from the God of heaven:

The priest:	O you sword! Is it your desire (to commit sin by cutting off the hands of the daughter-in-law)?
The sword:	It is not my desire but the desire of the spear.
The spear:	O no, it is not my desire but the desire of the bow
The bow:	It is not my desire; but the desire of the arrow
The arrow:	It is not my desire it is the will of the God of heaven
The priest:	O God of heaven! What should I do now?

The God of heaven [says,] cut a pig that has a slanted forehead into two halves. Throw one half of the pig towards the upward slope and the other half towards the downward slope of the village. The piece falling on the upward slope would push out the sins of the upper village and the other half landing on the lower slope would push down the sins of the lower village.

Having acted according to the direction of God, the priest pours wine on the ground and chants the following words:

> *Tunin phupi a keen tai phaipi a keen tai. Ka lei duppi hung thouvin kalei thaoui hung thouvin.* That is, 'the evil elements

have retreated today. O my fertile soil! May you be infused with life again'.[57]

The following can be observed from *Tol-theh*. Firstly, the institution of the ritual indicates the concept of sin as something that comes upon the community as a result of one's action. Related to this was the fact that human sin was understood to have caused the earth to become barren. Secondly, the remedy or salvation is imagined as something that is pushing or bulldozing the element of sin out of the village, clearing it from the community. The imagery must have been drawn from the way a pig clears the ground, which they witness every day, by clearing or bulldozing the ground with her forehead. Thirdly, the interrelatedness of human action and the creation is evident in the belief that the earth became barren because of human sin; the same is also reflected in the restoration of the fertility of the earth through the clearance of human sin from the village or community. Fourthly, and related to this, is the high reverence given to life and its deadly impact on the earth when it is harmed. This was further apparent in the fact that the priest never cuts animals for sacrifice on his own will but by the order given by God.

The theological insights reflected in the practice of *Tol-theh* ritual may include the following. One, the effect of human sin on nature: could the interrelatedness of human action and nature help address the present global ecological crises? Two, the concept of salvation: in what way does the understanding of salvation or remedy of sin as clearing the ground enrich the Christian understanding of the salvific work of Christ? Could the imagery of clearing the ground be another way of explaining God's work of salvation in addition to the existing analogies such as, Ransom Theory, Penal Substitution and so forth? Three, the impact of restoration from sin: How do we understand the traditional concept of salvation which includes nature? Could this, in some way, be related to Paul's teaching on an eschatological deliverance of creation from the bondage of corruption along with the sons of God in glory (Rom 8:19–22 NRSV)? In fact, Paul, reflecting on Genesis 3:17–19, made it clear that the earth came into the

---

57. Goswami, *Kuki Life*, 454–455. Reproduced and paraphrased.

present state of futility because of human sin. An exploration of this will lead to re-discoveries of resources for doing theology in a Kuki context. It was along the line of this argument that Joel B. Green and Mark D. Baker argued against the rigid understanding of the work of God in Jesus and wrote:

> No model of the atonement will fit all sizes and shapes, all needs and contexts where the church is growing and active in mission. This means, ultimately, that the next chapter of this book is being written in hundreds of places throughout the world, where communities of Jesus' disciples are practicing the craft of theologian-communicator and struggling with fresh and faithful images for broadcasting the mystery of Jesus' salvific death.[58]

Contemporary study of the theology and practice of Christian mission explores the marks of global mission in the present time and includes the issue of the integrity of Creation as one of the concerns. In his call for the broader understanding of mission, Dave Bookless, for instance, rediscovers missiological insights for non-human beings in the light of Noah's call to build an Ark and writes, "Mission that ignores creation will always present too small a vision of God and his purposes."[59]

6. 3. 4. 3. Cordial Relationship in Lha-kou: Key to Survival and Success

In chapter 3, we described the ways in which a person relates to everyone in the society through social relationship systems, such as *Upa-Naupa*, *Tucha-Becha -Sunggao* and *Jol-le-gol* relationships. Within the traditional worldview such a relationship was extended to non-human beings,

---

58. Joel B. Green and Mark D. Baker, *Recovering the Scandal of the Cross: Atonement in New Testament and Contemporary Contexts* (Carlisle: Paternoster Press, 2000), 221.
59. Dave Bookless, "To Strive to Safeguard the Integrity of Creation and Sustain and Renew the Life of the Earth (ii)" 94–104 in Andrew Walls and Cathy Ross eds., *Mission in the 21ˢᵗ Century: Exploring the Five Marks of Global Mission* (London: Darton, Longman and Todd, Ltd., 2008), 104.

showing that in the traditional Kuki society, a person is connected to all other members in the society, including nature, through this web of relationships. In that society, life was lived and shared in a community, effecting and being affected by both the present and the future. In such a situation, a cordial relationship was crucial for one's survival and success in this life and the life after. Here, we shall further show the importance of such cordial relationship reflected in the practice of *Lha-kou* and suggest how the traditional concept of relationship can be used as a resource for doing a theology of identity for the people.

The importance of cordial relationship for a person is evident in the practice of *Lha-kou* wherein a person seeks to establish a good relationship with, or approval of, the spirit/soul of the thing that is being sought after. The word *Lha* – spirit/soul and *kou* – call or invite, means to invite or to approach the spirit [of some thing that is being sought after] with a view to winning its cordial relationship or approval before it is sought after. Winning a cordial relationship with or approval of others, for instance with the spirit of grain/rice in this context was to harvest plenty of grains; or killing a wild animal, for a hunter, involved winning the spirit or soul of an animal.

There were different types of *lha-kou*: *Salha-kou*, an invitation of animals' spirits for a hunter, that is, a prayer for success in hunting wild animals; *Changlha-kou*, an invitation of the spirit of paddy/rice for cultivators; or *Moulha-kou*, an invitation of a bride's spirit for a young man, persuasion of a sick man's spirit and so forth. Letkhojam Haokip listed different kinds of *lha-kous* including the invitation of the spirit of Paddy/Rice, Animals, and that of the humans.[60]

Behind the practice of *Lha-kou* was a belief in the existence of the spirits of nature and the importance of living in harmony with them. We have discussed this under the section on a traditional Kuki worldview and pointed out how one lives in a way that does not harm the spirits of nature. It also indicates that a spirit of nature can be hurt or disassociated with a person as a result of his or her behaviour. In this case, the person or the

---

60. Haokip, *Thempu Ho Thu*, 53–60.

spirit of the creature being hurt by one's action was termed *Lha-se* [*Lha* – spirit, *se* – bad/hurt] and *Lha-kou* was the way to restore that relationship.

What is clear is the fact that a cordial relationship with others or nature was vital to one's survival and success: to get an animal for a hunter, plenty of grains for a farmer, a good wife for a young man and so forth. The practices of *Sa-Ai* and *Chang-Ai* referred to earlier also made this point clear. The point here is not to argue whether or not nature has spirit, or whether such a belief is scientifically provable, but rather it is to show the concept of community and the way in which one tries to live in peace with others. Relationship was a key to survive in the community. And it was in this light that the concept of 'success' was understood in terms of being able to relate with others well, including nature. For instance, *Sa-Ai* and *Chang-Ai* were regarded as successes that are achieved, not by being expert in shooting or working hard in the rice fields, but through a cordial relationship. That is, by being able to win the favours of animals and rice. In this way, cordial relationships with others, including nature, was considered the key to survival and success.

In the society which is increasingly violent and torn apart in the process of identity construction and assertion, there is an urgent need to evoke the power of the traditional concept of relationship, which also implies dialogue, as a crucial part of one's own identity for which the struggle is being endured. This is important for building a peaceful society in a multi-ethnic context of North-East India.

6. 3. 4. 4. Kuki Traditional View of Life

In a traditional Kuki culture, life was regarded as sacred. The understanding of life and the wishes for it needs to be understood in the light of the incantation of *Indoi* mentioned above and *Bul-tuh*, Kuki ethics. The words in the incantation include prayers for long life, for beauty, for God's care and so forth. The vision for life is for all the good things that can be imagined. For instance, before birth, a ritual ceremony called *kopkil-halho* or prayer for the couple, is performed so that they may be blessed with a child; at birth, a welcome feast called *Nao-Juneh* is organized; then *Lamsamvo*, or the first haircut ceremony; *Somge*, or ceremonial entry into a Common Hall for holistic learning; *kichen* or marriage ceremony; *gamlen* or hunting, and *loulho* or cultivation for women; *Sa-Ai* or celebration of victory over animal for men, and *Chang-Ai* or celebration of victory over paddy; *lhanlam-lhah* or farewell ceremony of the soul of the person after death. A successful life was understood in terms of being able to perform *Sa-Ai* for men and *Chang-Ai* for women and dying with a normal death or *Tehthi*, that is, a death not of diseases or by accident but due to old age. That, according to the traditional concept, was a life that one dreams of. A high reverence for life is most implicit in the practice of *Bultuh*, the Kuki ethics. *Bultuh*, or the stocks referred to earlier in chapter 3, was the highest level of penalty one could receive. There was no place for capital punishment in a traditional Kuki culture. This is substantiated by the obligatory act of justification in animal sacrifices before the act is performed.

Khankho, for these reasons, is close to the biblical concept of *Shalom* in terms of its outlook, vision, scope and approach. Drawing insights from both the Old and the New Testaments, the Old Testament scholar Walter Brueggemann argues that within the biblical worldview creation is one and every creature is to live in harmony with one another. He argues, "The central vision of world history in the Bible is that all of creation is one, every creature in community with every other, living in harmony and security toward the joy and wellbeing of every other creature."[61] The persistent vision here is for joy, wellbeing, harmony, and prosperity[62] hence, he argues, "*Shalom* is the substance of the biblical vision of one community embracing all creation. *Shalom* refers to all those resources and factors which make communal harmony joyous and effective."[63] Of course, we are reminded at this point that ancient Israel existed within a cultural context which was far closer to the primal world we are describing than it was to the modern, often secular, societies from which western missionaries came.

This explains why new Christians in primal societies have so often recognized the Old Testament as relating closely to many of their deepest concerns. To return to Brueggemann, he points out three dimensions of

---

61. Walter Brueggemann, *Living Toward a Vision: Biblical Reflections on Shalom* (Philadelphia: United Church Press, 1976), 15.
62. Ibid., 16–17.
63. Ibid., 16.

shalom: First, *shalom* is inclusive, encompassing all of reality expressed in the mystery and majesty of creation images, for instance, the harmonious living of all creatures in Isaiah 11:6–9a where the wolf is dwelling with the lamb, the leopard with the kid and so forth, and the calming of the storm in Mark 4:37–39. In this case, *shalom* is like the time of creation when all lived in peace and harmony. The second dimension is the historical political community where the absence of *shalom* was expressed in terms of social disorder, economic inequality, judicial perversion, and political oppression and exclusivism, against which the prophets called for righteousness and justice (Mic 2:1–2; Amos 5:14–15; Isa 1:16–17). In the same way, in the New Testament, Luke 4:16–21 records Jesus' work among the excluded people which includes healing the sick, forgiving the guilty, raising the dead and feeding the hungry. Besides the cosmic and historical-political aspects, Brueggemann points out the third dimension of *shalom*, that is, a sense of wellbeing experienced by the person who lives a caring, sharing, joyous life in community. Against this lifestyle, Brueggemann says, is covetousness, which Jesus opposed, for example, when he warned against the man who requested him to bid his brother to share with him the inheritance (Luke 12:13, 15, & 22). The point that Brueggemann stresses here is that wellbeing is received by living according to God's will and not by idolatrous covetousness at the expense of others.[64]

6. 3. 5. The Bible and the Gospel in Local Theology

6. 3. 5. 1. *The Need for Reading the Bible through the People's Eyes*

The roles of the Bible and gospel are important for a community, like that of Kukis of Manipur, who follow Christianity, their adopted religion. In the Kuki context, there are many aspects in which the Biblical worldview and stories are closer to their own tradition than they were to those in the affluent western world. Therefore, the main source for theology of identity must be drawn from the Bible and the gospel by reading the Bible through the eyes of the people. Prioritization of the Bible includes taking Old and

---

64. Ibid., 17–20.

the New Testaments equally seriously since this provides an integral approach to the issue of identity. Failure to do so is to repeat the tragic experience of Christianity in Africa where, as Schreiter observes, "The bitter irony, as African theologians have pointed out, is that African values and customs are often closer to the Semitic values that pervade the Scriptures and the story of Jesus than the European Christian values that have been imposed upon them."[65]

The way forward is to read the Bible through the eyes of the people. In other words, it is important to keep in mind the experiences of the people while reading the Bible and relate them to the situation of the people. In doing so, the people will find their own stories in the Bible and discover hope and resources for identity. Such a reading of the Bible has been undertaken in many parts of the Southern hemisphere. Jenkins shows how the Bible is read with fresh eyes, with new meanings, sometimes in surprising ways, in the context of issues such as famine, plague, poverty, and exile. In the primal cultures across the Southern hemisphere, people recognize the connection between the world of the Bible and their own situations. He writes, "the 'Southern' Bible carries a freshness and authenticity that adds vastly to its credibility as an authoritative source and a guide for daily living."[66]

The theologian James Cone has shown how the narrative of the Bible not only makes connections with primal religious culture, but also relates to the socio-political concerns of poor people and becomes a source for guidance in the struggles for human freedom and dignity.

When the Bible is read in the community of the poor, it is not understood by them as a deposit of doctrines or of revealed truths about God. Rather it becomes a living book that tells the story of God's dealings with God's people. Its importance as a source for creating theology cannot be overstated from black and Third World theologians.[67]

---

65. Robert J. Schreiter ed., *Faces of Jesus in Africa* (Maryknoll, NY: Orbis Books, 1991), viii.

66. Philip Jenkins, *The New Faces of Christianity, Believing the Bible in the Global South* (New York: Oxford University Press, 2006) 5–6.

67. Cone, *For my People*, 152.

The gospel truth is derived from a re-reading of the Bible, which cannot be communicated through others but by the histories and cultures of our peoples. Cone further writes, "Truth is embedded in the stories, songs, dances, sermons, paintings, and sayings of our peoples."[68] Similarly, Hseng-Chu Wang, professor of theology at Tainan Theological Seminary in Taiwan stated:

> Most European-American theologians treat the Old Testament as the interesting history of the Hebrews. The Taiwanese, however, view the Old Testament very differently. Living under domination of foreign power for four centuries, their history destroyed, their identity as a people diffused by colonization, the Old Testament is their story.[69]

While commenting on the differences between the western fundamentalists and ethnic minority groups' experiences, Gonzalez shares a similar view:

> Fundamentalism takes as its starting point the authority of Scripture, quite apart – at least in theory – from the degree to which it resonates with the experience and culture of the community. If there is dissonance, it is the experience and the culture that must be wrong and must be adjusted to the Bible. ... The ethnic minority community on the other hand, grants authority to Scripture precisely because Scripture resonates with the culture and experience of the group.[70]

Gonzalez's conviction is that,

> the authority of Scripture does not stand alone, but is closely related to, and grounded on, the manner in which the Bible

---

68. Cone, *For my People*, 153.
69. Quoted in Justo L. Gonzalez, *Out of Every Tribe & Nation: Christian Theology at the Ethnic Roundtable* (Nashville: Abingdon Press, 1992), 50.
70. Ibid.

resonates with our culture and experience, so that we find in Scripture the same Word of God that has been revealed to us and to our ancestors throughout the generations.[71]

In such a reading of the Bible, community is both the agent and the goal of hermeneutics with the view that truth belongs to the community and not to an individual. In this regard Stephen S. Kim proposes a move from 'I-Hermeneutics to We-Hermeneutics'[72] wherein he stresses that community is not only a hermeneutical tool or the context in which the text needs to be read, but also the goal of the hermeneutical task itself. In other words, the reading of the Bible is to benefit the community.[73]

The reading of the Bible through the eyes of the people is to help discover the gospel, which is about God and God's work for salvation for the people in and through Christ. In the context of the Masai in Africa, Vincent J. Donovan argues, "We must not force any particular interpretation of development on non-Western people. Otherwise, we might be aborting forms of development, still unknown to us and unseen by us, which can yet spring from that incredibly fertile gospel."[74] It is clear that the task of a people's reading of the biblical text in the light of both their own story and their present experience, still remains to be done. This publication aims to encourage that process, demonstrating the freedom Kuki Christianity has to respond to the gospel from within its own cultural and existential situation. The gospel must become good news in that context rather than pre-packaged patterns of belief and practice, presented as universally true, but in fact someone else's answer to questions other than those asked by the Kuki. Because this task is yet to be done it would be unwise to propose in advance which text may prove to speak into this

---

71. Ibid., 53.
72. Kim uses this phrase as the title of his paper presented at the Ethnic Minority Roundtable conference which was incorporated in Gonzalez's work, Gonzalez, *Out of Every Tribe*.
73. Represented by Gonzalez, *Out of Every Tribe*, 54.
74. Vincent J. Donovan, *Christianity Rediscovered: An Epistle from the Masai* (Maryknoll, NY: Orbis Books, 1982), 173.

context. However, we may suggest certain themes that can already be seen to have powerful relevance to the context we have described.

6. 3. 5. 2. *The Task for Future Research and Reflections*

The concern for liberation found in the book of Exodus, already so significant in the case of Dalit theology, provides the Kuki people a foundation and inspiration for their struggle for identity as a people. This includes a challenge to reflect on some difficult biblical passages, for instance, the song of Moses in Deuteronomy 32:8 and Acts 17:26 where God appears to have determined the time and the exact places for people to live, influencing the current identity movements. In fact, land or community land is an integral part of Kuki life and social order and we have shown in chapter 3 how land and clan identities are inseparably connected and play an important role in social orderliness and cohesion. In this case, loss of community land is considered an elimination of clan identity. One example is the experience of Tingkai Village, or Tingkai sub-clan, of the Haokip clan in the western part of Manipur to which the researcher belongs. Tingkai was destroyed on 6 September 1993. Although the identity of the sub-clan remains, the mark of that identity, the space and the feeling of belongingness and dignity through that space, were removed. Related to this is the role of the landscape in shaping the theological imagination of the people. We have pointed out that traditional Kukis approach God from 'known to unknown'. Environment and landscapes, including the hills, the plains and the rivers are significant in shaping their worldview through which they form the idea of God and God's revelation among them. In other words, their religious worldview is connected with the physical world. In fact, it was for that reason that Wati Longchar, a well-known Naga theologian writes:

> The land is seen as an integral part of the web of life, physical and spiritual, but not inert, empty and passive. . . . The strong sense of community rooted in indigenous view of life, when

interpreted properly, it would help the world communities in safeguarding the world from destruction and exploitation.[75]

The theological importance of the environment for indigenous people is an indication of the fact that they will be theologically impoverished if they are denied their traditional land and resources. This is a crucial point for the 'tribal' people in general, and for Kukis of Manipur in particular, whose traditional land and resources have become increasingly vulnerable in the face of assimilative government policies referred to earlier.

The question is "where is the land which God determined for the Kuki people to live in?" If that is where they are presently settled, then the related question is "how to claim it?" If a land is given or better put, their ancestors' land is politically recognized, for instance, by way of giving them statehood, how should such a land be viewed as, in the words of Brueggemann, "glorious and problematic"[76] and avoid the temptation to misuse it? Brueggemann reflects on the issue of land in the light of the biblical narratives and shows both the importance of community land ownership and the risk involved in misusing it. This is an important issue, however, it is not the immediate question in the sense that the Kukis first need to have the right to administer their traditional land in order to ask this question.

Two, as referred to earlier, the theme of *Shalom*, or *Khankho* in a local term, drawn from Leviticus 26:4–6, Isaiah 11:6–9; Luke 4:18–19 and Romans 8:19–22, will provide them both a hermeneutical bridge between the world of the Bible and traditional culture, and can form the basis for an integral concept of salvation. The theme of *Shalom* concerns the issues of equality, love, justice and peace that need to be articulated at different levels. At the local level, a fresh understanding must be sought in the context of an oppressive patriarchal culture as well as a hierarchical chief-villager relationship discussed in chapter 3. In a wider context, it needs

---

75. Wati Longchar, "Traditions and Cultures of Indigenous People: Continuity of Indigenous People in Asia", *Workshop on "Indigenous People – Spirituality and Peace" Asia Pacific Alliance of YMCAs and Interfaith Cooperation Forum* (Indonesia: October 19–24, 2007).

76. Walter Brueggemann, *The Land* (London: SPCK, 1978), 14.

to be reflected in the light of the people's experiences of alienation and impoverishment as a result of policies both at the state and national level. Similarly, the uncountable multitude drawn from every tribe and nation in the book of Revelation referred to earlier makes it clear that the praise of God has to be sung in community, showing the importance of peaceful co-existence with others. In re-reading the Bible in this way, the people will find their own stories in the Bible and discover a correct perspective and paradigm for their identity struggle.

Related to this is the task of asking some fundamental and risky question such as "Who did the traditional Kukis worship?" or "Who was the creator of those elements of *Indoi* they prayed to when they prayed 'bless me as you bless the *se* tree or the bamboo and so forth'?" "How do we interpret Jesus' life and work in the light of the concept of *Khankho*?" and "How do we understand *Khankho* in relation to Christian spirituality?" These questions may be elaborated here briefly.

To say that God participates in the people's history is to accept God's involvement in their culture at the same time. This is well expressed by Sanneh when he writes, "The fact of Christianity being a translated, and translating, religion places God at the centre of the universe of cultures, implying free coequality among cultures and a necessary relativizing of languages vis-à-vis the truth of God."[77] This naturally led him to argue that, "No culture is so advanced and so superior that it can claim exclusive access or advantage to the truth of God, and none so marginal or inferior that it can be excluded. All have merit; none is indispensable."[78]

Gonzalez's *Out of Every Tribe & Nation*[79] is based on a detailed report of discussions which took place among non-western theologians at what was called an ethnic roundtable. They concluded:

---

77. Lamin Sanneh, *Whose Religion Is Christianity: The Gospel beyond the West* (Grand Rapids, Michigan: William B. Eerdmans Publishing Company, 2003), 106.
78. Ibid.
79. Gonzalez, *Out of Every Tribe*. The book was the result of several years of dialogue participated by ethnic minority groups who met regularly for discussions from 1987 until the book was published in 1992. The ethnic roundtable conference was held in order to help the people's claim for identity and discover and affirm our cultural valued and contribute to a fuller understanding of the gospel.

> Our ancestors were told that there was a 'Christian' culture, and that in order to accept it they had to reject their own.... Such notions we unreservedly reject. We have come rather as Christian theologians who confess and rejoice that our cultural identities and experiences have given us particular perspectives and insights into the meaning of the gospel.[80]

The risky question is "did Kuki primal concept of God indicate that the people worshipped the God of the Bible who created the universe?" Bediako considers primal religion the "new theatre and arena of Christian vitality" and at the same time calls it, "revolution in itself".[81] The truth is that in the *Indoi* incantation, prayers were made to the One who created and sustains the elements such as a tree, a bamboo, an animal and so forth contained in *Indoi*. The question is, if those elements, which were used in the *Indoi* incantation, are part of the same creation that the book of Genesis says God created, was not this the same creator to whom the primal Kuki people prayed? Could this justify theologically the claim that the primal Kuki prayer found in the *Indoi* incantation was a prayer to the God of the Old Testament, the Creator of the universe? If not, in what way can this belief and practice of faith enrich the Christian worship of God?

The second fundamental question is to ask "who is Jesus in the context of Kukis?" As in Dalit theology discussed in the preceding chapter, the historical Jesus is meaningful to the tribal people because his lowly birth and peasant background can easily be identified with that of the tribal people. The way he lived and served – the meeting with the Samaritan woman at Jacob's well (John 4:1–26), healing the thirty-eight years sick man at Bethesda (John 5:1–15), the suffering and death on the Cross for the sake of others (John 19) – were easily identifiable with Kuki experience. The question here is whether or not we can say that Jesus was Kuki in the way that the Blacks and the Dalits have argued? Is it theologically sound to say that Jesus was someone who knows/practices and embodies *khankho* in a Kuki context? Elsewhere, we have developed the idea that

---

80. Gonzalez, *Out of Every Tribe*, 36.
81. Bediako, "Why has the summer", 6.

in a Kuki context Jesus was a *Kho-chaga*, or a suffering villager. That is to say, he was not only a Kuki, but also a suffering Kuki villager under the increasingly oppressive chief system of Kuki culture.[82] The point is that God experiences what the people have experienced and shows them the way forward. Kazoh Kitamori developed an understanding of God as the God who suffers pain because of his love.[83] This, for him, was both comforting news as well as an inspiration for Christian suffering for the sake of others. Suffering as the result of love for others is a necessary part of following Christ who was crucified outside of the gate. For Kitamori, knowing God is risking death, as he says, "Theology of glory can be understood only through theology of the cross."[84] Although his recent critics have found him guilty of ignoring the sufferings of those Asian nations under the hands of Japanese,[85] Kitamori's insight that God suffers pain with the people in their suffering is helpful for those under oppression. The task that lies ahead is to find ways in which Jesus is identified with the local people, experiencing the same experience they went through, and yet transforming the situation.

Connected to this is the understanding of *Khankho* in relation to the kind of Christian spirituality described in chapter 4. The point is that if in a Kuki context Jesus embodied and fulfilled *Khankho,* salvation or spiritual life is not to escape from the concerns of the world for a pietistic and privatistic life but it is to follow Jesus in practicing and embodying *Khankho* the way he did even to the Cross. Bonhoeffer writes, "The disciple looks solely at his Master", which for him, means the risks one has to take in radical imitation of what Jesus did for the sake of others. He continues, "But when a man follows Jesus Christ and bears the image of the incarnate, crucified and risen Lord, when he has become the image of God, we

---

82. Jangkholam Haokip, "Impact of Christianity: In Reference to Kuki Society", *Khanglai 2008-cum-KWS Gauhati Decade Celebration* (Gauhati, Assam: October 9–12, 2008).
83. Kazoh Kitamori, *Theology of the Pain of God* (Eugene, OR: Wipf and Stock Publishers, 2005, 5th Revised Edition). See, Chapter eleven in particular.
84. Kitamori, *The Pain of God*, 146.
85. Quoted in Anri Morimoto, "Foreword" 1–5 in Kitamori, *The Pain of God*, 2.

may at last say that he has been called to be the 'imitator of God'."[86] These are the tasks for future research and reflections

6. 4. Theology of Identity and Identity Construction

The question as to how a local theology relates to the people's quest for identity in this study lies in the preparation of the ground for identity construction. The main factor for Kuki identity crisis discovered in this work was the alienation of the people from their own cultural identity in the process of change brought about by the colonial administration, side by side with conversion to a westernized form of Christianity, and the subsequent impact of incorporation within Independent India. We argued that the people need to be reconnected to their cultural past and shown how such a reconnection is possible by revisiting the people's history and culture as a basis for theological articulation and expression in this given context. In this case, a local theology is a reconciling factor between the people's present experiences and their cultural past; an agent that prepares the ground for reunion as well as that which enables a smooth reconnection. In a 'Christian context' such as that of the Kukis of Manipur, such a critical theological reflection on the issue of identity needs to underlie all other responses.

While it is fundamental to affirm Kuki identity, it is equally important to remember the danger of romanticizing the identity by assuming it as static. Our study of the concept 'identity', in the light of insights drawn from literature in the fields of sociology and anthropology in chapter 2, led us to conclude that all identities, including Kuki, are social constructs reflecting a given socio-cultural, political and economic context. This is more so with the tribal people, the Kukis in particular, who are politically powerless and vulnerable. This, however, does not justify an identity construction at the expense of others, but only indicates the fact that the past cultural identity cannot be restored as it was, nor will it be possible to

---

86. Dietrich Bonhoeffer, *The Cost of Discipleship* (London: SCM Press, 1975), 275.

create a future identity which will remain static. Kuki identity will continue to influence, and be influenced by its given context, demanding a transformative imagination and creativity in identity construction and reconstruction, knowing that God is the ultimate ruler over all nations. For this reason, it is not only incorrect but also dangerous to presume or project identity as something that is static and of which we are custodians. Identity and local theology for these reasons need to be put in the right place or they can become more destructive than transformative. The second danger is to idealize one's own culture, ignore the evil of oppression of other peoples committed in the process of asserting an identity. Gonzalez rightly argues, "even though I love my language and the sentiments it can express, I must not idealize my own culture to such a degree that I forget the many oppressions and injustices through which it was forged. I expect that, if we go back far enough, we shall find similar origins to other cultures."[87]

Two points which are directly related to Kuki context from this quotation are the importance of self-retrospection and the issue of overemphasizing differences in identity assertion. Often the so-called majority clan or dialect group influences the formation of identity in the Kuki context, suppressing the aspirations of the minority group. The problem of nomenclature discussed in chapter 3 is precisely the outcome of this. Kuki identity assertion must be sensitive to the aspirations of all the clans, despite their sizes and tones of their voices, for their survival as a group. Related to this is the problem of overemphasizing, or inventing, cultural and linguistic differences in order to form a separate group. We noted this in the context of Bible translation in which often new words were invented in order to make a different Bible for a group concerned. At a different level in the context of Minjung theology in South Korea, Dong-Kun Kim observes a similar kind of problem when he writes that,

> minjung theologians wanted minjung theology to be treated as an independent and self-grown theology. This is one of the reasons why minjung theologians argued that their theology

---

87. Gonzalez, *Out of Every Tribe*, 34.

was not an Asian version of the liberation theology of Latin America. This attitude, which emphasized differences rather than mutual similarities, hindered minjung theology's abilities to dialogue with other theologies.[88]

Another form of romanticising identity, distinct to a 'Christian context' such as Kuki, and for that matter Naga, is what we called 'missionization of identity,' discussed in chapter 2. In a way, this is a confusion of Christianity with one's own socio-cultural and political identity, the mistake which the missionaries themselves had committed, particularly during World War I, as discussed in chapter 4. The problem of such an identity enterprise limits God into a particular group and possibly this is part of the reason why Christianity is seen as a religion of particular groups or nations. Christianity needs to transcend local identities and create one community of God, in the foretaste of the eschatological community God intends.

The way forward in the twenty-first century Kuki context is to hold the people's cultural past, their present experiences and the future hope in a transformative tension in a reconstruction of identity. Giving priority to the context in doing a local theology is important, however, it does not mean accepting culture uncritically, nor does it mean re-introducing the past culture as it was. Rather, once positive elements and values have been identified, they need to be understood and employed in the light of the present and the future hope. For instance, *Khankho* cannot be practised at present by imitating what the people did in the past but rather, its message can be applied in today's life situations. That is to say, if *Khankho* is used, for instance, to pacify the patriarchal structure of Kuki family discussed in chapter 3, that is to miss the message of the culture. In the same way, the chief system cannot be practiced as in the past. Thus, identity preservation is not merely re-introducing what was there in the past but rather drawing what is valuable from the past in dialogue with the present and the future. This is where the need for a critical theological reflection arises. Culture

---

88. Dong-Kun Kim, "Korean Minjung Theology in History and Mission" 165–182 in *Studies in World Christianity*, Vol. 2 Part 2 (1996), 177.

and cultural values need to be rediscovered in the light of the Christian message, indicating a constant task of reflection of the gospel in the light of every new context.

A theology of identity in a Kuki context also needs to prepare the way for the people to relate to 'others', within and outside the community, in order to form one universal family of God. The need for this is clear in the light of the fact that the great gathering of the multitude in the book of Revelation was to declare in unity, "Salvation belongs to the Lord". Moreover, God is the same so that no theology can be isolated from others, and our perception of God is determined by our time and place so that no understanding of God can be complete, Walls rightly argues.[89] Theology in a Kuki context is just one voice among the multitude of voices and it needs to be in harmony with others. In other words, theology in a Kuki culture should critique Kuki identity movement in the light of the Christian message when it becomes ethnocentric in nature. Walls writes:

> The faith of Christ is infinitely translatable, it creates 'a place to feel at home.' But it must not make a place where we are so much at home that no one else can live there. Here we have no abiding city. In Christ all poor sinners meet, and in finding themselves reconciled with him, are reconciled to each other.[90]

A theology for inter- and intra-ethnic relationship implies the importance of dialogue among the people. Dialogue basically means exchange of values with each other through words and action implying the needs for mutual acceptance and respect, active listening, and openness to other views and values and it is important in all aspects of life including theology and identity construction. This is important in North-East India, particularly for the Kukis and the Nagas, in their faith-backed identity movements described in this work.

---

89. Andrew Walls, *The Missionary Movement in Christian History* (Maryknoll, NY: Orbis Books, 1996), 12.
90. Ibid., 25.

It is important to show how a local theology stands in relation to theologies developed in other contexts. There cannot be a theology disconnected to other expressions of faith, since this would result in a contextualism, which merely repeated the errors of the past by arrogantly assuming that truth belonged within a single culture. This would be particularly tragic in the era of world Christianity in which the opportunity exists as never before for mutual enrichment within a multi-cultural and truly 'catholic' church. In the words of Ekka, "Any sustained and truthful effort at contextualization would not only revive the cultural manifestations of the communities but also would enrich the colourful mosaic of global Christian faith."[91]

The benefit of rooting the gospel into the people's culture will reaffirm the people's identity in the light of the gospel, which is Jesus the Christ, hence the culture is transformed, and at the same time enriches the understanding of God in a wider context of the church. For the Kuki people of Manipur and their allied groups across the border as described in chapter 3, an additional benefit of this will be the closer fellowship this would bring among them for mutual fellowship and enrichment for theological enterprises as they are linguistically and culturally intelligible to one another. A fresh theological articulation in a Kuki context of Manipur will have a wider impact across the borders.

---

91. Jhakmak Neeraj Ekka, "Cultural Deterioration", 19.

Conclusion

The aim of this publication was to investigate the tribal people's struggle for identity in North-East India with a view to proposing a theological response to the issue. We selected the Kuki people of Manipur in particular and investigated their history, cultural and religious traditions, and noted the enormous changes, which have created multiple crises for the people. Christianity, which came to fill the cultural vacuum created by the colonial power, further alienated the people from their own culture, and together created a grave identity crisis across North-East India. In the post-colonial era, the tribal people found themselves divided by international boundaries, and those on the Indian side became members of a nation-state whose majority culture is strikingly different from their own. It was in this light that we examined the question of identity and identity movements in North-East India and concluded that while they are social constructs, they are also signs of the people's search for liberation, reflecting the socio-economic, cultural and political context within which they emerge. We also examined the role of Christianity – the way it was brought, understood and practiced in this context – and concluded that the impact of Christianity was more negative than positive in terms of harm it caused to the cultural practices of the people. However, in the post-conversion period Christianity provided a new way of life, or 'vehicle', for the people to cope with the new situation, which the Kuki people still need to realize.

This publication argued that development of a local theology is an essential and urgent need to respond to the people's identity struggle. It was because of this that we studied Dalit theology, a pioneer theology of identity from an oppressed people's perspective, which provides valuable insights in the context of the tribal people of North-East India. It was noted that both Dalits and tribals share much in common, particularly in the fields of theological methodology, the emphasis and approach in theologizing. At the same time, it was argued that Tribal theology has an additional task of taking into consideration both the cultural and geographical realities of the people in an articulation of theology. The study showed how that could be done by proposing a local theology, or a hybrid theology – one that emerges as the result of a revisit of the people's history, culture and their present experiences in the light of the gospel.

In the context of the Indian sub-continent as a whole, the approach taken in this publicaiton clearly offers a challenge and a corrective to the assimilative approach of majority Hindu India, particularly the ideology of *Hindutva*. However, the approach proposed here, which involves the recognition of the validity of cultural plurality, can free peoples who found their own sense of dignity and identity to make a positive contribution to nation-building, enabling them to take their place within a broader and tolerant society and make their distinctive contribution to it.

Lastly, the Kuki struggle for identity reflects and represents the struggle of many peoples around the world. There is a global quest for values that respect differences and affirm the human dignity of all peoples. While a study of the Kuki struggle for identity is vital at the local level, it also contributes to the voice of the primal peoples around the globe for the recognition of identity and contribution of their values to the wellbeing of the human family as a whole. What was once silenced as primitive needs to be given a chance to speak for the good of all.

Bibliography

Books

Armstrong, Karen. *A Short History of Myth*. Edinburgh: Canongate Books Ltd, 2006.

Arokiadoss, P. "The Significance of Dr Ambedkar for Theologising in India" 290–313 in Devasahayam, ed. *Frontiers of Dalit Theology*, New Delhi: ISPCK/Gurukul, 1997.

Balasuriya, Tissa. "Divergence: An Asian Perspective" 113–119 in *Third World Theologies: Commonalities & Divergence*, K. C. Abraham, ed. Maryknoll: Orbis Books, 1990.

Barooah, Nirode, D. *David Scott in North-East India (1802–1831): A Study in British Paternalism*. New Delhi: Munshiram Manoharlal, 1970.

Barrett, C. K. *A Critical and Exegetical Commentary on the Acts of the Apostles*. Vol. II, Edinburgh: T & T Clark, 1998.

Barth, Fredrik. *Ethnic Groups and Boundaries: The Social Organization of Cultural Difference*. Boston: Little, Brown and Company, 1969.

Baruah, Sanjib. *Durable Disorder: Understanding the Politics of Northeast India*. New Delhi: Oxford University Press, 2005.

Bauckham, Richard. *Bible and Mission: Christina Witness in a Postmodern World*. Grand Rapids, Michigan: Baker, 2003.

Bauman, Zygmunt. *Identity*. Cambridge: Polity Press, 2006.

Bediako, Kwame. *Christianity in Africa: The Renewal of a Non-Western Religion*. Edinburgh/Maryknoll, NY: Edinburgh University Press/Orbis Books, 1995.

Bevans, Stephen B. *Models of Contextual Theology: Faith and Cultures*. Maryknoll, New York: Orbis Books, 1999.

Bhatt, Chetan. *Hindu Nationalism: Origins, Ideologies and Modern Myths*. Oxford: Berg Publishers, 2001.

Bonhoeffer, Dietrich. *The Cost of Discipleship*. London: SCM Press, 1975.

Bookless, Dave. "To Strive to Safeguard the Integrity of Creation and Sustain and Renew the Life of the Earth (ii)" 94–104 in Andrew Walls and Cathy Ross, eds *Mission in the 21st Century: Exploring the Five Marks of Global Mission*. London: Darton, Longman and Todd, 2008.

Boyd, Robin. *Indian Christian Theology*. New Delhi: ISPCK, 1969.

Brett, Mark G. "Interpreting Ethnicity" in Mark G. Brett, ed. *Ethnicity and the Bible*. Boston: Brill Academic Publishers Inc, 2002.

Brueggemann, Walter. *Living Toward a Vision: Biblical Reflections on Shalom*. Philadelphia: United Church Press, 1976.

———. *The Land*. London: SPCK, 1978.

Carey, Bertram S. and H. N. Tuck. *The Chin Hills: A History of the People, Our Dealing with Them, Their Customs and Manners, and a Gazetteer of their Country* Vol.1. Rangoon: Government Printing, 1896.

Castells, Manuel. *The Power of Identity*. Oxford: Blackwell, 1997.

Chirgwin, A. M. *Arthington's Million, The Romance of the Arthington Trust*. London: The Livingstone Press, 1936.

Chishti, S. M. A. W. *The Kuki Uprising: 1917–1920*. Gauhati: Spectrum Publications, 2004.

Chongloi, Hemkhochon. *Indoi: A Study of Primal Kuki Religious Symbolism in the Hermeneutical Framework of Mircea Eliade*. New Delhi: ISPCK, 2008.

Coe, S. "Contextual Theology" 10–24 in G. H. Anderson and T. F. Stransky, eds. *Mission Trends, No. 3: Third World Theologies*, New York/Grand Rapids, Michigan: Paulist/ William B. Eerdmans Publishing Company, 1976.

Cohen, Abner. "Ethnicity and Politics" in John Hutchinson & Anthony D. Smith eds. *Ethnicity*. Oxford: Oxford University Press, 1994.

Cone, James H. *For my People: Black Theology and the Black Church*. Maryknoll, New York: Orbis Books, 1984.

Connor, Walker. "A Nation is a Nation, is a State, is an Ethnic, is a . . . " 36–46 in John Hutchinson and Anthony D. Smith, eds. *Nationalism*. Oxford: Oxford University Press, 1994.

Copland, Ian. "From *Communitas* to Communalism: Evolving Muslim Loyalties in Princely North India" 23–50 in Gwilym Beckerlegge, ed. *Colonialism, Modernity, and Religious Identities: Religious Reform Movements in South Asia*. Oxford: Oxford University Press, 2008.

Cornell, Stephen and Douglas Hartmann. *Ethnicity and Race: Making Identities in a Changing World*. Second Edition, Thousand Oaks: Pine Forge Press, 2006.

Crawford, C. G. *A Hand Book of Kuki Custom.* Imphal: Printed at the State Printing Press, 1927.

D'souza, Joseph. *Dalit Freedom: Now and Forever, The Epic Struggle for Dalit Emancipation.* Foreword by Kancha Ilaiah and Udit Raj. Centennial, USA: Dalit Freedom Network, 2006.

Das, Bhagwan. "Reservations Today and Tomorrow" 234–275 in Walter Fernandes, ed. *The Emerging Dalit Identity: The Re-Assertion of the Subalterns.* New Delhi: Indian Social Institute, 1996.

Das, Rajat Kanti. "Tribal Identity in Manipur" 253–263 in Pakem, *Nationality, Ethnicity and Cultural Identity in North-East India.* Guwahati: Omsons Publications, 1990.

———. *Manipur Tribal Scene: Studies in Society and Change*, New Delhi: Inter-India Publications, 1985.

Datta, Sreeradha. *The Northeast Complexities and Its Determinants.* Delhi: Shipra, 2004.

Dena, Lal. *Christian Missions and Colonialism: A Study of Missionary Movement in Northeast India with Special Reference to Manipur and Lushai Hills 1894–1947.* Shillong: Vendrame Institute, 1988.

———. *In Search of Identity: Hmars of North-East India.* New Delhi: Akansha Publishing House, 2008.

Devalle, Susana B. C. *Multi-Ethnicity in India: The Adivasi Peasants of Chota Nagpur and Santal Parganas* IWGIA Document 41. Translated from Spanish by Elisabeth Soltau, Copenhegen: The Document Department of IWGIA, 1980.

Devasahayam, V. "Identity in Theology" 13–19 in Devasahayam, ed. *Frontiers of Dalit Theology*, New Delhi: ISPCK/Gurukul, 1997.

———. "The Nature of Dalit theology as Counter Ideology" 53–67 in Devasahayam, ed. *Frontiers of Dalit Theology*, New Delhi: ISPCK/Gurukul, 1997.

Donovan, Vincent J. *Christianity Rediscovered: An Epistle from the Masai.* Maryknoll, NY: Orbis Books, 1982.

Downs, Frederick S. *The Mighty Works of God: A Brief History of the Council of Baptist Churches in North-East India: The Mission Period 1836–1950*, Gauhati: Christian Literature Centre, 1971.

———. *History of Christianity in India*, Vol. V, Part 5: North-East India in the Nineteenth and Twentieth Centuries. Bangalore: The Church History Association of India, 1992.

———. "Administrators, Missionaries and a World Turned Upside Down: Christianity as a Tribal Response to change in North-East India", in *Essays in Christianity in North-East India*. New Delhi: Indus Publishing Company, 1994.

Eller, Jack David. *From Culture to Ethnicity to Conflict: An Anthropological Perspective on International Ethnic Conflict*. Michigan: The University of Michigan Press, 2002.

Elwin, Verrier. "The Nagas of Manipur" in Verrier Elwin, ed. *The Nagas in the Nineteenth Century*. Bombay: Oxford University Press, 1969.

Eriksen, Thomas H. *Ethnicity and Nationalism: Anthropological Perspective*. London: Pluto Press, 1993.

Esler, Philip F. *Conflict and Identity in Romans: The Social Setting of Paul's Letter*. Minneapolis: Fortress Press, 2003.

Fenton, Steve. *Ethnicity*. Cambridge: Polity Press, 2010.

Fernandes, Walter. "Conversion to Christianity, Caste Tension and Search for a New Identity in Tamil Nadu" 140–165 in Walter Fernandes, ed. *The Emerging Dalit Identity: The Re-Assertion of the Subalterns*. New Delhi: Indian Social Institute, 1996.

Flemming, Dean. *Contextualization in the New Testament: Patterns for Theology and Mission*. Leicester: IVP, 2005.

Furer-Haimendorf, Christoph von. *Tribes of India: The Struggle for Survival*, Berkeley: University of California Press, 1982.

Gangte, T. S. *Anglo-Kuki Relation from 1849–1937*, Churachandpur: Author, 1980.

———. *The Kukis of Manipur: A Historical Analysis*. New Delhi: Gyan Pubishing Company, 1993.

Geertz, Clifford. "Primordial Ties" 40–45 in John Hutchinson and Anthony D. Smith eds. *Ethnicity*. Oxford: Oxford University Press, 1996.

Ghosh, Lipi. "Ethnicity and Issues of Identity Formation" 187–207 in Bonita Aleaz, et al. eds. *Ethnicity, Nation & Minorities: The South Asian Scenario*. New Delhi: Manak Publications, 2003.

Gnanavaram, M. "Some Reflections on Dalit Hermeneutics" 329–335 in V. Devasahayam ed. *Frontiers of Dalit Theology*. New Delhi: ISPCK/Gurukul, 1997.

Gonzalez, Justo L. *Out of Every Tribe and Nation: Christian Theology at the Ethnic Roundtable*. Nashville: Abingdon Press, 1992.

———. *ACTS: The Gospel of the Spirit*. Maryknoll, New York: Orbis Books, 2001.

———. *For the Healing of the Nations: The Book of Revelation in an Age of Cultural Conflict.* Maryknoll, New York: Orbis Books, 2003.

Goswami, Tarun. *Kuki Life and Lore.* Haflong, Assam: North Chachar Hills District Council, 1985.

Green Joel B. and Mark D. Baker. *Recovering the Scandal of the Cross: Atonement in New Testament and Contemporary Contexts.* Carlisle: Paternoster Press, 2000.

Grierson, G. A. *Linguistic Survey of India,* Vol. III. Part III. Calcutta: Office of the Superintendent, Government Printing, 1904.

Guha, Ramachandra. *India After Gandhi: The History of the World's Largest Democracy.* London: Macmillan, 2007.

Hale, Henry H. *The Foundations of Ethnic Politics: Separatism of States and Nations in Eurasia and the World.* Cambridge: Cambridge University Press, 2008.

Haokip, Hawlngam. *Good News for Manipur.* Imphal: Kuki Baptist Convention, 1995.

Haokip, Letkhojam. *ThempuHoTh* [Oracles of the Priests], Churachandpur: Published by Author, 2000.

Haokip, P. S. *Zale'n Gam: The Kuki Nation.* np. Kuki National Organization, 1988.

———. *Zale'n-Gam: The Land of the Kukis.* First Edition. np, Kuki National Organization, 1995.

Haokip, T. Jamthang. *Manipur a Gospel leh Kuki ho Thusim* (The Gospel in Manipur and the Story of the Kukis). Churachandpur, Manipur: Published by Author, 1984.

Haokip, Thangkholim T. "Contesting Nomenclatures: The Kuki-Chin-Mizo of India and Burma" 308–322 in K. Robin, ed. *Chin History, Culture & Identity.* New Delhi: Dominant Publishers and Distributors, 2009.

Haque, Mahfuzul. *Ethnic Insurgency and National Integration: A Study of Selected Ethnic Problems in South Asia.* New Delhi: Lancer Books, 1997.

Haught, John F. *What is Religion?: An Introduction.* New Jersey: Paulist Press, 1990.

Hazarika, Sanjoy. *Strangers of the Mist: Tales of War and Peace from India's Northeast.* New Delhi: Penguin Book, 1995.

Hminga, C. L. *The Life and Witness of the Churches in Mizoram.* Serkawn, Mizoram: Baptist Church of Mizoram, 1987.

Hodson, T. C. *The Meitheis,* Reprint [First Published in 1908]. Delhi: B. R. Publishing Corporation, 1975.

Horam, M. "Foreword" in Hodson, *The Meitheis*, Reprint [First Published in 1908]. Delhi: B. R. Publishing Corporation, 1975.

Hutchinson, John & Anthony D. Smith. "Theories of Ethnicity" 33–34 in Hutchinson & Smith, eds. *Ethnicity*, Oxford: Oxford University Press, 1996.

Ilaiah, Kancha. *Why I am Not a Hindu: A Sudra Critique of Hindutva Philosophy, Culture and Political Economy*. Second Edition. Kolkata: Mandira Sen for Samya, 2005.

Jenkins, Philip. *The Next Christendom: The Coming of the Global Christianity*. London: Oxford University Press, 2002.

———. *The New Faces of Christianity, Believing the Bible in the Global South*. New York: Oxford University Press, 2006.

Jenkins, Richard. *Rethinking Ethnicity: Arguments and Explorations*. London: Sage Publications, 1997.

Jeyaseelan, L. *Impact of Missionary Movement in Manipur*. New Delhi: Scholar Publishing House (p) Ltd, 1996.

Joireman, Sandra Fullerton. *Nationalism and Political Identity*. London: Continuum, 2003.

Jusho, P. T. Hitson. *Politics of Ethnicity in North-East India With Special Reference to Manipur*. New Delhi: Regency Publications, 2004.

Khai, Sing Khaw. *Zo People and Their Culture: A Historical, Cultural Study and Critical Analysis of Zo and its Ethnic Tribes*. Lamphelpat, Imphal: BCPW, 1995.

Khupzago, *A Critical Historical Study of Bible Translations Among the Zo People in North-East India*. Churachandpur: Chin Baptist Literature Board, 1996.

Kim, Kirsteen. "India" 44–73 in John Parratt, ed. *An Introduction to Third World Theologies*. Cambridge: Cambridge University Press, 2004.

Kitamori, Kazoh. 5th Revised Edition. *Theology of the Pain of God*. Eugene, OR: Wipf and Stock Publishers, 2005.

Koyama, Kosuke. *Water Buffalo Theology*. Maryknoll, New York: Orbis Books, 1999.

Lalthangliana, B. *History and Culture of Mizo in India, Burma & Bangladesh*. Aizawl, Mizoram: Remkungi, 2001.

Lewin, Thomas Herbert. *Progressive Colloquial Exercise in the Lushai Dialect of the 'Dzo' or Kuki language with Vocabularies and Popular Tales*. Calcutta: Central Press Company Limited, 1874.

———. [First Published in 1912]. *A Fly on the Wheel or How I Helped to Govern India*. Aizawl: Tribal Research Institute, 1977.

Lloyd, J. Meirion. *History of the Church in Mizoram: Harvest in the Hills*. Aizawl: Synod Publication Board, 1991.

Lobo, Lancy. "Dalit Religious Movements and Dalit Identity" 166–183 in Walter Fernandes, ed. *The Emerging Dalit Identity: The Re-Assertion of the Subalterns*. New Delhi: Indian Social Institute, 1996.

———. "Visions, Illusions and Dilemas of Dalit Christians in India" 242–257 in Ghanshyam Shah, ed. *Dalit Identity and Politics*. Cultural Subordination and the Dalit Challenge, Vol. 2. New Delhi: Sage Publications, 2001.

———. *Globalization, Hindu Nationalism and Christians in India*. New Delhi: Rawat Publications, 2002.

Luikham, T. *A Short History of the Manipur Baptist Christian Golden Jubilee, 1948*. Ukhrul, Manipur: North-East Christian Association, 1975.

Lyall, C. J. "Introduction" in Hodson, *The Meitheis*, Reprint [First Published in 1908]. Delhi: B. R. Publishing Corporation, 1975.

Mackenzie, A. *The North-East Frontier of Bengal* [first published in 1884 as *History of the Relations of the Government with the Hill Tribes of the North-East Frontier of Bengal*]. New Delhi: Mittal Publications, 2005.

Marshall, I. Howard. *The Acts of the Apostles: An Introduction and Commentary*. Leicester: IVP, 1980.

Massey, James. "Ingredients for a Dalit Theology" 152–157 in R. S. Sugirtharajah and Cecil Hargreaves, eds. *Reading in Indian Christian Theology*. Vol. 1. London: SPCK, 1993.

———. "History and Dalit Theology" in Devasahayam, ed. *Frontiers of Dalit Theology*. New Delhi: ISPCK/Gurukul, 1997.

———. *Down Trodden: The Struggle of India's Dalits for Identity, Solidarity and Liberation*. Geneva: WCC Publications, 1997.

Mbiti, John. *African Religion and Philosophy*. London: Heinemann, 1969.

Melucci, Alberto. "Post-Modern Revival of Ethnicity", in Hutchinson & Smith, eds. *Ethnicity*. Oxford: Oxford University Press, 1994.

Michael, S. M. ed. *Dalits in Modern India: Vision and Values*. New Delhi: Vistaar Publications, 1999.

———. "Dalit Vision of a Just Society in India" 99–117 in S. M. Michael ed. *Dalits in Modern India: Vision and Values*, New Delhi: Vistaar Publications, 1999.

Misao, Paokhothang. *History and Customs of the Thadou Kukis*. Imphal: Published by Author, 1970.

Nag, Sajal. *Roots of Ethnic Conflict: Nationality Question in North-East India*. New Delhi: Manohar Publications, 1990.

Nash, Manning. "The Core Elements of Ethnicity" 24–28 in John Hutchinson & Anthony D. Smith, eds. *Ethnicity*. Oxford: Oxford University Press, 1994.

Newbigin, Leslie. "Religion for the Marketplace" 135–148 in Gavin D'Costa, ed. *Christian Uniqueness Reconsidered: The Myth of a Pluralistic Theology of Religion*. Maryknoll, New York: Orbis Books, 1996.

Nibedon, Nirmal. *North-East India: The Ethnic Explosion*. New Delhi: Lancers Publishers, 1981.

Nongsiej, T. *Khasi Cultural Theology*. New Delhi: ISPCK, 2002.

Omvedt, Gail. *Dalits and the Democratic Revolution: Dr Ambedkar and the Dalit Movement in Colonial India*. New Delhi: Sage Publications, 1994.

———. *Dalit Visions: The Anti-caste Movement and the Construction of an Indian Identity*. Hyderabad: Orient Longman Limited, 1995.

Pachuau, Joy Lalkrawspari. "*Chhinlung*: Myth and History in The Formation Of An Identity" 148–160 in K. Robin, ed. *Chin History, Culture & Identity*. New Delhi: Dominant Publishers and Distributors, 2009.

Pachuau, Lalsangkima. *Ethnic Identity and Christianity: A Socio-Historical and Missiological Study of Christianity in Northeast India with Special reference to Mizoram*. Frankfurt: Peter Lang, 2002.

Pakem, B. "Foreword" in Lucy Zehol, *Ethnicity in Manipur, Issues and Perspectives*. New Delhi: Regency Publications, 1998.

Pathak, Bindeshwar. "Gandhi, Ambedkar and Sulabh" 198–208 in Walter Fernandes, ed. *The Emerging Dalit Identity: The Re-Assertion of the Subalterns*. New Delhi: Indian Social Institute, 1996.

Porter, Andrew. "Introduction" 1–13 in Andrew Porter, ed. *The Imperial Horizons of British Protestant Missions, 1880–1914*. Cambridge: William B. Eerdmans Publishing Company, 2003.

———. *Religion versus Empire? British Protestant Missionaries and Overseas Expansion, 1700–1914*. Manchester: Manchester University Press, 2004.

Prabhakar, M. E. "Christology in Dalit Perspective" 402–432 in V. Devasahayam, ed. *Frontiers of Dalit Theology*. New Delhi: ISPCK/Gurukul, 1997.

Rad, Gerhard von. *Genesis: Old Testament Library*. London: SCM Press Ltd, 1970.

Raja, A. Maria Arul. "Inner Powers with Emancipation Agenda: A Probe into Dalit Roots" 151–160 in James Massey et al., *Breaking Theoretical Grounds for Dalit Studies*. New Delhi: Centre for Dalit/Subaltern Studies, 2006.

Raju, T. Swami. *Vira Cult in Fold Religion of Guntur District: A Dalit Perspective*. New Delhi: ISPCK, 2005.

[Ralte, Lalngurawna]. *The Presbyterian Church of Mizoram: The Testimony of a Self-supporting, Self-governing and Self-propagating Church*. Geneva: World Alliance of Reformed Churches, 1989.

Ramachandra, Vinoth. *Faiths in Conflict?: Christian Integrity and a Multicultural World*. Leicester: IVP, 2003.

Ray, B. Datta. *Tribal Identity and Tension in Northeast India*. New Delhi: Omsons Publications, 1989.

Ray, Basudeb Dutta and Asok Kumar Ray. "Editorial Notes" 11–45 in Basudeb Dutta Ray and Asok Kumar Ray, eds. *Dynamics of Power Relations in Tribal Societies of North-East India*. New Delhi: OM Publications, 2006.

Reddy, G. Prakash. *Politics of Tribal Exploitation*. Delhi: Mittal Publications, 1987.

Rizvi, S. H. M. "Introduction" 1–14 in K. S. Sigh, Gen. ed. *The People of India: Manipur*, Vol. XXXI. Calcutta: Anthropological Survey of India, 1998.

Rizvi, S. H. M. and Shibani Roy, ed. *Kuki-Chin Tribes of Mizoram and Manipur*, Delhi: B. R. Publishing Corporation, 2006.

Robin, K. *Chin History, Culture and Identity*. New Delhi: Dominant Publishers and Distributors, 2009.

Ross, Andrew C. "Christian Missions and Mid-Nineteenth-Century Change in Attitude to

Race: The African Experience" 85–105 in Porter, ed. *The Imperial Horizons of British Protestant Missions, 1880–1914*. Cambridge: William B. Eerdmans Publishing Company, 2003.

Roth, Guenther and Clause Wittich, eds. *Max Weber: Economy and Society*. Berkeley: University of California Press, 1978.

Rowney, Horatia Bickerstaffe. *The Wild Tribes of India*. Delhi: Low Price Publications, 1990.

Ruolngul, D. *Chanchintha Kalchawi* (Advance of the Gospel). Churachandpur, Manipur: Published by Author, 1982.

Saikia, Yasmin. *Assam and India: Fragmented Memories, Cultural Identity, and the Tai-Ahoms Struggle*. Delhi: Permanent Black, 2004.

Sakhong, Lian H. *Religion and Politics among the Chin People in Burma (1896–1949)*, Sweden: Uppsala University, 2000.

Sanneh, Lamin. *Whose Religion Is Christianity? The Gospel beyond the West*. Grand Rapids, Michigan: William B. Eerdmans Publishing Company, 2003.

Savarkar, V. D. Fifth Edition. *Hindutva*. New Delhi: Hindi Sahitiya Sadan, 2005.

Schreiter, Robert J. *Constructing Local Theologies*. London: SCM, 1985.

Schreiter, Robert J. ed. *Faces of Jesus in Africa*. Maryknoll, NY: Orbis Books, 1991.

Seidman, Steven. *Contested Knowledge: Social Theory Today*. Third Edition, Oxford: Blackwell Publishing, 2004.

Shah, Ghanshyam. "Introduction: Dalit Politics" 17–43 in Ghanshyam Shah, ed. *Dalit Identity and Politics*. New Delhi: Sage Publications, 2001.

Shakespear, J. *The Lushei Kuki Clans*. London: Macmillan and Co., Ltd, 1912.

Singh, B. P. *The Problem of Change: A Study of North-East India*. New Delhi: Oxford University Press, 1987.

Singh, R. K. "Emergent Ethnic Processes in Manipur: A Reappraisal", 233-254, in Pakem, ed., *Nationality, Ethnicity and Cultural Identity in Northeast India*. Guwahati: Omsons Publications, 1990.

Singh, K. M. *History of Christian Missions in Manipur and the Neighbouring States*. New Delhi: Mittal Publications, 1991.

Singh, K. S. "Concept of Tribe: A Note" 90–98 in H. S. Saksena, et al. eds. *Scheduled Tribes and Development*. New Delhi: Serial Publications, 2006.

Singh, S. K. *The Scheduled Tribes: People of India*. National Series, Vol. 3. Calcutta: Oxford University Press, 1994.

———. "Foreword" in Singh S. K. Gen. ed. *People of India: Manipur*. Vol. 31. Calcutta: Seagull Books, 1998.

Singson, Thangkholal. *HoubungKalsuon*. Churachandpur, Manipur: P. P. Printing Press, 2000.

Smith, David. *Hinduism and Modernity*. Oxford: Blackwell Publishing, 2003.

———. *Moving Towards Emmaus: Hope in a Time of Uncertainty*. London: SPCK, 2007.

Smith, James K. A. *Who's Afraid of Postmodernism?: Taking Derrida, Lyotard, and Foucault to Church*. Michigan: Baker Academic, 2006.

Song, C. S. *Third-Eye Theology: Theology in Formation in Asian Settings*. Maryknoll, New York: Orbis Books, 1979.

Soppitt, C. A. *A Short Account of Kuki-Lushai Tribes on the North-East Frontier* (In the Districts of Cachar, Sylhet, the Naga Hills, etc., and the North Cachar Hills). Shillong: Assam Secretariat Press, 1887.

Spalding, James C. "Foreword" in J. Stanley Friesen, *Missionary Responses to Tribal Religions at Edinburgh, 1910*. New York: Peter Lang, 1996.

Spence, Martin. "The Restitution of all Things in Nineteenth-century Evangelical Premillennialism" 349–359 in Peter Clarke and Tony Claydon, eds. *The Church, the Afterlife and the Fate of the Soul*. Suffolk: The Boydell Press, 2009.

Spencer, Stephen. *Race and Ethnicity: Identity, Culture and Representation.* London: Routledge, 2006.

Stanley, Brian. *The Bible and the Flag: Protestant Missionaries and British Imperialism in the Nineteenth and Twentieth Centuries.* Leicester: Apollos, 1990.

Sugirtharajah R. S. ed. *Frontiers in Asian Christian Theology: Emerging Trends.* Maryknoll, New York: Orbis Books, 1994.

Syiemlieh, Brightstar Jones. "The Viability of the term 'Tribe' in the light of Postmodernity" 17–28 in *In Search of Tribal Identity and Tribal Theology.* Jorhat: Eastern Theological College, 2001.

Takatemjen. *Studies on Theology and Naga Culture.* Delhi: ISPCK, 1998.

Taylor, John B. *Primal World Views: Christian Dialogue with Traditional Thought Forms.* Ibadan: Daystar Press, 1976.

Thanzauva, K. *Theology of Community: Tribal theology in the Making.* Aizawl: AICS, 2004.

Thomas, H. Lewin. *The Hills Tracts of Chittagong and Dwellers therein with Comparative Vocabularies of the Hill Dialects.* Calcutta: Bengal Printing Company Ltd, 1869.

Tilak, Shrinivas. "*Hindutva* – the Indian Secularists" 'Metaphor for Illness and Perversion' in Arvind Sharma, ed. *Hinduism and Secularism After Ayodhya.* New York: Palgrave Publishers Ltd, 2001.

Tinker, George E. *Missionary Conquest: The Gospel and Native American Cultural Genocide.* Minneapolis: Fortress Press, 1993.

Tschuy, Theo. *Ethnic Conflict and Religion: Challenge to the Churches*, Geneva: WCC, 1997.

Vaiphei, Kim. *The Coming of Christianity in Manipur: With Special Reference to the Kukis.* Imphal: Published by the Joint Women's Programme, New Delhi, 1995.

Vaiphei, Th. Lamboi. *Advent of Christian Mission and Its Impact on the Hill-Tribes in Manipur.* Imphal: Published by Author, 1997.

Vanlalchhuanawma. *Christianity and Subaltern Culture: Revival Movement as a Cultural Response to Westernisation in Mizoram.* New Delhi: ISPCK, 2007.

Vumson, Suantak. *Zo History.* Aizawl, Published by the Author, 1986.

Walls, Andrew. "Primal Religious Traditions in Today's World" 250–278 in Frank Whaling, ed. *Religion in Today's World: The Religious Situation of the World from 1945 to the Present Day.* Edinburgh: T & T Clark, 1987.

———. *The Missionary Movement in Christian History.* Maryknoll, NY: Orbis Books, 1996.

―――. *The Cross-Cultural Process in Christian History*. Edinburgh: T & T Clark, 2002.

Webster John C. B. et. al. *From Role to Identity: Dalit Christian Women in Transition*. New Delhi: ISPCK, 1998.

Webster John C. B. "Who is a Dalit?" 68–79 in S. M. Michael ed. *Dalits in Modern India: Vision and Values*. New Delhi: Vistaar Publications, 1999.

―――. *Religion and Dalit Liberation: An Examination of Perspectives*. New Delhi: Manohar, 2002.

Wenham, Gordon J. *Word Biblical Commentary, Genesis 1–15*. Texas: Word Books, 1987.

Westermann, Claus. *Genesis 1–11 A Continental Commentary*. Minneapolis: Fortress Press, 1994.

Whaling, F. *Religion in Today's World: The Religious Situation of the World from 1945 to the Present Day*. Edinburgh: T & T Clark, 1987.

Woodruff, Philip [Reprint]. *The Men Who Ruled India*, Vol. II. The Guardians. London: Jonathan Cape, Ltd, 1971.

Zehol, Lucy. *Ethnicity in Manipur: Experience, Issues and Perspectives*. New Delhi: Regency Publications, 1998.

Zelliot, Eleanor. *From Untouchable to Dalit: Essays on the Ambedkar Movement*. New Delhi: Manohar, 1992.

Journal

Bader, Veit. "Culture and identity: Contesting constructivism." *Ethnicities*, Vol. 2. no. 1 (2001): 251–285.

Baruah, Sanjib. "Confronting Constructionism: Ending India's Naga War." *Journal of Peace Research*, Vol. 40, no. 3 (2003): 321–338.

―――. "Postfrontier Blues: Towards a New Policy Framework for Northeast India." *East-West Center*, Policy Studies no. 33 (2007): 1–79. <http://www.eastwestcenter.org/fileadmin/stored/pdfs/PS033.pdf> [Accessed 30 May 2010].

Bediako, Kwame. "Why has the summer ended and we are not saved? Encountering the Real Challenge of Christian Engagement in Primal Contexts." *Journal of African Christian Thought*, Vol. 11, no. 2 (2008): 5–8.

Burman, B. K. Roy. "Problems and Prospects of Tribal Development in North-East India." *Economic and Political Weekly*, April 1 (1989): 693–697.

Chang, Eunhye et al. "Paul G. Hiebert and Critical Contextualization" in *Trinity Journal*, Vol. 30, no. 2 (2009): 199–207

Clarke, Sathianathan. "The Jesus of Nineteenth Century Indian Christian Theology: An Indian Inculturation with Continuing Problems and Prospects." *Studies in World Christianity*, Vol. 5 Part 1 (1996): 32–46.

———. "Hindutva, Religious and Ethnocultural Minorities, and Indian-Christian Theology." *Harvard Theological Review*, Vol. 95. no. 2 (2002): 197–226.

Ekka, Jhakmak Neeraj. 2008. 'Cultural Deterioration, a Threat to Indigenous/Adivasi Identity: Defining the Church's Theological Response for Cultural Restoration', 10 -20 in *Dharma Deepika: A South Asian Journal of Missiological Research*, Vol. 12. No.1, January – June.

Emberling, Geoff. "Ethnicity in Complex Societies: Archaeological Perspective." *Journal of Archaeological Research,* Vol. 5, no. 4 (1997): 295–344.

Gine, Pratap Chandra. "Doing Tribal Theology in North East Asia: A Retrospect and Prospect." *The Journal of Theologies and Cultures in Asia*, Vol. 1 (2002): 17–32.

Hale, Hendry E. "Explaining Ethnicity." *Comparative Political Studies,* Vol. 37, no. 4 (2004): 458–485.

Hiebert, Paul G. "Critical Contextualization." *International Bulletin of Missionary Research*, Vol. 11, no. 3 (1987): 104–111.

Hudson, J. H. "Introduction" in Shaw, "Notes on the Thadou Kukis." 1929. *The Journal and Proceedings of the Asiatic Society of Bengal*, New Series, Vol. XXIV, no. 1 (1928): 3–8.

Published by the Asiatic Society of Bengal on behalf of the Government of Assam, Calcutta: The Baptist Mission Press.

Jesurathnam, K. "Towards a Dalit Liberative Hermeneutics: Re-reading The Psalms of Lament." *Bangalore Theological Forum*, Vol. 34, no. 1 (2002): 1–34.

Karlsson, G. B. "Indigenous Politics: Community Formation and Indigenous Peoples' Struggle for Self-Determination in Northeast India", *Identities*, Vol. 8, no. 1 (2001): 7–45.

Kenrick, Justin and Jerome Lewis. "Indigenous peoples' rights and the politics of the term 'indigenous'." *Anthropology Today*, Vol. 20, no. 2 (2004): 4–9.

Kim, Dong-Kun. "Korean Minjung Theology in History and Mission." *Studies in World Christianity*, Vol. 2, Part 2 (1996): 165–182.

Kuper, Adam. "The Return of the Native." *Current Anthropology*, Vol. 44 (2003): 389–402.

Link, Bruce G. et al. "Real Consequences: A Sociological Approach to Understanding the Association between Psychotic Symptoms and Violence." *American Sociology Review*, Vol. 64 (1999): 316–332.

Mitchell, Claire. "The religious content of ethnic identities." *Sociology*, Vol 40. no. 6 (2006): 1135–1152.

Modood et al. " 'Race', Racism and Ethnicity: A Response to Ken Smith." *Sociology*, Vol. 36. no. 2 (2002): 419–426.

Nagel, Joane. "Constructing Ethnicity: Creating and Recreating Identity Culture." *Social Problems*, Vol. 41, no. 1 (1994): 152–176.

Oommen, George. "Dalit Conversion and Social Protest in Travancore, 1854–1890." in *Bangalore Theological Forum*, Vol. XXVII, nos. 3 & 4 (Sept–Dec. 1996): 69–84.

———. "The Emerging Dalit Theology: A Historical Appraisal." *Indian Church History Review*, Vol. XXXIV, no. 1 (2000): 19–37.

Pachuau, Lalsangkima. "Primal Spirituality as the Substructure of Christian Spirituality: The Case of Mizo Christianity in India." *Journal of African Christian Thought*, Vol. 11, no. 2 (2008): 9–14.

Phillips, E. G. "Missionary Conference in Assam." *Baptist Missionary Magazine*, Vol. LXXVI, no. 12 (1896): 72–75.

Shaw, William. "Notes on the Thadou Kukis." *The Journal and Proceedings of the Asiatic Society of Bengal*, New Series, Vol. XXIV, 1928, no. 1 (1929): 11–90. Published by the Asiatic Society of Bengal on behalf of the Government of Assam, Calcutta: The Baptist Mission Press.

Shils, Edward. "Primordial, Personal, Sacred and Civil Ties: Some Particular Observations on the Relationships of Sociological Research and Theory." *The British Journal of Sociology*, Vol. 8, no. 2 (1957): 130–145.

Smith, Kenneth. "Some Critical Observations of the Use of the Concept of 'Identity'." Modood et al., *Ethnic Minority in Britain*, in *Sociology*, Vol. 36. no. 2 (2002): 399–417.

Snaitang, O. L. "In Search of a Tribal History." *Asia Journal of Theology* 18, no. 2 (2004): 398–411.

Southall, Samuel. "An Uncommon Life in Friend." *Quarterly Examiner*, Vol. 35 (1901): 277–286.

Stanley, Brian. "'The Miser of Headingley': Robert Arthington and the Baptist Missionary Society." *Studies in Church History*, Vol. 24 (1987): 371–382.

Subba, Tank B. "Interethnic Relationships in Northeast India and the 'Negative Solidarity' Thesis." *Man In India*, (2) (1992): 153–163.

Wimmer, Andreas. "The Making and Unmaking of Ethnic Boundaries: A Multilevel Process Theory', *AJS,* Vol. 113, no. 4 (2008): 970–1022.

Pamphlet, Missionary Report, Newspaper, DVD and Magazine

A Report of Dr G. G. Crozier (cyclostyled) found in CBCNEI Office, Gauhati, Assam in *History of Christianity in Manipur: Source Materials,* compiled by Elungkiebe Zeliang, Imphal: Manipur Baptist Convention, 2005.

ABFMS 1917: One-Hundred-Third Annual Report in *History of Christianity in Manipur: Source Materials,* compiled by Elungkiebe Zeliang, Imphal: Manipur Baptist Convention, 2005.

Ashmore, William, "Evangelize the Heathen in Order to Save America" 567–568 in *Baptist Missionary Magazine,* Vol. LXXVI, 1896, no. 12, preserved at CBCNEI, Gauhati, Assam, India.

Census Report from Manipur State, India and Chittagong Hill Tracts, Pakistan, *North-East India Tidings,* 31 December 1954.

Daniel, Manodeep. "Eyes that can See: A way of reading the Bible from Dalit perspective", C. D. S. Pamphlet, no. 7, Published by C. D. S., New Delhi, 2004.

Evangelical Witness in South Africa: Evangelical Critique their own Theology and Practice, Published by Concerned Evangelicals, Dobsonville, 1865.

Foreign Mission Policies, ABFMS, New York, 1925, preserved at CBCNEI, Gauhati, Assam, India.

Foreign Mission Policies: American Baptist Foreign Mission Society & Women's American Baptist Foreign Mission Society, Massachusetts, 1917, preserved at CBCNEI, Gauhati, Assam, India.

Franklin, J. H. "Missionary Objectives as seen by the societies" 40–43 in Foreign Mission Policies of American Baptist Foreign Mission Society & Women's American Baptist Foreign Mission Society, Massachusetts, 1917, preserved at CBCNEI, Gauhati, Assam, India.

Haokip, Shonkhothong. 1996. *Thugilbu,* Imphal: Published by Author.

India's Broken People: *Three Documentary films,* DVD, dir. Michael Lawson, marketed and distributed by Authentic Media, 2005.

Kristian leh Indona [Christians and War], Editorial, 5–6 *The Herald of Truth,* no. 10. October 1942.

List of Indigenous Mission Workers and their Location, 2–7 in *Kristian,* November, 1926.

Lunkim, T. "Tribal Land and Heritage in the Northeast India Context" *National Workshop on Theologizing Tribal Heritage: A Critical Re-look, Aizawl Theological College*, (Aizawl, Mizoram, 2008).

Massey, James. 2008. "Dalit Roots of Christianity, Theology and Spirituality (Revised)", CDS Pamphlet 11, Published by CDS New Delhi.

Mission in Assam, 71–83 in the Ninety-Sixth Annual Report of the 1910 American Baptist Foreign Mission Society presented at the Annual Meeting held in Chicago, Illinois, May 6–13, 1910, CBCNEI, Gauhati, Assam, India.

Notes on Findings, Note 1. in Foreign Mission Policies of American Baptist Foreign Mission Society & Women's American Baptist Foreign Mission Society, Massachusetts, 1917, preserved at CBCNEI, Gauhati, Assam, India.

Pettigrew Centenary Celebration Committee, Imphal: Fraternal Green Cross, 1996.

Pettigrew, William, "The Year in Manipur" in *ABFMS*, 1922, preserved at CBCNEI, Gauhati, Assam, India.

Prasad, R. N. "Traditional political institution of chieftainship in Mizoram: Powers, functions, position and privileges." *International seminar, April 7–9* (Aizawl, Mizoram, 1992).

Report About Mission in Manipur (1913), Abstract from the editor's 'A Survey of the Field'

ABMC of the ABFMS, 1913, pp. 5–6; 16–17 in *History of Christianity in Manipur: Source Materials*, compiled by Elungkiebe Zeliang, Imphal: Manipur Baptist Convention, 2005.

Report of the Secretary for 1916, Supplement to the Minutes of the American Baptist Missionary Conference in *History of Christianity in Manipur: Source Materials*, Compiled by Elungkiebe Zeliang, Imphal: Manipur Baptist Convention, 2005.

Report on Christian Work in Manipur, *125* Anniversary Jubilee Reports of Baptist Work in North East India 1836–1961 preserved at CBCNEI, Gauhati, Assam, India.

Report on Christian work in Manipur, 49–52 in 125th Anniversary: Jubilee Reports of Baptist work in North East India 1836–1961, preserved at CBCNEI, CBCNEI, Gauhati, Assam, India.

Rev William Pettigrew's Mission Reports and Letters 1891–1932, n.d. Compiled and reproduced by Rev ChamphangJajo, Gauhati: Chandan Press.

S. T. Henpu, 1960. "*Kum 50 Jubilee Thu Belh* (The Jubilee Year)" 9–11, *Rest: Christian Magazine Issued by the Association of N.E.I.G. Mission Christian Workers*, Published Quarterly, March.

Savoma. 1960. "*Pathian Thu Lo Luh Dan* (The Coming of Christianity)" 5–7, *Rest: Christian Magazine Issued by the Association of N.E.I.G. Mission Christian Workers*, Published Quarterly, March.

Talks on Kuki plea next week, *The Telegraph*, Calcutta, India, Saturday 27 February 2010.

Thangkai, 'Bagnti'n a hung kipandawkem (How did it happened)' 7–8 in *Rest: Christian Magazine Issued by the Association of N.E.I.G. Mission Christian Workers*, Published Quarterly, March 1960.

Thangkai, "How The Light First Pierced Into the Darkness", *North-East India Tidings,* May 1960.

The Assam Mission, 127–142 in the Report of the American Baptist Foreign Mission Society 1924, compiled by Mr Cecil R. Fielder, preserved at CBCNEI, Gauhati, Assam, India.

The Assam Mission, 93–95 in the Report of the American Baptist Foreign Mission Society, 1918, preserved at CBCNEI, Gauhati, Assam, India.

The Contribution of Mission Fields to the War, the Report of the American Baptist Foreign Mission Society, 1918, preserved at CBCNEI, Gauhati, Assam, India.

The Emergence of Kuki Inpi Revision, n.d. Published by Kuki Movement for Human Rights.

The Herald of the Baptist Missionary Society, *Zenana Mission and Medical Auxiliary*, Vol. 94 (Vol. 1. New Series).

"The Missionary Aspect of the War" in *The Church Missionary Gleaner*, 1 February 1916.

U. M. Fox, 'Ukhrul' ABMC of the ABFMS Report of the Fourteenth Session, 1915, preserved at CBCNEI, Gauhati, Assam, India.

Ukhrul Field Report for 1910 in ABMC of the American Baptist Mission Union, 1910, 74–84 in *History of Christianity in Manipur: Source Materials*, Compiled by Elungkiebe Zeliang, Imphal: Manipur Baptist Convention, 2005.

Ukhrul Field Report for 1913 by William Pettigrew, ABMC of the ABFMS, 1913, 56–59 in *History of Christianity in Manipur: Source Materials*, Compiled by Elungkiebe Zeliang, Imphal: Manipur Baptist Convention, 2005.

Ukhrul Field Report for 1913, 56–59 by William Pettigrew, ABMC of the ABFMS, 1913, preserved at CBCNEI, Gauhati, Assam, India.

Ukhrul: Report of Rev Wm. Pettigrew, 56–59 in ABMC of the ABMFMS Report of the Twelfth Biennial Session, 1913, preserved at CBCNEI, Gauhati, Assam, India.

Vungthawn, "Children Evangelize Their Parents" in *North-East India Tidings*, Issued monthly by the North-East India General Missions, Inc, Philadelphia, PA, October, 1953.

William Pettigrew, "My Twenty-Five Years 1897–1922 at Ukhrul Mission School" Appendix in *Rev William Pettigrew (a pioneer missionary of Manipur)* Published by Pettigrew Centenary Celebration Committee (Imphal: Fraternal Green Cross, 1996).

Wynd, William, "The Status of Native leaders" 47–50 in Foreign Mission Policies of American Baptist Foreign Mission Society & Women's American Baptist Foreign Mission Society, Massachusetts, 1917, preserved at CBCNEI, Gauhati, Assam, India.

Archival Materials

A Letter from Peter Fraser to Rev R. J. Williams, Secretary, Calvinistic Methodist Mission Society, dated 14 September 1908, CMA, 27, 314 preserved at the National Library of Wales, Aberystwyth, UK.

A Letter of Major Cole to Fraser on 19 December 1910 in a File 'The Bawi System in Lushai. Dr Fraser's Case and Letters – 1909–1910'. CMA 27, 315 preserved at the National Library of Wales, Aberystwyth, UK.

A Letter of P. Fraser from Aijal to Rev R. J. Williams. CM Archives, 27, 314 preserved at the National Library of Wales, Aberystwyth, UK.

A Letter of P. Fraser to Rev R. J. Williams on 3 January, 1914 as an answer to the questions put forth by the Directors on 18 November, 1913. CMA, 27, 318 preserved at the National Library of Wales, Aberystwyth, UK.

A Report on Slavery in Lushai, CMA 27, 316, File III preserved at the National Library of Wales, Aberystwyth, UK.

An official letter of TKPM, CMA, 27, 318 preserved at the National Library of Wales, Aberystwyth, UK.

An official letter of Watkin Roberts to Rev Lloyd Jones in England dated 2 June 1912, CMA 27, 318 preserved at the National Library of Wales, Aberystwyth, UK.

Bibliography

Arthington, R. 'To the Church of Christ Jesus', Box H/31, a small booklet preserved at the Archive of Regent's Park College, Oxford, UK.

B.M.S. Report of 1910 written by Savidge in the absence of Lorrain entitled 'London Baptist Missionary Society, Lushai Hills' in Box IN/113 preserved at the Regent's Park College, Oxford.

Burma-Assam Frontier Rising, Indian Office Record (IOR): L/P,S/10/724 preserved at the British library, London.

Burma-Assam Frontier: Disturbances Among Kuki Tribesmen in Manipur, Indian Office Record (IOR) L/P,S/10/724 preserved at the British Library, London.

Doctor Fraser's Case, File V, CMA 27,318 preserved at the National Library of Wales, Aberystwyth, UK.

File No: 4895 Field Operations: 'Despatch on the Operations Against the Kuki Tribes of Assam and Burma. November 1917–1919 in Burma-Assam Frontier', Indian Office Record (IOR): /L/MIL/17/19/42 preserved at the British Library, London.

Letter of Fraser to Reese, 13 October 1911, CMA, 27, 314 preserved at the National Library of Wales in Aberystwyth, UK.

Letter of Roberts to Fraser, 11 October 1911, CMA, 27, 314 preserved at the National Library of Wales, Aberystwyth, UK.

Letter of the Directors to Revs. D. E. Jones and Dr Fraser, 16 February 1912, CM 27, 314 preserved at the National Library of Wales in Aberystwyth, UK.

Letter of Watkin Roberts to Rev D. Loyd Jones, dated 22 June 1912, CMA, 27, 318 preserved at the National Library of Wales, Aberystwyth, UK.

North-East Frontier: Operations in the Kuki Country, Summary of Operations, in Indian Office Record (IOR): L/MIL/7/16899 preserved at the British library, London.

North-East Frontier: Operation in the Chin Hills and Kuki Punitive Measures, 1918–19, Indian Office Record (IOR): L/MIL/7/16899 preserved at the British library, London.

Rev T. W. Reese's letter (nd), CM Archives, 27, 314 preserved at the National Library of Wales, Aberystwyth, UK.

Roberts, Watkin, *Yr Efengyglydd* [Sunrise in Manipur], CMA, 27, 318 preserved at the National Library of Wales, Aberystwyth, UK.

Telegraph Viceroy to Secretary of State, *Indian Bulletin*, No.20, preserved at the National Archives, London.

Telegraph Viceroy to Secretary of State, *Indian Bulletin*, No.21, preserved at the National Archives, London.

The South Lushai Mission, BMS India's Secretary's Report in 1913, IN/13 preserved at the Regent's Park College, Oxford.

The Thado-Kookie Pioneer Mission Official Statement, CMA 27, 318, preserved at the National Library of Wales, Aberystwyth, UK.

The Thado-Kuki Mission, CM Archives, 27, 314 preserved at the National Library of Wales, Aberystwyth, UK.

Electronic/Online Materials

Beatty, Rachel, "Review Essay: Primordialism versus Constructivism", <http://www.nationalismproject.org/books/bookrevs/beattyrev.htm>[Accessed 13 January 2010].

Clarke, Sathianathan, "Viewing The Bible Through The Eyes And Ears of Subalterns In India" in *religion-online* <http://www.religion-online.org/showarticle.asp?title=2450> [Accessed 2 Sept 2008].

Doungel, C. "Applicability of Tribal Forest Act 2006 in Manipur" posted at kukiforum@yahoogroups.com [Accessed 26 January 2010].

ECCI: Who Are We, <http://www.ecchurchindia.com/index_files/ecci.htm> [Accessed 26 March 2008].

Haokip, Seilen, "Rhetorics of Kuki Nationalism", <http://www.kukiforum.com/kuki-people/history/4136-rhetorics-of-kuki-nationalism.html> [Accessed 6 March 2010].

Haokip, Seilen, "What Price, Twenty Years of Peace in Mizoram (1986–2006): A Kuki Perspective", <http://www.dipr.mizoram.gov.in/index.php?option=com_content&task=view&id=779&Itemid=0> [Accessed 10 October 2010].

Hindu and Caste System, <www://vhp.org.uk/vhpcms/index.php?Itemid=44&id=27&option=com_content&task=view> [Accessed 14 November 2008].

Hindutva and Multi-Culturalism, *The Hindu*, Sunday, December 06, 1998, Col. a. <http://www.angelfire.com/al/appiuforum/hindutva.html> [Accessed 27 October, 2010].

Jacthanni, review of Y.T. Vinay Raj, *Re-Imagining Dalit Theology–Postmodern Readings* Tiruvalla: ChristavaSahityaSamithi: 2008. <http://www.shvoong.

com/books/1822256-re-imagining-dalit-theology-postmodern/> [Accessed 2 Sept 2008].

Jayaram, V. "The Hindu Caste System", <http://www.hinduwebsite.com/hinduism/h_caste.asp> [Accessed 18 November 2008].

Jesurathnam, K. "Towards a Dalit Liberative Hermeneutics: Re-reading The Psalms of Lament" in *religion-online* <http://www.religion-online.org/showarticle.asp?title=2452> [Accessed 2 September 2008].

Kamei, Gangumei, "Ethnicity And Politics In Manipur", A Speech given at the Talk on 'Ethnicity and Politics of Manipur', organized by the National Research Centre, at Manipur University on 16 September, 2003, <http://www.manipuronline.com/Features/December2003/ethnicityandpolitics21_1.htm> [Accessed 25 December 2008].

Kamboj, Anil, "Manipur and Armed Forces (Special Powers) Act 1958", <http://www.idsa.in/strategicanalysis/ManipurandArmedForcesSpecialPowerAct1958_akamboj_1004> [Accessed 11 September 2010].

Kuruvila, K. P. "Dalit Theology: An Indian Christian Attempt to give voice to the voiceless" <http://www.csichurch.com/article/dalit.htm> [Accessed 18 November 2008].

Maitra, Ramtanu and Susan Maitra "Northeast India: Target of British apartheid" <http://www.hvk.org/articles/1002/113.html> [Accessed 11 March 2010].

Mall, Jagdamba, "A Hindu renaissance in North-East region" <http://www.organiser.org/dynamic/modules.php?name=Content&pa=showpage&pid=384&page=37> [Accessed 13 April 2011].

MLR & LR Act <http://manipurrev.nic./Default.htm> [Accessed 6 December 2010].

Nabakumar, W. "The Inter Ethnic Relations Of The Different Communities Of Manipur: A Critical Appraisal", <http://www.manipuronline.com/Features/November2005/interethnicrelationship17_2.htm> [Accessed 9 October 2008].

Office of the Registrar General & Census Commissioner, India. 2001 Census of India. <http://www.censusindia.gov.in/Census_Data_2001/Census_data_finder/A-Z_index/A-Z_Index.html> [Accessed 14 August 2009].

Oommen, "The Emerging Dalit Theology" in *religion-online*, <http://www.religion-online.org/showarticle.asp?title=1121> [Accessed 2 Sept 2008].

"Population Figures of the North-East States, Census of India 2001", <http://mha.nic.in/nemain.htm> [Accessed 20 June 2007].

"Preamble of NSCN", <http://www.nscnonline.org/nscn/indext-2.html> [Accessed 28 October 2008].

Routray, Bibhu Prasad, "Manipur: Extortion Rules", <http://www.outlookindia.com/article.aspx?234914> [Accessed 27 October 2010].

Russell, William P. "Contextualization: Origins, Meaning, and Implications: A Study of What the Theological Education Fund of the World Council of Churches Originally Understood by the Term 'Contextualization,' with Special Reference to the Period 1970–1972", <http://web.ebscohost.com/ehost/pdfviewer/pdfviewer?vid=7&bk=1&hid=15&sid=75a5a071-5e98-4dcd-9e5a-a8153c96e6a9%40sessionmgr4> [Assessed 8 October 2010].

Sathianathan Clarke was interviewed by the Countercurrents.org on 7 October 2007, <http://www.countercurrents.org/sikand071007.htm> [Accessed 2 September 2008].

Shashikumar, V. S "Kuki outfit demands statehood" CNN-IBN News published on October 8, 2006 <http://ibnlive.in.com/news/kuki-outfit-demands-statehood/23463-3.html> [Accessed 11 March 2010].

Thawanthaba, Moirangthem "Manipur: A Case Study On Migration", <http://www.manipuronline.com/Manipur/February2006/migrationstudy26_1.htm> [Accessed 27 June 2007].

"United Liberation Front of Asom (ULFA) - Terrorist Group of Assam", <http://www.satp.org/satporgtp/countries/india/states/manipur/terrorist_outfits/Unlf.htm> [Assessed 30 May 2011].

"The Armed Forces (Special Powers) Act, 1958", <http://www.mha.nic.in/pdfs/armed_forces_special_powers_act1958.pdf> [Assessed 11 September 2010].

The report of Human Rights Watch, "Hidden Apartheid: Caste Discrimination against India's 'Untouchability' " to the UN Committeee on the Elimination of Racial Discrimination in 2007, <http://www.hrw.org/reports/2007/india0207/> [Accessed 9 October 2008].

"The South Asia Intelligence Review: Weekly Assessment and briefing", <http://www.satp.org/satporgtp/countries/india/terroristoutfits/index.html> [Accessed 28 October 2010].

Thimkhup Buiting, "The Advent of Christianity Among the Bawms", <http://bawm.info/bawmchristianity.htm> [Accessed 8 April 2010].

"UNLF Highlights Important Issues On Its 41st Birthday", <http://www.manipuronline.com/Features/January2006/militancy19_1.htm> [Accessed 9 October 2008].

"Violence, strikes mark panchayat, ZP polls in Manipur" in *Indianexpress*, Posted: Thursday September 20 2007, 00:00 hrs <http://www.indianexpress.

com/news/violence-strikes-mark-panchayat-zp-polls-i/218853/> [Accessed 4 April 2011].

Unpublished Thesis/Works

Haokip, Jangkholam, "Impact of Christianity: In Reference to Kuki Society", *Khanglai 2008–cum-KWS Gauhati Decade Celebration, October 9–12*, (Gauhati, Assam, India 2008).

Haokip, Peter. *Kuki Culture and the Christian Message: Theologizing in the Context of Kuki Culture* (Unpublished MTh Thesis, Jnana DeepaVidyapeeth Pune, 1979).

Haokip, Seilen. *Identity, Conflict and Nationalism: the Naga and Kuki peoples of Northeast India and Northwest Burma (Myanmar)* (Unpublished PhD Thesis, Liverpool University, 2001).

Haokip, Thangkholim T. *The Chieftainship among the Kukis* (Unpublished PhD Thesis, North Eastern Hills University, Shillong, 1996).

Jesurathnam, J. *Contextual Reading of Psalm 22 with Special Reference to Indian Christian Dalit Interpretation* (Unpublished PhD Thesis, University of Edinburgh, 2006).

Longchar, Wati "Traditions and Cultures of Indigenous People: Continuity of Indigenous People in Asia", *Workshop on "Indigenous People–Spirituality and Peace" Asia Pacific Alliance of YMCAs and Interfaith Cooperation Forum, October 19–24* (Indonesia, 2007).

Murry, Ezamo, "Bible and Culture–A Model of Christian Acculturation of Tribal Culture", *The Third Theological Educators' Symposium on Constructing a Relevant/Contextual Theology for the People of North East India*, held at Eastern Theological College 17–23 November (Jorhat, Assam, India, 2008).

Piang, L. Lamkhan. *Kinship, Territory and Politics: The Study of Identity Formation Amongst the Zo* (Unpublished PhD Thesis Jawahalal Nehru University, New Delhi, 2005).

R. N. Prasad, "Traditional political institution of chieftainship in Mizoram: Powers, functions, position and privileges", *International seminar, April 7–9*, (Aizawl, Mizoram, 1992).

Ruho, Rukuzo, "Concepts and Tribal Christian Theology", *The Third Theological Educators' Symposium on Constructing a Relevant/Contextual Theology for the People of North East India, held at Eastern Theological College 17–23 November* (Jorhat, Assam, India, 2008).

Dictionary, Encyclopaedia

Dictionary of Mission Theology: Evangelical Foundations. 2007. Nottingham: IVP.

Eliade, Mircea (ed.). 1987. *The Encyclopedia of Religion.* Vol. 4. London: Macmillan Publishing Company.

Roxborogh, John. 2000. "Two-Thirds World" 975–976 in A. Scott Moreau, ed., *Evangelical Dictionary of World Missions*, Carlisle: Paternoster Press.

The New Encyclopaedia Britannica, 1992. Vol. 21. 15th Edition, Chicago: Encyclopaedia Britannica Inc.

The Oxford Reference Dictionary. 1986. Oxford: Clarendon Press.

APPENDIX 1

The Tribal Population of Manipur in 2001[1]

Sl. No.	Name of the Tribe	Total Population
1	Aimol	2,643
2	Anal	13,853
3	Angami	650
4	Chiru	5,487
5	Chothe	2,675
6	Gangte	15,100
7	Hmar	42,690
8	Kabui: (i) Puimei (ii) Rongmei	62,216
9	Kacha Naga: (i) Zemei (ii) Liangmei	20,328
10	Koirao	1,200
11	Koireng	1,056
12	Kom	15,467
13	Lamkang	4,524
14	Mao	80,568
15	Maram	10,510
16	Maring	17,361

---

1. 2001 Census quoted in W. Nabakumar, 'The Inter Ethnic Relationship Of The Different Communities Of Manipur : A Critical Appraisal' in http://www.manipuronline.com/Features/November2005/interethnicrelationship17_2.htm Accessed on 20 March 2010. See also map showing the localities inhabited by these different clans on http://msme-diimphal.nic.in/images/manipur.GIF (Accessed on 20 March 2010).

17	Any Mizo (Lushai) tribes	10,520
18	Monsang	1,635
19	Moyon	1,710
20	Paite	44,861
21	Purum	503
22	Ralte	110
23	Sema	25
24	Simte	7,150
25	Sukte	311
26	Tangkhul	112,944
27	Thadou	115,045
28	Vaiphei	27,791
29	Zou	19,112
30	Tribe Unspecified	75,768
	Total	**713,813**

APPENDIX 2

Operations Against Kuki Tribes[1]

Results achieved by Troops employed on Kuki Punitive measures.

(A) Villages

(1) Surrendered	140
(2) Burnt	126
(3) Deserted	16
Total	282

(B) Guns obtained — 1,158

(C) Kukis killed — 120

This is an estimate figure. Details re: others killed and wounded not obtainable.

(D) Mythun destroyed — 576

(E) Permanent Posts established — 20

Also 1 reserved base.

(F) Miles of track prepared — 752

---

1. See, appendix III, p.26 of Confidential, Serial No. 9: 'Despatch on the Operations Against the Kuki Tribes of Assam and Burma. November 1917 to March 1919.' File No. 4895 Field Operations. Simla: Printed at the Government Monotype Press, 1919 Preserved at the British Library, London, IOR L/MIL/17/19/42

The following are the names of Rebel Chiefs placed on "Special List," guilty of notorious crimes, whose capture and punishment was especially desired by Government:

> Semchung of Ukha,
> Pakhang [Pakang] of Hinglep [Henglep].
> Ngulbul of Longya.
> Ngulkhup of Mombi [Lonpi].
> Leotang of Robok.
> Pachei [Pache] of Chassad.
> Ngulkhukhai of Chassad.
> Tintong of Laiyang.
> Enjakhup, renegade sepoy.
> Helashon [Helson] of Loibol.
> Mangkhoon of Tingkai.
> Khutinthang [Khotinthang] of Jampi.
> Chenjapao [Chengjapao] of Aishan.
> Lungkhulal of Chongyang.
> Chingakhamba of Senachauba.

All the above have been either killed or captured or have surrendered.

APPENDIX 3

The Five Hill Districts of Manipur and their Population[1]

SL	Name of District	Population	Major Communities in the five Tribal Districts.
1	Churachandpur	227,905	tribal folk belonging to Chin, Kuki, Mizo, Naga and Zomi ethnic groups – a mosaic of tribes.[2]
2	Chandel	118,327	Anal, Lamkang, Kuki, Moyon, Monsang, Chothe, Thadou, Paite, Maring and Zou etc.[3]
3	Senapati	156,513	Mao, Maram, Poumai, Thangal, Zemai, Liangmai, Roungmei, Tangkhul, Meetei, Kuki, Nepalese, Vaiphei, Chothe, Chiru, Maring.[4]
4	Tamenglong	111,499	Zeliangrong Nagas, Kuki, Chiru, Hmar, Khasi[5]
5	Ukhrul	140,778	Ukhrul district is the home of the Tangkhuls.[6]

---

1. http://manipur.nic.in/DistrictsinManipur.htm Accessed on 8 November, 2010.
2. http://ccpur.nic.in/distprof.htm Accessed on 8 November, 2010.
3. http://chandel.nic.in/ Accessed on 8 November, 2010.
4. http://senapati.nic.in/index.htm Accessed on 8 November, 2010.
5. http://tamenglong.nic.in/profile.htm Accessed on 8 November, 2010.
6. http://ukhrul.nic.in/People.html Accessed on 8 November, 2010. Other communities includes Kukis as per the list of District Electoral Roll found in the same website.

APPENDIX 4

Lists of Schedule Tribe in Different States of North-East India

Manipur

The Scheduled Castes and Scheduled Tribes Orders (Amendment) Act, 1976 (No. 108 of 1976, dated the 18 September, 1976)[1]

Scheduled Castes
1 Dhupi, Dhobi
2 Lois
3 Muchi, Ravidas
4 Namasudra
5 Patni
6 Sutradhar
7 Yaithibi

Scheduled Tribes
1 Aimol
2 Anal
3 Angami
4 Chiru

---

1. Census of India 1991, Series 1, PART II B (1), Volume 1, p. ccxlix.

5 Chothe
6 Gangte
7 Hmar
8 Kabui
9 Kacha Naga
10 Koirao
11 Koireng
12 Kom
13 Lamgang
14 Mao
15 Maram
16 Maring
17 Any Mizo (Lushai) tribes
18 Monsang
19 Moyon
20 Paite
21 Purum
22 Ralte
23 Sema
24 Simte
25 Suhte
26 Tangkhul
27 Thadou
28 Vaiphei
29 Zou

Meghalaya

The Scheduled Castes and Scheduled Tribes Orders (Amenment) Act, 1976 and the Constitution (Scheduled Tribes) Order (Amendment) Act, 1987.[2]

Scheduled Tribes
1. Boro Kacharis
2. Chakma
3. Dimasa, Kachari
4. Garo
5. Hajong
6. Hmar
7. Khasi, Jaintia, Synteng, Pnar, War, Bhoi, Lyngngam
8. Koch
9. Any Kuki Tribes, including:

(i) Biate, Biete	(ii) Changsan
(iii) Chongloi	(iv) Doungel
(v) Gamalhou	(vi) Gangte
(vii) Guite	(viii) Hanneng
(ix) Haokip, Haupit	(x) Haolai
(xi) Hengna	(xii) Hongsungh
(xiii) Hrangkhwal, Rangkhol	(xv) Jongbe
(xvi) Khawathlang, Khothalong	(xvii) Khelma
(xviii) Kholhou	(xix) Kipgen
(xx) Kuki	(xxi) Lengthang
(xxii) Lhangum	(xxiii) Lhoujem
(xxiv) Lhouvum	(xxv) Lupheng
(xxvi) Mangjel	(xxvii) Misao
(xxviii) Riang	(xxiv) Sairhem
(xxx) Selnam	(xxxi) Singson
(xxxii) Sitlhou	(xxxiii) Sukte

---

2. Census of India 1991, Series 1, PART II B (1), Volume 1, p. ccli–cccliii.

                (xxxiv) Thado   (xxxv) Thangngeo
                (xxxvi) Uibuh   (xxxvi) Vaiphei

10 Lakher
11 Man (Tai Speaking)
12 Any Mizo (Lushai) tribes
13 Mikir
14 Any Naga tribes
15 Pawi
16 Raba, Rava
17 Synteng

Mizoram

The Scheduled Castes and Scheduled Tribe Lists (Modification) Order, 1956 and as inserted by Act 81 of 1971.[3]

Scheduled Tribes

1 Chakma
2 Dimasa (Kachari)
3 Garo
4 Hajong
5 Hmar
6 Khasi and Jaitia (including Khasi Synteng or Pnar, War, Bhoi or Lyngngam)
7 Any Kuki Tribes, including:

(i) Biate, Biete	(ii) Sangsan
(iii) Chongloi	(iv) Doungel
(v) Gamalhou	(vi) Gangte
(vii) Guite	(viii) Hanneng
(ix) Haokip, Haupit	(x) Haolai
(xi) Hengna	(xii) Hongsungh
(xiii) Hrangkhwal, Rangkhol	(xiv) Jongbe
(xv) Khawchung	(xvi) Khawathlang
(xvii) Khelma	(xviii) Kholhou
(xiv) Kipgen	(xx) Kuki
(xxi) Lengthang	(xxii) Lhangum
(xxiii) Lhoujem	(xxiv) Lhouvum
(xxv) Lupheng	(xxvi) Mangjel
(xxvii) Misao	(xxviii) Riang
(xxix) Sairhem	(xxx) Selnam
(xxxi) Singson	(xxxii) Sitlhou
(xxxiii) Sukte	(xxxiv) Thado
(xxxv) Thangngeu	(xxxvi) Uibuh
(xxxvii) Vaiphei	

---

3. Census of India 1991, Series 1, PART II B (1), Volume 1, pp. ccliii –cclv.

8 Lakher
9 Man
10 Any Mizo (Lushai) tribes
11 Mikir
12 Any Naga tribes
13 Synteng

Nagaland

Scheduled Tribes
1 Garo
2 Kachari
3 Kuki
4 Mikir
5 Naga

APPENDIX 5

Letter of Directors to Revs. D. E. Jones and Dr Fraser on 16 February 1912

'Dear Brethren,

The Directors have recently received several letters from you and from the Secretary of the Disctrict Committee which contain references to the activities of Mr W. R. Roberts in Lushai and Manipur. Mr Roberts they are told has established an undenominational Mission in Manipur with a Treasurer in Wales and another in Calcutta, and has commenced work among the Thdo-kukis of Manipur. The Directors allowed Dr Fraser to take Mr Roberts with him to Lushai on the disctrict understanding that he was to be under his charge and control, which meant that Mr Roberts should not be allowed to do anything that would be an infringement of our Regulations, and of the understanding which exists between ourselves and other Missionary Societies working in contiguous districts.

The Directors therefore desire me to make it perfectly clear to you, and through you to all concerned, that in founding an undenominational Mission in Manipur, thereby breaking the comity of Missions, Mr W. R. Roberts has acted entirely on his own responsibility, and they wish to dissociate themselves from, and to repudiate, the steps which he has taken to begin work in a field which all Missionary Societies in Assam have looked upon as part of the field for which our brethren the American Baptist were responsible.

Moreover, we are given to understand that Mr Roberts is allowed to take part in the deliberations of the Lushai Presbytery, and presumably to vote on the questions discussed by the Presbytery. The Directors wish it to be clearly understood that they thoroughly disapprove of this, and of any interference on the part of Mr Roberts in the administration of the affairs of the Mission in Lushai.

Likewise, they desire to make it clear that he should not be allowed to compromise the Mission by taking any action in relation to the conduct or character of Government officials.

The Directors were exceedingly sorry to find that the Lushai Presbytery in the absence of the Missionaries had discussed the important question of the relations of the Christians to their heathen chiefs, and had the Missionaries to the Government, which proceeding is entirely contrary to the custom which prevails throughout our Mission field. In the present state of the young Church in Lushai the Directors consider it important that the Missionaries should be its guides and leaders, and it is they who should in all things when necessary intervene in its behalf with the rulers of the country.'

Found in National Library of Wales, Aberystwyth, Wales, UK. CM Archives, 27, 314.

APPENDIX 6

Letter of Roberts to Fraser

Aijal 11 Oct. '11

Dear Dr Fraser,

As you are likely aware, previous to our opening up the Thado Kuki district, no Xn [Christian]. work had been done among these people. It was a response to a heathen Chief's request, which came on the fly leaf of a Gospel which I had personally sent him, that we first visited the District, & the works did not commence there until full permission had been given by His H. the Prince of Manipur, thro' the political Agent. I may say that no work whatever had been opened up amongst these people except by ourselves so far. I am sorry that the Dist. Comm. shd [should] have been caused the trouble of discussing the matter at their recent sitting, but they will radily [readily] understand that any business regarding these Mission can best be done by ourselves – the members of the Mission. I shall be glad if you will please pass on to them an earnest request for prayers for these poor people who are groping in the dark & waiting for the message of Calvary. The proclaiming of this message is much harder for the fact that their language is not reduced to writing.

Yours vy. Sincerely in the blessed one who said "Go ye",
Watkin
Dr P. Fraser,
Aijal.

Found in National Library of Wales, Aberystwyth, Wales, UK. CM Archives, 27, 314.

APPENDIX 7.

Letter of Fraser to Rev T. W. Reese

Aijal 13 Oct. '11.

Dear Mr Reese,

I am enclosing a letter re the Thado-kuki Pioneer Mission from Mr Watkin Roberts. I do not think it wd. [would] be right to do anything now which might obstruct the work of this Pioneer Mission, now preaching the Gospel among the Thado kukis.

With kin regards to you all

Yours faithfully

(sd) P. Fraser

Found in National Library of Wales, Aberystwyth, Wales, UK. CM Archives, 27, 314.

APPENDIX 8

Sunrise in Manipur

By Watkin R. Roberts

(Being a translation from a Welsh article in *Yr Efengylydd*)

My dear brother,

Thank you from the bottom of my heart for the interest shown by you and our brothers and sisters, readers of the Evangelist, in our work amongst the Thado-Kook.

Only a little over two years has passed since we first met this dark and needy people. As we look back, our mouths are filled with praise for Him who has acknowledged the message so distinctly, indeed, the outward fruit is much greater than we expected. We had believed that God would make speedy His work amongst these peoples, but we must admit that our faith did not expect what we have received of the readiness of God to touch so deeply the hearts of a people so used to immorality and paganism. The land of the Thado Kook had been completely ignored but, today, Jesus rides there successfully and the enemy has become uncomfortable there and tries to put obstacles in the way – is this not a good sign? 'For it is inevitable that stumbling blocks come;' (Matt XVIII :7).

Two years ago, we had the privilege of leading the first two natives to Christ. Today, these two dear brothers are themselves evangelists and have led many of their fellow country – men to Christ. These two have been on a missionary tour a few weeks ago, and they had some pretty striking stories when they last returned here. In one village, the chief wanted them to stay there and he promised to build them a school. For all they wished to do so, this was not possible then. One of these evangelists is the son of a pagan priest and he told me of his visit home. He tried to tell his ignorant mother something of the sacrifice of the Cross. She was astounded by his teaching. There was for her so much charm in 'the old, old story' that she pleaded with him to stay at home to teach her to pray. She pleaded with him not to leave them 'We could die while you were away from home and what if we were to die without believing in the Gospel!" It is a frightening thing' he said. Some of the villagers were too afraid to work in their fields without giving themselves to Christ. One wife called her husband – and him taking part in a sacrifice to evil spirits in a nearby house – so that he had a chance to hear the Gospel. In another village, all the men were in the fields, only the women and children were home. The Gospel and the resurrection of the Lord was preached to these women and the two men then went on to a village some six or eight miles further away. The following day two young stranger came forward and, on questioning them, they said that the women in the previous village had said to them about the evangelists and that had led them to want to hear more about the Word of God. Hearing this, one of the evangelists returned to that village and stayed there a day or two. There was so much joy in the blessed old Gospel for these people that some of them could not go to work while the evangelist stayed there.

A few days ago, a number of the Christian students that we have staying in one of the villages came here and they also had good news to report. The schoolmaster of that village sent word that the Holy Spirit was clearly at work there. He said that the Lord put such a burden on him one time that, as they met to pray, the needs of the mission field, the burden of the work, the scarcity of workers, and the thought that millions were without the Gospel had made him weep. He pleaded that the students should pray more for their pagan country and the result was that people who had never prayed publicly before started taking part in meetings an all increased their efforts to read and learn the Scriptures. Pray with us that the Holy Fire will take a clear hold there.

While these students were at Aijal, the youngest of them – a boy of about sixteen – had to have an operation. While he was being given the chloroform but before he became unconscious, we could hear him praying 'Lord, lead me to Thee'. He sang

> 'I've found a friend in Jesus – He's everything to me;
> He's the fairest of then thousand to my soul!
> The 'Lily of the Valley' in Him, alone I see,
> All I need to cleanse and make me fully whole'
> (Sankey, 545)

And also

> 'There's a land that is fairer than day,
> And by faith, we can see it afar' &c
> (Sankey, 9)

This touched our hearts greatly and it was very difficult to keep the tears at bay. About a year ago, he was an absolute pagan, having never heard of the Gospel or seen a missionary. He was told about Christ by people who themselves had only just heard the 'Good News'. But he had then left his home and his parents and had walked 250–300 miles to learn more about Christ. Today, he is a happy Christian, whose heart is obviously full of Christ and His love. I have heard of civilised people, those born in a 'Christian country', who have sworn and cursed under the influence of chloroform to the embarrassment of all who heard them. But here is a boy, born and brought up in the middle of the immorality and dreadful darkness of cruel paganism, who did not swear but prayed and sang of his 'New Friend'. Thank God for the Gospel which can give the pagan rebirth and for the One who is always ready to give of his happiness to the simple believer whether the believer is in Wales or dark Manipur.

Since I last wrote to you, we have had the privilege of creating an alphabet of one of the Thado-kook dialects and we have printed a small pamphlet of some forty pages which contains a catechism, a few prayers including the Lord's Prayer, a picture of Christ on the Cross, a few hymns etc. This, of course, would have been totally impossible without the assistance of one of the native evangelists.

May I pray most earnestly yet again for your readers' prayers? Prayer is our greatest need. Hundreds of Thado Kook die without Christ, they face the cold dark grave without ever learning about the 'Resurrection and the Life': they face long eternity without a Saviour. If only the 'Spirit of the Lord' made the needs of these people such a weight on His people that they insisted, through prayer, freedom, in the name of Christ, for this people who are still in the hands of the Devil and his angels.

Dear brothers and sisters, pray, pray, PRAY for us.
Faithfully yours in Him,

Watkin H Roberts
Aijal, Lushai Hills#
Assam, India
Mawrth 15 1912

Found in the Calvinist Missionary Archives, unclassified, in the National Library of Wales, Aberystwyth, UK.

Translated by Lona Jones on my request and received via email on 20 May 2008, at 5.40pm at International Christian College, Glasgow, UK.

Langham Literature and its imprints are a ministry of Langham Partnership.

Langham Partnership is a global fellowship working in pursuit of the vision God entrusted to its founder John Stott –

> ***to facilitate the growth of the church in maturity and Christ-likeness through raising the standards of biblical preaching and teaching.***

Our vision is to see churches equipped for mission and growing to maturity in Christ through the ministry of pastors and leaders who believe, teach and live by the Word of God.

Our mission is to strengthen the ministry of the Word of God through:
- nurturing national movements for training in biblical preaching
- multiplying the creation and distribution of evangelical literature
- strengthening the theological training of pastors and leaders by qualified evangelical teachers

Our ministry

Langham Preaching partners with national leaders to nurture indigenous biblical preaching movements for pastors and lay preachers all around the world. With the support of a team of trainers from many countries, a multi-level programme of seminars provides practical training, and is followed by a programme for training local facilitators. Local preachers' groups and national and regional networks ensure continuity and ongoing development, seeking to build vigorous movements committed to Bible exposition.

Langham Literature provides majority world pastors, scholars and seminary libraries with evangelical books and electronic resources through grants, discounts and distribution. The programme also fosters the creation of indigenous evangelical books for pastors in many languages, through training workshops for writers and editors, sponsored writing, translation, strengthening local evangelical publishing houses, and investment in major regional literature projects, such as one volume Bible commentaries like *The Africa Bible Commentary*.

Langham Scholars provides financial support for evangelical doctoral students from the majority world so that, when they return home, they may train pastors and other Christian leaders with sound, biblical and theological teaching. This programme equips those who equip others. Langham Scholars also works in partnership with majority world seminaries in strengthening evangelical theological education. A growing number of Langham Scholars study in high quality doctoral programmes in the majority world itself. As well as teaching the next generation of pastors, graduated Langham Scholars exercise significant influence through their writing and leadership.

To learn more about Langham Partnership and the work we do visit **langham.org**

www.ingramcontent.com/pod-product-compliance
Lightning Source LLC
Chambersburg PA
CBHW052011290426

44112CB00014B/2195